# Korelitz
# The Life and Destruction
# of a Jewish Community

## Translation of

## *Korelits:*

## *hayeha ve-hurbana shel kehila yehudit*

## Karelichy, Belarus

**Published by JewishGen Press**

**An Affiliate of the Museum of Jewish Heritage - A Living Memorial to the Holocaust
New York**

Korelitz -The Life and Destruction of a Jewish Community
Translation of the Yizkor (Memorial) Book: *Korelits: hayeha ve-hurbana shel kehila yehudit* (Karelichy, Belarus)

First Printing: March 2018, Adar 5778
Second Printing, March 2019, Adar II 5779

Editor of the original Yizkor Book: Michael Walzer-Fass
Translation Project Coordinators: Ann Belinsky and Merle Horwitz (*emerita*)
Layout: Ann Belinsky
Image Editor: Larry Guam and Nili Goldman
Cover Design: Nili Goldman
Indexing: Adar Belinkoff

Published by JewishGen, Inc.
An Affiliate of the Museum of Jewish Heritage
A Living Memorial to the Holocaust
36 Battery Place, New York, NY 10280

"JewishGen, Inc. is not responsible for inaccuracies or omissions in the original work and makes no representations regarding the accuracy of this translation. Digital images of the original book's contents can be seen online at the New York Public Library Web site."

The mission of the JewishGen organization is to produce a translation of the original work and we cannot verify the accuracy of statements or alter facts cited.

Printed in the United States of America by Lightning Source, Inc.

Library of Congress Control Number (LCCN): 2018939049
ISBN: 978-1-939561-66-4 (hard cover: 574 pages, alk. paper)

Front Cover Photo: Korelitz, before 1906, photo courtesy of David Abelson
Back Cover Photo: Drama Club and Orchestra of Korelitz

# JewishGen and the Yizkor-Books-in-Print Project

This book has been published by the **Yizkor-Books-in-Print Project,** as part of the **Yizkor Book Project** of **JewishGen, Inc.**

**JewishGen, Inc.** is a non-profit organization founded in 1987 as a resource for Jewish genealogy. Its website [www.jewishgen.org] serves as an international clearinghouse and resource center to assist individuals who are researching the history of their Jewish families and the places where they lived. JewishGen provides databases, facilitates discussion groups, and coordinates projects relating to Jewish genealogy and the history of the Jewish people. In 2003, JewishGen became an affiliate of the **Museum of Jewish Heritage - A Living Memorial to the Holocaust** in New York.

The **JewishGen Yizkor Book Project** was organized to make more widely known the existence of Yizkor (Memorial) Books written by survivors and former residents of various Jewish communities throughout the world. Later, volunteers connected to the different destroyed communities began cooperating to have these books translated from the original language—usually Hebrew or Yiddish—into English, thus enabling a wider audience to have access to the valuable information contained within them. As each chapter of these books was translated, it was posted on the JewishGen website and made available to the general public.

The **Yizkor-Books-in-Print Project** began in 2011 as an initiative to print and publish Yizkor Books that had been fully translated, so that hard copies would be available for purchase by the descendants of these communities and also by scholars, universities, synagogues, libraries, and museums.

These Yizkor books have been produced almost entirely through the volunteer effort of researchers from around the world, assisted by donations from private individuals. The books are printed and sold at near cost, so as to make them as affordable as possible. Our goal is to make this important genre of Jewish literature and history available in English in book form, so that people can have the personal histories of their ancestral towns on their bookshelves for themselves and for their children and grandchildren.

A list of all published translated Yizkor Books in the project with prices and ordering information can be found at:
http://www.jewishgen.org/Yizkor/ybip.html

*Lance Ackerfeld, Yizkor Book Project Manager*

*Joel Alpert, Yizkor-Book-in-Print Project Coordinator*

JewishGen
# Yizkor Book Project

This book is presented by the
Yizkor Books in Print Project
Project Coordinator: Joel Alpert

Part of the
Yizkor Books Project of JewishGen, Inc.
Project Manager: Lance Ackerfeld

These books have been produced solely through volunteer effort
of individuals from around the world. The books are printed and
sold at near cost, so as to make them as affordable as possible.

Our goal is to make this history and important genre of Jewish
literature available in English in book form so that people can have
the near-personal histories of their ancestral towns on their bookshelves for themselves and for their children and grandchildren.

Any donations to the Yizkor Books Project are appreciated.

Please send donations to:
Yizkor Book Project
JewishGen
36 Battery Place
New York, NY 10280

JewishGen, Inc. is an affiliate of the
Museum of Jewish Heritage
A Living Memorial to the Holocaust

חייﬨ וﬨרבﬡﬣ �‎ל קﬣﬡﬥﬨ

קﬡﬧﬠﬥﬡﬨש

בּﬨ זﬣﬧﬡﬡﬨ

Cover of the Original Yizkor Book

# קורליץ - קארעליטש

## חייה וחורבנה של קהילה יהודית
## קיום און חורבן פון א ייִדישער קהילה

חלק ראשון - עברית ויידיש

ערשטער טייל - העברעיש און ייִדיש

הוצא לאור על ידי ארגוני יוצאי קורליץ בישראל ובארצות הברית

אַרויסגעגעבן דורך די פאַרבאַנדן פון קאַרעליטשער לאַנדסלייט

אין ישראל און אין אַמעריקע

ישראל. ה'תשל"ג – גדסו

Title Page of the Original Yizkor Book

# KORELITZ

## The Life and Destruction of a Jewish Community (Karelichy, Belarus)

First Part – Hebrew and Yiddish

[Second Part – English]

[Edited by: Michael Walzer-Fass]

Published by the Korelicze Societies in Israel and the U.S.A.

Tel- Aviv, 1973

Translation of the Title Page of the Original Yizkor Book

Compiled and Edited by

**Michael Walzer-Fass**

Translated by

**Israel I. Taslitt**

Publication Committees :

**Israel** — ABRAMOWICH, Yaacov; CASPI, Chiena; MALKIELI,
Mordecai; OBERZHANSKY-TURTEL, Hassia; POLUZSHKY,
Malka.

**U.S.A.** — GULKOWICH-BERGER, Fruma; KESSLER, Morris;
SIMON-SHIMONOWITZ, Gutl.

Printed in Israel

**"ACHDUT"** Offset and Letterpress Printers, Ltd.
5, Levontin Street, Tel Aviv

CUTS : "Hazinkografiyot Hameuhadot"
12, Lilienblum Street, Tel-Aviv

# Foreword by the Translation Project Coordinator Ann Belinsky

It is my pleasure to present below the completely translated Korelitz Yizkor Book.

In the words of Michael Walzer-Fass, Editor of the original book:

*…This volume…brings us into communion with our dear ones and our town, for a twofold purpose: to perpetuate the memory of those who were taken from us by the most brutal destruction recorded in human history since the fall of the Temple, on the one hand, and to portray to the younger generation the images of its progenitors, whence they came, what brought them there, and who were their preceding generations. The young people in Israel and abroad should be told about this other life, more modest but intensely civilized, of dreamers and fighters, of pious and honest people whose lives mirrored their creed.*

One of my aims in translating and helping prepare the Yizkor Book for publication was indeed to perpetuate the memory of a town that is no more and the life of its townspeople. I wanted to obtain and insert more narratives, more photos, and more material that could be shared to all interested.

I have participated in the annual Novogrudek and Surroundings Memorial meetings in Israel, which in recent years includes the towns of Korelitz, Lubtch and the surroundings, and requested help in adding more information into this book. From these meetings I met or corresponded with several Korelitzer descendants in Israel and overseas and recorded information and photos.

Chance enquiries to me by three Americans with roots in Korelitz led to very interesting email correspondence, a detailed list of New York Korelitzer Society members in the 1930's, gravestone information from Korelitzer cemeteries, and surprise recognition of relatives in photos taken in Korelitz before the Holocaust.

From all this material I have prepared 15 appendices, each giving a new, interesting and different perspective of the Korelitzer story, which I hope will add to the emotional experience of the reader.

I hope that this book will be read by as many descendants as possible of the townspeople from Korelitz and that by the translation appearing below, we have indeed kept alive the memory of our town and families.

# Additional Notes by the
# Translation Project Coordinator Ann Belinsky

## The Translations:
### Spelling of the town name
Although the official name is now **Korelichi** (Belarussian pronunciation), the town was always called and pronounced **Korelitz** (or **Karelich**) by the Jewish inhabitants and, as such is transliterated throughout the book.
### Spelling of names
In this book, because there were several translators, names are sometimes spelt in different ways, but the reader should be able to identify them as matching, e.g. ending of names could be transliterated as *itz*, *ich*, *itch* or *icz*, depending of the Hebrew, Yiddish or Polish spelling. However, I consider that the endings are interchangeable, and should be treated as such for genealogical research. For example Yaacov Abramowich could also be Abramowitz or Abramowicz. Since the name in the English section was written as Abramowich, it was decided that this would be the way it was written throughout the translation.

In this context I would also like to mention that in several chapters, the **author's name** is given as *Ben Ir*. This is a pen name = "A son of the town", and it relates to Yaacov Abramowich. It is unclear why he wrote under a pen name (easily recognizable) in some chapters, while in others he used his own name.

## Translation of Yiddish/Hebrew words:
Within the texts, the translators have also included words which are acceptable in their original language, such as *Yeshiva, Bet Midrash, Kolel, Melamed* etc. The English definitions/translations of these and other words are usually given in square brackets [ ] in the texts.

## The English Section (Part II)
The English Section of the original Yizkor Book contains abridged chapters translated by Israel Taslitt. In addition, there are several chapters which were written only in English (for example "The Bielshchiks").

The abridged chapters, while adhering to the spirit of the original chapters written in Hebrew or Yiddish, did not always contain all the information written in the original language, but on the other hand sometimes contain extra information! In many cases, the translators have noted that *The Yiddish text (Page...) is similar to the English text (Page ...), but **includes additional information***. In several cases, the original English text is that which has been inserted into the main translation. For these reasons, I suggest that readers read both versions if they appear in full. In all relevant cases, the original page numbers of both texts appear to the side of the chapter titles.

## Page Numbering

The page numbers of the original Yizkor book are written in *italics* on the side of the chapter titles.

References to page numbers as they appear in this book are written in **bold** characters.

# KehilaLinks Webpage for Korelitz

If anyone is interested in setting up a virtual webpage about Korelitz, JewishGen KehilaLinks (formerly "ShtetLinks") is a project facilitating web pages commemorating the places where Jews have lived.

KehilaLinks provides the opportunity for anyone with an interest in a place to create web pages about that community. These web pages may contain information, pictures, databases, and links to other sources providing data about that place.

The goal is to develop a kind of grass-roots atlas of Jewish life, a way to share the stories and histories of the cities, towns and villages where our ancestors lived.

If you have memoirs, historical material, photos, maps, or anything else that can illuminate a particular community, you're invited to contribute.

The link is: https://kehilalinks.jewishgen.org/

It would be a wonderful project for someone to create and as mentioned on the webpage, you would be able to get help from the coordinators. This would be a type of extension of the Yizkor Book, where new materials can be added in as they become available. Once it is created, an announcement will be made on the Belarus SIG (special Interest Group) online forum (belarus@lyris.jewishgen.org). This last is also recommended for all persons interested in Jewish gencalogy.

# Acknowledgements for the Publication
# of the English Translation

**My maternal grandparents** were born in Korelitz, and migrated to New Zealand at the turn of the 20th century. We knew about the relatives from the "old country" from several letters received from them, but after 1934 there was no more communication. These letters formed a basis for my genealogical curiosity and the desire to find out more about Korelitz.

**Allen Katz** originally brought attention to my family that many of our ancestors had lived in the nearby town of Lubtch and indeed started a success story of tracing a whole group of new relatives. He introduced us to the Yizkor books of Korelitz and Lubtch (Lyubcha). Thus I was exposed to the JewishGen Yizkor Books website (https://www.jewishgen.org/Yizkor/translations.html), and saw that very little of the Korelitz book had been translated. Several chapters had been translated by **Vitaly Charney**, while the Table of Contents was translated by **Sara Mages** [Hebrew] and **Gloria Berkenstat Freund** [Yiddish].

**Merle Horwitz**, the original co-ordinator of this translation, was unavailable to continue at this stage, so I took over. I thank her for her initiative in beginning the translation project, and for information and photos of modern Korelitz. It is very fitting that Merle, the first coordinator of the Korelitz Yizkor Book, is also the last contributor to it, with an Appendix of photographs of her visit there in 2010. Sadly, she did not find any plaque in the town marking the centuries-long presence of Jews in Korelitz and their terrible massacre in the Holocaust.

I gratefully thank **Harvey Spitzer** for translating the Yiddish chapters of this book, as well as his proficient translations of Hebrew chapters concerning Rabbis and religious institutions. At the same time I started to translate other Hebrew chapters. All chapters in Hebrew were sent to Harvey for final editing and polishing, and his professional approach has enhanced the quality of the final translations in both languages. Without his devoted and constant help, this Yizkor Book translation could not have been completed.

# Appendices:

I thank all the contributors to these Appendices, which give additional glimpses of the life both in Korelitz and in America with the Korelitzer Society.

**David Abelson** contributed the story of his family who emigrated to the United States in 1906, a photo of Korelitz taken before that time, and a very interesting list of Korelitzer Society members and their addresses, prepared in the late 1930's.

**Zehava** and **Dina**, daughters of Yaacov **Abramowich**, kindly and enthusiastically hosted me several times to pass on information about their father, who joined the Bielski camp and was a daring partisan. From them I received photographs and interesting documents attesting to his participation in many partisan operations against the Germans.

Fruma Gulkowich Berger was one of the first women partisans in the Bielski camp. After the war she emigrated to New York with her husband Murray, also a partisan. She wrote poetry in Yiddish to express her feelings about the horrors of the war in Korelitz. Their story is told in a memoir edited by her sons **Ralph and Albert Berger**, who gave permission to use several photos and the translations of Fruma's poems which appear in the Korelitz Yizkor book.

**Ken Domeshek** contributed two interesting chapters about his United States family, and their connection to Korelitz and to the Korelitzer Society in New York.

**Hana Golan**'s parents Feivel and Fruma Nissilevitz arrived in *Eretz-Yisrael* in 1932, but the rest of her family remained in Korelitz and were murdered there. Hana has published poems lamenting the fate of Korelitz and her family, and they are translated and appear in her chapter.

The Faivelovitz family, my grandparents who emigrated from Korelitz to New Zealand in 1912, always thought that their relatives had all died in the Holocaust. However, with the advent of the internet, we discovered a whole clan in South Africa, Australia, the USA and Israel. The story is briefly told here by **Solly Faine** and myself. Three other accounts of Faivelovitz families from Korelitz are also included, by **Hillel Orgad**, **Paulette Lubelsky** and the **Targum, Pagano, Duchan** and **Musikar** families in the USA.

**Merle Horwitz** and her cousin **Marion Nakash-Polusky** contributed the story of the Polusky (Poluzhsky) family who emigrated from Korelitz to South Africa at the beginning of the 20th century. They knew that there were relatives in the USA, but hadn't manage to find them until **Bradley Nash, Karen McQuillan and Mary Goodman** contacted Merle in 2004, and added family tree information, Korelitzer Society and cemetery photographs. The story remains unfinished, but one never knows when the next piece of the puzzle will be found. This year **Mark Tobias** from Connecticut, USA, sent me the story of his Korelitz family, which fits into the Polusky narrative. Merle and Marion have contributed family photographs, while Mark has donated cemetery photographs which have added more genealogical information. Merle's visit to Korelitz in recent years is also recorded.

**Leah Lubchansky** describes the expulsion from Korelitz in World War I for four years, Russian antisemitism, the return to Korelitz, and participation in the youth group *Hashomer Hatzair* until 1932, when she emigrated to *Eretz-Yisrael*, where she met her husband and built a new life. Her parents and three of her four siblings perished in the Holocaust. Material was provided by her daughter-in-law **Rosemarie Koren** and grand-daughter **Nurit Buchweitz**.

**Malka Poluzhsky** tells of life escaping Korelitz and spending World War II years as a refugee in Russia and Uzbekistan, followed by the post-war years in displaced person's camps in Europe before finally making *aliyah*. Thanks to **Yogev Bargad** and **Gershon Poleg** who made the material available.

**Channa Messer** wrote about her parents Tova and Hertzel Nohomovski, who joined the partisans of the Bielski camp in the Naliboki forests during the Holocaust, and eventually made *Aliya* to Israel. She also contributed several photos.

I thank **Bella Rubin**, niece of Tuvia Bielski, **Assaela Bielski** Weinstein, daughter of Assael Bielski, and **Tova Gershoni** for help in identification of photos.

Special thanks to the **National Yiddish Book Center** in Amherst, Massachusetts and the **New York Public Library** for supplying the high resolution images used in this book.

I especially thank **Lance Ackerfield**, Yizkor Book Project Manager, and his dedicated team for putting the original translation online in the JewishGen Yizkor Books website.

I especially thank **Joel Alpert**, Yizkor-Books-in-Print Project Coordinator, for his guidance and patience with me during preparation of the book text for publication.

**Ann Belinsky, Translator and Translation Project Coordinator**

# Geopolitical Information:

Alternate names: Karelichy [Bel], Korelicze [Pol], Korelichi [Rus], Korelitz [Yid], Kareličai [Lith], Kareličy, Karelic, Karelits, Korelits, Korelitsh, Koreliche, Korzelice, Kozhelitse

Located at: 53°34' North Latitude and 26°08' East Longitude

| Period | Town | District | Province | Country |
|---|---|---|---|---|
| Before WWI (c. 1900): | Korelichi | Novogrudok | Minsk | Russian Empire |
| Between the wars (c. 1930): | Korelicze | Nowogródek | Nowogródek | Poland |
| After WWII (c. 1950): | Korelichi | | | Soviet Union |
| Today (c. 2000): | Karelichy | | | Belarus |

Jewish Population in 1900: 1,840 (in 1897), 1,300 (in 1931)

Notes: Belarusian: Карэлічы. Russian: Кореличи. Yiddish: קארעליץ/קארעליטש
14 miles E of Navahrudak (Nowogródek), 16 miles NW of Mir.

## Nearby Jewish Communities:

Negnevichi 6 miles NNW
Yeremichi 8 miles E
Turets 8 miles ESE
Dolmatovshchina 10 miles SSE
Tsirin 12 miles S
Navahrudak 13 miles W
Lyubcha 13 miles NNW
Mir 16 miles ESE
Delyatichi 16 miles NNW
Vselyub 17 miles NW
Haradzishcha 18 miles SSW
Naliboki 18 miles NE
Nesvizh 35 miles SE

Derevna 20 miles ENE
Novoyel'nya 24 miles WSW
Haradzieja 24 miles SE
Stolovichi 25 miles S
Molchad 25 miles SW
Bakshty 25 miles N
Novy Svyerzhan 26 miles ESE
Stowbtsy 26 miles ESE
Dvorets 26 miles WSW
Snov 27 miles SSE
Gav'ya 29 miles NW
Iwye 29 miles NNW
Kamen' 30 miles NE

ESTONIA

LATVIA

2012 Border

1940 Border

BELARUS

0 25 50 75 km

0 25 50 75 miles

RUSSIA

LITHUANIA

RUSSIA

VILNIUS

BELARUS

• Delyatichi

Lyubcha •

• KORELICHI • MINSK

Novogrudek •

1940 Border

• Slonim

• Ruzhany

POLAND

UKRAINE

Korelichi in Belarus

# A Short History of Jewish Korelitz

Korelitz (Karelichi), a town in the county of Novogrudek, in the Minsk District of present-day Belarus, is located on the banks of the Ruta River. Until the First World War, Korelitz was included within the northwestern region of the boundaries of Jewish settlements of the Russian Czarist rule.

The beginnings of the Jewish community in Korelitz are from the 17th century. In 1765 the Korelitz community had 336 taxpayers who paid a *per capita* tax to the "Committee of the Four Lands" - a fact indicating a well-known community with a large population. For internal matters, the Korelitz community bound to community leaders, assisted by nine dignitaries, who were rotated every month. The Assembly (*Hakahal*) ruled aggressively and any attempt of revolt or disobedience was repressed in all strictness including ostracism and boycott.

The Jews of Korelitz suffered from all those legal restrictions, discrimination and persecutions that were part of the Jewish life in Czarist Russia. Most of the livelihood was from small trade and crafts, and most of their customers were the farmers from the environs who would come to the town on the weekly market days and the annual fairs.

In the town there were two synagogues and a Hassidic *kloiz* [house of worship]. The Korelitz community was famed as a Torah-abiding community, but even this orthodox and mitzvoth-keeping community could not completely hide itself from the winds of advancement and knowledge. In the summer of 1881 the branch of *Mefitzey-Haskalah* (Disseminators of Enlightenment) was founded in Korelitz, and 1897 the local branch of "Lovers of Zion" *(Hovevei Tzion)* was established in Korelitz.

Many charitable societies were also active in the town: the Bridal Fund for poor girls, Lodging for the Poor- for both men and women, the Burial Society and the Charity Fund to support the needy.

Education for the youngest pupils was in the hands of the *melamdim* [teachers] who maintained *hederim* [classes] Talented youth went to the well-known *yeshivot* in Mir, Volozhyn and Slobodka. Towards the end of the century there were already progressive youth in the town, who read Hebrew and Russian literature. In 1902 young public activists established a school for girls without means.

According to the first census of the Russian-Czarist Empire in 1897, there were 2559 inhabitants in Korelitz, of which 1840 were Jewish (71.9% of the total population).

xv

In World War I, when Korelitz was close to the war front, the civilian population was evacuated from the area. The Jewish population found temporary shelter in Novogrudek. After the Peace Treaty was signed in 1918, the Jewish refugees began to return to Korelitz, which had been almost completely destroyed. Houses were rebuilt, and the basis for re-establishing the community began.

In 1921, Korelitz was annexed to Poland after the Polish-Soviet Russian War. In the 1921 census there were 799 inhabitants, of whom 535 were Jews. Over next 18 years, two Hebrew schools and the Hebrew *Tarbut* School were founded. Children also went to the elementary Polish school. Some parents sent their daughters to the Polish-government Gymnasium in Novogrudek and to the Hebrew teachers' *Tarbut* seminar in Vilna. In the 1920's, branches of all the Zionist Youth Movements were established - *HeChalutz, HeChalutz HaTsa'ir, Hashomer HaTsa'ir, Betar, Zukunft-Bund.* The young people organized dances, parties and a dramatic circle. A Hebrew and Yiddish library was established. Before 1939, some members of the youth movements succeeded in making *aliyah* to *Eretz-Yisrael.*

The economic situation of the community was difficult. Most of the livelihood was from small business, crafts, gardening, especially from cucumbers, from leasing fishponds and fruit orchards. Most of the Jews of Korelitz were supported by their overseas relatives. In early 1939, the local population numbered about 2000, of whom 1300 were Jews.

With the outbreak of the Second World War, the non-Jewish population began to be hostile towards the Jews. On the 15th September 1939, - after the Molotov-Ribbentrop Pact - the Soviet forces entered Korelitz and the Jew-hating atmosphere calmed down a little. For close to two years, the town was under the rule of the Soviets. On the 21st June 1941, the Germans attacked Russia and within a few days White Russia, including Korelitz, was flooded with a wave of the conquering German army. Some of the population joined the frightened fleeing Red Army. With the entrance of the Germans to the town the life of the Jews became hcll. The Germans did not hide their plans - complete annihilation of the local Jewish population - which were passed onto the Belarus authorities to carry out. The Belarussian Gentiles in the town ruled the Jews, treated them cruelly, beat them, murdered and robbed them.

In July 1941, the Nazis called the heads of the community and ordered them to set up a *Judenrat,* (Jewish Council) to "govern" its affairs. Orders and new decrees were daily imposed on the Jews - to wear the yellow *Magen David* on their clothes, to hand over their jewelry and other valuables. Anyone refusing to do so faced the punishment of death. The Nazis rounded up 105 men, old people and youth and imprisoned them in the synagogue. The next day they were loaded onto trucks and shot to death.

Next, Rabbi Yisrael Viernik and ten more Jews were ordered to take out all the furniture, Torah scrolls, prayer books, prayer shawls and other holy articles from the two synagogues, and set it on fire. The Rabbi was brought to Novogrudek, tortured for several days in the prison and finally murdered.

The fear of death enveloped the town. Public prayer took place only in private houses. And even so, a cell of Jewish partisans was organized in the town. They purchased weapons and made contact with the Russian partisans in the forest, but because the Germans had warned that if even one person was missing there would be a general massacre, they waited till the time would be right to escape from the town to the forest.

In February 1942 the Jews of Korelitz were ordered to leave their houses. They were crowded into a ghetto with more than 50 people in each house, and terrible sanitary conditions.

On the 2nd June 1942, carts driven by peasants appeared and immediately began the loading of elderly, the children and their belongings. All the Jewish population was expelled from their houses and concentrated in the marketplace and its surrounds. Local peasants came in hordes to loot the houses and the carts loaded with belongings. With no choice, the banished community trudged forward, covering the 21 kilometers to Novogrudek in the course of a whole day in intense heat and under the whip and bayonets of the police. When they entered Novogrudek in the evening they were taken directly to Perishika - the large ghetto in Novogrudek. Several of the Korelitz youth exploited the first opportunity, and ran out of the ghetto or from their work camps to the forest to join the partisans. The craftsmen amongst the Korelitz Jews were transferred with their families to the workshops in the Courthouse building.

On the 8th August 1942, all the Jews were loaded onto trucks and brought outside of the city to pits which had been prepared in advance, where they were mown down by machine guns. After the massacre, the ghetto in Novogrudek was almost emptied. The craftsmen and their families, among them Korelitzers, were concentrated in the town Courthouse.

In September 1942, another *aktzia* was carried out, where 3000 Jews were murdered. Those left in the Courthouse dug a tunnel under the building and on a dark night a couple of hundred escaped to the forests.

On the 7th May 1943 the third and final massacre took place of the prisoners in the Courthouse - among them the last Jews of Korelitz.

Those who fled to the forests of Naliboki joined the partisans either in the Bielski camp or as active militants. Most went later to *Eretz-Yisrael* or to the USA. Thus came to an end the once vibrant community of Korelitz.

# Notes to the Reader:

The original Yizkor (Memorial) Book was written in Hebrew, Yiddish and English and had 416 pages.

The original book can be seen online at the NY Public Library site:
http://yizkor.nypl.org/index.php?id=1200


and at

https://www.yiddishbookcenter.org/collections/yizkor-books/yzk-nybc313827/walzer-fass-michael-korelits-korelitsh-hayeha-ve-hurbanah-shel-kehilah-yehudit


A list of this book and all books available in the Yizkor-Book-In-Print Project along with prices is available at:
http://www.jewishgen.org/Yizkor/ybip.html

# TABLE OF CONTENTS
**Translated by Sara Mages [Hebrew]**
**and Gloria Berkenstat Freund [Yiddish -Y]**

***Please note that the* pages are numbered as they appear in this book, not as in the original**

## Part One – Hebrew and Yiddish

## History and Recollections

## Torah and Rabbinate

## Torah Scholars born in Korelitz

# Before and Between the Two World Wars.
# From the Jewish Press, recollections and way of life

## Personalities and Figures

## Destruction and Heroism

# The Fallen

# The Korelitzer Societies in Israel and the World

# In Memoriam

# Part Two – English - Abridged and original articles*

*Coordinator's Note: All the texts below were written and printed in **English** in the original Yizkor book. In the present book, they were either used in their entirety as the official translation, or because most were abridged versions, the translation from the original Hebrew/Yiddish texts were used, and differences between the two versions are noted in the texts. **Note** that not all of the articles in English appear in the Hebrew/Yiddish version (e.g. the Bielski brothers, and others).

## Personalities

## The Holocaust

## Aftermath

## Index

# Appendices to the Korelitz Yizkor Book

1. Early Emigration from Korelitz
    - A. The **Polusky-Turetzky** families (including connections with **Nash, Goodman and Tobias** families) in South Africa and the USA *(Merle Horwitz, Marion Polusky-Nakash, Bernard Paul, Bradley Nash, Mark Tobias)*
    - B. The **Sapolsky and Kolczycki** families in the USA *(David Abelson)*
    - C. The **Kartorzynski** family *(Ken Domeshek)*
    - D. The **Faivelovitz** family in New Zealand *(Solly Faine, Ann Belinsky)*
    - E. The **Fajwelewicz** family in France *(Paulette Lubelski)*
    - F. The **Fivelevitz** family in the USA *(Targum, Duchan, Pagano and Musikar families)*

2. Korelitz Between the Wars
    - G. Leah **Lubchansky** *(Rosemarie Koren, Nurit Buchweitz)*
    - H. Berl **Domesek** *(Ken Domeshek)*
    - I.  The **Nisselevitz** family *(Hana  Golan)*
    - J. The **Fivelovich** family in Korelitz in WWII *(Hillel Orgad)*

3. World War II – the Partisans
    - K. Fruma **Gulkowich** *(Ralph and Albert Berger)*
    - L. Yaacov **Abramowich** *(Zahava Elbaz and Dina Abramoviz Karmy)*
    - M. Gutke **Gantzevitz** (Tova **Nohomovski**) *(Chana Messer)*

4. World War II and After – Escaping to Life in Russia and then in the DP Camps
    - N. Malka and Yaacov **Poluzhsky** *(Gershon Poleg, Avigail Poleg-Dvir, Yogev Bargad)*

5. Korelitz today
    - O. **A visit to Korelitz** in 2010  *(Merle Horwitz)*

# PHOTOGRAPHS

# Family Notes

**Write this as a Memorial in a Book**
(*Exodus, XVII, 14*)

**I shall give him
An everlasting name
That shall not be cut off**
(*Isaiah, LVI, 5*)

*[Pages 13-14 - Hebrew]*
*[Page VI –VIII - English – below and* **page 349***]*

# EDITOR'S FOREWORD

SEFER KORELITZ is intended to serve as a monument to this old and elite Jewish community which, for centuries on end, was the center of vibrant and variegated Jewish life, a community of Diaspora Jews who bore the heritage of their people for many generations, struck root in alien soil, made steadfast their Jewish way of life, and maintained the continuity of their traditions.

The volume is meant to eternalize the memory of the dear ones who perished in the holocaust which overtook European Jewry during the Second World war, the memory of the town and its inhabitants, so that Jewish Korelitz may forever remain a star in the sky - a small shining star, someone's star.

SEFER KORELITZ will always be a fountain of inspiration to the men and women of Korelitz who were born there, were reared in the town, were part of its life and tribulations, and who, at an early age joined the Zionist chalutzim who went to the Land of Israel to rebuild its ruins. The volume will strengthen the townspeople who remained there until destruction stuck and escaped miraculously, after long and agonizing experiences. It will serve as a family album for those  former residents of Korelitz who left the town before the war and found their places in other countries on the face of the globe, struck root there and went on to live traditional lives, and for those who were saved from destruction but have not as yet come to Israel.

Editing a memorial volume involves many problems. Each passing day makes gathering the material more difficult; a townsman who passed on takes with him recollections which then become lost forever. Also, this material must be studied, edited and reworked, so as to achieve a certain balance, since the purpose of the editing is to project not only the life of the town as a whole but also to emphasize the role of the individuals who lived there, particularly if they contributed something unique to its cultural and social experience.

The volume is also a history of sorts of regular events. In history, as a rule, the farther one gets away from the period, the better equipped is he to write its annals. Here the situation is quite the opposite: the nearer one finds himself to the events, the more accurate and authentic is the compiled material. Pre-war Poland had about 2,800 Jewish towns and cities. Of these, about 600 have been memorialized in "Yizkor" volumes of one type or another. Each volume is in communion with its town and its dear ones. So is this volume. It brings us into communion with our dear ones and our town, for a twofold purpose: to perpetuate the memory of those who were taken from us by the most brutal destruction recorded in human history since the fall of the Temple, on the one hand, and to portray to the younger generation the images of its progenitors, whence they came, what brought them there, and who were their preceding generations. The young people in Israel and abroad should be told about this other life, more modest but intensely civilized, of dreamers and fighters, of pious and honest people whose were lives mirrored their creed.

In ordinary times, the Jews of Korelitz would not have thought of photographing their town and its personalities, for future generations. It would never have occurred to them that the history of the town should be written in order to preserve the elite reputation of the locality. There have been people who jotted down reports of events, particularly in times of distress (and these were not rare in the history of Poland's Jews), but these generally became lost. Even the records of the "Four Lands Committee" did not remain intact. However, it so happens that Korelitz maintained a written community record, part of which has survived and has served as a genuine source of information. An attempt to keep the record going and to preserve the information has been made by Hassia Turtel-Oberzhansky of Korelitz. Thus SEFER KORELITZ is able to present a broad tapestry of the town and constitute a worthy monument to its memory.

*

It is a pleasant duty for me to acknowledge the aid and assistance of those who were helpful in the compilation of this volume - particularly Moshe Cinowicz, Yitzhak Alperowicz, and Yad Vashem, and of Israel I. Taslitt, who abridged the material and translated it into English. My thanks to the Achdut Press, its managers and crew, for their fine work, to United Platemakers, and finally to the members of the publication committees in Israel and the U.S. and to all who once called Korelitz their home.

**Michael Walzer-Fass**

---

*[Page 15 -Yiddish]*

# THE POEM OF MY LITTLE TOWN OF KORELITZ

## (Unrhymed Translation)

## Yitzhak Katzenelson

### Translated from the Yiddish by Harvey Spitzer

\*    \*    \*

From childhood on, fate has driven me away
from my quiet, modest corner to a foreign world.
And yet I haven't remained a stranger in that foreign world,
and foreigners have not shamed me in my life.

Nevertheless, I've been drawn to the place
where my cradle once stood.
I have longed for, longed for... I have longed for my home.
What use are rich streets and brick houses for me?
I've been drawn to the little houses of wood and mud.

I've been far away at a wedding... but I felt
as guests do at a wedding...
I longed to come back here, to my poor possessions –
The little bird hasn't changed its nest.

I've come back! Already somewhat tired...I've been,
as I said, at a wedding, dancing in a circle. ...
I've come back - and I am refreshed and enlivened.
The little town gives back what the city has robbed from us.

You ask what I find here?  Well, don't ask. Don't ask.
I don't need any palaces, villas with bowers -
I'll give away a world for hilly Zapole paths!
An emperor's castle for a house on Zalamanke Street.\*

Oh! My little town! Oh! My desolate corner!  -  How you are in ruins!
You lie before me like a treasure, sunken and buried,
but I believe, I believe you will soon come back to life,
because he who gives me life, must have a life....

\* A small street in Korelitz
*Heint, 9 Mar-cheshvan, 5696.*  Issue: 264 (November 15, 1935)

---

[Page 16]

MAP OF THE TOWN (DRAWN FROM MEMORY)

Winter Fish Ponds

Estate Palace

Boulevard

?

Korelitz Estate Area

Steam-Powered Flour Mill

Estate Fruit Tree Garden

Estate Areas

Karnitza (?Pump)

Zapula Road

Church Lane

Zalmanke Street

Feigel Tziras (Hotel)

Estate Ornamental Tree Garden

Chaim Beimes

Vegetable Gardens

Vegetable Gardens

Ahuza (Estate) Street

Russian Orthodox Church

RUTKA RIVER

Lane To The Synagogues

Chassidic Prayer House

Toilets

The Hole (Well)

Old Study Hall

Bath House

School

Slaughter-House

Market Square

New Study Hall

Mill Street

Rabbi's House

Zissel's Alley

Keidar (Potter) Street

Galutcha Street

Putzuba Street

Fire Station

Well

Potters

Christians

Greenfeld (Blacksmith)

Christians

Road To Radin (Radun)

Canal To The Fish Ponds

Town Council

[Page 17]

# HISTORY AND RECOLLECTIONS

**At the entrance to the town...
Post Street**

*[Page 18]*

SCALE

Cities ◉
Small Towns ○
Stations and other points ○

Russian-Polish Border (until 1939)
Railway Line
Small Railway Line
Rivers

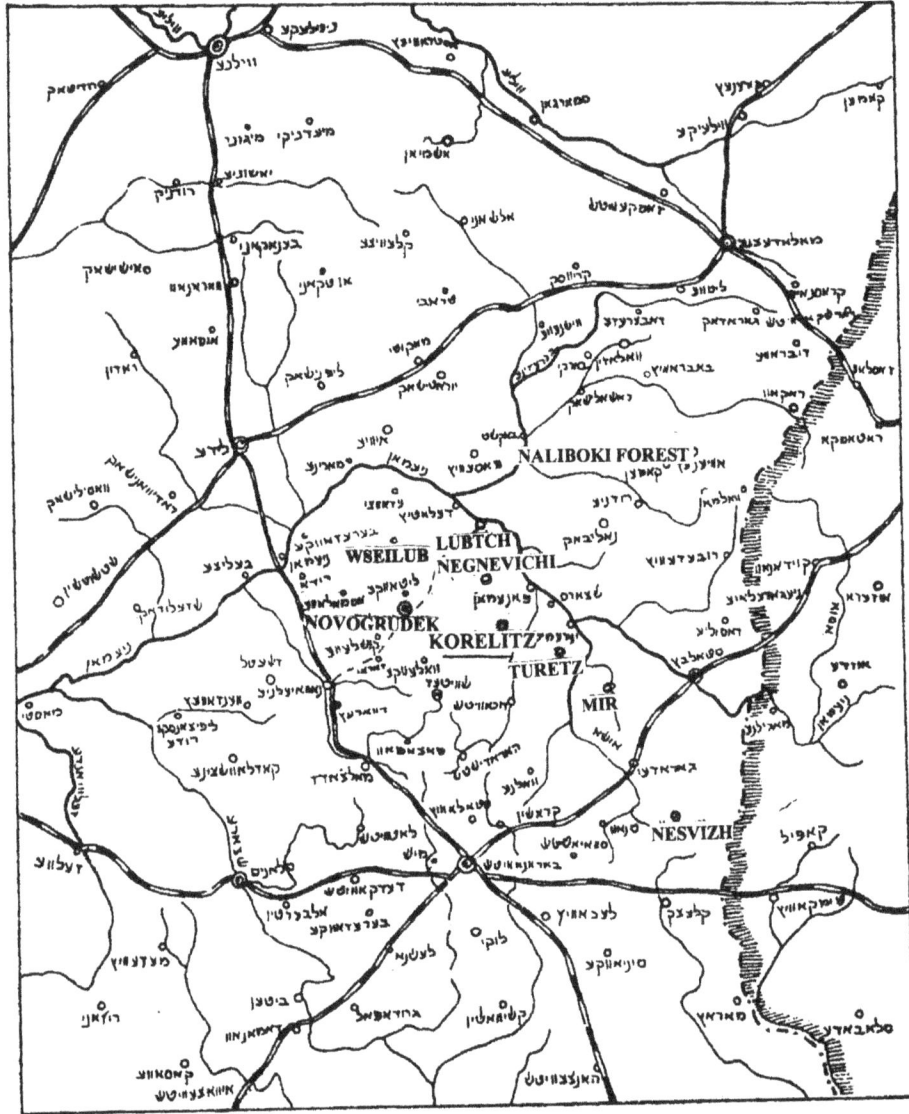

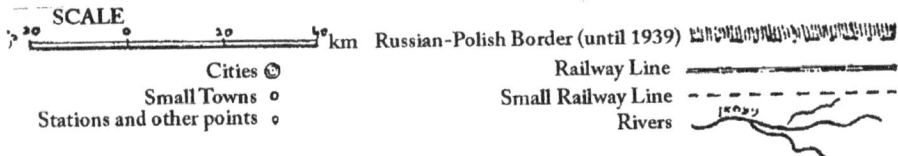

MAP OF NORTHEAST POLAND (1939)

*[Pages 19-34]*
*[This is similar to the abridged articles on* **pages 31** *(Yiddish) and* **351**
  *(English)]*

# A History of the Jews of Korelitz

## Hassia Turtel-Oberzhansky

### Translated from the Hebrew by Ann Belinsky

### Part A
### The History of the Town

Korelitz* (Korelice), a town in the Novogrudek Vyboda (*wojewodztwo nowogrodzkie*) during the Razitzpostpolita period, in the county of Novogrudek, the Minsk District, White Russia - during the rule of the Russian Czar. Korelitz is located on the banks of the Ruta River in a picturesque, fertile and forested area, on the Slutzk-Niesviezh-Mir highway and at a distance of 3 miles on the north-eastern side of Novogrudek, on the highway leading to Lithuania and to the other crown lands of former historical Poland. During the Polish kingdom, Korelitz was the possession of the great Lithuanian Princes of the dynasty of the Tchartoriskis (*Czartoryski*) and the Radziwills (*Radziwillowic*). Afterwards it passed by dowry of the Princess Stephania to the House of Radziwill (*Radziwillowna Stefania*) to the authority of the princes of the house of Wittgenstein. In the 16, 17th and 18th centuries Korelitz was a focus for important historical events of independent Poland.

In 1505 it was used as a passing station for the Tartars who robbed and looted it. In 1655 it fell victim to the Swedish troops who invaded Poland .In 1705 the Czar Peter the Great stayed there for 24 hours, on his way from Grodno to Moscow.

In 1733, following the death of King Augustus II, the Polish nationalist patriotic representatives of the nobility came to Korelitz, for consultations about crowning a king from the Piast Dynasty. In 1812 the remnants of the defeated Napoleon Army passed through during their retreat from Russia. After the first division of the Polish kingdom in 1772, the western districts and Lithuania were annexed to the Czarist monarchy under the rule of Catherine the Second (1729-1796). From then onward for 142 years until the First World War, Korelitz was included within the northwestern region of the boundaries of Jewish settlements of the Russian Czarist rule - until it was abolished in 1916.

*In Jewish sources: Korelitz, Karelitz, Karelitch, Karelichi

## Part B
## The Jewish Settlement in Korelitz

The beginnings of the Jewish community in Korelitz are some time in the 17th century. However the official documentation about Jews is from the first quarter of the 18th century.

**Part of Zalamanka Street**

Leasing contract documents (*Kontrakt*) have been preserved from the years 1723, 1726, 1730-1733 between the Princes Anna, Michael, Kazimierz of the House of Radzwill and the local Jews Avraham Chaimovitz, Shmuel Itzkovitz and others, who received by lease flour mills, taverns, inns, the right to trade in wool and flax, sugar, salt etc - for several years, renewed according to mutual agreement.

In 1772 a lease-contract was made between the princes of the House of Radzwill and between 2 Jews from Korelitz - David Ben Yitzchak and Yosef Ben Yaacov.

Even in 1807 - 35 years after the annexation of Korelitz to the Russian Czarist monarchy - representatives of the House of Radzwill, whose permanent place of residence was in Niesviezh collected land taxes from the Jews of Korelitz.

## Life in the Community during the Polish Reign

During the time of Independent Poland, the community of Korelitz was subject to the authority of the "Committee of the Four Lands" and regularly paid a *per capita* tax.
In 1752 the "committee of counts, governors and officers chosen from the leading communities" met in the city of Mir and imposed a *per capita* tax of "two hundred and two and ninety Polish gold coins".

In 1765 the Korelitz community had 336 taxpayers who paid a *per capita* tax to the "Committee of the Four Lands" -a fact indicating a well known community with a large population. From the point of view of conducting internal matters - the Korelitz community was bound to the Slutzk *kahal*, the leadership in the community was composed of "community leaders" as well as nine "dignitaries", who were rotated every month *(Parnas hachodesh)*.

From sections of the *Pinkas Hakehila* (Community Records) from the end of the 18th century, which have been preserved to this day, we learn that it was a pious community, keeping the commandments, where all aspects of daily life were based on religion and tradition. The Assembly (*Hakahal*) ruled aggressively and kept a strict eye on the lawfulness of every detail, and any attempt of revolt or disobedience was repressed in all strictness including ostracism and boycott. Thus for example, according to a judgment of *Hakahal* in *Tammuz* 5540 (July 1780), the woman Batya daughter of R' Yitzhak Eizel was punished with a "great ostracism" after being found guilt of travelling alone in a cart with a farmer from Novogrudek to Korelitz with no chaperone.

Thus according to the *Pinkas Kehilah* at the same time, - 2 other members of the community R' Yaakov and R' Gershon, apparently scholars, were punished because "they opened their mouths against a *P"h Parnas Hahodesh* (dignitary) and against the rest of the honorable people in the *Bet Midrash* [study hall or synagogue].

*Hakahal* also determined the economic way of life of the community which, from the point of view of the socio-economic level, was divided into two statuses, as defined - landowners - on one hand and tradesmen on the other hand. During the last quarter of the 18th century, "community leaders" discussed and decided that "as the outcry of our people in the community is growing and has reached our ears due to the increasing pressure of the tailors' craft which exists extensively in the business of sewing garments", *Hakahal* has therefore determined the level of payment for work which the tailors are to receive and, if it becomes clear that one of the tailors of the community is transgressing the aforementioned regulation and is showing contempt for one of the members of *Hakahal*, he will be penalized with a fine, the amount of which will be deemed appropriate by a meeting of *HaKahal*.

**A portion of Taube (Pigeon) Street**

**Part of the Market Square**

The tailors gave in and accepted the judgment and didn't take more that was specified "on the price list". The Jews of Korelitz made a living from small trade, shops, peddling, leasing taverns, inns and from crafts. Almost half of the community from the 19th century until the outbreak of the First World War made a livelihood from crafts of various types - they worked mainly for the internal market and farmers of the environs.

It should be pointed out that the craft passed on as an inheritance from father to son: generations of tailors, saddlers, capmakers, bootmakers etc were a regular phenomenon in the socio-economic structure of the community. Only thanks to the democratization process that began after the First World War was there a type of "transition" from the status to status: sons of landowners were not ashamed to learn a trade and on the other hand sons and daughters of the tradesman infiltrated the branches of trade, shop keepers, brokerage services etc.

## Part C
## The Community in the 19th Century

The Jews of Korelitz suffered for all those legal restrictions, discrimination and persecutions that were part of the Jewish life in Czarist Russia.
Also in this period most of the livelihood was from small trade and crafts, and most of their customers were the farmers from the environs who would come to the town on the weekly market days and the annual fairs, The community did not have an official status - and all its expenses were covered by collection of the meat tax (*karobke*) that was collected by one of the community members who was given this responsibility by lease.

In the town there were two synagogues and a *kloiz* [house of worship], called a *Chassidishe shtibil* [Hassidic little house] that went up in flames during the great fire in the 18th century, as it was made of wood. This synagogue, which replaced the *Alteshule* [Old Synagogue] was called the *Bet Midrash* [study hall] since until the First World War yeshiva boys regularly studied there, supported with *achilat yamim* "eating days" - in the homes of the town's well-to-do families. This Bet Midrash was used also as a hostel for groups of students of *Eyn Yaacov*, *Mishnayot* and *"Psalm Reciters"*.

The following charitable societies were also active in the town: *Hakhnasat Kala* - the Bridal Fund for poor girls, *Linat Tzedek* - Lodging for the Poor - for both men and women (founded in 1898), the *Chevra Kadisha* Burial Socicty. In the community there was also the *Kupa Tzedaka* - Charity Fund - to support the needy, so that they would not have to seek charity in other towns and would not humble themselves in front of others.

On 2 *Sivan*, 5659 (11 May 1899), *HaMelitz* newspaper published a letter signed by one of the community, M.A. Aberzhansky, announcing that in the year

1898 the "Lodging for the Poor" was founded by several of the honorables of the community. The number of members was 150. The women also banded together into one society to come to the help of sick women and the number of members was 110.

The Korelitz community was famed as a Torah-abiding community, religious and with a high public-moral level and many well known rabbis and illustrious scholars considered it a privilege to serve as rabbi or judge in the town.

Already in the thirtieth year of the 17th century there was a rabbi of the community called Rabbi Yosef. In the 60th year of the same century, there was a president of the rabbinic court by the name Rabbi Yosef, and towards the close of that century and beginning of the 18th century - there was a head of the rabbinic court in Korelitz - a scholar named Mordechai.

His successor was his son-in-law Rabbi Haim - father of the Rabbi and *Gaon* (Genius) R' Yisrael Michal from Minsk. In the 19th century the most excellent rabbis R' Eliyahu Proziner, R' Iliya-Baruch Kamay, who was head of the Mir Yeshiva and in 1887 Rabbi Mordechai from Bitten, known as Mordechai'le sat on the chair of the rabbinate in Korelitz.

The people of that generation saw him as a holy and exemplary man and both Jews and non-Jews flowed to Korelitz to request his advice and become intoxicated from his personality.

Since the many guests and visitors became a bother to the townspeople, the community published on *Rosh Hodesh Av* 5649 (23rd August 1889) an announcement in *HaMelitz*, signed by four of the most important house-owners and leaders of the community: R' Avraham Yitzchak Oberzhansky, Dov Tzvi Maeyerovitz, Yeshayu Kushelivitz and Mordechai Poluzshsky, in a request to the public, to "stop coming to Korelitz seeking advice from the *Gaon*, may he live long and happily, Amen! , because guards had been placed outside his house... so that not everyone could come to see him..., and so that they would not come in vain... for they would not be permitted to see the *Admor*, may he live long and happily".

In 1890 Rabbi Mordechai'le left Korelitz in order to preside as the rabbi of the Slonim Community.

His departure – caused "the ways to Korelitz to mourn. Without holiday travelers, her houses are silent, their owners are sighing", as one of the men of the community, Zalman Yudelvitch, lamented in a letter in *Humelitz* of *Elul* 5650 (2 September 1890).

The community - which remained without a spiritual shepherd - sent messengers to negotiate with the Rabbi the *Gaon* R' Avraham-Yitzchak Cohen from Plashnitz, *Der Pleshnitzer Ilui* [The Plashnitz Genius]. And it came about that Rabbi Mordechai'le changed his mind and expressed his desire to return to Korelitz. But he made two conditions: "that all the women will shave their heads and that there will be a meat tax.

The community became divided into two rival camps, but in the end those siding with Rabbi Avraham Yitzchak Cohen had the upper hand, and he was appointed Rabbi of the flock until the First World War.

Even this orthodox and *mitzvoth*-keeping community -could not completely hide itself from the winds of advancement and knowledge.

In the summer of 1881 the branch of *Mefitzey-Haskalah* (Disseminators of Enlightenment) was founded in Korelitz, with a library, as it appears from thank you letters appearing on the 30th August of that year in *Hamelitz*: "The enlightened youth thank the committee of *Mefitzey-Haskalah* for sending good and necessary books to read."

In 1897 the local branch of Lovers of Zion *(Hovevei Tzion)* was established in Korelitz. On the anniversary of its founding - that is on 27 *Iyar* 5658 (19 May 1898), its members organized a grand celebration, a detailed report of which appeared in *Hamelitz* as follows: "In a town as small as Korelitz they managed to gather over the year one hundred and sixty rubles for the benefit of our lofty idea... and the heads of the members can be happy that they have seen laudable results of their hard work". Even more, members of the branch also managed propaganda for the Zionist idea in the nearby towns and, thanks to their initiative, branches of *Hovevei-Zion* were established in Novogrudek, Mir and other places.

The head of the Zionistic branch was Moshe Haim Cohen - the local rabbi's son, who was famous as a writer, journalist and one of the editors of *HaOlam*. He describes in detail the celebrations of the first anniversary of the branch: "On Monday ,the second of the Intermediate Days of Passover, many of the townspeople came together to one of the *Batei Midrash* [study halls, synagogues] and there they gave a financial account... read booklets.... about the Zionist idea".

"But the many listeners marveled at the pleasant sermon of one of the heads of their group - the full-time yeshiva student, Moshe Haim Cohen, son of the local rabbi who is also a writer and edits the letters sent abroad".

"After we refreshed their hearts with fruit, produce of our holy land, the assembled people returned home happy and in a cheerful mood with Zion engraved on their hearts".

Education of the young generation was in the hands of the *melamdim* [teachers] who maintained *hederim* [classes for the youngest pupils] - amongst these, teachers of beginners - and also teachers of Talmud and rabbinic authorities. Sharp-witted and talented youth moved to the well-known *yeshivot* [seminaries] - Mir, Volozhyn and Slobodka.

Towards the end of the century there were already progressive youth in the town, who read secular books, literature in the holy tongue and also in Russian. Those who were especially active in field of enlightening the youth in the town were the sons of the local rabbi, Avraham Yitzchak Cohen - the above Moshe Haim, Shalom and his daughter Braina, who spent hours with boys and girls thirsting for knowledge in Hebrew and Russian.

On the other hand, there were girls of the poor classes without any education. And here we learn that in 1902 young public activists established a school for girls without means.

On Purim of the same year a party was held, the proceeds of which went towards this school, as was described in a letter of M.Tz. Hirshavitz in *Hatzfira* from the 6th April 1902.

We do not know the number of members of the Korelitz community in the 19th century.
According to the first census of the Russian-Czarist Empire in 1897 - there were 2559 inhabitants in Korelitz - of which 1840 were Jewish (71.9% of the total population).
On 16 *Sivan* 5671 (12th June 1911), a fire swept through the town and within a few hours destroyed 150 houses -more than half of the town - including the "Old" Synagogue *(Di Alte Schule)*, the *Bet Mirchatz* (bath-house) and other public institutions.

Among the casualties of the fire were dozens of wretchedly poor families who did not have even enough money to insure their homes, who were forced with no roof over their heads to sleep in the cowsheds, stables and under the open skies, as the rabbi of the congregation, Rabbi Avraham Yitzchak HaCohen, described the situation in the town in an appeal published in *Hatzfirah* of 23 *Sivan* 5671 (19th June 1911) - to come and help those burnt and help rebuild the ruined town.

## Certificate to Yitzhak Katzenelson

**LEGEND AROUND THE PHOTO:**
*Writers*                                    *of Israel*

*Yitzchak Katzenelson*

**LHS TEXT:**
Born in the city of Korelitz, (District of Minsk) in the year 5645 in the month of *Tammuz*, an original Hebrew poet and writer.

"If a pleasant hour falls upon you
If the hour of play comes - become addicted to it, devote your soul to it. -
For the hour may never come again"

**Under the scroll, LHS:** - the illustrator's name in Russian

The community of Korelitz produced from its ranks important people in various areas including: the martyred Yitzhak Katzenelson (1885-1942), who was killed in the Warsaw Ghetto; the poet David Einhorn, may he live long! (1885). Korelitz was the birthplace of the well known bacteriologist Prof. Shaul Aharon Adler (1895-1965), among the first scientists of the Hebrew University*, and also the architect Baruch Ben Yonah Hirshovitz, who was active towards the end of the 19th century and the beginning of the 20th century in Petersburg – as a first rate architect and in the public and Jewish fields especially in an organization for spreading the acquisition of skills of crafts and agriculture amongst Russian Jews.

* At a young age he came with his parents to England. He studied medicine at the University of Leeds and specialized in the Institute for Research of Tropical Diseases at the University of Liverpool. He worked in research of tropical diseases in the Jones Laboratory in Sierra -Leone in Africa. From 1924 he was stationed in Eretz-Israel and from 1928 served as Professor of Parasitology at the Hebrew University of Jerusalem. His important research in tropical diseases and their cures, and especially his achievements in cutaneous leishmaniasis - *Shoshanat Yericho* and visceral leishmaniasis *Kala Azar* - diseases gained him international fame. Since 1957 he has been a member in "The Royal Society of London for the advancement of Natural Sciences". (Massada General Encyclopedia, published by *Alumot*, 5718, (1958) Volume 1. Page 111)

**Haim Yossilovitz, grandfather of Prof. Adler**

**Prof. Shaul Aharon Adler**

## Part D
## The Community During the First World War

When the German armies broke through to White Russia, and since the front was close to Korelitz and its surroundings - the civilian population was evacuated from the area. The non-Jewish residents mostly tried to escape to Russia and the Jewish population found temporary shelter in Novogrudek.

When the battles subsided and the Peace Treaty was signed in 1918, the Jewish refugees began to return to Korelitz. The town was completely destroyed and ruined and only a few houses remained standing without windows or doors.

Also the two synagogues remained standing and were not very damaged.

The work of rehabilitation began, the houses were rebuilt - and the basis for re-establishing the community began. The economic situation was very bad.

These were the first years after the October Revolution of 1917, and the new regime repressed any attempt of independent-economic rehabilitation. All types of commissars appeared, who expropriated everything in order to "avoid speculation and exploitation of the working class".

According to the agreement signed in Riga in 1921, Korelitz was annexed to Poland after the Polish-Soviet Russian War. In Korelitz, according to the census there were 799 inhabitants, of whom 535 (66.9%) were Jews.

For the next 18 years - until the Soviet invasion of the area in September 1939, the Jewish community looked towards its spiritual continuity. Two *heder*s were founded - which became the nucleus for the Hebrew School *Tarbut* and the children also went to the elementary -Polish school. Those parents who could afford it, sent their daughters to the Polish-government Gymnasium in Novogrudek and to the Hebrew teachers' seminar *Tarbut* in Vilna. In the 1920's, branches of all the Zionist Youth Movements were established - *HeChalutz, HeChalutz HaTza'ir, HaShomer HaTza'ir, Betar, Zukunft-Bund*, which were the moving spirit of all the Zionistic activity for the National Funds - The Jewish National Fund (*Keren Kayemet LeYisrael*) and the *Keren HaYesod*.

The young people would organize dances, parties, a dramatic circle -where artistic talents were discovered, and a library with many volumes of books in Hebrew and Yiddish.

Members of *HeChalutz, Hashomer HaTza'ir* and *Betar* were privileged to make *aliyah* [emigrate] to Eretz-Israel where they joined kibbutzim, worked on road construction, etc. From that time until the Soviet invasion in 1939 the stream of those making *aliyah* did not stop - the best of the sons and daughters of the community.

The economic situation of the community was difficult. Most of the livelihood was from small business, crafts, gardening, especially from cucumbers, from leasing fishponds and fruit orchards. Apart from a small minority - most of the Jews of Korelitz were supported by their relatives overseas. In the town there was a cooperative bank, which gave loans at low interest rates.

On the eve of the Second World War the local population numbered about 2000 souls, of whom 1300 (65%) were Jews.

When the area was annexed to Poland in 1921, Poles came - soldiers of the Pilsudski legion -  and settled on the lands that had been confiscated from the Russian and Polish nobility who had fled the area when the First World War broke out.

These settlers (*Osdaniks*) began to incite anti-Semitism, and to call for an economic boycott of the Jewish traders.

## Part E
## The Second World War and the Destruction of the Community

With the outbreak of the Second World War on 1 September 1939, the Germans distributed leaflets from aeroplanes announcing that their aim was to annihilate the Jews.

The non-Jewish population was encouraged and began to be hostile towards the Jews. They did not hide their intentions - when the time would come - to rob and pillage the Jewish property.

On the 15th September 1939, - after the Ribbentrop-Molotov Pact - the Soviet forces entered Korelitz and the hostile, Jew- hating atmosphere calmed down a little.

Close to two years - until the 21st June 1941, the town was under the rule of the Soviets, and the Jews of the place tried as best they could to accustom themselves to the new conditions. The young people found work. And here on the 21st June 1941, came a lightening attack of the Nazi Germans on Russia and within a few days White Russia was flooded -and with it Korelitz - with a wave of the conquering German army. Part of the population joined the frightened fleeing Red Army, while the Germans were bombing them from the air and blocking their paths of retreat to greater Russia .With the entrance of the Germans to the town, the life of the Jews became hell and an inferno.

.

Every day as darkness descended, bands of peasants from the surrounding villages would infiltrate the town, break into the houses of the frightened Jews, steal and pillage whatever they could.

There were also cases of opposition to the robbers by daring courageous Jewish youth.

The Germans did not hide their satanic plans - complete annihilation of the local Jewish population - which were passed onto the Belarus authorities to carry out.

The entire administrative machine - including the police, was put into hands of the Gentiles, the supposed neighbors and friends of the Jewish population for centuries.
The Belarussian Gentiles in the town ruled the Jews, treated them cruelly, beat them, murdered and robbed them.

**The courtyard of the Synagogue in Korelitz**
**Translation of Yiddish handwriting: Synagogue Courtyard in Korelitz**

There are known cases of assault on the tailor **David Nissilevitz** and another community member **Yoel Mayerovitz** by the Belarussian police, who tortured them, robbed them and almost killed them.
**Yoel Mayerovitz** being healthy and strong, remained alive and even managed after the war to emigrate to the United States.

Towards the end of July 1941, a division of Nazis appeared from Novogrudek. They called Rabbi Yisrael Viernik and various other Jews and ordered them to set up a *Judenrat*, (Jewish Council), at whose head was Shimon Zaleviansky. One of the first decrees that the *Judenrat* was ordered to carry out was the institution of the Jewish Star (*Judenstern*) on the front and back of their outer garments and a Jew who dared to appear in public without the Jewish Star was shot on the spot.

And thus orders and new decrees were issued to the supervisors who imposed them on the *Judenrat* - as mediators between the Nazis and the Jews.

Thus they were ordered to hand over their jewelry, and other valuables - and anyone refusing to do so faced the punishment of death.

On one of the days in July 1941 men of the Nazi S.A. (Storm Troopers) appeared in Korelitz and ordered the *Judenrat* to immediately bring together all the men, old people and youth to the marketplace.

After the Jews appeared, they were stood in dense rows and the Nazi soldiers took out 105 men, old people, youth - including members of the *Judenraat* - and imprisoned them in the synagogue which was surrounded by a guard of Belarussian police who did not let anyone come close, not even to bring food to the prisoners. The next day trucks arrived in Korelitz, on which the hundred and five prisoners were loaded and taken to an unknown location. Afterwards the cruel and bitter truth was discovered -they had been shot to death.

On the 15th August 1941 the Germans passed through Korelitz, invaded houses on the pretense of looking for weapons, but they robbed and pillaged everything they laid their hands on. They also treated the Jews cruelly. And when a Jewish woman requested permission to travel on one of their trucks to another place, she was thrown into a cellar together with her husband and their 8 year old child and shot to death.

On another day the *Judenrat* was ordered to call Rabbi Yisrael Viernik with another ten Jews. When they came -they received an order to take out all the furniture from the two synagogues, and to pile it up and set it on fire. Also into the fire were thrown Torah scrolls, prayer books, prayer shawls and other holy articles [*Sifrey Torah, siddurim, talitot,* and other *tashmishey kodesh*] .The Germans planned to throw Rabbi Viernik himself into the fire. But some disagreed, because the fire would burn for too long. So it was decided to throw him into a nearby well, but they changed their minds, and made content with pulling out the hairs of his beard together with his flesh - and mortally wounded - sent him home. The Nazis tried to throw other Jews into the fire, they escaped and ran towards the synagogue - but were shot on the spot. The next day Rabbi Viernik was brought to Novogrudek, tortured for several days in the prison and finally murdered.

The fear of death enveloped the town. With nightfall, the Jews shut themselves in their houses. The synagogues stood silent and wide open with no Torah scroll or holy articles. Public prayer took place in private houses.

Life carried on in the shadow of the array of decrees and orders, one worse and more humiliating than the other such as the prohibition to be seen on roads outside the town, and anyone violating the order was abandoned to the cruelty and wickedness of the Belarussian police.

And even so, a cell of Jewish partisans was organized in the town. They purchased weapons, made contact with the Russian partisans who were active in the area, but because of the warnings of the Germans, that if one person was missing from the place, there would be a general massacre and all the Jewish population would be destroyed, they desisted at that time from joining the partisans and waited till the time would be right to escape from the town to the forest.

## The Establishment of the Ghetto in Korelitz

In February 1942 the Jews of Korelitz were ordered to leave their houses in the marketplace and the central streets - and move to a side road. They even received orders that they must take out their belongings - only once, with strict orders not to return to their houses a second time.

All the Jews were crowded into all sorts of houses, with terrible crowding and awful sanitary conditions. In each house there were more than 50 people. Slowly they got used to life in the ghetto - the craftsmen even were permitted to go to the market and receive orders from the local peasants, who in most cases didn't pay anything, except for those farmers who gave in exchange potatoes, bread, and other necessary foodstuffs.

In May 1942 the Germans ordered the *Judenrat* to make an exact list of all the craftsmen, who were ordered to move with their families to Novogrudek.
But the craftsmen were convinced that the move to Novogrudek meant death. So they decided not to move from Korelitz.

## The Liquidation of the Community

Towards the end of May and the beginning of June 1942, the Germans called the members of the *Judenrat* and ordered them - that within three days the Jews must make all the preparations to leave the place, in order to make it *Judenrein* - free of Jews. They said that the elderly and the children would be loaded together with their belongings on carts, and all the rest - would go by foot. Within minutes the rumor spread to the local villages about the imminent departure of the Jews, and for all of the three days - peasants came to the town in hordes, wanting to buy all sorts of things from the Jews, but actually taking whatever they fancied without any payment whatsoever. In the morning hours of the 2nd June 1942, carts driven by peasants appeared in the town and immediately began the loading of elderly, the children and their belongings onto the carts.

All the Jewish population was expelled from their houses and concentrated in the marketplace, and its surrounds – the gaping, jeering Gentiles rejoicing at their calamity. The sick and the frail were murdered in their beds and buried in the cemetery.

And here began the tragic and fateful exodus from the town - their birthplace and that of their forefathers - for many generations.

The expelled people burst into tears and the cries of the women and children filled the space of the murdered Jewish town. There were even those that turned back to their houses, preferring to die in the town. The police, however, began to shoot - and immediately the dead fell down on the spot. With no choice, the townspeople trudged – forward.

The carts loaded with Jewish belongings left before the masses towards Novogrudek and once they were at a distance - the peasants driving them stole valuables that they liked. The police, too, took part in the looting.

The banished community covered the 21 kilometers to Novogrudek in the course of a whole day - and all this in intense heat and under the whip and bayonets of the police. When they entered Novogrudek in the evening they were taken directly to Pereshika - the large ghetto in Novogrudek where, apart from the local Jews, Jews from the surrounding towns were concentrated. They stood at the gates of the ghetto in pouring rain and in the sinking mud for many hours, and were finally taken to cowsheds with ramshackle roofs. It rained all night and many of them - especially the children and babies were chilled and got badly sick.

In the Novogrudek ghetto they met Jews from the towns of Volma and Ravzavitz - Rubiezewicze - who lamented that before they were brought here all the elderly and children were murdered. After one day of rest the young and healthy people were sent to work camps to the nearby towns, to work on roads etc.

Several of the Korelitz youth exploited the first opportunity, dodged out of the ghetto or from their work camps and ran to the forest - to the partisans.

Pereshika (Perisica)

## The Liquidation of the Ghetto in Novogrudek

The craftsmen amongst the Korelitz Jews in the Novogrudek ghetto were transferred with their families to the workshops that had been set up in the Court of Peace building in the city.

And here at the beginning of August 1942 there were gloomy rumors of a great massacre which would take place in the coming days.

This time the Germans deceived their victims: they circulated a rumor that they were going to send Jews to forced labor in Smolensk and accordingly the *Judenrat* and the police were ordered to urge the Jews to leave the ghetto and appear at 6am in the morning of the 8th August 1942 - in the marketplace of Novogrudek - from there they would be sent to Russia. The Jews, carrying backpacks - together with their wives and children appeared at the city marketplace - and immediately the Gestapo and the police came and ordered them to take off their backpacks and lie of the ground - with their faces downwards.

From the masses of people lying on the ground, a hundred Jews were chosen - and transferred to an unknown place and murdered.

After a few hours, trucks came to the market place, on which the Jews were loaded and brought outside of the city to pits which had been prepared in advance, where they were mown down by machine guns.

After the massacre on the 8th August 1942 the ghetto in Novogrudek was almost emptied; still about 2000 people were living there - craftsmen and their families, among them Korelitzers - in the town Court House.

In September 1942, another *aktzia* was carried out was carried out, where 3000 Jews were murdered.

In this operation of death, very precise searches were carried out by the Germans under the direction of Reuter, the acting Regional Commissar, in the workshops within the Court House. They were looking for children who had been hidden by their parents. The above German, Reuter, would throw the children that were discovered from the windows of the second floor to a truck that stood outside, but instead of falling inside it, they fell on the pavement and were mortally wounded, and their blood splashed all over the stones.

The massacre in September 1942 brought in its wake the complete destruction of the Novogrudek ghetto. The ghetto still existed in the Court of Peace which was securely locked and surrounded by the police on all sides. The remnants of the craftsmen and their families were imprisoned in the Court House.

Those imprisoned in the Court House dug a tunnel under the building and on a dark night several hundreds of them succeeded in escaping to the forests. Amongst those that succeeded to escape was also the carpenter - the artisan R' Tzvi Hirsh Shkolnik, may his memory be blessed, who remained alive, came to Eretz Israel and lived until his death with his daughters Vital Tzipporah Arieli and Esther Horovitz. On the 7th May 1943 the third and final massacre took place of the prisoners in the Court of Peace - among them the last Jews of Korelitz.

The very few who fled to the forests of Naliboki joined the partisans, remained alive -amongst them were those who came to Eretz-Israel or to the United States .Thus came to an end on the gallows the once vibrant community of Korelitz with its glorious historical past - a jewel in the chain of towns, or *shtetelach* in White Russia.

We, the last remnants - are ordered - to cherish their memory and pass it on to our children - for the future generations.

# Bibliography:

*Hamelitz,* St. Petersburg: Volume 17, Issue 32, 30th August, 1881, Page 683.

*Hamelitz,* Volume 19, No. 61, 20th August, 1883, Page 979.

*Hamelitz,* Volume 27, 9th October 1887, No. 211, Page 2,250.

*Hamelitz,* Volume 29, No. 179, 25th August, 1889, Page 2.

*Hamelitz,* Volume 30, No. 188, 2nd September, 1890, Page 5.

*Hamelitz*, Volume 39, No. 96, 11th May, 1899, Page 4.

*Hamelitz*, Volume 38, No. 100, 19th May, 1898, Page 3.

*HaTzfira*, Volume 29, No. 70, 6th April, 1902, Page 278.

*Hatzfira*, No. 128, 19th June, 1911, Page 3.


**Yad Vashem Archives**

1. *Zichronot shel Mordechai Mayerovitz* (Memories of Mordechai Mayerovitz) 032/106.

2. *Zichronot mighetto Novogrudek vehisulo* (Memories of the Novogrudek ghetto and its destruction) a) 04/17 - 3 -5; b) 03/1786; c) m 11/b 283; d) m 1/e 807

Black Book of Localities whose Jewish population was exterminated by the Nazis.


**Bibliography - Yad Vashem**

Yad Vashem - Jerusalem, 1965. p. 135

In the file: the General Archive of the History of Israel, The Hebrew University of Jerusalem.

3. *Slownik geograficzny Krolestwa Polskiego. Warazawa.* Tom. IV 1883 pp. 400-401 [*A.B.*- Translation from the Polish: Geographic dictionary of the Polish kingdom]

4. Encylopedia Judaica Berlin Vol. 10, 324.

Dubnov, Shimon : *Pinkas Hamedina* (Notebook of the State), Page 259

*Zeitshrift far Yiddishe Geshichte, Demographia un Economik*, Minsk, 1928; Vol. II-III, page 367

2. *Sprawy Zydow dotyczace arendy propinacyjnej w kluezu korelickim* 1722-1807. [*A.B.* - Translation from the Polish: "Cases pertaining to Jewish tavern leases in the Karelichy region 1722-1807"]

---

*[Pages 35-38]*

# One Hundred And Fifty Years Ago *

## Ch. A Kaplan

## (Excerpts from the Book of Records *[HaPinkus Hakehila]* of the Holy Community of Korelitz)

### Translated from the Hebrew by Harvey Spitzer

If you wish, a period of 150 years is not the longest. A Jew who has merited a long life and is still going about among us had dealings with people of that generation who took part in its events. In any case, the spirit of that period has not yet disappeared; we are still influenced by its customs and miss the romanticism of its way of life. In moments of repentance, we lament, in the recesses of our heart, the good, old days, stamped with the seal of our great-grandfather, days which have long gone by, never to return. Let's observe, then, how our ancestors lived – not from hearsay and the conversation of the elderly – which are not accurate, but rather from instructive letters from ancient documents which, though covered with dust, are alive with the feelings of men and women; and the echo of their joys and aspirations, sighs and annoyances still reaches our ears through the space of the generations. Here, for example, in the Book of Records of the holy community of Korelitz, the souls active in the events related in the book are forever silent, for they have gone the way of all the world, but when you read the clauses that tell about them, despite the low level of their culture and their faulty and stammering Hebrew, we can still appreciate the value of this written list for future generations – behold this entire nearby and far off period comes to life before your eyes, and the distant echo of loving, strange sounds which still hover in the air of two neighboring periods, seeking their correction, reach your ears.

## A.

The excerpt concerning the woman Batya, daughter of Reb Yitzchak Eizel "who performed an irreligious act, travelling from Novoredak to Korelitz with a Gentile – may his name be erased! – without a chaperone", is a human document from a time of suppression of personal freedom, and the desire to live erupts when both the body and soul were put in chains. Batya was not, God forbid, a dissolute woman, flirting with a Christian fellow. She certainly had no other way of getting to her hometown of Korelitz and when this "Gentile - may his name be erased!" happened to come by travelling alone and let her

* *HaOlam*, volume 18, pg. 274-6, 11 May, 1933. Thursday, 15 *Iyar* 5693, London

get into his wagon for a few cents, she took advantage of this opportunity. The woman Batya was not so familiar with the laws of "privacy". The clause in the Book of Records itself calls her sin "folly", but the community leaders have no mercy. The "scandal" was entered into the records with her severe punishment beside it "so that people would hear and fear." The clauses relate in the following words:

"As the woman Batya, daughter of Reb Yitzchak Eizel, performed an irreligious act, travelling from the holy community of Novoredak with a Gentile without a chaperone and nevertheless added to her sin, daring to open her mouth wide and speak illegally and contemptuously against the leaders of our community in the committee and in the community room, the community leaders have therefore placed the aforementioned woman Batya under the ban of excommunication, and she may not be summoned to a judge's decision and may not even be involved in the commandment of burying a deserted corpse, nor may anyone do business with her until she appeases the community leaders and promises never again to repeat the scandal of performing the aforementioned act, transgressing Jewish law . We have come as witnesses. Signed, Sunday, 6 *Tammuz* 5540 (1780), here in Korelitz."

The woman Batya committed two transgressions for which any offender is guilty: first, she travelled alone with a Christian man, may his name be erased!, without a chaperone; and secondly, she "opened her mouth wide and spoke illegally and contemptuously against the community leaders." Therefore, she was punished with "complete excommunication" – not less and not more - that is to say, she was removed from the community entirely and was rebuked and made liable to malice, disgrace and insults, and after her death, she would likewise be made liable to shame seeing that no one would be involved in her burial. Such an unbearable situation compelled her to surrender and accept the judgment. The community leaders were victorious. The wickedness of the heart of the woman Batya was suppressed. And although it was in her nature to be loud and vocal – she could easily "speak illegally" – nevertheless, she could not argue with those who were more aggressive than she was. The second clause, which is undated, relates:

"As the aforementioned woman Batya admitted that she had sinned and promises never again to repeat the scandal caused by performing the aforementioned deed, we, the leaders of the community, have therefore cancelled the aforementioned ban of excommunication, which is henceforth like a piece of broken pottery without any substance to it."

There is, however, another surprising and unexpected epilogue to Batya's dispute with the leaders of the Korelitz community. On Tuesday, eve of the month of *Menachem Av* 5540 (1780), it is recorded in the third clause:

"As the woman Batya has gone back to being rebellious and continues to exhibit heretical tendencies (heresy and lawlessness - editor) against the leaders of the holy community of Korelitz and has cursed them with grievous curses and has also maligned and cursed the new leader in his month of office, the community leaders, joined by the nine town elders, have therefore agreed, according to the regulations clarified above, that the woman Batya should again be placed under the ban of complete excommunication until she appeases the community leaders. 24 leaders and community heads joined by the abovementioned town elders in the community room."

The feelings of anger and wrath on the part of the insulted woman increased, apparently, at the expense of her sensible reasoning, and she fought against her enemies with her weapons – grievous curses. We can suppose that the woman died while still under the ban and was given a contemptible burial. She stood in rebellion until the day of her death, for had she repented, the fourth clause would have protested against the victory of the community leaders.

## B.

Even in that controlling period, there were "insolent" and "brazen" men and women who stood up against the community and quarreled with the powerful leaders in the community room. The quarrel would sometimes reach dramatic moments as in the case of the woman Batya or would sometimes be temporary, instantaneous "among faithful friends" and would frequently come to an end with an expression of regret and acceptance of authority. It is clear that a brave individual finally surrendered and was compelled to grovel before those more powerful than he – the community, which had power and dominion. Here, before us is a dispute of two moments. The first moment:

"As, among our many transgressions, Zvi son of Yaakov and Gershon son of Rabbi Yitzchak spoke contemptuously against the community leader in his month of office and against other honorable people in the study hall and during the prayer service - therefore, in order to make this matter known so that the Children of Israel shouldn't be like a flock without a shepherd, we have unanimously decided to punish the men as explained here, namely: that the abovementioned men should henceforth not be called up to the reading of the Torah by the name "our teacher", but rather by the name "member". The aforementioned Moshe Gershon is henceforth (not) permitted to serve as *gabbai* (synagogue treasurer) and transfer money collections and they may never again be appointed to any position, and even one member of the assembly can prevent them from returning to their former status. "

And we learn a very important thing from this - and precisely in praise of the community leaders: they punished without mercy only when the offender acted contrary to Jewish law. The community leaders did not allow the honor of the God of Israel to be disparaged. On the other hand, they easily relinquished their own dignity and did not punish to the full extent of the law. The punishment of being called up to the reading of the Torah by the name "member" instead of "our teacher" is not the most severe. The "transfer of money collections" and "preventing appointment to a position forever" is more perceptible, but cannot be compared to "complete excommunication".

## C.

In these days, when elections for any important community are on the agenda, disagreements break out between the ultra-orthodox and the secular. The secular aspire to a completely secular community or to a community that has modern orthodox functions, while the ultra-orthodox want to reduce precisely the community functions and establish them solely - on the basis of religion. There are grounds for supposing that the ultra-orthodox have taken this stand regarding the Jewish community out of a lack of knowledge about the history of communities and their functions. The clause brought down below is exemplary proof that the ultra-orthodox of the past generation- contrary to the ultra-orthodox of our days – expanded the boundaries of the community, imposing on it not only religious and cultural functions, but also economic – functions which, by their nature, belong to the authority of the government and in their name, the government sets up special offices. The "community leaders" were concerned with the body as much as they were concerned with the soul.

Let's read the interesting clause in its source and language:

Due to the great outcry from the town which has reached our ears in reaction to the tailors' oppressing the residents with the high prices they charge for sewing clothes (they take high prices unheard of in communities around us), we, the community leaders, called a meeting where it was decided from now on to institute a strict regulation so that no such outcry will ever, God forbid, be heard again in our borders. Namely - that no one of the local residents- whoever it may be – should dare give a tailor more than the fee regulated by us as stipulated in the price list in exchange for his sewing. And here are the details:

> A) gabardine without rows (seams) – 2 guilder, and with rows – 2 guilder and 15 groschen; silk gabardine – 3 guilder; cloak – 3 guilder; silk cloak - 4 guilder. B) fur coat with cat trim - 2 guilden and 15 groschen; with fox or grey squirrel trim - 4 guilder; fur coat with *"platzaynike"* (?) with fur - 3 guilder; magpie –one guilder and 13 groschen; jacket from any cloth – one guilder. These prices are all for large sizes. For smaller sizes, it will be proportional to the prices stated above.

And prices were likewise set for other kinds of apparel which the clause enumerates one by one regardless as to whether the tailor made them before or after the holiday. And the clause continues:

"This was all done in agreement with all the community leaders as an immutable law and it is required of all the town residents –whoever it may be - to obey the law, and it is likewise required of all the tailors not to charge more than the prices stipulated in the aforementioned list. And even just one member of the abovementioned assembly can protest to make sure that the regulation is carried out properly, and if it should become clear that one of the tailors is not in compliance with the regulation explained above and is disparaging any one in the community, he will receive a heavy fine as seen fit by the members of the assembly."


Why did precisely the tailors overcharge for their "sewing craft" in the holy town of Korelitz? As the clause remarks, "So such a thing won't be heard about in neighboring towns?" And why tailors of all people and not the other craftsmen? We can't find any clue to that in the clause which is unique in the entire book of records because a listing of prices for other kinds of craftsmanship was not set. This is a sign that everything was as it should be. And although it is not stated explicitly, it is very likely that the tailors were forced to accept the decree and not charge more than the prices set in the price list "so that they would not be penalized with a heavy fine", and if they were penalized, some clause would have testified to this. But there is no clause to this effect.

---

*[Pages 39-41]*

# Little Pages Of History

## Hassia Turtel-Oberzhansky (Jerusalem)

### Translated from the Yiddish by Harvey Spitzer

The town of Korelitz is situated in a fertile environment on the banks of the Ruta River, on the main Slutzk-Niesviezh-Mir highway leading to Lithuania and to the other crown lands of former historical Poland. Korelitz was then in the possession of the great Lithuanian princes, the Tchartoriskis and the Radziwills. As a dowry for Princess Stephanie Radziwill, control of the place was transferred to the authority of the princely family - Wittgenstein. In addition to this event, many other happenings in the history of Poland and Lithuania took place in Korelitz.

In the 14th century, Korelitz was a passing through station for the Tatar hordes, who destroyed it. The Swedes also left signs in Korelitz during their wars with Poland in the 17th century. In 1705, Korelitz was honored to have as a guest for 24 hours the Russian Czar, Peter the Great, on his way from Grodno to Moscow. Korelitz served as a place of assembly for the Polish nobility who gathered there to hold an election (after the death of King Augustus II) in order to restore a king of the Piast Dynasty to the Polish throne. In 1812, the remnants of Napoleon's Grande Armée passed through Korelitz during their retreat in the wake of their defeat in Russia. After the division of Poland (1772), Korelitz came under the rule of Czarist Russia, to which it belonged until the First World War (1914).

## The Old Jewish Community

Unfortunately, we lack historical documents relating to the establishment of the Jewish community in Korelitz. The oldest tombstones in the Jewish cemetery are from the 18th century. It is nearly a certainty, however, that there was already a Jewish settlement in Korelitz many years earlier. According to a census from the year 1765, the Jewish community had 336 taxpayers (adults only); that is to say, the Jewish population in all numbered about 1,000 souls. According to a census of 1897 (under Russian rule), the Jewish population numbered 1,840 souls out of a general population of 2,259.

The Jewish community had no official status under Russian rule. The community's expenses were covered by a tax on meat (*karobke*), which was collected by one of the Jews who was given this responsibility on lease from the Russian authorities.

The old community supported two synagogues and a small place of worship for Chassidic Jews. One of the synagogues was called the "Old" because it was erected on the site of the "old" synagogue, which had been in existence since the 18th century and had burned down in 1911. Many yeshiva boys regularly studied in the "Old" synagogue until the First World War. They received their meals at the homes of the town's well-to-do families. The "Old" synagogue also served as a hostel for various groups of students: *Eyn Ya'akov, Mishnayot* and psalm reciters. The following charitable societies were also in the town: bridal fund, hospice for the poor, burial fund and a free loan society for the needy. The Jewish community was concerned about and supported the poor and saw to it that they didn't have to seek charity in other towns lest they humble themselves before "strangers"...

## Between Both World Wars

According to the Riga Treaty of 1921, Korelitz reverted to Polish rule following the Polish-Bolshevik War. In the period of renewed Polish rule (1921- 1939), the Jewish community was involved with organizing spiritual-social life. Their first concern was - education of the younger generation. Two elementary schools were set up and later a *Tarbut* school. Jewish children also attended the local Polish public school. Parents of means sent their children to pursue their studies in the government high school in Novogrudek as well as in the Hebrew High School or the Teacher's College in Vilna.

Lively social activity developed in the town of which young people were generally the leaders. All the Zionist youth movements were active: *HeChalutz* (Pioneers), *HeChalutz HaTza'ir* (Young Pioneers), *HaShomer HaTza'ir* (Young Guard), *Beitar* as well as the *Zukunft Bund* (Future Union) youth movement. Many of the pioneer youth realized their dream of moving to the Land of Israel. Starting in the 1920s, there was a steady emigration to the Land of Israel on the part of Korelitz's sons and daughters, who had first undergone training and preparation for kibbutz living on the farms of the *HeChalutz* and *HaShomer HaTza'ir* movements.

## Worsening Economic Situation

On the eve of the Second World War, Korelitz numbered 1,300 Jewish souls out of a general population of 2,000 residents. The Jewish population made a living from small business, crafts, gardening and from leasing fish ponds, gardens and fruit orchards. These economic groups established a "Cooperative Workers and Trade Bank", which provided low interest loans. The economic situation of the Jews was very difficult and, with few exceptions, most of the people were in need of support from relatives living abroad. The situation in the last years before the Second World War was especially difficult, during the period of increased anti-Semitism and the boycott of Jewish business. The Polish "settlers", who came from western Poland, led a campaign against Jews - among the local White Russian population who had lived peacefully with the Jews for generations.

## The Destruction

Under German occupation, Korelitz experienced the same tragic road to death as did hundreds of other cities and towns in Poland. In February 1942, after a series of death *aktions* in the town itself, the Jews of Korelitz were transported to the ghetto in Novogrudek. In the great slaughter that took place in Novogrudek on August 8, 1942, the Jews of Korelitz were murdered, together with the Jews from surrounding neighboring little towns. Only a small group of 20 Jews from Korelitz succeeded in escaping to the partisans in the dense forest around Naliboki. A few of the surviving remnants were fortunate to make their way to Israel.

---

*[Pages 42-48]*

# FROM THE COMMUNITY RECORDS OF KORELITZ

## A. Litvin

### Translated from the Yiddish by Harvey Spitzer

### A. A woman ostracized for travelling with a non-Jew without a chaperone

Whereas the woman, Batya daughter of R' Yitzchak Izik[1], performed a shameful act, namely travelling to Novogrudek with a Gentile man without a chaperone; and as, in addition, she committed another sin – opening her big mouth and reviling the leaders of the congregation at a meeting in the synagogue, we, the undersigned leaders of the community, have, therefore, issued a judgment and a punishment to the effect that the woman Batya should be thoroughly ostracized: she must not be called upon for any reason, nor must she participate in performing the *mitzvah* of burying a deserted corpse and no one should do any business with her until she apologizes to the leaders of the congregation and takes it upon herself not to commit such crimes.

Signed: Saturday night, *6 Tammuz 5540* (1780)
(4 signatures of the members of the community)

---------------

   (1)  Korelitz Community Records, *Pinkasey Kehilat Korelitz*, p.137, side 2

A few lines written further:
Since the aforementioned woman has corrected her errors and has taken upon herself to refrain from doing such things, we, the "chiefs of the community"[2], have decided that the ban of excommunication should be entirely cancelled like a broken clay vessel.

## B.   A court house attendant – a thief and his punishment

In memory of and as testimony for later generations - it is recorded on the next page how Zvi Bar Chaim "Segal" used his "hand-work" to steal from other people in the community, including several property owners, as it has become clear to the chiefs of the community and of the court of justice, so that we, the "chiefs of the community" and of the court of justice, have decided that this "runner"[3] (that is, the attendant) should be disqualified from giving testimony and for taking an oath, from today and henceforth, until he swears, wearing his prayer shawl and burial shroud, that he will no longer steal.
(*Signed*, members of the congregation and court, *5554, 1794*)

## C.  A Tax (Fine) for Tailors

Regarding the great outcry from the town which has reached our ears[4] in reaction to the tailors' oppressing the residents with the high prices they charge for sewing clothes (They take high prices unheard of in communities around us), we, the "chiefs of the community", therefore, called a meeting where it was decided from now on to institute a strict rule so that no such outcry will ever again, God forbid, be heard in our borders. Namely – that not one of the local residents –whoever it may be – should dare give a tailor more than the fee regulated by us in exchange for his sewing. And here are the details:
**Men's apparel: A)** Gabardine [5] without rows [6] – 2 guilder, and with rows – 2 guilder and 15 groschen; silk gabardine – 3 guilder; cloak [7] – 3 guilder; a silk cloak – 4 guilder. **B)** fur coat with cat trim - 2 guilder and 15 groschen; with fox or grey squirrel trim – 4 guilden; fur coat with "*platzaynike*" ? with fur – 3 guilder; *sarako* (article of clothing) - one guilder and 13 groschen; jacket from any cloth – one guilder. These prices are all for large sizes. For smaller sizes, it will be proportional to the prices stated above.

------------------------

(2) "Chiefs of the community" - title borne by the leaders of the Jewish community
(3) In the book of records – runner, Hebrew "*ratz*". He is also called "special emissary" who was the usual attendant or an extra attendant who served the congregation as an "extra postman" in case they had to announce something in another city or town regarding a decree or some other distressful thing about to befall the Jews.
(4) Community records, p.118, side 2
(5) long cloak without a split
(6) rows of velvet around the edges
(7) a kind of lady's coat

**Ladies' apparel: A)** *tchuhai* [8] with cat trim- 3 guilder; with fox – 3 guilder and 15 groschen, with grey squirrel – 4 guilder; smooth *tchuhai* - 2 guilder; *tchuhai* with *abnav* ( i.e. a blouse with a fur collar) – two guilder and 15 groschen. **B)** *tchuhai* from *mareh* (flowered silk) and covered with *kradishur*? - 3 guilder, and a smooth _____ - 2 guilder and 15 groschen. **C)** garment made of calico and *nankeen* ( thick black cotton material in lattice) – one guilder; a garment edged with *mareh* – 2 guilder; garment edged with *kradishur* – one guilder and 15 groschen; smooth garment - one guilder and 15 groschen. **D)** *Vist* [9] made of *mareh* covered with golden spangles - 13 groschen; made of *liama* (golden pieces) – 2 guilder; other *visten* in proportion to these. **E)** waist jacket made of *liama* [10] - 2 guilder; from other kinds of silk – one guilder and 13 groschen; from calico – one guilder; weekday body jacket with rabbit or cat trim – one guilder; jacket and *zaleshkesh* [11] stitched with fox - one guilder; *zaleshke* from good material with gold, or a _____ from *mareh* with _____ - 15 groschen; other *zaleshkes* in proportion to these.

All these regulations were approved by all the community representatives so that there would be a law which none of the town's residents should transgress, no matter who he or she may be. The tailor must not take more from this "instructor". Even just one of the assembled representatives can protest[12] to make sure that these rules are strictly obeyed. And if it appears that a tailor is violating these regulations and is taking more from one of the residents, whoever he or she may be, that tailor is to be punished with a substantial "fine" according to the judgment of those attending the meeting.

(Signed: two synagogue treasurers, the beadle and trustee)
*28 Tishrei 5565* (1805)

----------------------------

(8) a "*shuba*" –from Russian, a fur (coat), an overcoat of silk and satin cotton cloth sewed at the waist from the front with little buttons, in the back without a seam. The sleeves were at first wide and later narrow according to the new style.
(9) This was also called "*figara*" or "*bezrukovnik*" - a kind of small, sleeveless jacket. A kind of "sausage" was sewn in the back at the waist with wadding so that the garment would hold tight.
(10) a kind of small under jacket called "*zeleverm*" (?) In Russian, "*dushegrayka*"
(11) a kind of woven piece of gold cloth with lining which women used to wear on their chest while nursing a child.
(12) At the Jewish meetings, just as in the Polish parliament (*Siem*), the "right of veto" prevailed. In other words, one could change a decision already taken only if the assembly was unanimous. If, however, one of the representatives was opposed, no decision could have any effect.

## D.  For not making a ceremonial meal following a circumcision

It was once customary to invite all one's relatives- close and distant with their wives, children and grandchildren- to a joyous event. Since half the town was "bound" together through marriage, it is easy to understand that, for an ordinary person in times of poverty, arranging a meal was like experiencing a pogrom. Therefore, many people were actually afraid to announce a wedding, circumcision, a congratulatory occasion, etc. to the public at large. They would make the meal for a "few people", in short, those closest to those celebrating the joyous event. The "community", however, did not let themselves be duped. What do you mean not having a party? Going behind their backs?

And thus it was written in the Korelitz records book in 5568 (1808):

Because something terrible happened in the congregation due to our many sins to cancel the meal following a circumcision ceremony (regarding which it is hinted at in certain holy books that one should have a meal for all the invited guests) and even a person who is in a position to make a meal doesn't do so either, it is therefore unanimously decided that whoever doesn't make a meal – for at least 10 people – a ban of excommunication will be placed on the sexton of the synagogue if he invites anyone to a congratulatory or happy occasion and a ban of excommunication will be placed on anyone who goes to a congratulatory occasion including even the "circumcisers" and the greater and lesser godfather, and even the very own brothers of the person making the joyful event must not go. Finally, the congregation relaxes its stand and places an obligation on the circumcisers and on all those involved in the circumcision to endeavor to make a festive meal for anyone who is not himself in a position to make a meal.

Signed: Two synagogue treasurers, Eve of *Purim, 5568* (1808)

## E.  A payment made by the "godfather" and "circumciser"

In former times in Russia, it was a great honor to be a "godfather" and "circumciser". Later, this was also a good livelihood. Sometimes, however, those involved in performing a circumcision were required to provide a ceremonial meal out of their own pockets for a poor person celebrating the joyous event. We find such a regulation in the Korelitz book of records:

"It has been agreed upon and decided in the "committee" of the meeting of the "community leaders" that whoever is a godfather at a circumcision ceremony is required to give *chai*, that is 18 groschen; the circumciser, 9 groschen: uncovering the membrane of the corona of the baby's penis - 6 groschen, sucking out the circumcision blood – 3 groschen. All this money is to be given to the wives of the synagogue treasurers with which to help poor mothers giving birth. At every wedding, the groom must also give 18 groschen for charity to the wives of the synagogue treasurers for the stated purpose. "

## F. A Jewish man was caught with a married woman in a "closed room"

As a shameful act was committed in our holy community due to our many sins –namely, the man Mordechai was found in a closed room with the woman, Leah daughter of Reb Chaim Segal, the woman being married, and this was confirmed by witnesses, therefore, we the "community leaders", have decided to pay them back for their evil deeds and have pronounced a judgment on her, such a licentious woman, as she. Meanwhile, however, the matter has come to naught. That is to say, the woman ran away like a refugee that very night and we were unable to carry out the decision as planned. We are afraid, however, that this "licentious woman" may return one day. Therefore, we, the "community leaders", in the presence of the rabbi and the members of the local court of justice, have all decided to issue a great ban of excommunication on anyone of the people of our community, whoever it may be, who lets this "licentious woman" into their house, even for a minute - this person will henceforth be separated from the Jewish People and the Jewish religion and from all activities which are performed among the People of Israel. This has all been decided by a majority of votes of the "community leaders" and selected fine people, in the presences of the rabbi and members of the court of justice. The meeting was held in the community synagogue and I signed the decision on the rabbi's orders:

Tuesday night, *12 Shvat 5570* (1810)
Signed: Ze'ev Wolf, cantor, and trustee of the local congregation

What is interesting about this account found on this page of the records book is the fact that nothing was done to the man. The entire ban of excommunication was imposed on the woman.

## G. No one is eager to be a *kvater* at a circumcision or an usher at a wedding

*Kvater* (one of the participants at a circumcision ceremony) and the usher who accompanies the bride and groom to the wedding canopy are the loveliest of honors among religious Jews. Yet in Korelitz 100 years ago, no one eager for these honors could be found. The synagogue ministrants (rabbi, beadle and cantor) were responsible for this. They would put out collection plates at every joyous event. These plate payments were called *tzushrayich* in Korelitz. This laid such a heavy burden on the common resident that he had to forgo the honor as well as the festive meal. Such a regulation is discussed in the records of Korelitz.

"As it was an old custom that every *kvater* at a circumcision ceremony and every usher at a wedding had to give *tzushraylich* (payments) to the synagogue ministrants and, as a result of which, the good deed of serving as a *kvater* or usher at a wedding is in danger of falling by the wayside, this has become a very big problem for the person making the happy event, as he can no longer find a *kvater* or an usher. Therefore, in order to prevent this good deed from disappearing entirely and to raise it from the ground, where it has fallen until now, it has been decided among the "community leaders" in the presence of certain exceptional individuals and members of the court of justice and the rabbi to institute a prohibition on making payments to synagogue ministrants so as not to embarrass anyone who doesn't have the means. From today on, a complete prohibition has been put into effect forbidding any *kvater* or usher at a wedding to give *tzushraylich* (payments) to any synagogue official, and anyone who transgresses this rule will- in addition to being ostracized- be penalized with a considerable fine and suffer great disgrace. The same ban is also imposed on synagogue ministrants if they do not let everyone know who has transgressed the prohibition of giving *tzushraylich*. Whoever knows that someone has transgressed this rule is required to inform the *parnas hachodesh*[13], the leader representing the community during that particular month."

## H. For mocking the "community leader for the month"

"Whereas two of the townspeople, Zvi ben Yehuda and Gershon Behari, opened their mouth and reviled the community leader in his particular month [14] and other fine people in the synagogue study hall and at prayer time, we have unanimously decided - in order to make a fence so that the "Children of Israel" should not be "like a flock of sheep without a shepherd" - to impose a punishment on these individuals, as enumerated here – namely, not to call these people up to the reading of the Law with the title *morenu* ( "our teacher") [15], but rather with the title *chaver* ("friend", "member") [16], from now on, and Gershon will be forbidden to serve as synagogue treasurer forever, and they will never again be chosen for any congregational or social position. And even one of those present at any meeting can, with his protest, keep these people

------------------

(*13*)   One of the twelve community leaders who were also called *alufei hakahal* (leaders of the community), each of whom was a kind of representative for a month. When one was in charge that month, none of the other leaders had the right to get involved. Only at meetings would all twelve come together and have the right to vote.
(*14*)   The "community leader for the month" was considered an official person only "in his month". In the other months, he was the same as everyone else.
(*15*)   The title *morenu* ("our teacher") was given to any young man, a "fine Jew", a scholar or a simple person when he had earned certain merit for the community.
(*16*)   The title *chaver* ("friend", "member") was given to every man soon after his marriage. This title indicated that he had equal rights with others in the community. These titles were usually used when a man was called up to the reading of the Torah in the synagogue and when the person bearing this title was mentioned in writing.

from being chosen again. And in order to ratify the congregation's decision, which was formulated in the community synagogue, and to give it more power, we have signed it: Sunday, *2 Nissan 5544* (1784)
(5 signatories)"

Exactly a month later, on the same side and page of the record book, there is an addition to the aforementioned decision:

"Since the abovementioned individuals have bowed to the" Great Court of Law", which was convened here, and have asked the leaders of the congregation for forgiveness, we have decided to pardon them for what occurred here and from now on, these people may return to their former standing."
(5 signatories)
---------------

## I.  Smaller attendance, more happiness

A wedding, more than a circumcision ceremony, was a joyful occasion on one hand and a source of misery on the other. According to a custom of earlier times, people invited close and distant relatives - even the farthest removed – on both sides in addition to friends, acquaintances, neighbors and synagogue ministrants. For an average person, therefore, making a wedding was a real disaster. Consequently, the community of Korelitz was compelled to issue an order as recorded in the Book of Records:

"It was unanimously decided by the representatives and leaders of our community, in the presence of several fine people (distinguished individuals), regarding the needs of our community according to the rules recorded in our record book: that whoever makes a wedding, whoever it may be from our community, must not invite any but his closest relatives up to his nephews and nieces on both sides. One may also invite the community representative for that particular month, the closest neighbors on both sides, synagogue ministrants, wedding ushers and the host of the house where the wedding is taking place. And whoever has a *mechutan* (father of a son-in-law or daughter-in-law) living in town, may invite him as well to the banquet (where they are making the meal). Also the relatives up to the nephews and nieces of the groom's father may be invited to the wedding. However, regarding invitations to a meal following a circumcision ceremony, he must invite more than those included above as well as the circumciser and synagogue ministrants, precisely those who serve the congregation. Each and every member of our congregation, whoever he may be, is obligated to obey this requirement. This rule does not apply to those living in surrounding settlements which do not fall under the restrictions of this regulation. The synagogue ministrants are also excluded from obeying this regulation. All of this was decided upon at a meeting of the congregation including the threat of ostracism from the community, and whoever transgresses this rule will be subject to great punishments and fines. Should any congregation of our community wish to cancel this regulation, three valid Jews (i.e., those with voting rights) suffice to protest the ruling.

Recorded, Thursday, *18 Marcheshvan 5554* (1794)
Four signatories

As is easy to imagine, according to this regulation, which greatly limited the number of invited guests, there still remained a considerable number of family members to invite to the joyful event.

---

*[Pages 49-53]*

# YITZCHAK KATZENELSON'S NATIVE TOWN

### Zippora Katzenelson - Nachumov
**Translated from the Yiddish by Harvey Spitzer**

Among the endless, dense forests of the State of Minsk by the Empress Katerina great highway, a broad, paved road which leads to the capital city of Minsk - 24 *verst* from Mir, 22 *verst* from Novogrudek and 20 and some *verst* from Baranovitch – was once located Korelitz... one of the lovely small towns

pulsating with the vibrancy of the warm blood of Jewish life. The town was so intimate, cordial, ours...
*[Note: Verst is a Russian unit of measure, equal to 3500 feet - HS]*

One of the famous, great noblemen of that region, a friend of the Jews whose name was Korelitch, decided to develop his property. In the State of Minsk, in Minsk alone, he found a very honorable Jewish man whom he settled here as a lessee. This first resident brought along other Jews, first of all his relatives, one of whom was a tavern owner, and if there is a tavern, Christians show up right away. They leased forests from the nobleman, out of which they made villages and fields. Jews began trading in wood and later in grain, and that is how the famous town of Korelitz first became a respectable, a very, very respectable small town. The old, very old cemetery, the old synagogue with its artistic, fine woodcarvings, gave evidence of vibrant Jewish life going back 600 years.

The small town of Korelitz was colorfully built and offered a splendid panorama outwards from its very center, that is to say from the marketplace, which stood on the highest place in the area, and all the little streets extended downward from there. People would say "downhill" at the end of the town, where peasants already lived, and especially owners of orchards and gardens. Whenever heavy rains fell, there would be a flood and the trees would be nearly submerged, but this didn't cause any harm. On the contrary, Jews would be doubly happy: first, on account of the trees, which revived after a recent hot spell, and secondly, because they were protected, thank God, from the deluge, living, as they did, on the hill. The fate of the orchards and gardens was closely linked to the livelihood of the majority of the Jews because they were the local lessees. Korelitz also had many Jewish craftsmen and a considerable number of storekeepers. The peers of the town dealt in wholesale wood and grain. They were the old, most respected property owners, the aristocrats of Korelitz but, as said, most of the Jews, ordinary Jews, were involved in small trade with products from orchards and gardens. People also did business in dairy products. Cheese from Korelitz had a very good name in the entire statc.

With regard also to *Yiddishkeit* (Judaism), Korelitz did not lag behind the other distinguished small towns. The position of town rabbi was formerly held by the finest personalities. The town had synagogues, *yeshivot* (rabbinical seminaries) and religious elementary schools where all, definitely all Jewish children drew knowledge from Torah and wisdom. No ignorant people, God forbid, were to be found in Korelitz. Even the water carriers knew a chapter of Jewish oral law.

On all sides of the big, boisterous market place, on the top of the hill, there extended long rows of stores and shops of all kinds, especially dry goods merchandise. But was anything lacking, God forbid, of other things? Our Jewish brothers had thought of everything. Anything a man could eat and whatever a head, a Jewish head, could remember – you could find in all the stores and shops.

At the start of one of these rows of stores stood the only traditional town well, the pride of Korelitz. Every guest arriving from the state capital, i.e. from Minsk itself, would be shown, first of all, that well which was a reminder of the first inhabitant of Korelitz, the founder of Korelitz, the town's first Jew. The first well in Korelitz is located near the first tavern. For hundreds of years, that was always the gathering point for people and horses. The horses would get fresh water and the people would drink fresh liquor, often diluted with water, on account of which disputes often broke out between the Christians and the tavern owner. Therefore, one of the few town policemen was stationed there. The *gorodovoi* (policeman) watched the drunkards to make sure they wouldn't kill one another seriously. He would do his job thoroughly, although he was tipsy himself .... Taverns were not places where you would meet people with sober thoughts to get information, but the well, the town well, was really a source of the latest news, especially at a time when people had not yet begun reading newspapers. The living newspapers were then the wagon drivers. Jewish wagon drivers used to travel around distant places, bringing back the freshest news reports from all over the country. Especially when pogroms against Jews used to take place in the far off sections deep inside Russia, as far as distant Moscow, where the first expulsion then occurred...and the inhabitants of Korelitz, thirsty for news, would soon surround them, the first arrivals, when they would water their horses at the well. The wagon drivers would immediately and gladly transmit all the news. Seldom, however, was there good news... They knew that Jews become distressed upon hearing about the troubles that befall other Jews, the torments which they have to endure in the bitter exile... and the Messiah still refuses to come... Apparently, the cup of suffering which we deserve for our sins is not yet full... Elderly Jews would shake devoutly and their lips would recite psalms while doing so... Women, especially elderly Jewish women, would weep aloud and also young women, charming girls, would sob but would quickly wash their faces with the crystal clear water from the well, and their faces again shone brightly and they swiftly smiled.

Further down the street, the one in disrepair which, in fact, is called Zalamanke Street, leading to Novorade (Novogrudek), on a second hill on the side of the nobleman's house, stood the only Russian Orthodox church. Here, entire groups of Christians used to move along the way, going to the prayer service on Sundays and holidays and would buy a garment or very long candles for the numerous saints of the Church. The dry goods merchants had a great opportunity to do business on important Christian holidays and weddings. This made the storekeepers very happy and they prepared themselves in advance with a large selection of red dresses and bright red kerchiefs for the young Christian girls who attracted the attention of the discharged imperial soldiers who also needed a wife of their own, besides stocks of live cattle. The whole market place and the road to and from the church would fill with the loud chattering of carefree Christian youth. Everything around would also be covered with the red color of the red kerchiefs which would sparkle from the burning glow of the sun and blind the eyes of the storekeepers themselves. They would point to this red panorama and say, "Look! Everything around is red...like blood...like..."

The narrowest lane of the town opened from one of the sides of the market place, but it was also the most distinguished - the Rabbi's Lane – at the end of which stood the rabbi's house. This house, the largest in Korelitz, was the pride of the Jews of Korelitz because, for many generations, it was the seat of the town rabbi and also served as a community center. The rabbi's house was always open in order to give a cordial welcome to all distinguished guests as well as merchants from out of town who showed up for business and to welcome others who came simply to visit the old Jewish town and look at its remarkable sights.

During the Napoleonic War, when the French world conqueror fought against the Russian general, Kutuzov, the Jews of the large city of Bobroisk ran away throughout the surrounding areas. A part of the many branched Katzenelson family also tore itself away from this stream of refugees from the city of Bobroisk. Through its direct and indirect members, this eminent family occupied the position of town rabbi in many cities and small towns in White Russia and Lithuania.

In Korelitz, as well, the town rabbi, Rabbi Yitzchak Yechiel, of blessed memory, was from that important family. And when his lovely and intelligent daughter, Hinde, grew up and became the dream of the best young men from far, far around, the rabbi couldn't find any more suitable groom than his own cousin – "Who is then from greater, distinguished lineage than our family?", and so it was decided to make a match between the rabbi's daughter, Hinde, and his nephew, the prodigy, Binyamin- Yaakov Katzenelson from Kapulia. (My mother would always say with a laugh that that was her first "hint of Kapulia"!)

This occurred in 1882 in the years of the first revolutionary movement of the *Narodnaya -Volia* (People's Freedom) after the assassination of Czar Alexander II. The successful assassination stirred the minds of the entire Russian intelligentsia and made an impression on the pioneers of our *Haskala* (Enlightenment) movement. However, the mighty reaction of Czar Alexander III suppressed the revolt, sent its leaders to the harsh labor camps in Siberia and persecuted the smaller revolutionaries in cities and towns throughout all of Russia. The Christian revolutionaries were even concentrated in the villages, where they became teachers. This movement was called "Going into the people".

Jewish supporters of the "People's Freedom" movement, however, settled almost exclusively in towns and small towns, that is to say, among the common people. There, they began to instruct the youth. Libraries were set up everywhere, and young men and girls gathered there. The serious young people began to read about sociology and political economics. The majority, however, preferred to read polite literature in Russian, Hebrew and Yiddish. They began to swallow up novels from world literature, and girls would practically choke reading Sh.M.R's (?) works so quickly. This renaissance did not avoid the small town of Korelitz either.

**Right to left: Binyamin-Yaakov Katzenelson, Avraham, Yitzchak, Hinda and Gershon Katzenelson**

---

*[Pages 54-56]*

# THE TWO TIMES I VISITED KORELITZ

## Dovid Einhorn

### Translated from the Yiddish by Harvey Spitzer

When a person is born, an invisible note is hung on him which he carries on his person all his life – that is his name and the place where he was born.

I was born in Korelitz in 1882. A year later my parents moved to Novogrudek. When I was seven years old, my father took me for a walk on Castle Hill in Novogrudek. On the horizon, you could see roofs and trees.

Pointing this out to me with his finger, he said:

"Look, Dovid! You were born there!"

It was a bright, warm day at the end of the summer. The grain crops in the field were already ripe. The rye waved in the breeze. The wheat bent under the load of its ripe spikes. The barley with its hairy ears shone like small bands of rays and, among them, the fields of buckwheat with their little white flowers looked as if someone had poured milk over them. Together with the green chickpeas, they looked like woven carpets.

This colorful picture was etched in my memory together with my Korelitz - a memory from my youth which has never been erased.

The second time, I saw Korelitz in another light: It was already late in autumn. My father, Dr. Binyamin Einhorn, decided to settle in Rubiezhevitch. The house which the small town had built for the doctor was nearly finished and my father wrote to my mother to come with the children.

Communication with the town was, of course, made possible by wagon drivers who carried passengers and merchandise in their large wagon booths. My mother quickly ordered two wagon booths and we soon set out on our way.

The road to Rubiezhevitch led through Korelitz.

I remember that it was a cool, clear autumn night. A big moon poured its silvery light over the whole town and everything was quiet. The lamps in the windows were out. Only a bright light from the tavern where we stopped lit up part of the street.

Suddenly, my mother drew open the curtain of the wagon and said to me: "Come, Dovidke. Let's take a walk and have a look at the small town. You were born here".

Our walk didn't last long. The elderly wagon driver, an old acquaintance of our family, was already standing next to the wagon. He looked at me and said to my mother: "Is this the pale little boy whom the good Jew of Korelitz blessed?"

"Yes", answered my mother with a sigh.

Meanwhile the wagon and carriage drivers had come out of the tavern, looked around their wagons to see if everything was alright, tying the ropes around the boxes and bags more tightly. Then they got up on the coach box, gave a crack with their whip and the whole caravan began moving from the place. My mother, who was sitting by the open curtain, suddenly began calling:

"Look! The whole sky is burning!"

The caravan stopped and everyone got off the wagon and began wondering which little town was burning. Finally everyone agreed that Mir was the little town that was burning, and we would pass by Mir on our way.

When I looked at the red sky, all my limbs began shaking. My mother could hardly calm me. The fright of a red sky remained with me for a long time.

That was the last time I saw Korelitz. Today it's a dead town for all Jews.

---

**Korelitz after a fire**

*[Page 57]*

# TORAH AND RABBINATE

The New *Bet Midrash*, Korelitz

*[Pages 58-59 Yiddish]*
*[Pages XXI-XXII English –Below]*
**As on page 361**

# The Poem of Korelitz's *Bet-Hamidrash*

## Yitzhak Katzenelson
### (unknown translator)

There it stands, your *Bet-Hamidrash*! Deep in my heart
I feel a tug - you are known to me, yet unfamiliar...
This is the sacred spot where I used to romp abut,
Where portly young men used to chat, and the pious prayed.

This is the sacred site to which Jews once came
With aching hearts, and emerged requited;
This was the place where the speechless were heeded
And the weak refreshed with strength.

O Jewish Bet-Hamidrash, home for every Jew,
Recipient of supplication, repository of pain;
To you the Jew his joys recited,
Within your walls the exile lost its edge.

In summertime the birds chirped their song of praise,
Their melodies came through the open windows
Like birds on the wing and sunlight streaming in,
And in the winter nights we sought your warm comfort.

O Jewish *Bet-Hamidrash*, home of all homes!
O our only guardian - can anything replace you?
We the wanderers, you our guiding light.
The comforter who soothes our weary wandering.

Your door is ever open - whene'er I wish, I enter.
Your kindly *shamash* does not ask: Who and wherefrom are you?
If I wish, I pray; if not, silent I remain;
No other home so warms the heart.

Your Holy Ark is filled with Torah scroll,
Its curtain by pious brides embroidered;
A preacher's stand for quoting Scripture,
A lectern with two lions, carved into gentleness.

Your shelves are lined with ponderous volumes,
Ancient Talmud tomes and Rambam folios, books on end!

Over which pallid students pore and sway -
No! No house with such treasure troves is poor.

Your study lecterns, where wars are waged,
Was more worthy than most tranquil peace;
Your benches, for soul and body restful,
For slumber sweet and the best of dreams.

Lowly built, you rise above all others!
Unbeautiful, your beauty all exceeds!
Your loyal roof reflects the brightest sunshine,
The warmest ray through your windows stream.

**Published in "Hajnt", Warsaw, 1935, No. 265**

---

*[Pages 60 - 61 Hebrew]*
*{Pages XXIII-XXIV English -below]*
**As on page 363**

# Once there was the Rabbi's House

Small and of meager means as it was, the town knew how to safeguard its way of life, its spiritual wholesomeness, its inner light and atmosphere, quietly spinning the continuous fabric of faith and tradition. It withstood adamantly the barbed shafts of assimilation, an island beset by an inimical environment.

The town's weapons in this relentless struggle were the institutions which it created and maintained: the houses of prayer, the schools and academies, the societies and organizations founded to support and supplement them: the Talmud Study group, the Visitation Society, Free Loan Aid, and others.

The Rabbi's house was one of these institutions, singular and outstanding, the center of kindliness and the core of understanding. Owned by the community, this house was the rabbi's residence during his tenure, which in many cases meant for life; (rabbis left at times to assume positions elsewhere; rarely was a rabbi dismissed). Within the walls of this house dwelled, in the course of many decades, Torah luminaries whose decision and impact was felt in the community's religious, social and cultural life. Theirs was the decisive voice in litigations between man and his neighbor, and their esteemed personality lent weight and credence to their judgment.

The Rabbi's House, in itself, lent a distinctive charm to the town, in comparison with the external aspect of Korelitz. The town's appearance was drab, at best. Its plainness was accentuated even more sharply by the beautiful expressions of nature all around it: hills, glades, meadows, and the bright blue skies above - all of which combined to show up the mossy houses and their crooked walls, their ragged roofs and smoke-stained windows, a blot on the creation of the Almighty.

Nor did the appearance of the town fare any better from its mundane life. The days were filled with the rasping sound of people engaged in earning a living, the harsh tumult of the masses, the peasants and the hangers on of the market place, uncouth, boorish and often closer in appearance to the animal world.

In this depressing atmosphere the Rabbi's House stood out in magic relief. It was located on the town's boundary line, on a tract of land adjoining the open fields. Its dignified exterior was matched by the serenity within its walls, by its cleanliness and soothing atmosphere. Here one could readily shed the barnacles of gray reality, straighten up, and face an uncontaminated world.

This was the Rabbi's House that I knew, the gathering place for the cleansing of the soul. Now it is gone, and the heart weeps over the destruction that overtook it, as it shared the fate of the town and its Jewish inhabitants.

**HADOAR, 3 *Tevet* 5703, Vol.6. Poland Edition**

(*AB:* The Hebrew date translates to 11th December 1942)

---

*[Pages 62-63 –Hebrew]*
*[Pages XXIX - XXX English - Below]*
**As on Page 369**

# The Korelitz Shochet
### (abridged English version)

## David Cohen - Kibbutz Alonim

*/ Reality and Legend/*

**\*In memory of the Korelitz community which was annihilated in the Holocaust**
years and its martyrs who were buried in a mass grave in the city of Novogrudek*

This happened two or three generations ago. Korelitz, pursuing its life at the
slow pace of its Ruta River, the power source for the flour mills in the area,
was already famous for the many sages and scholars in its midst. But the man
whose fame spread with the advent of Zionism was R' Moshe Avrohom Volfin,
the *shochet* of Korelitz, a pious man of learning whose soul yearned for
Jerusalem and whose heart wept for it, in the midnight prayers which he
offered for its redemption.

One wintery night the cold penetrated his lungs and laid him low with a high
fever. The town physician, an expert on pneumonia, prescribed several drugs,
plus goat's milk. Thus was a goat added to the *shochet's* household, a white
goat which R' Moshe Avrohom prized greatly.

The news of the forthcoming First Zionist Congress reached Korelitz and at
once R' Moshe Avrohom became an "active Zionist". During the days of the
Congress he donned his Sabbath clothes and greeted his fellow Jews with
*Mazeltov*. As soon as the Congress proclaimed the establishment of the
Palestine Bank *on the initiative of Dr Herzl\**, he began campaigning for the
purchase of its stock. His main concern was to set an example for the others,
but the shares cost money - a rare commodity with R' Moshe Avrohom.

The white goat! True R' Moshe Avrohom had grown attached to the animal but
he would do it! He would sell the goat and buy a share, and let the people of
Korelitz thus know how dearly he regarded the Zionist idea! He sold the goat,
went to Novohorodok to acquire the share, and read what it said in Hebrew to
the delighted congregants in the synagogue. They applauded heartily - and
bought shares.

The story about the goat and the shares reached Vilna, and the Zionists there
tendered lavish praise to Korelitz and its energetic and devoted Zionist. When
the Second Zionist Congress came around and the shekel campaign was

proclaimed, it was again R' Moshe Avrohom who spurred shekel sales in Korelitz. When the authorities got word of it, they issued a warrant for R' Moshe Avrohom's arrest. As the constables came to get him, R' Moshe Avrohom stood up and pronounced the *Shehecheyonu* benediction, thanking the Almighty for having given him the privilege of being arrested for selling the Zionist shekel.

It is said that when Dr. Theodor Herzl was told about it, he said: "If I have such Zionist Jews as the shochet of Korelitz, it will be much easier to surmount all the difficulties that the Jewish nation will encounter on its way, to Zion and Jerusalem".

**\*** added in from the Hebrew version

*[*

---

*Pages 64 – 89 - Hebrew*
*[Most of the following below appear also in very abridged versions on Pages XXIV-XXVIII]*
**See also pages 365-368**

# Rabbi Moshe Son Of Rabbi David

## Moshe Cinowicz – Tel Aviv

### Translated from the Hebrew by Harvey Spitzer

Rabbi Moshe was the son of Rabbi David, head of the religious court in Novogrudek, who was considered one of the geniuses of Lithuania in his generation. When Rabbi David took ill, his son Rabbi Moshe served as his assistant until his father's death in the year 5597 (1837). In his book of *responsa*, *Ateret Yitzchak* by Rabbi Yitzchak Isaac, head of the religious court in Shavli, a special letter by Rabbi Moshe Denan is brought down regarding the mutual relations between him and Rabbi David close to his death (*Ibid*, section 75). Rabbi Moshe Denan's letter is dated Friday, 22 *Tevet* [year *nimtzativ*= 597, without the Hebrew letter *hey* whose numerical value is 5,000].

After his father's death, Rabbi Moshe, newly appointed head of the rabbinic court in Korelitz, took pains to prepare his father's book of *responsa* and sermons for publication in order to carry out his father's wishes to him before his death. However, the matter did not succeed, for the rabbi's son, Rabbi Moshe, also died a short time later in the prime of life, before reaching the age of 30. And the book, *Gelia Masechet*, was printed in the year 5604 (1844), by Rabbi David's grandson – Rabbi Zemach, newly-wed yeshiva student.

Rabbi Moshe's new interpretations of the Torah are brought down in *Geza Tarshishim*, [Vilna, 5608 (1848)], containing words of eulogy for Rabbi David.

The author of this book was Rabbi David's student, Rabbi Chaim bar Eliahu Krinksi. With regard to Rabbi Moshe's position in the rabbinate in Korelitz, we can note that his father, Rabbi David, head of the rabbinic court in Novogrudek, was in contact with the community of Korelitz and he knew at close hand the former rabbis in Korelitz who would visit Novogrudek, the district town, from time to time and would come to the town's religious court on matters relating to community needs and religion and on complex matters of handing down decisions regarding Jewish law in their small town. Thanks to Rabbi David's connections with Korelitz, his son Moshe was appointed head of the religious court in their small town, although he was still a young yeshiva student and hadn't served previously in any other community.

---

[Pages 64-66]

# Rabbi Chaim Tur

## Moshe Cinowicz – Tel Aviv

### Translated from the Hebrew by Harvey Spitzer

Rabbi Chaim Tur was head of the religious court in Korelitz from approximately 5600 (1840) to 5616 (1856) and was later called to honor as the head of the yeshiva *Gemilut Chassidim* in Vilna where he was active for 18 years and died there in the year 5634( 1874), as is brought in *Levanon*, 1873-74, issue 48.

Rabbi Chaim Tur was great in Torah, an outstanding innovator and a master of instruction in deciding matters of Jewish law, as his book, *Tiv HaChaim* testifies. This book was published in Vilna in 5633 (1873) and contains new interpretations on *Orach Chaim*, *Yoreh Deah* and *Even HaEzer* on the *Shulchan Aruch* (Code of Jewish Law) as well as clarifications and new interpretations of several tractates of the Talmud.

In regard to the question of allowing a "chained" woman (a woman whose husband deserted her without giving her a Jewish divorce) to remarry, as was brought down in matters of deciding questions of Jewish law with Rabbi Yitzchak Eliahu Landa, a preacher of the city of Vilna, and especially with Rabbi Bezalel HaCohen, head teacher of righteousness in Vilna, Rabbi Tur reacts to several ideas of this well known genius in an independent way, with all due credit to him.

In the preface to his book, Rabbi Chaim transmits facts to us concerning his distinguished lineage and his family's origin. His father, Rabbi Dov, was a great and erudite scholar, assiduous in his learning, logical and known for his charity. His grandfather was the genius and righteous man, Rabbi Aryeh Leib, head of the religious court in Volpi, replacing his pious father-in-law (his mother's father's father), Rabbi Chaim, head of the religious court in Volpi, (a small town in the district of Grodno). And Rabbi Aryeh was the son of the righteous Rabbi Gavriel, head of the religious court in Liubishoi (district of Pinsk). The rabbi and author also notes that his grandfather's uncle was Rabbi Yehuda Leib, head of the religious court in Horodishtz near Baranovitch).

With regard to Rabbi Tur's special connection to the rabbinate in Korelitz, his decision making relating to practical application of Jewish law is brought down in his book, *Tiv HaChaim*, which reviews one branch in the field of business and Jewish law as it applies to the Jews of that small town in those days. He writes that "I was asked a question while I was in the holy community of Korelitz regarding the fact that there are grain merchants who send their merchandise to Vilna and who generally hire non-Jews on Thursday or Friday to transport the grain to Vilna, and these non-Jews come to Korelitz to take the grain and measure it on the Sabbath and then they take the grain and measure it for their bags and transport them from there. I was asked if there is some dispensation for Jews to sell their grain entirely to a non-Jew by means of a monetary acquisition or barter so that the grain is theirs and that the non-Jews understand that the intention of the Jews selling their grain to a non-Jew is only to circumvent the prohibition of performing work and conducting business on the Sabbath and that they are transporting grain to Vilna at the owner's expense". The rabbi from Korelitz believed "that there can be no dispensation regarding this matter, since one must measure and take the grain from a Jew's house or storeroom on the Sabbath. In the *Levanon* of the 18th of the month of *Menachem Av*, 5634 (1874) issue 48, we find words of estimation of Rabbi Chaim Tur, the former rabbi of Korelitz. According to the writer of this column (Rabbi Baruch Epstein, author of *Torah Temimah*, a commentary on the Pentateuch), the late rabbi was only 22 years old when he was appointed head of the religious court in Korelitz, where he was active - with blessed results - for sixteen years. The above mentioned writer is correct in noting that Rabbi Chaim Tur was a great orator who "imparted knowledge to the people in his lovely and pleasant sermons and instructive lessons and that the synagogue was filled with those coming to hear a lesson from his mouth and although he was afflicted with serious illnesses, he nevertheless endeavored with all his strength to lead his pupils (as head of the *Yeshiva* in Vilna) on the path of Torah and in making decisions pertaining to matters of Jewish law". According to the writer of this column, Rabbi Chaim Tur died as a stranger in Koenigsberg (East Prussia) on 14 *Tamuz* 5634 (1874) on his way to seek medical advice from doctors there.

When the report of his death reached Vilna, the whole city was stunned. Everyone was in mourning. Lamenting was heard in every corner. It was as though people of kindness were gathering and asking: "Who will teach us knowledge in the sea of *Talmud*, answer difficult questions and clear up discrepancies arising from intricate methods of understanding the text and who will express words of reproof and knowledge to cure the ruined places of our heart? And from whom shall we obtain advice and understanding in the ways of instruction in deciding matters of Jewish law and knowledge of God?"

The author of the abovementioned column includes the town of Korelitz as well regarding Rabbi Tur's passing. Here is what he says on this subject: "Raise your voice, too, and put on a covering of grief, for he also led you in the way of the Lord, and he also turned upwards from then on and bore the burden of directing the *yeshiva* here in Vilna and he satiated your hunger for counsel and understanding, and his wisdom also supported you."

The column ends with words of comfort for the rabbi's widow and children whom he left behind and he also speaks to the heart of his students to whom this rabbi and head of the *yeshiva* taught knowledge of Torah as well as instruction in deciding matters of Jewish law, and they saw his many righteous acts, his simple piety, his pure Torah, over which we lament in the passing of this great rabbi and *yeshiva* head.

We can also point out another connection that Rabbi Chaim Tur had with the town of Korelitz while he was head of the *yeshiva* in Vilna. He would draw close to many young men from Korelitz who came to study in Vilna and took an interest in their adjustment to the various *yeshivot*, whether his own *yeshiva* or study hall *Gemilut Chassidim* or other *yeshivot* such as Remiles Yeshiva, the *yeshiva* in the synagogue *Zovchai Zedek* (the butchers' *yeshiva*) and in their personal arrangements. He would likewise recommend a number of *prushim* ("abstainers" - married men who left their wife and children to study Torah) in Vilna to move to Korelitz for a specified period of time to study with a group of students from Korelitz in the local study hall.

*[Page 66 (middle)]*
**Lineage of Rabbinic Families in Korelitz (mentioned on pages 62-68)**

**THE SONS** of Rabbi Yaakov: Our Teacher, Rabbi Chaim Turetzer, and his brother-in-law, Rabbi Chaim from Korelitz, father of the Rabbi and Genius (*Gaon*) Yisrael Michel from Minsk, (from the opening of my book, *Zecher Yehosaf*, printed recently but written some time ago. Rabbi Yaakov, son of Rabbi Chaim of Korelitz, is written there by mistake according to hearsay, not intentionally and it only became known to me later that Rabbi Yaakov's father was Rabbi Chaim from Turetz, (and not Korelitz), who was called Rabbi Chaim Turetzer and his brother-in-law was called Rabbi Chaim from Korelitz, and both were sons-in-law of the Rabbi and Genius, Rabbi Mordechai, head of the religious court in Karlin), and the sons-in-law of the Rabbi, Genius and Mystic, Rabbi Mordechai, head of the religious court in Korelitz, who was used to reconciling contradictions of the commentators of the later generations on the *Levush* (compilation and analysis of Jewish laws, etc. by Rabbi Mordechai Yaffe of Prague (d.1612), which he would refer to and_____ (meaning unclear) and, according to a story from his grandchildren, he said about the *Sha'agat Aryeh* ("The Lion's Roar", volume of *responsa* by Aryeh Leib ben Asher Ginsburg) regarding one of his *responsa* in opposition to some *halacha* (Jewish religious law): "The lion has roared, who will fear?, (Hebrew:(M)i, Who, (Y)ireh, will fear) Rabbi (M) Mordechai (Y) Yaffe will NOT fear [from the verse, (Amos 3:8.): "The lion has roared, who will fear?]

**THE SISTER** of the aforementioned Rabbi Dov, wife of the great rabbi, Rabbi Yitzchak Yehoshua from Slonim, father-in-law of the Rabbi and Genius Rabbi Eli' Noach, head of the religious court in Ostrin and later in Simiatin, wife of the above mentioned Rabbi Dov, Her name was Ruchama and she died on 16

*Kislev*, daughter of Rabbi Mordechai Gimpel Turetzer and sister of the Great Rabbi Shlomo Zalman Turetzer and his wife Zartel, granddaughter of Rabbi Yisrael, preacher in Vilna for thirty years and is mentioned in *Chayai Adam*, book of Jewish laws (end of 18ᵗʰ century or beginning of 19ᵗʰ century).

**THE RABBI AND GENIUS**, Rabbi Mordechai of Korelitz, son of our teacher and rabbi, Rabbi Shmuel, and son-in-law of the Rabbi and Genius Rabbi Yosef, head of the religious court in Korelitz, lived there before the registration of their family and their family pedigree in full detail from several great rabbis, and I was unable to clarify and certify the family transplantations, since the facts are from different people and so I put them aside for the time being.

---

*[Pages 67-68]*

# The Jaffe Family In Korelitz

## Binyamin Benari Jaffe – Jerusalem

### Translated from the Hebrew by Harvey Spitzer

Rabbi Mordechai Jaffe, author of *Levushim* died in Posen in 1612. He had two sons and two daughters. Several years later we find in Korelitz Rabbi Yosef, who was the head of the town's religious court. Rabbi Yosef had a son-in-law, Rabbi Shmuel, who was the father of Rabbi Mordechai from Korelitz. Rabbi Shmuel and Rabbi Mordechai were the "great-grandson and grandson" respectively of the author of *Levushim*. These details are known to us from *Megillat HaYachas* (genealogical record), which Rabbi Zacharia Stern of Shavli recorded and which was included in his book of responsa *Zecher Yehosaf.*

It is not clear how many generations elapsed from the author of *Levushim* to Rabbi Mordechai of Korelitz, nor is it clear which one of Rabbi Mordechai (Jaffe's) sons was the ancestor of Rabbi Mordechai of Korelitz. Apparently, it was Rabbi Aryeh Leib, one of the two sons of Rabbi Mordechai, most of whose offspring were in White Russia, Lithuania and Besserabia.

Rabbi Mordechai of Korelitz was the son-in-law of Rabbi Yaakov Ben Chaim Turetzer, who lived in the town of Turetz close to Korelitz. Details relating to Rabbi Yaakov or his father, Rabbi Chaim, are not known to us, except for one item of information (the source of which I cannot verify), namely that Rabbi Yaakov was the brother-in-law of the Chassidic rabbi of Chernibyl (Twerski?).

More numerous are the facts relating to Rabbi Yaakov's son, Rabbi Dov Ber Turetzki, who was apparently the first to be called by the family name, "Jaffe". (In general, family names were not in use in Russia before then.) Rabbi Dov Ber was born in the second half of the 18ᵗʰ century. He was among the most outstanding students of Rabbi Chaim of Volozhin and one of the first students of the Volozhin Yeshiva. He served as rabbi in Korelitz, Lubtch and Otian. Rabbi Dov Ber was married to his cousin, Ruchama, daughter of Rabbi

Mordechai Gimpel Turetzer. According to the aforementioned Rabbi Yosef, the uncle of Rabbi Dov Ber and his wife Ruchama was Rabbi Dov Ber Trivsh (1724-1804), the son of a famous family of rabbis. He was the head of the religious court in Zagar and the *safra d'dina* (writer of law) in Vilna at the time of the Gaon of Vilna. Rabbi Dov Ber was the author of the *Revid haZahav*, a commentary on the Pentateuch, and *Shir Chadash*, a commentary on the "Song of Songs".

Rabbi Dov Ber died in the year 5589 (1829) and was buried in the old cemetery in Vilna, not far from the grave of the abovementioned Gaon, Eliahu. Inscribed on his tombstone: "This is the monument of the rabbi who was great in Torah and piety, practicing what he preached, our teacher and master, Rabbi Dov Ber, son of our teacher and master, Rabbi Yaakov, Teacher of Righteousness, of the holy communities of Korelitz, Lubtch and Otian. Died, 15 *Shvat* 5589 (1829), may his soul be bound in the bond of life" (*Kiryah Ne'emanah* by Rabbi Fein, Vilna, 5675 (1915).

Rabbi Dov Ber and his wife Ruchama had several sons: Rabbi Yaakov, Rabbi Chaim Zalman, Rabbi Yehosaf, Rabbi Yehoshua and Rabbi Mordechai Gimpel and also several daughters, two of whom were married to the brothers, Yona and Natan-Neta Luria, rabbis who were the sons of Rabbi Moshe Mishel Luria, rabbi of Karkinova. One daughter, Freida-Batya, was married to Rabbi Nachum Kook, progenitor of the Kook family of rabbis.

Rabbi Dov Ber's son, Rabbi Zalman Jaffe, emigrated to the Land of Israel and died in Jerusalem in the year 5630 (1870) and is buried on the Mount of Olives. His son Baruch also went to live in the Land of Israel. He was the progenitor of the Dinovitz family in Petach Tikvah. Rabbi Chaim Zalman's brother, Rabbi Mordechai Gimpel, who was born in Otian in the year 5580 (1820), was the famous rabbi of Rozhinoi and one of the leaders of religious Zionism and one of the founders of *Moshav* (collective settlement) Ekron. He immigrated to the Land of Israel in 5648 (1888) and settled on Moshav Yehud near Petach Tikva, where he died of malaria in the month of *Cheshvan*, 5652 (November, 1892).

Among the progeny of Rabbi Dov Ber Turetzer, who also served in Korelitz, we find several rabbis who left Korelitz to become pioneers in Israel, including the first chief (Ashkenazic) rabbi of pre-state Israel, Rabbi Avraham Yitzchak HaCohen Kook and also the Zionist leaders, the brothers Bezalel and Leib Jaffe, as well as many others who were pioneers in the *yishuv*, the Jewish population of Mandate Palestine. They were its builders and fighters who lived in the cities, towns, kibbutzim and moshavim of the State of Israel.

---

*[Pages 68-71]*

## Moshe Cinowicz – Tel Aviv

# A. The "Luminary Of The Exile" Naftali Hertz

### Translated from the Hebrew by Harvey Spitzer

This rabbi, as the Rabbi of Korelitz, appears with his signature on the purchase of the book, *L'zecher Yisrael*, by Rabbi Yechiel Michel.

This book was printed by the jointly owned Vilna-Horadanai printing press in the year 5594 (1834). We are talking here about the period of this rabbi's term of office in Korelitz during the years 5589-5594 (1829-1834) following Rabbi Dov Ber Jaffe's tenure as the town's rabbi.

In the aforementioned book, *L'zecher Yisrael*, one can find many Korelitz names including Rabbi Avraham Hertz, son of Rabbi Binyamin Yaakov; Moshe, son of Our Teacher Rabbi Elikum Ketz; Mordechai, son of Our Teacher Yosef Segal (HaLevi); Yehuda Leib, son of Our Teacher Menachem Mendel; Issar, son of Our Teacher Tuvia; Natan Neta, son of Our Teacher David; Yaakov, son of Our Teacher Shraga, the father, and the son, Mordechai, son of Yosef Katz and Yitzchak, son of Our Teacher Mordechai Moshe, son of Our Teacher Aharon; Natan Neta, son of Our Teacher Avraham, the father, and the son Shlomo, son of Our Teacher Dov and his son Moshe; Elikum, son of Our Teacher Avraham; Bezalel, son of Our Teacher, Chaim.

The very fact of his being in Korelitz to obtain the aforementioned signatories for his book further strengthened the connection of the people of the small town to the Volozhin Yeshiva, something which was evident well before then with the activity of the previous rabbi, Rabbi Dov Ber Jaffe. Closer to Korelitz, the Mir Yeshiva also sparkled and this, too, had both a direct and indirect effect on strengthening the students' Torah learning

In Korelitz itself, a Torah group was founded made up of young people and needy *porshim* ("abstainees" i.e. young married men who left their wives to study Torah) who established a place for their learning in the local study hall. Included among the students were brilliant Torah scholars who found the quiet Torah atmosphere of the study hall suitable for their diligent learning during the intermediate period of their student years.

## B. Rabbi Yitzchak Yechiel Davidson

He was the son of the *Gaon* (Genius), long in his generation, Rabbi Dov Ber Kapolier, head of the religious court in Starobin, son of the rabbi, Master of the Torah, Rabbi Yehuda, son of Rabbi Yitzchak in Skidel (small town in the District of Grodno), author of the book, *Beit Yitzchak*, who calls the author of the book *Me'irat Eynaim* (commentary on the *Choshen Mishpat* section of the *Shulchan Aruch*) by the name, "My Uncle, the *Gaon*" (according to *Nachalat Avot* by Rabbi Levi Avotzinski).

Rabbi Yitzchak was among the most famous rabbis of his generation in knowledge of Torah, wisdom, religious investigation, administration of the rabbinate together with fine qualities, and he brought fame to the small town of Korelitz, where he was the head of the religious court from 5617-5634 (1857- 1874), watching over the Torah group in the local Beit Midrash (study hall) and excelling as a fine Talmud pedagogue whose aim was to improve the studies of the young men and *porshim* who came from near and far to attend the study hall in Korelitz. Among those who studied in the Beit Midrash in Korelitz at that time, one should note in particular Rabbi Malchiel Tenenboim – author of *Divrei Malchiel* and Rabbi Y.Y. Reines. With regard to Rabbi Reines, it is worth noting that Rabbi Yitzchak Yechiel knew him previously when he himself was a *poresh* yeshiva student in Pinsk (Rabbi Reines' native town) and when this *poresh* moved to Korelitz to serve as the head of the town's religious court, Rabbi Reines stayed a certain time with Rabbi Yitzchak Yechiel in the town and was greatly influenced by this rabbi's logical way of teaching.

Rabbi Mordechai Slonimski, a resident of Turetz, prefaced his book, *Haker Elohi* (Vilna 5665, 1905) with words of approval from the leading rabbis of Lithuania, among whom were Rabbi Mordechai Gimpel Jaffe and also Rabbi Yitzchak Yechiel from Korelitz.

Rabbi Yitzchak Yechiel died in Korelitz in the year 5634 (1874) without reaching old age.

He was honored to have three *Gaonim*-geniuses as sons-in-law: a) Rabbi Eliahu Feinstein, who replaced him in the rabbinate in Kletzk; b) Rabbi David Feinstein, head of the religious court in Starobin; c) Rabbi Yaakov Kantrobitz, rabbi of the towns of Shatzk and Ozdah.

## C. Rabbi Eliahu Feinstein

He was widely known in the rabbinic world by the name "Rebbi Elinka Prozhiner" after the name of the place where he last served in the rabbinate, the town of Prozhan (State of Grodno). Rabbi Eliahu Feinstein was born in the year 5603 (1843), son of Rabbi Aharon Halevi, head of the religious court in Starobin (District of Slutzk).

Rabbi Eliahu studied at the Volozhin Yeshiva and became acquainted with two eminent *yeshiva* heads of those days: Rabbi Naftali Zvi Yehuda Berlin (HaNetziv) and Rabbi Dov Ber Yosef Soloveitchik and there he rose in stature as a respectable, sharp-minded expert in Torah and Talmud. In the years 5623-5630 (1863-70), Rabbi Eliahu served as replacement for his late father in the rabbinate in Starobin. Shortly thereafter, he became the son-in-law of the Rabbi and Gaon Rabbi David (son), head of the religious court in Korelitz. In 5630 (1870), he served as head of the religious court in Kletzk.

In 5634 (1874), he was compelled to accept a position in the rabbinate in place of his father-in-law, who passed away at that time. Although Korelitz was small compared to Kletzk, he was forced to build the "rabbi's house" there and to make arrangements for the rabbi's widow, who remained there with her young sons and daughters, all of which required immediate attention, a task which Rebbi Elinka carried out devotedly, faithfully and satisfactorily. Rebbi Elinka occupied the important position of rabbi and head of the religious court in Korelitz for five years. His name was exalted and he gained prestige as a rabbi great in knowledge of Torah, as an exemplary community leader and as a person wise in sacred and worldly affairs. In the later years, his name became a blessing in the mouths of the elders of Korelitz who knew him at close hand in their youth and merited to gain wisdom in his light.

In 5639 (1879), Rebbi Elinka was accepted as head of the religious court in the community of Chislovitz in the State of Mohilov, and in 5644 (1884) he was called to honor as head of the rabbinic court in the community of the aforementioned town of Prozhan as substitute for the Rabbi and Gaon Yerucham Yehuda Leib Perlman, chief rabbi of Minsk, and was known as the "Great Scholar of Minsk".

After Rabbi Eliahu Feinstein's death in 5689 (1929), his son-in-law, Rabbi Ben-Zion Menachem Krakovski, published a list of information regarding the life and activity of this genius in the ultra-orthodox weekly, *Dos Vort* in Vilna, and here are some excerpts:

At the age of seven, "Elinka" was already an expert in the entire Talmudic Order of *Nezikim* (Damages). He was amazingly diligent. When Elinka was ten, Rabbi Yosef, head of the religious court in Slotzk, took him under his wing and supervised the development of this prodigy. At the age of fifteen, when he was at the Volozhin Yeshiva, he learned Torah from the mouths of the great and famous heads of the yeshiva, Rabbi Yosef Ber Soloveitchik and the *Netziv* (Rabbi Naftali Berlin). He was diligent, modest and lived in penury. When Rabbi Yosef, head of the rabbinic court in Slotzk, visited Volozhin and inquired about the teenager from Slotzk and about his situation, the administration of the yeshiva began to take special interest in him.

In the year 5634 (1873), his father-in-law, the rabbi of Korelitz, died, leaving behind a large orphaned family. The deceased's son turns at once to Rebbi Elinka, asking him to accept the position in the rabbinate in Korelitz. He doesn't refuse and moves to the small town, where he lives for five years. He is active in community affairs, arranges matters regarding the recruitment of Jewish boys into the Russian army, registration of children, etc. And everyone relates to this great personality with reverence and respect.

As a safeguard against the spread of *Haskala* ("enlightenment") he establishes groups for the study of *Talmud* and *Mishna* (Oral Law) for Torah clubs and societies: *Eyn Yaakov*, Psalms and *Midrash* and *Chayei Adam* - for wide circles of students and for the masses. Simultaneously, he supervises matters of education and Talmud-Torah on a local level and is concerned with religious education organized into levels in Talmud-Torah classes. Likewise, he sends the most gifted pupils to the higher *yeshivot*, especially to the Volozhin Yeshiva, where he studied in his youth. He tries as much as possible to reduce the gap between those providing work and their hired workers and laborers. In his special letter to Baron Horatio Ginzburg, he turns his attention to the question of hiring God-fearing people and those who observe religious commandments. The Baron hastened to respond that he would devote special attention to the matter and would fulfill his request to the greatest extent possible.

Rabbi Eliahu was known as the "Wise Jew". He was held in high esteem due to his incredible knowledge of Torah. He was a public worker in many areas. He was a public figure in the economic sphere and one of the first Torah personalities on the rise among Russian Jewry. He would call restricted conferences and meetings of Torah geniuses in Russia and general assemblies of Jews, such as the well-known conference of rabbis that took place in St. Petersburg in 1910. His words and opinions were highly regarded at these meetings.

Rabbi Eliahu Feinstein's sons-in-law were four famous rabbis of the last generation: Rabbi Menachem Ben-Zion Krakovski; Rabbi Moshe Soloveitchik; Rabbi David HaLevi Feigenboim; Rabbi Eliezer Yitzchak Meizel.

Rabbi Eliahu passed away in the year 5689 (1929) at the age of 86. Eulogies were given in all the cities and all of them emphasized the worth of this genius. He was the "Last of the Mohicans" of the survivors of the Lithuanian *Gaonim* of that Golden Age.

Rabbi Eliahu's book, *Halichot Eliahu*, was printed in 5693 (1933). It contains matters of *halacha* (Jewish law), clarifications and new interpretations on the

*Rambam* (Maimonides) and on the four sections of the *Shulchan Aruch* (Code of Jewish Law) - and this is only a small part of his numerous writings in all branches of the Torah which have survived him. In this book, Rebbi Elinka is revealed to us as a genius who rules over the "Sea of Talmud" with his direct understanding logic and subtle feeling.

It is to be noted that his grandson, Rabbi Dr.Yosef Dov Ber, son of Rabbi Moshe Soloveitchik, head of the Yitzchak Elchanan Rabbinic College of Yeshiva University in New York, often introduces words of Torah in his lessons, talks and Torah research in the name of his maternal grandfather, Rebbi Elinka, head of the religious court in Korelitz, Kletzk, Chislovitz and Prozhan.

It is likewise to be noted that Rabbi Eliahu's connection to Korelitz remained strong even after he had already become rabbi in Chislovitz and Prozhan and that he would sometimes stay in the former small town to attend to family matters, as his widowed mother-in-law continued living there for many years. She was the beloved wife of the Rabbi and Gaon (Rabbi Yitzchak Yechiel Davidson) in his youth.

---

[Page 71]

## Rabbi Zvi Menachem Tsizling

# Rabbi Eliahu Baruch Kamai

### Translated from the Hebrew by Harvey Spitzer

Our city, you can now be considered and numbered among the cities which planted faithful saplings within. From the time he was appointed rabbi of our community, the Rabbi and Genius, Rabbi Eliahu Baruch Kamai, may he live long and happily!, in whose light we will see light, brought new life to the youngsters of the Talmud Torah. This school had previously been conducted in an orderly way but in more recent years stumbled on the path. And Rabbi Kamai saw the need to correct this important matter with all his might. First of all, he appointed an effective teacher who would lead the pupils on a straight path and in the right way. And he encouraged the property owners to support and aid the school generously, each person whose heart impelled him to contribute to the cause.

The rabbi greatly aroused the conscience of the townspeople, asking them to build a shelter for the poor and needy who came from afar to seek aid, and the property owners responded to his appeal and built a refuge. He likewise was encouraged to set up a clinic for the town's poor residents who could not afford to pay a doctor's fee or buy medicines.

*HaLevanon*, **28 *Nissan* 5641 (1881), (17th year, No. 35).**

---

[Page 72]

# Sketch In Ink Of Rabbi Mordechai

## Made by Yehuda Leib Tzluch from the town of Ivyeh 16 *Kislev* 5727 (December 1967)

### Translated from the Hebrew by Harvey Spitzer

**Semi-Circle of Words beneath the sketch:**
"The rabbi, the *Gaon* (Genius) of his generation, the great mystic, Rabbi Mordechai'ele Weitzel (Rosenblatt); the beginning of his career In the rabbinate was in **Korelitz** and later in the town of **Oshmana** and he finally served in the town of **Slonim**.

It is also worth mentioning that the *Chofetz Chaim* relates that Rabbi Mordechai'ele once apologized to him for being involved in giving remedies and blessings to women in the following words: "When I converse with women, some of their transgressions and sins are made known to me and I bring them back to repentance."

*[Pages 72-73]*

...Concerning the new rabbi, whom will they choose? Some say: Let's go and serve Rabbi D. (referring to Rabbi David Feinstein, son-in-law of Rabbi Yechiel Yitzchak Davidson, who was supported by his mother-in-law, the rabbi's wife and widow in Korelitz) because he had precedence as the older son, according to the tradition of our forefathers. Others say: Let's prostrate ourselves before Rabbi A. Meir A...because the position befits him, for he is holy and stronger in piety and abstinence. And thus the dispute broke out. The people's voice was set on evil. The house of prayer became a battlefield as they came to blows and vilified one another like women in a fish market. It's easy to understand that due to such disturbances and quarrels, disorder has increased in our community and no one can tell us if and when the disputants will compromise and the fighting will stop. Indeed, once or twice they came together and tried to put things in order, but just as they came, so they left, for dissension consumes the House of Jacob like a moth and has brought them to differences of opinion. Nothing has resulted from these meetings, and weeks will pass and months will go by and there will be meetings after meetings and there will be no salvation for the matters of the town.

It is therefore appropriate that the Rabbi, the Great Luminary, who has remained for a few more weeks in our town before parting from us to move to the town of Vekshno, should pay attention to this matter and restrain the people and that he alone should choose four wise men (as he advised in his sermon on the Sabbath) who have never deceived anyone nor have defiled their hands – and these four men will choose a respected rabbi because after he leaves, the quarreling will flare up even more vehemently, for each person will want to be among the four chosen. Therefore, let the rabbi undertake this good task and may he receive a complete reward from the Lord who recompenses man with kindness according to his deeds, and may there be peace in our town!

**"*HaYom*" 23 *Tevet*, 5647 (Jan. 19, 1887), No. 5**

The residents of our town, who have been accustomed to seeing great men, men of renown on the seat of the rabbinate, will not choose just anyone and therefore I consider it my duty to announce at the outset that any person unsuited to wearing the crown of the rabbinate will not have the honor of sitting in his place and not trudge here needlessly nor waste his money, for in an adorned town such as ours, where geniuses have always sat on the chairs on judgment, the residents will only accept someone who has become world famous, and only such people have the hope of being welcomed with love and inheriting the seat of honor.

**"*HaYom*" 17 *Shvat* 5647 (1887) No. 25**

*[Pages 73-75]*

# Rabbi Mordechai as Rabbi in Korelitz

### Translated from the Yiddish by Harvey Spitzer

In the year 5647 (1887), when Rabbi Eliahu David Kamai left Korelitz and moved to Vekshne, the leaders of the Korelitz community invited Rabbi Mordechai to assume the position of town rabbi. When the leaders of Bitten found out about this, they absolutely refused to let Rabbi Mordechai leave, and a dispute broke out between the two communities.

Finally, Rabbi Mordechai was spirited out of Bitten in the middle of the night. When the residents of Korelitz found out that Rabbi Mordechai was on the way, the whole town travelled several miles to greet him in the middle of the night and they brought him into the town, marching in a parade with bright candles and music.

Rabbi Mordechai conducted the rabbinate autocratically. Everyone was afraid of him and gave him great respect. As was his wont, he did not show favoritism to anyone and treated everyone cordially without exception. He was especially approachable to the poor and to scholars. They say he would seat poor scholars at the head of his table, and the wealthy property owners at the back.

Rabbi Mordechai also established a large *yeshiva* in Korelitz for young men students and for young scholars, and he himself would impart the lessons.

Rabbi Mordechai became famous in Korelitz as a sage and miracle worker, and people would come from everywhere for his advice and blessings. Because of his heavy workload, he had to place notices in the newspapers requesting people not to come to Korelitz as his health would not allow him to tend to so many matters. This, however, was of little avail. Here we must add that Rabbi Mordechai did not consider himself as a miracle worker, and he would explain that the wondrous signs were not miracles at all and that his fine memory and exceptional knowledge of medicine often enabled him to come up with various kinds of advice. Still, many things have been told about him which cannot be explained by simple logic.

A Christian squire from Korelitz, well disposed to Jews, suddenly became paralyzed. He had been to many doctors, but none could help him. His innkeeper advised him to see Rabbi Mordechai. Rabbi Mordechai had a conversation with the squire and asked about his illness and gave him several remedies which actually helped him, and the squire got better in a short time. The squire returned to the rabbi and wanted to give him a lot of money, but the rabbi began putting the money in a charity box for the poor. From then on, the squire would throw in double that amount for poor people on the eve of Passover.

When it became known that Rabbi Mordechai'el was leaving Korelitz, after serving four years as town rabbi, the townspeople were very sad. Wagon drivers and simple people besieged his house in an attempt to prevent him from leaving. A group of community leaders from Oshmena headed by Rabbi Yosef came to Korelitz in the middle of the night and secretly took Rabbi Mordechai'el and his household away on special wagons. It is said that as they were leaving Korelitz, with Rabbi Yosef in one wagon, Rabbi Mordechai laid down a condition that he should be paid only 15 rubles a week, which was the amount he needed to live on, and not more.

Since the Korelitz townspeople had been guarding the highway so that Rabbi Mordechai could not travel to Oshmena, Rabbi Mordechai did not go directly to Oshmena but rather to Slonim, and from there he went on to Oshmena a short time later. In order to avoid parades, which Rabbi Mordechai, a modest person, found unacceptable, he didn't inform anyone about his coming, and he arrived in a peasant's cart, only asking the cart driver to inquire as to where the rabbi's house was located.

When the residents of Oshmena found out that the rabbi had arrived, there was great commotion in the town – storekeepers closed their stores and craftsmen closed their workshops, and everyone went to welcome the rabbi.

Rabbi Mordechai was the rabbi in Korelitz until 5651 (1891).

**"*Dos Vort*", Friday, 13 *Elul*, week of Torah reading "*Ki Teitzei*", 5694 (1934), No. 667.**

---

*[Page 75]*

# Rabbi Mordechai As "Righteous Rabbi" In Korelitz
### Translated from the Hebrew by Harvey Spitzer

We are hereby informing the many readers of this periodical that due to the considerable increase in the number of people travelling to the town of Korelitz from near and far every day to seek advice from our esteemed rabbi, Rabbi Mordechai (Weitzel), may he live a long and happy life, Amen!, and due to the fact that these numerous visitors do not let the rabbi rest and have actually become a burden on the rabbi, who is so busy that he can no longer attend to matters in the town, we have therefore been compelled to place guards at the rabbi's house with his consent so as not to allow anyone- whoever he or she may be- to come to see him.

And the rabbi has likewise ordered us to notify the public in periodicals read by the Children of Israel that it will be in vain for anyone to come and try to see him and speak to him and that any visitor will be wasting his time and money if he expects to have an audience with the rabbi. Moreover, it will be a *mitzvah* for all those who read our words to inform fellow members of the Covenant wherever they may live that it will be useless for them and an unnecessary expense to travel to Korelitz, since no one will be allowed to see the distinguished rabbi, may he live a long and happy life, Amen!

May the Almighty spread his wings of kindness over our brothers, Children of Israel, in all the lands of their dispersion and may He protect and save them from all trouble and distress and from every plague and disease, and may there be peace over Israel! - as they so desire and is likewise the wish of their brothers of the Covenant of the community of the town of Korelitz headed by the Genius, Rabbi Mordechai, may he have a long and happy life!

The undersigned, the day on which "...and you live in security" (Deuteronomy 12:10) is read, 5649 (1889), Korelitz:
Dov Zvi Mayerovitch, Yishayahu Kishelevitch, Mordechai Polozhesky, Avraham Yitzchak Oberzansky

And as a sign and testimony that our words are true, we have sealed our letter with the seal of the community of Korelitz.

I hereby also attest to the fact that everything mentioned above was done with my consent, as I can no longer bear this- may there be peace on Israel!

**HaMelitz, 28 Av 5649 (Aug.25, 1889), No. 179**.

Signed by Mordechai, aforementioned community spokesman (Signed and sealed in the Town Council.)

---

*[Pages 76-77]*

# The Departure Of The "Righteous Rabbi"

## Zalman Yudelevtich

### Translated from the Hebrew by Harvey Spitzer

The streets of Korelitz are in mourning without any visiting pilgrims. Its houses are desolate, the residents are lamenting and embittered.

For three years the esteemed rabbi and miracle worker, Rabbi Mordechai Weitzel, the eminent rabbi from Bitten, lived among us. Our town was an important place. People from all over flocked here – the lame and the blind, every person in distress and desperate, barren women as well as mothers with many children.

People from all over trembled at the mention of this exemplary individual. The roads were filled every day and the residents welcomed people coming to the town to see the rabbi, some on horses and in vehicles, some poor people walking with their canes to the joyful and bustling town. All the houses of the town were filled with guests from near and far, some eating and drinking, and others sitting and rejoicing as the rabbi sat on his holy chair answering each person, including a foreigner who came from a distant city. The rabbi despised no one, rejected no question and made no distinction between Jew and Gentile. Moreover, he refused to take gifts from anyone, even though they urged him to accept a present. Also those who were saved by his words of advice and remembered him for good sent him money and donations from their homes, but the rabbi accepted nothing from them, not even a gift worth a penny. Therefore, his fame spread far and wide, and he gained a fine reputation. And who can count the number of Jacob's children and the number of Gentiles who came here?

**The "Community" Board**
**Inscription on table: "Community" of Korelitz together with the Rabbi"**

Seated (from left to right): Rabbi Moshe Yoselovitch, Rabbi Avraham Yitzchak Cohen, Rabbi Nachum Lubtzky, Yisrael Efroimsky, Moshel Pomerchik, Yoel Becker, _____, Yershel Shkolnik; Standing (from left to right): Pesach Kaplan, Shalom Cohen, Kharlop Slavin, Leibel Pereveluzky, Moshe Rozovsky

And not only did the town of Korelitz see a blessing during the rabbi's tenure, but also the neighboring smaller towns and villages, as well as hotels and wagon drivers received a blessing from the Protector of Jacob, who dwelt in their town. The streets of Korelitz bustled with crowds of people, and they all ate, drank and were merry.

Now, however, that the righteous and exemplary man has left the town, its splendor, beauty and glory have faded and waned, for a few months ago the rabbi left and chose to live in the town of Slonim. He lives there all alone and occupies himself with the study of Torah. As soon as he left Korelitz and gave up being the shepherd of Jewish people, the butchers, slaughterers and cooks began to yearn for him because he usually approved anything that was doubtfully *kasher* [suitable for consumption by Jews], as he was careful about a Jew's money and would always find a way to permit the use of food and utensils and make these things pure thanks to his genius and casuistry.

On the other hand, he took up arms against the new generation of young people and persecuted violators of the Sabbath and Jewish law, and while he was in Korelitz, no one was ever found reading an irreligious book, nor did a young man and girl ever go out together to talk by themselves. The ways of this man were amazing!

And now today, when Korelitz has been left without a rabbi, its eyes are turned towards an exalted rabbi from Minsk, head of a rabbinic college, whose salary is sufficient, for the town of Korelitz will support the rabbi with proper honor and dignity, and emissaries have already left to write up a contract with the head of the rabbinic college in Minsk.

But we have suddenly become important because the first rabbi wants to return to us.

**HaMelitz, 17 Elul 5650 (September 2, 1890), No. 188**

---

[Page 77]

# Rabbi Meir, Son Of Rabbi Yosef Feimer

## Moshe Cinowicz

### Translated from the Hebrew by Harvey Spitzer

He was born in the year 5594 (1834) in Slutzk, son of Rabbi Yosef Feimer, head of the rabbinic court in that community. Rabbi Meir was known as a remarkable authority on matters of Jewish law. His house was open to anyone passing by. He made do with little. When he was accepted as rabbi and his wages set at 18 rubles a week, he took only 10 for himself and divided the rest among the town's judges. He subsequently gave up his position as rabbi in Minsk. In the summer of 5650 (1890), he returned to serve as rabbi in Lechivitch. Rabbi Meir became rabbi in Korelitz after Rabbi Mordechai'le moved to Oshmena. He was active in that small town from 5653- 5656 (1893-1896) and the community of Korelitz was proud of the fact that they merited to have the rabbi of the city of Slutzk serving as head of the rabbinic court in their small town. He died on Thursday, 20 *Iyar* 5671 (1911).

Rabbi Yosele (the second) Feimer, son of Rabbi Meir, was close to his father in Korelitz in his youth. He perfected his Talmudic knowledge in the town's *Beit Midrash* (study hall) and became a specialist in matters of prohibition and permission and in all matters pertaining to the rabbinate. He came to the United States in 5685 (1925), serving as rabbi at Congregation Beth-El in New York, where he died on the first day of the month of *Kislev* 5699 (1939)

---

*[Page 78]*

# Rabbi Avraham Yaakov Bruk

## Moshe Cinowicz

### Translated from the Hebrew by Harvey Spitzer

He was born in Novogrudek. He received a traditional Torah-Talmudic education. He studied in his native town and likewise at the Mir Yeshiva, which was then under the direction of Rabbi Chaim Leib Tiktinski, who was also the main Talmud lecturer at the *yeshiva*. (His son, Rabbi Avraham Tiktinski, was also head of the college in the *yeshiva* and was the father-in-law of the writer and editor, Mr. Moshe Cohen, son of Rabbi Avraham Yitzhak Cohen from Korelitz. M.C). Rabbi Avraham Yaakov was ordained as a rabbi by Rabbi Yechiel Michel Epstein, head of the rabbinic court in Novogrudek, author of the "*Aruch HaShulchan*". He was also ordained by Rabbi Mordechai Weitzel, whose daughter he married in the meanwhile. When Rabbi Mordechai moved from Bitten to serve as rabbi in Korelitz, his son-in-law, Rabbi Avraham Yaakov also moved with him and was supported by his father-in-law, who trained him in rabbinic decision making and in the practical application of *halacha* (Jewish law).

Rabbi Avraham Yaakov distanced himself from the yoke of the rabbinate and refused to exploit the rabbinate for his personal gain, just managing to earn a living by doing other kinds of work. He eventually moved back to Bitten (the town where his father-in-law, Rabbi Mordechai'le had served previously as rabbi) and earned a living as a glazier. It was only in his later years that he consented to accept a small payment of a few rubles from the residents of the community as their judge and "Teacher of Righteousness" (rabbi).

Rabbi Avraham Yaakov Bruk was great in knowledge of Torah, well versed in religious philosophy and was familiar with Hebrew research literature and streams of modern Hebrew literature. He was a public activist, coming to the aid of the suffering and needy and served as delegate to the JCA (Jewish Colonization Association).

He was an enthusiastic *Chovev Zion* (Lover of Zion) in Korelitz and in Bitten. His fund raising and donations on behalf of *Chovevei Zion* in Korelitz became a household word in the entire area. He especially influenced the young ritual slaughterer and examiner, Rabbi Mordechai Avraham, in Korelitz to be faithful to the *Chovevei Zion* movement (later political Zionism), and when he moved away from Korelitz, he left the strengthening of the movement in the hands of the aforementioned local ritual slaughterer. Despite the persecutions on the part of the extreme ultra-orthodox, especially the *Chassidei Slonim*, he would always show up at the meetings of the Zionist youth in these places and in adjacent small towns and even in Mir. He founded Zionist associations in the districts of Novogrudek and Slonim and travelled to Zionist conferences – at his own expense. Despite his poor means, he managed to support his family, albeit with difficulty. He also signed an appeal on the part of a group of young rabbis in support of the *Po'alei Zion b' Eretz Yisrael* (Workers of Zion in the Land of Israel) for the purpose of their settling the land by establishing colonies.

Rabbi Avraham Yaakov Bruk passed away in the year 5674 (1914). His relative, Chaykel Lonsky, a librarian at the Shtrashon Library in Vilna, wrote and article of appreciation about him in the Hebrew periodical, *HaZman*, which appeared in Vilna. The writer, Avraham Litvin, also dedicated a short article in his memory in his book, *Yiddishe Neshamot* (Jewish Souls)

---

*[Page 79]*

# An Appeal For Help

### Translated from the Hebrew by Harvey Spitzer

God's anger struck our town yesterday, 16 *Sivan*, when fire went forth from On High and consumed some one hundred and fifty homes within hours. More than half of the town went up in flames. And not only did the best houses serve as fuel (and even though they were insured, it is still cause for sorrow), but among the houses that burned down were also dozens of homes belonging to poor and wretched families who could not afford to purchase insurance for their homes. And now, hundreds of families are wallowing in holes and stables under the open sky – and many of these poor people have no hope of building a tent – even a small one – to serve as a shelter from the rain and cold. And how our hearts shudder at this sight of poverty and paucity, wandering and bereavement, which has suddenly befallen so many impoverished families in our town! And the Lord's hand further chastised us severely in that the four houses of prayer which we had also went up in flames and we no longer have a place to pour out our complaints before the Lord. And the remaining public institutions such as the bathhouse, etc. also burned on the altar, and here we are, standing poor and empty on the smoldering coals, and in this hour of distress, we appeal to our brethren with groaning from the heart and we call out to them:

Dear brethren! May your compassion be stirred upon those of our people who survived the terrible fire! Take pity on us and be generous with your charity! Come to our aid and lend a hand in rebuilding our destroyed temples and also in building houses for dozens of families from among our poor and needy. Have pity on us and come from your city to help and support us as much as possible so that we can repair our ruins, and may your reward be complete from Him Who has chosen Israel, and may you be blessed by the poor and unfortunate in our town and the world.
Requesting your help with a broken and pained heart,

Avraham Yitzchak HaCohen, the holy community of Korelitz, District of Minsk.

*"HaTzfira"* **22** *Sivan* **5673 (June 19, 1913)**

---

*[Pages 79-80]*

# Torah Personalities- Native-Born Sons Of Korelitz

## Moshe Cinowicz

**Translated from the Hebrew by Harvey Spitzer**

### A. RABBI NISSAN BROIDAH (5617- 5664, 1857-1904)

Rabbi Nissan Broidah was born in Korelitz in the year 5617 (1857). He was a teacher at the *yeshiva* in Rozhenoi (Grodno district) under the supervision of Rabbi Mordechai Gimpel Jaffe (1820-1890).

He served for several years as head of the rabbinic court in the small town of Shiniavski (near Nesvizh), 13 years as head of the rabbinic court in Krevel, a small town in the province of Vilna and 13 more years in the small town of Horodok in the district of Bialystok, where he was accepted as rabbi at the recommendation of Rabbi Mordechai Weitzel, who was closely acquainted with Rabbi Nissan Broidah when he was the head of the rabbinic court in Korelitz, Rabbi Nissan's place of birth.

Rabbi Nissan Broidah was famous as a scholar, a man of imposing figure and an industrious public and religious activist. He established a splendid synagogue and other public buildings in Horodok. He was involved in benevolent institutions, took care of neglected sick people and, together with all this, frequented "tents of Torah" and gave scholarly lessons to groups of students of Talmud.

He was an enthusiastic *Chovev Zion* (Lover of Zion) and devoted much of his spiritual and physical energies to strengthening this movement in the towns where he served as rabbi and in surrounding towns. The incentive to do so came from his teacher, Rabbi Mordechai Gimpel Jaffe. From the time he became head of the rabbinic court in Horodok, he was close to Rabbi Shmuel Mohilever, who was among those coming to his house in Bialystok and was influenced by him. Afterwards he gave his support to political Zionism by giving sermons and in practical work. He organized Zionist meetings in his house and encouraged young people to join the Zionist movement.

The leaders of the Zionist movement appreciated Rabbi Broidah's activity and chose him as delegate to the Third Zionist Congress, which took place in London in the year 5660 (1900) and which was also attended by Rabbi Y.Y.

Reines of Lida and by Rabbi Yaakov Rabinowitz of Sofotskin. In the framework of this trip, Rabbi Broidah gave sermons on behalf of Zionism in several synagogues in London and Warsaw and took part in the Zionist Conference in Minsk in the year 5662 (1902) and belonged to the *Mizrachi* faction at this conference. The *Mizrachi* faction was founded in the month of *Adar* 5662 (1902) in Vilna, and Rabbi Broidah established a branch of *Mizrachi* in his small town and worked on behalf of *Mizrachi* in Bialystok and, thanks to his efforts, the group, *Shlomei Emunei Zion* became a branch of the *Mizrachi* center in Vilna.

In one of his articles on behalf of Zionism which appeared in *HaTsfira* (1900, Vol. 141), Rabbi Nissan Broidah writes: " The Zionist spirit is a pure spirit in whose power even those who have gone away and turned their back on Judaism are now returning and coming close to their people and religion." He expresses the hope that when the rabbis and the ultra-orthodox community awaken to Zionist activity: "then there will be no more fear of the religious being swallowed up by the free-thinkers who presently stand at the head of the Zionist movement." Only good will and joint enquiry and discussions will help, according to him, to bring the leaders of the ultra-orthodox and the irreligious closer to working in partnership for the sake of Zionism. At the conclusion of the article, Rabbi Broidah proposes an assembly of rabbis who are sympathetic to the Zionist cause for the purpose of consultations: how to broaden the idea of Zionism and how to enlarge the national treasure. This great rabbi passed away in the year 5664 (1904), when he was only 47 years old.

*[Page 80]*

# B. RABBI YISRAEL MICHAL YESHURUN

Rabbi Yisrael Michal Yeshurun was born in Korelitz. His father, Rabbi Chaim, saw to it that his son received a strong Torah education. Rabbi Yisrael Michal Yeshurun was a disciple of Rabbi DovBer Jaffe, when the latter was head of the religious court in Korelitz. He also arranged and prepared his writings for publication. He moved to Minsk, where he was appointed head of the *yeshiva* attached to the *Beit Midrash HaGadol* (Great Study Hall or Synagogue).

Rabbi Yisrael Michal Yeshurun is described by the author of the book, "Rabbis and Sages of Minsk" as "a perfectly wise and erudite man, great in understanding and a great genius in Torah... magnanimous, active in many fields and resourceful." Rabbi Yisrael Michal of Korelitz gave his approval to the book *Derech Tvunot* (Way of Reason) [Minsk, 5595 (1835)]

Rabbi Yisrael Michal Yeshurun died in the prime of life. One of his associates, Rabbi David Tevli, chief rabbi of the Minsk community, said the following about him: "This rabbi and great luminary was a giant in Torah and a toiler in

Torah. And he had nearly no other occupation than studying Torah. He was a kind of great thinker who plumbed the depths of Torah with his common sense. And he taught many pupils, for he gave a regular lesson at the *Beit Midrash HaGadol*, covering *Magen Avraham* and *Yoreh De'ah* (sections of the *Shulchan Aruch*, Code of Jewish Law). His fame spread far and wide as a result of his *responsa* and, in addition, he possessed many fine qualities, and all matters pertaining to the administration of the city and general public were articulated by him."

*[Pages 81-82]*

# C. RABBI URI DAVID BEN YOSEF

Rabbi Uri David Ben Yosef was born in Korelitz. He received a Torah education and studied several years in the town of the *porshim* ("abstainers" - men who left their wives to study Torah) – Eishishok. He was the head of the rabbinic court in Niemaksht and later in old Zager. He gained fame in the world of rabbis and yeshivot through his book, *Aperion David*, which was published in Vilna in the year 5633 (1872).

According to the preface of this book, we know that the author, Rabbi Uri David, was a native of Korelitz and that his father's family name was - Aperion. In addition, the author informs us that he is from the family of the sharp and well-versed rabbi, Rabbi Moshe Yosef, of saintly memory, head of the rabbinic court in the community of Oshmena and from the family of the sharp, well-versed and clever late rabbi, Rabbi Our Teacher Moshe, son of Avraham Ne'eman, of saintly memory from the community of Turetz. His mother, Chaya Devorah, was the daughter of Rabbi Shlomo Zalman, a relative of the righteous late rabbi, Rabbi Our Teacher Moshe Yosef, of saintly memory, head of the rabbinic court in Eishishok.

Rabbi Uri David's brother-in-law, Rabbi Ephraim who, some 40 years ago (before the publication of the aforementioned book, *Aperion David*), was appointed rabbi of the community of Paritsh, described Rabbi Uri David as "the venerable, renowned, great expert in both Talmuds (Babylonian and Jerusalem) and also in deciders of questions of Jewish law and who never left the "tents of Torah" all his days."

We have brought down here the lineage of Rabbi Uri David in mentioning names of spiritual personalities who branched out from this precious stock. Our purpose in recalling the names of these Jewish scholars and men of renown is to make known the remarkably high level of scholarship and piety that characterized the community of Korelitz in those days 150 and more years ago. And as a classical example: the respected family of Rabbi Yosef Aperion. In his book, *Aperion David*, the young author brings the Talmudic intercourse which he had with Rabbi Yitzchak Yehoshua, a judge in Mir, who was also a native son of Korelitz.

Rabbi Uri David was inclined to the *Chibat Zion* movement which, at that time, was just at its inception and was a matter of interest to exceptional individuals only. We see how this abovementioned rabbi contributes on behalf of the *Mazkeret Moshe* operation in Jerusalem, (named for Sir Moses Montefiore) and thanks to his influence, some one hundred people contributed to this aim from the small town of Zager and the surroundings.

Rabbi Uri David's offspring: Rabbi Eliahu Dov Rabinowitz, (died in Jerusalem), Rabbi Yosef Yaakov Rabinowitz, ritual slaughterer and examiner in Rostov on the River Don and Menachem Mendel Aperion. His daughter was married to Rabbi Shabbtai Chaim, expert ritual slaughterer and examiner and outstanding teacher in Boisk, Latvia, author of the book, *Zahav Shachut* [new interpretations of legends, Berlin 5676 (1916)].

**[HS: Note: The following paragraph refers to <u>Rabbi Yitzchak Yechiel Davidson</u> (page 68).]**

Children born in Korelitz in the year of Rabbi Yitzchak Yechiel Davidson's death were named after him. Among them was the author, Rabbi Yitzchak Yechiel, son of Rabbi Naftali. This Rabbi Yitzchak devoted himself to the study of Torah. In his youth, he knew both local rabbis, Rabbi Mordechai Weitzel and Rabbi Meir Feimer, who encouraged him in his path. He wrote a book, *Yad HaTalmud*, on the tractate Baba Kama and another book, *Yesodai Torah* on the six orders of the Mishna, which he lived to see published in the year 5690 (1930). The approvals of the two aforementioned rabbis of Korelitz appear on this book. These were given as early as 5670 (1910). We find Rabbi Yitzchak Yechiel in Jerusalem, frequenting "tents of Torah" in the old Jewish colony.

[Pages 82-83]

# RABBI AVRAHAM YITZCHAK COHEN

**Left: Rabbi Avraham Yitzchak Cohen**
**Right: Wife of Rabbi Avraham Yitzchak Cohen (née Rapaport)**

Rabbi Avraham Yitzchak Cohen, son of Rabbi Shalom Cohen, was born in the year 5612 (1852) in the small town of Pleshtsenitz (Minsk region) to upright and God-fearing parents. From the time of his birth, he excelled in lofty skills and gained fame as "the child prodigy from Pleshtsenitz". When he was 14 years old, he married the daughter of the respected and beloved rabbi, Rabbi Avraham Ze'ev Rapaport, from his town and in whose house his son-in-law studied Torah day and night and rose higher and higher. When he came to Volozhin at the age of 18, he was already great in knowledge of Torah and occupied the most honorable place among the students at this great *yeshiva*, where the Genius Rabbi Naftali Zvi Berlin (the *Netziv*) and the Genius Rabbi Chaim Soloveitchik – may they live long and happily, Amen! – showed him respect and recognized his worth. He subsequently frequented the home and attended lessons of the Genius and "Great One", Rabbi Yerucham Yehuda of Minsk, who involved him in all matters of Torah and *halacha* (Jewish law), and this above-mentioned genius mentioned him several times as being wise in regard to his new interpretations. He served as rabbi in 5646 (1886) in the town of Pisatsneh (Minsk region) and a few years later was called to honor and occupy the seat of the rabbinate in the respected town of Korelitz. This notable rabbi excelled in his marvelous expertise of the Talmud and deciders of matters of Jewish law. He takes a place among the great rabbis of Israel with his honest intellect and ability to grasp ideas quickly.

*Oholei Shem*, pg. 175, **Shmuel Noah Gottlieb**

---

*[Page 83]*

# Rabbi Abrazhansky
## Moshe Cinowicz
### Translated from the Hebrew by Harvey Spitzer

Rabbi Abrazhansky lived in Korelitz, having moved there from the nearby town of Mir. He was a walking encyclopedia, a man of diverse interests, a brilliant scholar. He didn't stop studying from the dawn of his youth to the day he died. He was familiar with general science, knew Russian perfectly and his knowledge of the Hebrew language and literature was a model for all the Ultra-Orthodox in the surroundings. He also excelled as a man of deeds and as a merchant. He died in the year 5700 (1940). His daughter, Nechama, is the wife of M. Gvirtzman, one of the veterans of the *HaPoel HaMizrachi* movement in Israel and former Deputy Mayor of Jerusalem. His daughter Nechama received a general education and, like her husband, is also one of the veterans in the vanguard of the *HaPoel HaMizrachi*.

# Rabbi Yosef From Korelitz

Rabbi Yosef **Shimshelevitz** from Korelitz moved to Eishishuk when he was 15 years old. He studied at least 18 hours a day. His exemplary diligence and his excellent memory served him well and even as a young man was an expert in Talmud and in authorities in matters of Jewish law, eventually becoming one of the outstanding rabbis of his generation with his superior erudition. He could quote Rashi and the Talmud without any hesitation. He would review his studies a hundred times. He was perfectly familiar with the Talmud and authorities in matters of Jewish law, yet he was modest and shunned people and publicity.

Rabbi Yosef Shimshelevitz went to live in the Land of Israel and settled in Jerusalem, where he taught Torah for its own sake at one of the yeshivot without being conspicuous. The élite knew about him, held him in high regard and admired him. He was especially admired by Rabbi Avraham Yitzchak HaCohen Kook, head of the Jerusalem rabbinic court and Chief Rabbi of the State of Israel.

Rabbi Yosef of Korelitz passed away in Jerusalem in the year 5694 (1934). The Genius Rabbi Kook said in his eulogy: "The Scroll of the Oral Law has fallen to the ground and its sheets of parchment have been scattered about." He died at the age of 70. In the ultra-orthodox weekly, *Yisod*, 25 *Tammuz* 5694(1934), Rabbi Stolitz wrote an article of appreciation in memory of this great man and described him as "the eternal, diligent student".

---

*[Pages 84-85]*

# My Father, Rabbi Idel Isaac (Alter) Osherovitz

## Bat-Sheva Shula Osherovitz

### Translated from the Hebrew by Harvey Spitzer

**Rabbi Idel Isaac Osherovitz**

My father, Rabbi Idel Isaac (Alter) Osherovitz, was born in Korelitz in the year 5645 (1885). He was the son of Rabbi Moshe Avraham and Leah-Deibeh. My grandfather, a copyist of Scriptures, was an upright and God-fearing Jew, a decades-long resident of Korelitz, who lived his last years in the Land of Israel, where he died on 7 *Nissan* 5693 (1933) and was brought to eternal rest in Petach Tikvah. My grandmother died in the prime of life in Korelitz and left behind three daughters and three sons, the oldest of whom was my father. Already as a child, my father stood out with his keen mind and ability to grasp ideas quickly, and everything he learned was absorbed in his memory and bore fruit. Likewise, he was deeply impressed by everything his eyes saw and his ears heard in his parents' house in his hometown of Korelitz and would often tell his own family about these things until the end of his life. When my grandfather became aware of his oldest son's abilities, he gave much thought to providing him with a good education. My father left Korelitz at a young age and went to study Torah at the Mir and Slobodka *yeshivot*, where he gained renown as a child prodigy, well-versed in Talmud and in authorities of matters of Jewish law until he was ordained as a rabbi. After his marriage in the small town of Shkidel (Skidel?) which is in (Greater) Lithuania, he went into business but did not derive any satisfaction from this occupation, for all his thoughts were given to Torah and knowledge. The young man likewise turned down an offer to serve in the rabbinate, preferring instead to devote his time and energy to teaching Torah. He was afforded this opportunity when he was appointed director of the yeshiva *Ohel Yitzchak* in Kovno. He would draw pearls of wisdom from treasures of the Torah and its commentators, and his words remained engraved in the hearts of his students and audiences for a long period.

My father was tall and majestic in appearance, and all those who came into contact with him were enchanted by his personality which overflowed with charm and kindness. It was difficult for him to see anyone in hardship and he never turned down anyone's request. Besides his devotion to teaching Torah to his many pupils, his soul was given to dreaming about the final redemption and the glad tidings of national revival which made his heart throb. He took part as a delegate in conferences of the *Mizrachi* movement in Lithuania and educated his family to love the Jewish People and the Land of Israel. He was fluent in Hebrew and yearned all his life to go and live in Israel with his family, but death put an end to the fulfillment of his aspirations, as he passed away in the prime of life at the age of 48. He had always wished to go back to Korelitz to see his family and the townspeople, who were dear to him and were preserved in his memory, but he was unable to realize this ambition as well, due to the severing of relations between Poland and Lithuania in those days. I, the sole survivor of our family which perished in the Holocaust, was privileged to go and live in Israel and know my grandfather, of blessed memory, and my Uncle Bezalel and my cousins (my aunt's children) Shaul, Leah and Dov – may they be set apart for a long life!

The opportunity I have been given to recall the memory of my father, of blessed memory, makes me feel, all the more intensely, the beautiful life we had in our pleasant and dear home which was destroyed together with all the homes of the Jewish People in the sorrowful Diaspora. I can see with my own eyes the image of the little town of Korelitz, abounding with tenderness, warmth and love of people – the small town where my father was born and spent his childhood years.

*Beit Midrash* (study hall) in Korelitz

*[Page 86]*

# THE TALMUDIC GROUPS IN KORELITZ

### Translated from the Hebrew by Harvey Spitzer

**Told by the writer and Hebrew teacher, Y. Ovsi (Yehoshua Ovseyewitz), native of Korelitz and well known in the *yeshivot* of Mir, Novogrudek and Maltsh, where he studied as a young man and was known as *Alter Korelitzer*, - in his article, "Rabbi Yosef Yozel" about various Talmud groups:**

The *mitzvah* to strengthen Torah learning was one of the most beloved commandments performed by all the Jewish People. Already in the generations just prior to our generations, many of the rabbis, who were invited by community leaders to bring honor to their town, insisted on the consent of the community leaders to support a certain number of Torah students according to the importance of the town, and the communities very gladly fulfilled this condition.

These groups of students were free of all supervision. In every study hall or synagogue which the groups frequented, there was someone (especially the beadle of that study hall) who would try to find "meals for a day" for the young men students of the group who came from other small towns. Every family of whatever means – even a poor family – considered it its duty to share their meals with one of the members of the group, and well-to-do families would feed two or three at their table.

These groups, some of which would gather together from the town itself, were free of all administration – unlike at the *yeshivot* where they were supervised by the head of the *yeshiva*. Instead, they were under the supervision (indirectly) of the head of the local rabbinic court who knew (together with the best of the scholars of the town) the power of perseverance, ability and manners of each and every one of the students in the group.

There were also charitable women in several of the small towns who would feed any young man of the group who lacked a place to eat on any day. There was such a woman in Korelitz whose name was Devorah Shimshelevitz. She deserved to be called "Mother of the *yeshiva* boys". Every day, whether sunny or rainy, she would trudge through the lanes of the small town on her old legs and collect money and all kinds of food, and any young man who needed a meal would turn to her house, where he would find what he required.

---

## Moshe Cinowicz – Tel Aviv

## A.    Rabbi Zvi Menachem Zisling

### Translated from the Hebrew by Harvey Spitzer

Rabbi Zvi Menachem Zisling was among the students in the group of *prushim* ("abstainers") in Korelitz. He was born in Shkod in the year 5626 (1866), son of Rabbi Ben-Zion Aryeh Leib Zisling, one of the writers for the Hebrew periodical *HaLevanon* and one of the most active religious public workers in that generation.

Rabbi Zvi Menachem Zisling was an ardent *Chovev Zion* and went to live in the Land of Israel in the year 5674 (1914). He received a position as teacher of Talmud in the *Tachkemoni* school in Tel Aviv and served in that position until almost the end. He was also a very active public worker and was a member of the board of the Tel Aviv Community Council and Municipal Council. He died on 2 *Tevet* 5692 (1932) at the age of 66.

**(According to: "*HaHar*", *Tevet* 5692, Issue 4)**

*[Page 87]*

## B.    Rabbi Meir Levin

### Translated from the Hebrew by Harvey Spitzer

Rabbi Meir Levin was also one of the students in the Korelitz Talmud group and was later appointed rabbi in Vilaika close to Vilna. As an "abstainer" (after his wedding) in Korelitz, he was taken under the wing of Rabbi Yitzchak Yechiel Davidson, from whom this "abstainer" student learned the ways of leadership in the rabbinate and of guiding a Jewish community. He later became an active *Chovev Zion* and also joined political Zionism. He used to say in public that he had a rabbi from Korelitz, Rabbi Yitzchak Yechiel Davidson, who was also – as he was closely acquainted with his mentality and inclination of spirit - faithful to this movement. He also helped the young rabbi, Rabbi Moshe Avigdor, to establish his yeshiva which opened in the year 5671 (1911) in the town of Svantzian, where he first served in the rabbinate.

## C.    Rabbi Yehuda Leib Davidson

### Translated from the Hebrew by Harvey Spitzer

Dr. Yehuda Leib Davidson was also included in the "group" of students in Korelitz. He was a nephew of Rabbi Yitzchak Yechiel Davidson, head of the small town's rabbinic court. He was born in the year 5617(1856) in the town of Kapulia. His father, Rabbi Aharon, who was an expert in Torah and also a religious intellectual, put his son in the charge of a teacher who knew Hebrew grammar very well and who taught him Torah with the commentary of *HaBiur* (Moses Mendelsohn). He studied at the Mir Yeshiva for two years and was then taken into the home of his uncle, his father's brother, Rabbi Yitzchak Yechiel, who was a man of the world and shunned fanaticism. He found satisfaction in the young man's flowery language and poetry, encouraging him to gain perfection in the language of the past. After his uncle's death, the young man went to live with relatives in Minsk. He devoted himself to secular studies as well in order to obtain a matriculation certificate. It was then that the young Davidson published his first work in the Hebrew weekly, *HaKol*. It was entitled "Confronting the Evil" (in four installments) and dealt with the urgent need to establish a high school for Jewish studies in Russia. This essay drew the attention of many writers including Moshe Leib Lilienbaum.

He likewise published articles about agriculture and manufacture among Russian Jews. In 1882 Davidson went to Warsaw, where he lived in penury. His perseverance, ambition and patience enabled him to obtain a matriculation certificate as an outside student. He went on to study medicine at Warsaw University. The well known Polish writer, Clemence Jonusha, suggested that he translate for him some of the finest Yiddish books into Russian, which he would then translate into Polish. He translated two books by Mendele Mocher Sefarim (a native of Kapulia and a childhood friend of the two brothers, Rabbi Aharon and Rabbi Yitzchak Yechiel): "My Horse" and "The Travels of Benjamin the Third" and Clemence translated them into Polish. In 1890 Davidson was awarded a doctorate in medicine. In Paruzhani, Davidson was close to his cousin, head of the local rabbinic court, Rabbi Eliahu Feinstein, who was previously head of the rabbinic court in Korelitz, where they both spent their early years. Dr. Yehuda Leib Davidson published many articles in *HaMelitz*, *HaTsfira*, *HaPardes*, *HaShiloach* and others. He also encouraged his relative, the young Yitzchak Katzenelson, on his way to becoming a future poet among the Jewish People. He died in 1912.

*[Page 88]*

# D.  Rabbi Malkiel And His Connection With Korelitz

### Translated from the Hebrew by Harvey Spitzer

Rabbi Malkiel Tannenbaum, author of a collection of responsa, *Divrei Malkiel* (5 volumes), studied as a young married man at the local *Beit Midrash* in Korelitz during Rabbi Yitzchak Yechiel's term of office in the rabbinate. Rabbi Malkiel was born in the small town of Motileh, the hometown of President Chaim Weizman and his family, according to the President's memoirs. He married a girl in her teens when he himself was quite young. His father-in-law owned property between Yarimitz and Korelitz, and he lived with his father-in-law for a number of years. However, because the tumult and noise of doing business during the six weekdays were very disturbing to this diligent child prodigy, the young Malkiel agreed to study from Sunday to Thursday at the *Beit Midrash* in Korelitz, just a few kilometers away from his father-in-law's home. He studied constantly and several stories have been preserved by the elders of Korelitz about the way the young married student applied himself. On the days he was in Korelitz, he managed to review all Six Orders of the *Mishna* and *Talmud* by sheer concentration, and he mastered all four sections of the *Shulchan Aruch* (Code of Jewish Law) as well as all rabbinic literature, something which astounded all the rabbis in the area. Already then, the head of the rabbinic court could see that this young rabbinic student was destined for greatness. Whenever Rabbi Malkiel's father-in-law came to Korelitz to arrange for provisions for his son-in-law, he would also show generosity to the local *prushim* who studied in Korelitz. He was like a regular member of the head of the rabbinical court's family in Korelitz and would honor the town's rabbi by providing for his needs and for many years continued to do likewise for the rabbi's widow. In this way, he would respond to the needs of the community and was considered a resident of Korelitz at the community level. In his preface to *Divrei Malkiel* part 2 (5657- 1897), he praises his respected father-in-law.

Rabbi Malkiel served 14 years in the town of Bodki. In 5647 (1887), he was invited to accept a position as rabbi of the town of Lomze which he held for 13 years. He died on 8 *Nissan* 5670 (1910).

*[Page 89]*

# Rabbi Meir Hillel Zunser

### Translated from the Hebrew by Harvey Spitzer

In the town of Lubtch (State of Minsk, District of Novogrudek), the joy of Passover turned into deep mourning when an excellent and unique man of inestimable worth was suddenly taken from its residents. He was a great rabbi who had a perfect mastery of languages and sciences, Rabbi Meir Hillel Zunser, of blessed memory.

The deceased was born in Vilna and studied much Torah in poverty and diligently studied Talmud day and night. And in those days, he also studied books of the grammar of our holy language and searched for hidden things. He also set aside time for learning other languages and basic knowledge of mathematics. He studied earth sciences and general history until his knowledge of these subjects was as complete as that of a scholar's.

About 13 years ago, while he was still residing in the town of Korelitz, studying books of authorities of Jewish law, he was ordained by the head of the rabbinic court in Korelitz. Later, however, he went into business and enjoyed the benefits of his toil. In his last years, he was an accountant for companies in Lodz and Warsaw. Few of his friends and acquaintances knew that a living treasure of books was walking among them, for besides his expertise in Talmud and authorities of Jewish law, he read many books in Hebrew, Russian, German and French, and he knew all these languages perfectly and retained everything.

On the first day of the Intermediate Days of Passover, towards evening, he was enjoying himself at home in the company of friends. Then he went to bed but didn't get up again and the doctors' efforts to save him were to no avail, for his soul departed and returned to its Creator. He died at the age of 42 and left behind a wife and seven children. May his dear soul abide in the shadow of the Almighty! And may the Lord comfort his mourners and all his friends who esteem the memory of this great rabbi.

*HaTsfira* 5649 (1889), No. 93                    **Signed: G.**

**Moshe Cinowicz** adds: What is written above that the sage, Rabbi Meir Hillel Zunser, was ordained by the late rabbi of Korelitz, refers to Rabbi Yechiel Yitzchak Davidson, father-in-law of the Genius Rabbi Eliahu Feinstein and father of the mother of the poet, Yitzchak Katzenelson.

Regarding this sage, we must add that he was related to the members of the Meizel family, one of the most splendid and distinguished in Lubtch, including Rabbi Eliahu Chaim Meizel, head of the rabbinic court in Lodz, the Genius Rabbi Baruch Dov Leibowitz, head of the college at the Yeshiva "Knesset Beit Yitzchak" in Slobodka-Kamenitz and - May he be set apart for a long life! – the Genius Yechezkel Avramski, author of *Chazon Yechezkel.* Zunser was also related to the respected Shimshelevitz family, which originated in Lubtch. Several members of this family were residents of Korelitz. One of the female members of the Shimshelevitz family, Mrs. Laske, was an intimate friend of the wife of Rabbi Yechiel Yitzchak Davidson, head of the rabbinic court in Korelitz.

In *HaTsfira* 1896 (No. 38), a "thank you blessing" is transmitted from Korelitz to Mrs. Devorah Shimshelevitz, a generous woman from Korelitz who agreed to establish a Torah supporters group whose aim is to feed 40 young men studying Torah every single day.

---

*[Pages 90-91 - Hebrew]*
*[Pages XXXI-XXXIII – English - below]*
**As on page 371**

# DVORAH AND THE TALMUD ASSOCIATION

## Alter Gitlin

Dvorah, the provider for the *Kibbutz* (Talmud Association) in Korelitz, was well on in years, and so was her dwelling, a rambling structure so low that it seemed to be bowing before the Torah students that kept crossing its threshold. Inside, however, there was a sense of spaciousness. A long table, covered with a spotless white cloth, ran down the middle of the main room, and white benches paralleled it on either side. The room was bright even on bleak winter days, and the scholars (young men who were not invited by other households in town for meals) couldn't tell whether the light came from the pert white curtains at the small windows or from the fond look in Dvorah's eyes.

Dvorah had a system: each weekday morning she would make the rounds of the well-to-do and generous homes in the town and collect the funds which their owners had pledged. Then she would proceed to the market place, purchase the commodities she needed, and prepare a meal for the young men "worthy of Solomon's table". She knew who liked what, and delighted in preparing the special dishes. The scholars also knew what Dvorah liked - the lively sound of pilpulistic disputation, and they engaged in Talmudic debate as Dvorah kept refilling their plates. Then, as they recited the Grace After Meals, she received her reward: "May the Compassionate One bless the mistress of this house". Her eyes would fill with tears of gratitude for the privilege of serving Jewish scholars.

Dvorah also fried potato pancakes for all the *Kibbutz* scholars, poor and rich alike, and none dared not to partake of them, for to have done so was to run the risk of being charged with heresy. The scholars gathered at 1pm at Dvorah's home, crowding each other to get at the morsels. Dvorah apportioned the pancakes to each according to his scholarliness, and the largest portions went to those who spent longest hours on their studies. Amazingly, she knew exactly who was studying how hard, for, in the course of her rounds, she would go up to the women's gallery in the Beth-HaMidrash and look down at her charges, as they argued over a jot and fought over a title. If she spied a group sitting behind the stove and simply chatting, her face would darken and she would cry out: "Bums! Robbers! Why are you wasting your time? Back to your studies!" At the sound of her voice, all the young men in the place would rise to their feet and yell: "Long live Mama Dvorah", at which their benefactress, contrite because of the break in study that she had caused, would hastily withdraw.

Such was Dvorah's custom, for thirty years on end. When she died, the young men took apart the table and fashioned a coffin out of it. The entire town was at the funeral and three rabbis eulogized her. Many have since forgotten her - but not the young men whom she had fed so lovingly, and I, one of them, am paying her this tribute.

**"*Hamizrachi*" 18 Shvat, 5681 (Third year, No. 4), 1921**

---

*[Pages 92-94 - Yiddish - below]*
*[Pages XXX-XXXI - English - slightly different and abridged]*
**See also page 370**

# History Of Korelitz's Ritual Slaughterers

## Sarah Beigin (Gal)

### Translated from the Yiddish by Harvey Spitzer

Korelitz is one of the small towns in White Russia where Jews settled around the 15th century. Victims of persecution, they were driven from place to place and finally began to develop Jewish communities in the Novogrudek region. Wherever a Jewish settlement developed, the leaders of the community were foremost concerned with maintaining religious life. They saw to it that each town had a rabbi, *shochet* (ritual slaughterer), *mohel* (circumciser), *chazzan* (cantor), etc. People who remember the circle of the *shochetim* in Korelitz have surely heard of the very popular *shochet*, Reb Moshe-Yitzchak Volfin, who was everything- a ritual slaughterer, cantor and circumciser. He was brought to Korelitz because he had all the qualities and thus saved the community a lot of money. The town was small and could not afford to support a *shochet* and a *chazzan* separately. It is not known where Reb Moshe-Yitzchak Volfin came from, nor how many children he had. The only thing that was known was that one of his sons was a rabbi in Baksht and his name was Rabbi Zvi. His second son, Chloineh, took over the legal claim to serve as *shochet* in Korelitz when Reb Moshe-Yitzchak was already very old.

In the course of time, Korelitz grew in size and developed. The Jews living there fulfilled the commandment "to be fruitful and multiply" despite the difficult economic situation. The families were burdened with many children.

*Chloineh the Shochet* was a clever Jew and a Torah scholar. He lived out his years in Korelitz. It is not known how many children Reb *Chloineh the Shochet* had, but it is known that, in his old age, he gave one half of his legal claim to serve as *shochet* to his son, Reb Bertche, and the other half as a dowry to his daughter, Duskeh, when she married the son of the rabbinic judge in Kletzk, Reb Yitzchak Dovid Katzenelboigen.

Reb Yitzchak Dovid had 8 children: 4 sons and 4 daughters. His son Avraham Katzenelboigen was a household name. He was a rabbi in the city of Rostov in Russia. He was also very wealthy. A second son, Reb Kalman Beigin, was Reb *Chloineh the Shochet*'s son-in-law. (He changed his family name so as to avoid having to serve in the army.)

Reb Yitzchak-Dovid gave his children a fine education. My grandmother, Freide Hinde, who was Reb *Kalman the Shochet*'s sister, was even able to read a *blatt Gemorah* [a page of Talmud]. Reb Kalman was a scholar with a very sharp mind. He was known throughout the region as a Torah scholar. Reb Kalman had two sons: Reb Yitzchak-Dovid and Reb Nachum-Eizik and five daughters: Sarah-Devorah, Chana, Chana-Mereh, Malkeh and Etta-Tzireh.

Reb Yitzchak Dovid's oldest son became self-supporting early on. He left the small town and moved to Minsk where he had dairy concessions. Before his death, Reb Zalman called his father-in-law, Chloineh, and his brother-in-law, Bertche, and gave them a handshake in the presence of the rabbi, Reb Eli-Baruch, signifying that he was transferring one half of his share of the legal claim to serve as *shochet* to his son, Nachum-Eizik, and the second half as a dowry for his daughter Sarah-Devorah. By doing so, Reb Kalman wished to avoid arguments after his death.

After Reb Kalman's death, Reb Bertche remained the only *shochet* in Korelitz. Nachum-Eizik was not particularly eager to carry out the will of his late father. That was because Nachum-Eizik, a quite modern young man, was influenced by the enlightenment movement and soaked up Zionist literature. He strove to go far away from the small town but was compelled to keep his beard and *peot* [earlocks] and learn the skill of slaughtering animals. Nachum-Eizik had inherited all his father's good qualities. He had a sharp mind, was blessed with a fine sense of humor and was known as a wise man in the town. After marrying off his sister Sarah-Devorah to the son of the rabbi from Baksht, Reb Alter Morduchovitch, Nachum-Eizik transferred the entire legal claim to serve as *shochet* to his sister and moved to Minsk by himself where he joined his brother in business.

It happened that at the end of the First World War, an argument between butchers and the *shochet* broke out in a small town near Minsk. The rabbis from that town decided that a *shochet* from another place should judge the case involving Torah law and hand down a ruling. Since Reb Nachum-Eizik was officially no longer practicing ritual slaughtering, he was invited to be the arbiter of that quarrel. The morning after the judgment was handed down, they found Reb Nachum-Eizik stabbed to death on the ground, wrapped in his prayer shawl and phylacteries. The report of Reb Nachum-Eizik's murder quickly spread through the district but, for various reasons, the matter was hushed up. As the army controlled the roads at that time, the deceased could not be laid to rest in Korelitz and was buried in the Minsk cemetery. Thus did Reb Nachum-Eizik the *Shochet* tragically end his life.

When Reb *Bertche the* Shochet grew weak in his old age and could no longer perform ritual slaughtering, he transferred the legal claim to serve as *shochet* to his son, Reb Moshe-Avraham Volfin, and from that time until the destruction of the Korelitz Jewish community, there were two ritual slaughterers in Korelitz who lived in unity. Reb Moshe-Avraham returned to Korelitz from Poltava, where he was active in Zionist life. However, due to the respect he had for his father, he came back to Korelitz.

Despite his difficult private life and the "pain of raising children", especially "the pain of raising daughters", he was abundantly blessed by the Lord. He led a full cultural life and was socially active in Zionist life in Korelitz. He was the representative of the Jewish National Fund and all the Jews held him in great esteem.

An altogether different sort of person was Reb *Alter the Shochet* - Reb Avraham-Yitchak, an imposing figure with burning, black eyes and with a long, white beard. His whole being recalled the appearance of the Patriarchs. He was very active in religious life in Korelitz. His clothing was neat and clean and he was always seen with a black hat or skullcap on his head, wearing a white collar. Jews gave him the proper respect and he was held in high repute among the Jews of Korelitz.

Both ritual slaughterers lived, as was said, in peace. When they played chess, they would forget the weekday troubles. In this way, both *shochetim* shared the fate of all the Jews in Korelitz.

The children of the *shochetim* did not follow in their fathers' footsteps and did not want to forge the chain of the Korelitz ritual slaughterers. The Zionist movement took them away from their homes. They became pioneers in the Land of Israel.

With the annihilation of the Korelitz Jewish community, the lovely chain of Korelitz ritual slaughterers was also torn asunder and with their death, the dynasty of Korelitz *shochetim* came to an abrupt end.

---

*[Pages 95-96-Hebrew - below]*
*[Pages XVI-XVII –English – abridged -* **See also page 357***]*

# A SHORTCUT TO THE PAST

## Yechezkel Zaks – Tel Aviv

### Translated from the Hebrew by Harvey Spitzer

I see you now my small town of Korelitz, a small town in White Russia. I see you with your little houses and narrow lanes. The people in the small town are seemingly drawn by an artist's hand - each one with his image and fixed character: the "petit bourgeois" storekeeper hopelessly yearning to make a sale; the craftsman owns a workshop and can hardly make a living; the industrialist owns a small factory.

The sound of a trilling melody of young men students pours out from the study hall and penetrates every single place and comes to say that help does not exist for everyday matters only, but is involved with matters from above, in other worlds.

All this is said regarding the world of the town's boys and young men students. The girls attended the *cheder* (religious elementary school) of Moshe *Shreiber* and learned neither Talmud nor Bible, but just Yiddish script and spelling and simple addition, a kind of incidental learning without content and without enthusiasm. And the teacher was called Moshe *Shreiber* because, in addition to being the teacher of girls, he used to be the town's letter writer (*shreiber*). If a letter reached a person who had trouble reading small letters of the alphabet, he or she would bring the letter to Moshe, who would read out the letter to the person who received it and would also write a reply written in lovely, curly letters with the wording according to each one's needs and affairs. The Hebrew letters *lamed* and *feh sofit* still stand before my eyes, and it is on account of his special handwriting that I admired him so much.

This is to point out that if a teacher of boys was not considered to be an important professional, a teacher of girls was ranked even lower professionally, for while a teacher of boys has to maintain order and discipline in order to impart knowledge of Torah to his pupils, a teacher of girls would only place before each girl a kind of a copy of script - and each girl tried to copy what was written, but they never dealt with pertinent matters or real learning. Even the content of the material the girls had to copy was not related to the Bible or any other subject.

Reuven *der rotshetzer* (one who values the rod to maintain discipline) used to teach the girls "Hebrew" and "Hebrew translation", but he too was satisfied with superficial teaching and learning while Yache, his tall and thin wife, helped him, and her voice intermingled with her husband's voice in the translation of words from the prayer book, as her pointer, indicating the letter or word, accompanied her every movement.

The periods of learning in the *cheder* were set according to "seasons", namely winter or summer and, in general, the girls did not spend many "seasons" in the *cheder* of Moshe Shreiber and Reuven Rotshetzer together. Thus passed the "seasons": the girls going and girls coming, and the "method" of teaching remained unchanged. Something finally happened, however, that brought about an essential change in the education of girls in the small town of Korelitz and, of course, a change in all the education in the town. One morning, the rabbi's young daughter, who was also one of the girls in the *cheder*, came and told us that her brother Moshe, who was considered a *maskil* (follower of the enlightenment movement) and a "Zionist" and who studied in a large town, was getting ready to come home for the holidays and intended to stay in town for some time after the holidays. There were hectic preparations for the arrival of Moshe, the rabbi's son, as the town was fond of him and he was known as a Zionist preacher and a good organizer. And indeed, with his coming for the holidays, he introduced a drastic change in the method of teaching and learning in the town. He influenced his friend, Alter-Herzl, to take on the responsibility of educating the girls, and a new period in our lives began all at once. Our learning was no longer incidental and without content. Suddenly we began to learn Bible stories like all the boys.

At the same time, the adults organized into various Zionist groups: "Sons of Zion", "Daughters of Zion" and just Zionists. Torah proceeded from the rabbi's house and reached our *cheder*, which was now called an *advanced cheder*. Our teacher was the rabbi's son's right hand and they were both supported by the enlightened ritual slaughterer whose house became a center of Zionism and enlightenment. Our teacher let us participate in what was going on and we swallowed every word that came out of his mouth. The rabbi's son himself visited our school and supervised the instruction and even tested us. Each one of us tried not to disappoint him and indeed we did not put him to shame.

The school term ("season") passes. The rabbi's son returns to his studies in the big city, but he comes back to the town for every holiday, and the town rejoices when he comes. We organize parties, and pictures of Herzl and other Zionist leaders decorate the walls of the house where the parties are to take place. I remember in particular a visit by the rabbi's son on his return from one of the Zionist Congresses. The first part of his visit was at our *cheder*. He spoke before us and in our eyes it was as though Herzl were standing there alive in person before us.

\*\*\*\*\*

Years passed and the vicissitudes of life took me away from my small town. And behold, one day, in one of the halls, I met the very son of the rabbi from Korelitz, the son whose vision was the dream of our life in our childhood. I recognized him and the vision of the small town of those days passed before my eyes, the small town with the "style" of life of that time and with the cares of those days, many days before the great Holocaust.

These recollections are called to my mind in light of the meeting with Moshe Cohen, the son of the rabbi of Korelitz, who brought me back to those days. I saw our small town again in a hasty glance only for 24 hours in 1930 after an absence of 23 years. I recognized everyone, and everyone remembered me as if we hadn't parted at all. Of course, the young people I met were different from those of my period. This time I encountered young people who were consciously Zionistic, educated, speaking Hebrew and knowledgeable about world affairs. The school was already normal with a full curriculum of subjects. I saw our small town and the young people who were preparing to go to live in the Land of Israel. I saw young people studying in big cities and I thought that a new period had awakened my small town, but that was a vision of illusions: it was an awakening before the great tragedy which had been hovering over the heads of European Jewry for many years and which destroyed everything, nearly everything.

---

*[Pages 97-99 Hebrew - below]*
*[Pages XVIII-XIX - English - abridged version -* **See also page 358***]*

# HOW DID WE STUDY?

## Esther Shkolnik-Hurwitz

### Translated from Hebrew by Ann Belinsky

How did we study in Korelitz? How were we educated from a young age and until we became independent? In order to answer these questions, I first have to describe briefly the image of our town during that period. Korelitz was situated far from the large cities. The biggest city close to us was Novogrudek - which also was not considered to be large.

This was in the period between the two World Wars. After the First World War, many cities had normal educational systems with qualified teachers and study programs - which was not the case with us. Our life did not yet suit these demands. When a child reached the age of three or four, he met with the realities of life at that time: parents troubled with their livelihood, who had no time to worry about the child or his education. Who knew then about children's games? A child's education was haphazard and influenced by the environment, the street and the child's friends.

At the age of 6 -7 he was sent to *cheder*. I well remember mine, in the home of R' Aharon Yaakov Dovidovitz - a large room, long table, benches on either side. R' Aharon Yaakov wore a skull-cap, he was serious and attentive all hours of the day; he taught "reading, writing, as well as arithmetic" (the primary steps of addition and subtraction). It was called an *advanced cheder*. We studied from morning till evening, reading and transcribing entire pages of the *Chumash* (Pentateuch), after having learned their contents, word by word, in Yiddish translation. And woe to the pupil who failed to remember! A male miscreant was placed in a corner with a dirty *shtreimel* dunce cap on his head to be the object of ridicule by all the pupils. For girls, the usual punishment was to put their name on the blackboard and write a large zero filled with smaller zeros next to the name. On the other hand, a good student was rewarded with 5's next to her name. Naturally the children were ashamed of the bad punishment and tried to delete the negative grades from the wall, but were also scared that the punishment would be doubled.

The next, higher *cheder* was R' Yitzhok's. He was well-versed in the Bible, Talmud and grammar; he was very aggressive to the pupils, especially to the boys whom he would punish for the slightest thing, pinching them or even slapping their cheeks. He had a much better relationship with the girls, treating them tenderly and with affection and would praise them for their diligence and knowledge.

In the *cheder* the terms of "games" or "entertainment" did not exist - only "to study" and "to study". But with time - a Yiddish-Hebrew elementary school was established. The teachers were local youth with expert knowledge in different fields - each was invited to teach the subject that suited him: Accountant Yitzhok Klatzki taught arithmetic, Poet Zvi Kivelevitz was invited to teach Hebrew, R' Itzke taught Talmud and grammar, and Mr Shuster taught nature studies.

The pupils sat examinations before entering this school and were divided into classes as in a real school. We opened our eyes and breathed a sigh of relief: we had left the darkness for the bright light: here was a school like "the others" with recesses, bells, and naturally games during the recess. The school did not have a study program or a standard; none of the teachers were qualified; the standard of the studies was different from other schools, but we pupils were happy because we had returned to childhood, which the *cheder* had stifled. We hiked during the holidays, we organized classroom dramatics and felt the pulse of life.

But even with this school, matters were not finished; our parents were worried: how would their children fare, in a foreign land? What would we get with all these studies in Hebrew and Yiddish? One needs to know Polish for the future, for advancing in life, and so we were transferred to the Polish elementary school, with all the *shiktzim* and *shiktsas* gentiles. This was a difficult transition period - The adaptation to the mixed group of Poles, Russians and Jews; learning the Polish language, different study subjects and a different life. The teachers here were qualified. Here we studied new subjects that we previously did not know existed: singing, art, gymnastics. The Jewish students enthusiastically took up their studies and soon outdistanced their Polish fellow students. The result: envy and hatred.

The principal of the Polish school, named Dolemba, was a good-natured but far from being a good educator: he was also a pleasure-hunting drunkard, rolling around the streets at nights and being a bad example to his pupils. But we Jewish students tried to obtain only the good from the school and ignore the bad, damaging side. The aim of the Jewish students was to finish their studies successfully, so as to go on to higher education in the big cities. Together with these aims, we did not forget our origins and we tried as much as possible to deepen our knowledge in the Hebrew language and culture. Here appeared the noble Benjamin Ovseyvitz who privately taught us Hebrew. He was the complete opposite of the Polish school headmaster Dolemba: an inspired man, with a delicate soul who succeeded implanting in us love for the national language and the desire to continue to study.
 [Those of us who managed to continue with our studies always recalled him with love and affection. Other Korelitz teachers who held classes in their homes were Hershel Dobkes, Berl Feivel from Eishishuk, Zelig der Schorser (who also did watch repairing) and Zvi Hirsh Chessler. - *written in the English version only -AB*]

Only a few managed to realize their desires. But those who did and left the town for the large cities felt a strong spiritual connection to the town where they grew up and took their first steps - the town with the friends and the people that we loved so much.

---

בית־ספר עממי עברי, קורליץ. התרפ״ח

[Page 99]     The elementary Hebrew school, Korelitz, 5688 - 1928

*[Pages 100-101] Yiddish*
*[Pages XIX-XXI] English (below)*
**As on page 360**

# R' Zvi-Hershel Hacohen Boyarsky

## by Zippora Katzenelson-Nachumov

Ignorance had no place in the "Old Shul". There the folks studied Torah and Talmud day and night. Around it were the public institutions of the community: the Rabbi's home (the "Cold Shul", so named because the temperature inside was always cooler than outside - summer <u>and</u> winter). Beyond was an even cooler spot - the cemetery, with its headstones sunken into the ground among the weeds - except for the modest mausoleum of the deceased Rabbi, R' Yitzhok Yechiel, for whom Yitzhok Katzenelson was named. On the other end of the courtyard was the warmest spot in town - the *schvitzbad*, the Turkish bath, so-called.

Opposite the Old Shul and the cemetery was the Hassidic *shtibel* [a place for prayer and also a place for community gathering] of the Koidanover Rebbe. The first *Gabbai* of the *shtibel* was R' Zvi-Hershel Hacohen Boyarsky, a teacher by occupation and understandably a man of modest means. He was a jolly person, rotund and built close to the ground, and he sported a short black beard. He had unbounded faith and was ever in good spirits. His fine singing voice resounded through the alleys and lifted the hearts of his listeners. No *simcha* [joyful occasion] in the *shtibel* was worth the name without his presence, and his preparations to visit the Rebbe in his town was an event in Korelitz.

He was beloved for his gaiety by all his students. He was also a born teacher and knew how to handle the children; the pupils who lagged behind were taken into the smaller room for "private instruction" as in the main room the older pupils taught the younger ones. Yitzhok Katzenelson often spoke of the influence that these surroundings had upon him in his childhood days. This was the background of his future folk poem, "The Sun in Flames is Setting". He often returned to it in later years, visiting the Rabbi's house where his cradle was still standing. And on each occasion he would remark, sadly, that R' Zvi-Hershel was no longer among the living.

**Coordinator's note:** Harvey Spitzer notes that the **Yiddish text** (Pages 100-101) is almost identical to the above English text. At the bottom of the <u>Yiddish</u> text, it is noted that the article is derived from:

**Zippora Katzenelson-Nachumov: Yitzhak Katzenelson: His Life and Works. Ch. 7, Pages 55, 56, 57. [In Yiddish].**

---

*[Page 102]*

**The Pedagogic Council and Parents Committee at the Hebrew School
in the year 5687 (1927)**

**From right**: Yaacov Galwitzky, Shamai Klatzkin; Moshe Avraham Volfin; Tzvi Kibelevitz;
Spokoyna; Rabbi Vernik;; -------; Chaim Bussel; Baruch Shimshelevitz; Yitzhak Meir Kaltzitzky;
Tuvia Kaltzitzky (Kolczycki).

**The "*Kehila*" (Community) Executive Board with Alexander Harkaby**

**From right:** Bakar; Pesach Kaplan; Shalom Cohen; A. Harkaby; Rabbi Moshe Yossilevitz;
Bakar; Michael Shuster; Nissan Rakovitsky.

*[Page 103]*

# BEFORE AND BETWEEN THE TWO WORLD WARS

## FROM THE JEWISH PRESS

## RECOLLECTIONS & WAY OF LIFE

[Pages 104-105]

## *From the Jewish press*

# Love Of Zion In Korelitz

### Translated from the Hebrew by Ann Belinsky

Korelitz announces: that at the recent Festival of Pesach they celebrated the anniversary of the establishment of their *Chovevey Tzion* (Lovers of Zion) association, and indeed they can be happy. For their hope was not disappointed and, in a town as small as theirs, they managed to collect over the year one hundred and sixty rubles for the benefit of their lofty idea. An amount of money that they never dreamed they would collect. And the heads of their association can be happy that they saw fruits of their labor. And indeed they labored and toiled very much, and not only in their own town, but they also worked to spread their ideology to other places. They wrote arousing letters and sent them to other towns in their area, so that they too would be aroused. And indeed their words were successful, and people as far as Novogrudek, Mir and other towns were aroused by their call and honorable associations were established in these places as well.

**"*HaMelitz*", 27 *Iyar* 5658 (Edition 100, 19th May, 1898)**

*** 

**Moshe Haim Cohen**

On the second intermediate day of Passover many of the townspeople gathered in one of the *Batey Midrash* where the accounts were presented to them, and they also read from some pamphlets which discussed Zionism. And the people were satisfied. The listeners were surprised by the pleasant sermon of one of the heads of the association, the scholar, Moshe Haim Cohen, son of the local Rabbi, who is both the writer for their association and also the editor of the florid letters which were sent around the country. Although Mr. Moshe Cohen spoke a short time, his words were very effective. And after refreshing their hearts with fruit of the produce of our Holy Land, the assembled people returned home happy and goodhearted with the name of Zion engraved on their hearts. Mr. Cohen agreed to the request of those imploring him, and promised to preach his words another time on Zion, and on the seventh day of Passover a huge mass of people gathered again in a private house. And after they read the speech of Dr Herzl, who had lectured in London in the Maccabee Hall, Mr Cohen spoke for two full hours. His words spoke to hearts of the listeners and were very effective, for on the day following Passover many more joined the association. Those who had never imagined that they would support the organisation, did so.

**"*HaMelitz*", 25 *Elul* 5658, (12th September, 1898, Edition 195)**

\*\*\*

The representative of the Odessa Committee in Korelitz, Moshe Avraham Volfin, the ritual slaughterer, collected contributions from the people of Korelitz as follows, for the good of the settling the Land of Israel for the aims delineated below.

On Shabbat Nachmo 5658 (1898) the *Chovevey Tzion* assembled here in the synagogue to pray and when they were called to the Torah, they thought of Jerusalem and donated for the good of *Gan Shmuel*.
These included: the Rabbi, head of the local rabbinic court, Yeshayahu Kishelevitz, Shmuel Baltermantzer, Nissan Veinshtein, Moshe Avraham Volfin, Haim Issar Shimshelevitz, Aharon Davidovitz, Reuven Leib Mesliavsky, Leib Polack, Yosef and Nechemia Friedman, Gershon Zochovitzky, Shlomo Volpovitz, Moshe Pomerchik, Moshe Yitzchak Toybsh, Shimon Yitzchak Greenfeld, Yaacov Karelitzky.

Avraham Meyerovitz from Korelitz married Osnat Rivkah the daughter of the Rabbi, head of the rabbinic court in Rakishok, and his brother Dov David Meyerovitz donated to *Gan Shmuel* on this occasion.

Nissan Veinshtein mentioned above appears again as a donor to *Gan Shmuel* on the occasion of the marriage of his cousin, the daughter of his uncle Mordechai Veinshtein. The above mentioned Leib Polack donated to *Gan Shmuel* on the occasion of the marriage of Pessia Beilin's son Moshe.

The above mentioned Shlomo Wolfovitz again donated to *Gan Shmuel* on the occasion of the wedding of his cousin Moshe Greenvald, the prayer leader, in Turetz.

At the wedding of a daughter of the Chorgil family to her chosen bridegroom, Yitzchak Shimonovitz, which took place in a hall in Erozevitz, a donation was made to *Gan Shmuel* by Gershon Leib Ostashinsky and Yitzchak Yossilevitz and also by Rachel Halavnovitz and Sarah Kaplan and Rivka Tzonzer.

An anonymous donor donated a total of 150 rubles to *Gan Shmuel* in memory of the Second Zionist Congress in Basel.

*Chovevey Tzion* made a special donation by planting a citrus tree in the name of the Gaon Eliyahu from Vilna on the centenary of his death (5558 - 5658) and also donated towards our commitment to plant a tree in the name of the late Professor Tzvi Shapira from Heidelburg. The trees planted are ethrog (citron) trees.

---

*[Page 106]*

# A visit to Korelitz in the year 5661 (1900)
## Rabbi Y. Nissanboim

### Translated from the Hebrew by Ann Belinsky and Harvey Spitzer

At a distance of three parasang *[a parasang is about 4 miles - AB]* from Novogrudek stands the city of Korelitz. A small town numbering about 400 Jewish households. Its houses are low and poor and the "poverty" is discernable in every direction. If you desire to see in actuality the model of a small town in Lithuania that Dr Mandelstam spoke about in his speech to the Congress which you conceive in your mind's eye, so come here and this model will be in front of you.

The most attractive building is the *Bet Mirchatz* (Bath-house), which cost five thousand rubles! Where did they obtain this amount of money, Korach's fabulous wealth? Did they get it in K(orelitz) itself or from other towns which came to their aid? Whoever knows, knows! But either way, a large, two-storey high building stands ready for people of the town to wash their bodies and to remove their grime and no-one can ever say that it is cramped.

Also the *Talmud Torah* and all the other charity organizations are found in K(orelitz) as in all Jewish towns.

The Zionists in K(orelitz) do their loyal work and especially outstanding in his work is the representative of the supporting company - an honest and innocent man, loving the settlement in Eretz Israel with a pure, strong love, and without external enthusiasm, without thunder and noise, he does his onerous work most quickly and skillfully.

This man is the ritual slaughterer, grandson of a ritual slaughterer and great-grandson of a ritual slaughterer, but he didn't like his trade and did not think to try to be officially appointed the ritual slaughterer of the town until several people came and thought of robbing him also from his "rightful claim", and in order to defame him in the eyes of the community, several townspeople began to say that he was a heretic who was sending letters that he received from Zionist centers. The Zionists heard this and did not rest until he had been appointed the official ritual slaughterer. The Zionists in K(orelitz) are down-to earth-people, innocent in their ways and practices, "simple Jews" without the addition of (the extremes) of either "abstinence" or "enlightenment" and they are as all of the House of Israel.

***HaMelitz* 3, *MarCheshvan* 5661 (26th October 1900, No. 223)**

***

*[Pages 106-108]*

***HaTzfirah*, 1912, Issue: 134**

A Mazal-Tov greeting to Mr Baruch Shimshilevitz from Korelitz on the occasion of his marriage with his fiancée Ms Chana Ostashinsky, from his friends in Korelitz: Shalom and Breina Cohen, Mordechai and Binyamin Yosilevitz, Sarah and Liebeh Kliatzkin and Yisrael Cooper.
**"A group of Zionists in the above town"**

***

A large meeting in the town of Korelitz was arranged in honor of the confirmation of the Mandate. The local Rabbi R' Yosilevitz, may he live a long and happy life!, spoke about the significance of the Mandate. During the prayers, Psalms *[Excerpts from Hallel - M.Tz,]* were recited by the ritual slaughterer R' Moshe Avraham Volpin and the secretary of "Mizrachi" of our town, Mr Shlomo Volpovitch. Two hundred and ten thousand marks were collected at this meeting for the benefit of the Jewish National Fund.

***HaMizrachi,* 6 Tishri 5683 (No. 39, 1922)**

***

A letter of congratulations from Korelitch - on the occasion of the Jubilee of *Hatzfirah* (1862-1912, 5622-5672) from a faraway town, far from man and city, to which only *Hatzfirah* brings us light and pleasure, we send our most sincere blessings to the great author and noble individual, Mr Nachum Sokolov, and his honorable assistants for the celebration of the Jubilee of *Hatzfirah* we bless the periodical and pray that it will continue with its fertile work to fight the true war and protect our persecuted and unfortunate people, to encourage our spirit and to stand against the flow of hardships and distress which have surrounded us from every side. May *Hatzfirah* be worthy of lightening our way also when our people soon will be in our dearly beloved land.

The readers of *Hatzfira* and its admirers: Moshe Avraham Volpin; Yisrael Cooper; B. Shimshilevitz, A.M. Avramavitch, Lieba Kliatzkin, Sara Kliatzkin; Sh. and B. Cohen, G. Yellin; Chaya Hirshavitz.

### *HaTzfirah,* 13 *Tammuz* 5672 (28 June, Issue 134, 1912)
***

**A.** Ten measures of poverty were given to the world, nine of which were taken by our town Karelich; for there is no poorer town in all the Country of Greater Lithuania than our town (*Today Korelitz is in Belarus, which was once part of Greater Lithuania. H.S.*). Traders will not succeed and will go overseas, and all the people of our town have joined those who sit idly at the street corners. And little does it matter if a man celebrates his wedding. It's only a sign that a new store has been created, and if he's the son of a rabbi, he'll become a teacher and a few weeks later, "this bridegroom" will become a storekeeper or a teacher of beginners.

There are nearly as many stores as there are residents. And seven women or townspeople hold one buyer, one on his left side and one on his right side. It is obvious that the competition is great and there is little profit to be had. The wise men would have done well if they had made peace between them and decided on a price for every item. Then they would not do business in vain and God's name would not be desecrated in public. And competition, which is not useful but rather a source of heartache and pain, would come to an end. But instead of peace, everyone is trying to make a livelihood.

**B.** As is the material situation, so is the spiritual situation: the stomach is empty, and the soul is unable to soar. And therefore the paths of education are languishing in our town. Hebrew periodicals will not come (except one subscriber to *HaMelitz*) and the greater deficiency is that there is no library in the town. Several times we thought of requesting the "Disseminators of Education" [*Mefitsey Hazkalah*] company to support us with educational books, but we knew that our toil would be for nothing and that our request would be rejected because ten years ago the above company sent books here to read and it was the fault of the head of the library that the books were lost.

The first youths sinned and should we suffer for their iniquities?

### *"HaMelitz"* 24 *Shvat* 5650 (Issue 28, 1890)
## Levi Berman

*

## KARELITCH

The Hospice for the Poor [*Linat-Hatzedek*] society was founded a year ago by several of the honorables of the town who put all their attention into the project and made every effort to set it on a firm base, and their work paid off, for many of the townspeople took upon themselves the obligation to sleep over in the house of a sick person and anyone who couldn't carry out the order of the *gabbays* will pay back the association, and they will send someone else, or he himself will hire another person to do this.

Every week the collectors will walk around the thresholds of the houses to collect the weekly payment from the members and this money will buy the essential equipment needed by the sick person.

The number of members is one hundred and fifty people, and women, too, have joined forces to come to the aid of sick women, and the number of members in our society is one hundred and ten women.

*HaMelitz*, 2 *Sivan* 5659 (Issue 96, 1898)
## M.A. Oberzhansky

---

**The Library Committee in 1930**
**From right to left**: Nechama Kaplan, Alter Greenfeld, Leah Kaplan, Yitzchak Stoller, Mordechai Shimshilevitz

*[Pages 109-111]*

# My little town Korelitz
## (Unrhymed translation)

## Malka Poluzhsky– Kfar Saba

### Translated from the Yiddish by Harvey Spitzer

1. A small town – Lithuanian, on the bank of the Rootke.
   A little river –small, turning like a ribbon.
   Without ships, without barges, even without boats.
   Jews lived there and were happy.

2. Just a little town, as usual as others,
   paved, full of stores.
   A little tree, a blade of grass, a flower, a rock.
   A street intertwined with a lane.

3. What did the Jews live on in that small town?
   Only on what you hear and think:
   On trade, crafts, baking a small bread,
   On whatever is worth a penny.

4. A few Jews - were gardeners.
   They were occupied with planting and harvesting.
   Every morning they hurried with fervor
   to do business with their cucumbers.

5. On a winter morning, the snow falls,
   decorates the windows with frosty flowers.
   Two lady shopkeepers are wrapped in shawls.
   People take a walk along the stores.

6. Calmly, measured, life flows
   in the small town of Korelitz, framed in the river.
   It hardly enjoyed great wealth,
   not very poor, and not rich enough.

7. The youth in the small town – united in friendship,
   in pioneer work sought their goal.
   Social dividers disappeared,
   the same hora, the same quadrille.

8. They danced the fiery hora, all as one
   in pioneer clubs with much feeling.
   They held each other's arms, swinging and warming their bones,
   moving noisily and impetuously with much energy.

9. Rabbi Moshe Avraham in his old age
   can hardly drag himself around, is almost half blind.
   Yet he comes regularly to arrange (order) the _____
   for the Jewish National Fund, his holy deed.

10. They hold a bazaar for Zionist purposes.
    The old man comes again with the gang at the same time.
    He has already come to your house to awaken you at dawn.
    He absolutely has to know if the cash box is rich.

11. The teachers of the Jewish schools take part
    in life here in the place.
    They educate the pioneers and more and more raise
    the spirit of the time in spiritual sport.

12. They hold seminars, give lectures.
    A lively newspaper, very cordial jokes.
    Is anyone insulted? It won't do any harm either.
    People walk with pleasure and laughter in the street.

13. Life would have gone on in this way
    were it not for the terrible misfortune
    when Hitler [?the Kaiser] destroyed Poland and shot
    and put the country entirely under the yoke.

14. This horrible episode passed Korelitz by,
    and the town became a child of Russia.
    Our customary life immediately changed.
    Everything was gone with the wind.

15. The pioneer then became the proletariat.
    He was made to work with tooth and nail.
    He lost the spiritual possessions which he had from before.
    He didn't find any new ones, he had to go with "them".

16. Life would have still gone on slowly,
    were it not for the devil in Hitler's form,
    were it not for the extermination, the horrible terror,
    consisting of death and annihilation.

17. The little houses stand silent, no more sounds are heard.

No Jewish faces are seen in the street.
No laughter is heard, no familiar singing
of children running home from class.

18. Everything has vanished, as though it had never been.
The small town is forgotten, the Jews are already dead.
The Jewish presence has completely disappeared.
The ashes of the martyrs are sown and spread about.

19. At the memorial ceremony, by the black candles,
I remember everyone together...
I see you, my brother; your dear face...
Let me be joined with you, mother and father...

---

*[Pages 112-113]*

# My Town

## Hassia Turtel-Oberzhansky

### Translated from the Hebrew by Ann Belinsky and Harvey Spitzer

My birthplace, Korelitz, which was set, like a pearl, within the patchwork of small Jewish towns spread around the forests, swamps, hills and rivers of White Russia, can serve as an example of the classical historical phenomenon of a tapestry of original Jewish life. From within the ruins of thousands of Jewish towns, the city of my birth is depicted in all its glory, its beauty and its tragedy, its roots buried within the historical background of Polish and Lithuanian princes, heads of the Czarist regime, anti-Semitic clerks and German executioners.

Despite all the restrictions and the persecutions of the foreign regime, the town succeeded in creating a web of life and forging link after link in the chain of generations. Here is the market place square with its two rows of shops. Here is my father's old-new house, which over the years became a type of public institution. Here is the *Tarbut* school, the Rabbi's house and the other public institutions in the town. The trait that characterizes the town is the shared and unifying awareness of the spiritual and national war of existence for the sake of the continuance of the generations.

The Jewish youth were the center of gravity where the memories of the long historical past and the daily struggle for material existence merged and crystallized, placing the proud young generation opposite the hostile foreign regime. The young people strove towards a future in which they would shape their own personal life within the framework of a general national, social and spiritual revival. Their awareness and experiences, their whole soul and spiritual face, suckled inspiration from the feeling of national Zionism.

Zionism did not come to the youth as a result of propaganda and education. Zionism was transferred as a family and national possession and constituted its entire general essence. Its energy, soul and spiritual strength were invested in the Zionist youth movements: *HeChalutz, HeChalutz HaTza'ir, HaShomer HaTza'ir*, etc. The youth were active. Every move and step was directed towards one aim - personal and national redemption.

The life in the town was bustling, alert and flowing. All our activities had an impact on the community. The youth organized the library and enlarged it with the purchase of children's books; the dramatic club; evenings dedicated to discussions on all sorts of literary and political subjects were part of the living spirit and the stimulus of my town.
I see the Jewish youth on the rise in Korelitz, boys and girls, friends from school days, the youth movements - together we wove the golden dreams of redemption of the nation, freedom of man and building of the Land of Israel, *Eretz-Israel.*

The youth of Korelitz was consistent, to the point of self-sacrifice on the altar of its idealism. The youth of Korelitz contributed much to *aliyah*, to pioneering and to building the L
 and of Israel. It may be that the desire to move out of the narrow framework that filled the souls of the youth raised them also outside the boundaries of the national redemption. The Russian Revolution overflowed and flooded also the Jewish youth, whose eyes were blinded by the historical event of shaking the foundations of the Czarist regime and the establishment of a new society, enthusiastic and endearing young people who wanted to force the issue of the coming of the Messiah. There are those who went astray within the fields and acquaintanceship of the national Zionist environment and moved over to the Russian revolutionary movement.

The nationalistic feeling was the strongest and most original. In *aliyah* and pioneering, they saw the realization of the ideal of National-Jewish Revival and the establishment of a society based on justice and honesty.

My town of Korelitz, destroyed and ruined. We, the remnants that were saved in various ways and had the privilege to come to Eretz-Israel, let us bow our heads before our slaughtered brothers and sisters.

Let us unite in the memory of our friends, together with whom we dreamed the dream of Jewish heroism and National Redemption.

---

*[Page 113]*

**Sign – The *HeChalutz* Organization in Korelitz, 5685 (1925)**

**Sitting from Right: - Row A**: Mordecai Malkieli (Krolavetzky), Bracha Kaplan, Gittel Londin, Haim Kaplan.
**Row B:** Yitzchak Stoller, Sonia Kaplan, Yosef Portnoy, ---, Moshe Eliyahu Shuster, ---, David Portnoy, Pessia Ephroimsky, Mordechai Levine, Shaindel Perevolotsky (Kuznitz)
**Row C:** Moshe Gershonovsky, Berel Lipshitz, Royza Lipshitz, Hershel Zalamansky, Yehuda Levitt, Abramowich, Noach Gershonovsky, Matel Lipkin, Lama Ben-Haim, Kalman Bezalel Osherowitz (2 names are missing).

*[Page 114]*

**HeChalutz HaTza'ir** in 1928

**From right - 1<sup>st</sup> Row:** Chaim Stoller, Abba Nisselevitz
**Row B**: Avraham Gorodisky, Chaya Mordechovitz, Henia Izralit, Fanya Lipshitz, ----, Leah Troyvitsky, Chaya-Leah Sharshevsky, Itay Lipshitz
**Row C:** Moshe Stoller, Miriam Shkolnik, Menucha Abramowich, Yehudit Berkowitz, ----, Shirka Dushkin, Yosef Portnoy, Elka Berkowitz, Sarah Zalmansky, Leah Gershonovsky, Michael Yellin
**Row D**: Chaim Bolutnitzky, Hassia Oberzhansky (Turtel), ----, Freidel Kuznitz, Friedel Shapira, Yeshayahu Bolutnitzky, Sarah Zalmansky, Yona Yellin, Leah Kaplan, Yehuda Meyerovitz.

**Hashomer HaTza'ir** in 1936

*[Pages 115-118 - Yiddish]*
*[Pages XIV-XV – English abridged -* **see also page 355***]*

# Korelitz Before The First World War

## Alter Boyarsky

### Translated from the Yiddish by Harvey Spitzer

Korelitz had a lovely landscape. Surrounded by mountains and valleys, with smaller and larger forests and numerous villages and hamlets, the small town was home to a few hundred Jews who led a quiet, traditional life.

Regarding the founding of the small town, it is known that, hundreds of years ago, a nobleman by the name of Karelitz -a friend of the Jews - decided to develop his estate in the area. For that purpose, he brought a Jew from Minsk and he settled him there as a farmer with a lease. The Jew brought his relatives and they opened a tavern by the highway and Gentiles began to show up. Later, Jews began to settle in the small town. They leased fields and woods and they dealt in wheat and garden produce, and the Jewish population grew from year to year.

The most important ways of earning a livelihood were trading in produce from orchards and gardens, owning larger and smaller stores, and working as craftsmen, "the common people". The grain merchants and wood traders were the most privileged in the small town. Jews also dealt in dairy products. The cheeses from Korelitz were renowned in the whole region.

Before its long history, the little town developed nicely and built up. Korelitz had very lovely panorama. The center- the market place- was located on a hill, and all the streets and lanes extended downhill from there. At the end of the small town, the huts of the better-off Gentiles spread out with their orchards and gardens.

A wide road cut through the Zalamanke Streets, the market place and the Post Office Street. The road to Novogrudek started from there, and in the other direction, to Turetz and Mir. The distance to Minsk, the capital city, was 110 km *(70 miles – HS)*.

*[Page 116]*

**Post Street**

Korelitz had a very old cemetery with tombstones of Jews of noble lineage. The old synagogue was a great work of art, built of wood and decorated with lovely artistic carvings. The synagogue was high and spacious. The Holy Ark was a great, lovely work of art in the old style, adorned with various figures. This was the only *Kalte* synagogue in the area, and the Jews of Korelitz were very proud of it.

Opposite the *Kalte* synagogue was the large study hall. This was the synagogue for the "common people". The small shopkeepers and craftsmen prayed there. Above the market place, across from the rabbi's house, was the second study hall. The wealthiest Jews of the town prayed there: the grain merchants, dry goods merchants and other privileged people. Opposite the cemetery and downwards was the little Koidinav prayer house for *Chassidim*. Only *Chassidim* prayed there. Most of them were butchers, cattle merchants and just plain Jews. Downwards from the *Chassidic* synagogue as far as the cemetery fence was the town bath house. Further downwards, past the cemetery, was the town slaughter house. At the corner of the lane, by the synagogue yard, stood the rabbi's house, and the Rabbi's Lane started from the rabbi's house and ended at the market place.

The market place was the town's center and was paved. In the middle of the market place, stood rows of stores which belonged exclusively to Jews. One could buy whatever one needed in the stores. Gentiles from the villages would come on market day - Wednesday - and buy everything they needed: salt, herring in ____, _____, sugar, soap, kerosene and other things. The Gentiles, on the other hand, sold their wares: wheat, chicken, eggs, butter and cheese. Market day gave the Jews a livelihood for the entire week.

At the beginning of the rows of stores, as far as the church and between the houses at the beginning of the market place, was a big town well which had to be monitored all the time and people seldom drew fresh, pure water from it. The Jews of Korelitz, however, had their own big well filled with fresh water in the synagogue yard, and the water was clean. Down Zalamanke Street, which led to Novogrudek, there was no well, but only a spring. It was called a spring because one could draw spring water from it. The spring was located between the two taverns which Korelitz possessed. That was always the gathering point for people and horses. The horses could drink up the cold water and the Gentiles -brandy. The Korelitz police were always there. Both taverns were a source for the latest news – especially when, at that time, it was not customary to read a newspaper. Jewish wagon drivers, who used to travel to distant places, would bring the latest news from the world. In those years, people talked about pogroms, persecutions and misfortunes and occasionally one would hear good tidings.

On Zalamanke Street, on the hill, next to the Korelitz nobleman's courtyard, stood the only Russian Orthodox church with its tall steeples. On Sundays and on Christian holidays, the area around the church was filled with Gentiles and wagon drivers in their national dress. After the prayer service, the Gentiles would go to the Jewish stores to buy various items.

Jewish life throbbed with intensity: there were many *chederim* (religious elementary schools) where young boys studied Torah: Bible and Oral Law. From the *chederim*, the boys moved on to the *yeshivot* (schools of higher religious learning). Jews would also study in the study halls. There were several groups of learners: Psalms group, traditional laws group, Oral Law group. One would study a page of *Gemara* (Talmud) or a chapter of *Mishna* (compilation of traditional laws and their interpretations) between the afternoon and evening prayer service. Some of the leading rabbis of the time always occupied the position of town rabbi.

Prior to the first revolution in Russia, the "Enlightenment" movement had also reached Korelitz together with the first sprouts of socialism. Various political groupings were established which were laden with various ideas: socialism and Zionism. Working men and poor people dreamed of better times: liberty, equality, fraternity. A library was founded in the town. Young people started reading pamplets. Money collection and discussion evenings were organized. People attended lectures on various subjects: sociology, political economy, Jewish, Russian and Hebrew literature. A dramatics club which performed various plays was also set up.

At that time, illegal circles would gather to read illegal literature. Former yeshiva students would give fiery speeches about revolution. Every Sabbath, people would go into the forest and have "meetings". The Roodishtch forest was the center of freethinkers and radical socialists who wanted to topple the Czar. Friday night, after welcoming the Sabbath, when their parents were already asleep, young people would pull off the lock to the study hall and would discuss various subjects, mainly about the Czarist regime.

On a summer Sabbath afternoon, after taking a nap induced by eating *tcholent* (Sabbath stew), the Jews would walk downhill to Mill Street to get some fresh air in the forest. The road was always crowded, especially with young people. This was how the Jews of Korelitz lived with their joy and sorrow, with their aspirations and worries and hopes for better times. This was the manner of the hundreds of Jews from Korelitz and of the Jews from the hundreds of little towns in the area.

Korelitz produced many great personalities, both scholars and fighters. They knew how to live but also knew how to fight for the existence of the people and their country.

---

*[Pages 119-125]*

# Memories Of The Old Home

## Mordechai Meyerovitz

### Translated from the Yiddish by Harvey Spitzer

Prior to the First World War, Korelitz was a small, lively Jewish town. About 2,000 Jewish people lived there. As in all small Jewish towns, there was a rabbi, ritual slaughterer and just plain Jews -scholars who had received rabbinic ordination. In the center of the town was a synagogue quarter, with a synagogue, two study halls and a small synagogue house for *Chassidim*. Many Jews, *yeshiva* students, would always sit and "learn" in the study halls.

There were various societies and charity organizations in Korelitz such as a people's bank, a hostel for the poor, a burial society, a group of reciters of Psalms, a free loan society, a Zionist organization, thanks to which many Jews left to settle in Palestine, the Land of Israel.

Every year on the 15th day of *Kislev*, the burial society would hang up fruit on the walls of the study hall and after the Fast, and when the penitential prayers were over, the burial society members prepared a lavish meal. Women were also in the burial society and would make their separate feast.

There was a fire brigade in Korelitz which was organized and run by Jews. The fire brigade musical band had a good reputation in all the surrounding villages and small towns of the area. Korelitz would hire out the band to play at weddings.

The town itself was situated in a lovely, rich area, surrounded by forests, orchards and fields. There were many villages around Korelitz and every week, on market day, hundreds of wagons would arrive at the market place and business was lively. Besides that, there were 15 fairs every year. The fair in Korelitz had a particularly good name in the area. Merchants from far and wide would travel to Korelitz together. The small town profited from these fairs.

## Personalities and events in Korelitz

There was a shopkeeper in Korelitz whose name was Shaye Brankes. He was a good prayer leader. He organized a choir made up of many boys. His praying was renowned in the area. On the eve of the holidays, many Jewish farmers who lived in the villages would travel to Korelitz with their families to hear Shaye Brankes the Cantor with his choir. One could feel the holiday spirit in the small town.

There were sons-in-law in Korelitz who would "sit on the boards". Prominent Jews would travel to *yeshivot* to choose *yeshiva* students for their daughters. Shaya Brankes had 7 daughters and he took *yeshiva* boys who were ordained as rabbis for each of them. He gave them the opportunity to sit and study until they became a rabbi and found a position.

There was a righteous woman in Korelitz - Devorah Farashiskar. She helped the *yeshiva* students in whatever way she could: she arranged "eating days" for them at the homes of wealthy Jews, washed their linen and saw to it that they had something nice to wear.

My father, may he rest in peace, as well as Aharon-Yankel the Teacher, would devote themselves to helping *yeshiva* boys, or "monks", as they were called.

I remember a certain Pupko. He was a well-read, conscientious, cultured young man. He was nearly blind. Young men with revolutionary ideas (this was before the first revolution in Russia in 1905) used to come to him and hold meetings and also read prohibited books and pamphlets. When he died in 1907, many young men and women arrived from the surrounding small towns to attend his funeral. He was eulogized and his social activities were recalled.

There was a Zionist in Korelitz, R' Moshe-Avraham, the ritual slaughterer. He was very active before WWI. He used to collect money for the JNF (Jewish

National Fund) and organized a Zionist organization in the town, which made the police very suspicious. One Sabbath afternoon in 1907, R' Moshe-Avraham noticed through the window the police chief with policemen coming to his house. He understood that they were going to conduct a search. In the house were books, material and blank forms for the JNF. Before they managed to open the door, he stood by the wall and pretended to be praying and didn't even call out a word to them. The police chief and policemen waited for him to finish praying.

At the same time, his wife went out of the house and called a few little boys. I was also one of those boys. We sneaked through the stable into the house and from a side room, unnoticed by the police, we carried out the bookcase with the books and material and brought it into the stable of a neighbor, R' Asher-Moshe, the glazier. We covered it with hay and dung and put the cow there.

R' Moshe-Avraham finished reciting the afternoon prayers, went over to the police chief and asked him what he wanted. The police chief replied that he came to conduct a search. They looked in every little corner and, of course, found nothing. They also looked in R' Asher-Moshe, the glazier's stable. It never occurred to them that the materials they were looking for were hidden in the place where the cow was standing! The police chief ordered R' Moshe-Avraham to appear before the inspector in the small town of Mir. In our small town there was a well-to- do man, R' Leib-Eliahu, who spoke a fine Russian. He convinced the police chief to let him stay home. R' Moshe-Avraham continued his work for Zionism. After the incident with the search, Zionism became even dearer to him. He asked the Jews of the town to help him collect money for the JNF.

After World War I, the Polish authorities allowed the Jews to carry on Zionist activities. It became legal. They rented a place, arranged meetings, listened to lectures and readings about Zionism and Palestine. Zionist thought had a great influence on the Jews in Korelitz.

There was a tradition in Korelitz that following the afternoon prayer service on *Yom Kippur*, they would sell the honor of opening the doors of the Holy Ark for the *Ne'ilah* (closing) service. A fellow Jew, Berl-Dovid, lived on Mill Street near the river. Year after year, he would buy the honor of opening the Holy Ark. Once, the congregation got together and would not let him buy the honor of opening the Holy Ark for the closing service. They purposely bid such a high amount of money that Berl-Dovid could not afford to pay. There was a commotion in the synagogue. Berl-Dovid got angry, but the congregation would not give in to him.

That *Yom Kippur*, a very wealthy man who had stopped in Korelitz on Yom Kippur was attending the service in the synagogue. Since there was a great tumult, he asked what was going on. They told him that every year R' Berl-Dovid had the claim on opening the Holy Ark for the *Ne'ilah* service, but this year he had become poor and couldn't afford to outbid the others. The rich man thereupon called out that he would pay the sum of money on Berl-Dovid's behalf so that Berl-Dovid could open the doors of the Holy Ark that year as well. And so the rich man would send Berl-Dovid the money every year so that he could carry on the tradition of buying the honor of opening the Holy Ark for the service of *Ne'ilah* on *Yom Kippur*. This went on until Berl-Dovid's death.

A rabbi came to Korelitz. This was Rabbi Kagan, who took over the position of town rabbi. R' Chaim-Nata, the teacher, came to see him one day. He stayed there a little while and left. After he left, Rabbi Kagan noticed that 100 rubles had vanished from the table. The rabbi gave orders to call R' Chaim-Nata back. As soon as R' Chaim-Nata came into the rabbi's house, the rabbi told him that he suspected him of taking the 100 rubles from the table. Thereupon, R' Chaim-Nata the teacher, took a *Gemara* (holy book) off the table and swore that he never saw any money on the rabbi's table. The rabbi gave R' Chaim-Nata a powerful slap and said that he was the only one who could have taken the money. R' Chaim-Nata became ill because of the great shame.

One Friday, Mrs. Farashiskar, the lady who looked after the *yeshiva* students, came to see a *yeshiva* boy who was staying at the home of a resident for his period of "lodging". She brought him clear underwear. The lady noticed that the *yeshiva* boy was ill. He asked the kind Jewish lady to take out 20 kopeks from his pants and buy castor oil. The lady took out 99 rubles, took the money and came to my father and said, " "R' Nachum-Kopel, I found 99 rubles in the "monk's" pants. This must be the rabbi's money which disappeared." In former times, 100 rubles was a considerable amount of money and how is it that a "monk" should have so much money? My father took the money from her. He understood that the rabbi had wrongly suspected R' Chaim-Nata of theft. On Sunday, my father went to the rabbi and told him that the money which had vanished from his table was found in the possession of the "monk" and not with R' Chaim-Nata, the teacher. The rabbi remembered that on the same day that R' Chaim- Nata came to his house, the "monk" had also been there. The rabbi exclaimed, "What should be done with R' Chaim-Nata? I wrongly suspected him of stealing." My father replied that the rabbi had to ask R' Chaim-Nata's forgiveness before all the people and the community. And so R' Chaim-Nata was called to the pulpit in the synagogue and the rabbi publicly apologized to him. The rabbi added that R' Chaim-Nata was a righteous man and that the righteous must suffer in this world - this was R' Chaim-Nata's suffering in this world.

A short time later, R' Chaim-Nachum passed away. The whole town gathered at his funeral. He was given many eulogies. After that incident, the rabbi himself became ill from a lot of aggravation and never had any pleasure from his life until his death. This happened in 1899. My father told me this story.

My father related another incident to me: in 1870, on the first day of *Shavuoth* (Feast of Weeks), the sexton went to open the synagogue. Entering the synagogue, he saw that the window was open and near the window stood a small basket. The sexton was frightened and went to the rabbi, Rabbi Eliahu-Baruch (that was his name). The sexton told him that someone had thrown a small basket into the synagogue. The rabbi ordered the sexton to bring him the basket. The sexton took the basket and, wrapped in a prayer shawl, brought it to the rabbi. The rabbi opened the small basket and saw that there was a silver crown with golden bells and a silver pointer lying inside the basket. The rabbi ordered the sexton to put all these things on a Torah scroll in the synagogue. When the Jews came to the synagogue to pray and when the Torah scroll with the beautiful crown with bells with taken out of the Holy Ark, no one knew where such a treasure had come from.

Forty years passed. Many Jews of that old generation had already died and no one solved the riddle of the silver crown.

Merchants from the surrounding small towns would travel together to the fairs as well as horse traders from Ivenitz.

Once, after a fair, the horse traders from Ivenitz remained in Korelitz to spend the night and, as is customary among Jews, they went to the synagogue to pray. When the Torah scroll with the silver crown was removed from the Holy Ark during the morning service, the horse dealers from Ivenitz noticed that it was the crown which had been stolen from the synagogue in Ivenitz many years earlier. There was a great commotion in the synagogue.

The rabbi said that since 40 years had already gone by, the thing was already considered abandoned without any hope of being found and that this was a matter of Jewish law. The Ivenitz horse dealers related the incident to their own rabbi. The rabbi from Ivenitz immediately came to Korelitz and insisted on having a rabbinic court decide the matter. A few more rabbis were invited to the court of Jewish law, including the rabbis from Novogrudek and Mir. The rabbis decided that the matter of the stolen crown was a case where the missing item was considered hopelessly lost with no chance of being recovered and that the silver crown with the golden bells should, therefore, remain in the synagogue in Korelitz.

In 1908, a Gentile baker came into Korelitz. He would display his baked goods for sale in the market place and in other places. His baked goods had a good name and, besides that, he would give every buyer a free glass of tea. At that time, things were going badly for Jewish bakers and they couldn't make a decent living.

A Christian man, a big drunkard, then lived in Korelitz. His name was Mikolai Maritchevski. He lived near the bathhouse and all the Jews in Korelitz knew him. This drunkard would incite the Gentiles against the Jews, telling them to shop only in Christian stores and buy baked goods from Gentile bakers only. The Jewish bakers took a few other Jews with them and went to the rabbi in Slonim, who was renowned in the district as a great scholar and very righteous man.

The bakers from Korelitz poured out their embittered hearts before the rabbi from Slonim, and they asked him to bless them. The rabbi blessed them and told them they could go home calmly.

When the Jewish bakers returned to Korelitz, they found out that the drunkard, Mikolai Maritchevski, had hanged himself. The Gentile baker died a short time later. And thus Korelitz was rid of both anti-Semites - the Gentile baker and the Maritchevski, the drunkard. The Jewish bakers once again earned a suitable livelihood.

In 1915, the Germans seized Korelitz. The Russians built fortified positions near the Beroza River, and the war front remained there for three years. Nearly all the Jews from the small town had been evacuated to various towns because living there was very dangerous, due to the incessant shooting from both sides of the front.

After the 1917 revolution, the Jews from Korelitz began returning home, but there were no homes for them to live in. The Germans had taken apart the wooden houses and built trenches. Some houses were burned. The Jews took apart the trenches and used the wood again to build the houses.

Life returned to normal. Commerce flourished and the craftsmen also had something to do. However, as after every war, various epidemics broke out and spread and many people died.

Jewish relief committees were formed and people were helped with medicines, clothing and loans as well. The small town quickly built up and Korelitz became lovelier than ever. Korelitz also suffered from fires. After every fire, the small town would be built up and become prettier and better.

---

[Page 125]

**Members of the Korelitz-Lubtch community committee in 1934**

**Seated from right to left:** Getzl Yellin, Pesach Kaplan, Yitzchak Aharonovsky (ritual slaughterer and examiner), Rabbi Yitzchak Weiss, Tobolsky (cantor), Tuvia Shimshelovitz.
**Standing from right to left:** ---, Berl Basel, Leibel Perevolutsky, ---, Hershel Jishin, Yitzchak Berkovitz, Avraham Chaim.

[Pages 126-128]

# Korelitz During And After The First World War

## Reuven Ovseywitz

### Translated from the Yiddish by Harvey Spitzer

Prior to the outbreak of the First World War, life in Korelitz was similar to the life of Jews in many cities and small towns. The opportunities that people had to reach their goals were limited. For some Jews, small town life was too confining, and so they tore themselves away and ventured into the wider world. There were then no special difficulties involved in emigrating. Whoever had money to purchase a ship ticket could leave, as the borders were open. It didn't matter whether one was travelling with or without a visa. Jews found a way to leave and it was especially easy to emigrate if one had an invitation from a relative living abroad.

The situation was quite different after WWI. The world was closed and the doors of many countries were hermetically sealed. In order to emigrate, one needed a passport with a stamped visa as well as an invitation from a close relative in the country where the emigrant wanted to live. An exception was Brazil and Argentina, but few people were eager to go to these countries. Finally, even these countries began to impose certain restrictions with regard to immigration, so that in the last few years before the Second World War, the doors of both these countries were also tightly shut.

Korelitz had the "privilege" of being the place where the war front stopped in 1915, and the Jews were actually very happy about that. That was because the air was so poisonous in the last years before the outbreak of the First World War that the situation became unbearable. There was a new decree every day. It began with the uprooting of a long established Jewish family from the place, or a pogrom in the city or small town, a blood libel and the Beilis trial, which shook the whole world. The village hooligans would throw stones at every Jew going through the village and would sing anti-Semitic songs at the same time.

When the Germans came into Korelitz during the Intermediate Days of the *Sukkot* festival, the Jews breathed more freely. First of all, they were rid of the better-off Gentiles, drunks and Jew haters. The Jews thought they could get along with the Germans, but they were quickly disappointed.

The front stopped permanently in the town so that the positions of the combatants on both sides - Russian and German - were situated on both sides of Korelitz and, as a result, the shooting was heard incessantly every day.

About three weeks after the arrival of the Germans, the German commander ordered the evacuation of the entire population. Those who left the town in time and moved to Novogrudek were lucky. At first, one could still get an apartment, but later the evacuees had no place to rest their weary heads. It was still possible for those who had a horse and wagon to save the little they possessed, but most people left whatever they owned in their houses and went out of the small town with nothing. Three years went on in this way. The elderly and feeble died off little by little from want and hunger, and the survivors began returning to Korelitz little by little.

Korelitz was entirely destroyed. The wooden houses were taken away, the wood being used to build trenches. With the exception of Zalamanke Street, not one house remained in the small town. However, nothing but the walls and roofs remained even of the houses on Zalamanke Street. The Germans had dragged out everything from the houses. They even took apart the ceiling.

Little by little, the small town began to be rebuilt. The first to return were those who had suffered the most being away from Korelitz. Among these was my family: my brothers, sisters, my mother and grandmother and I myself. At first, life in Korelitz was very hard, but people accepted the hardships with love. We had tortured ourselves so much on foreign beds that our own little corner was now very dear to us. Korelitz built up year after year. Various institutions again began to function such as the people's bank and study halls with two rabbis instead of one as before. The sources of livelihood were very limited so that the young people, who were mostly attuned to Zionism, strove to go to Palestine, the Land of Israel. However, only a few had the privilege of obtaining a certificate enabling them to settle in Palestine. The doors were locked in other countries so young people went around the streets idly and had no way to expend their energy.

Many jokes circulated about Zalamanke Street. People joked that there was only one pair of shoes on Zalamanke Street. Therefore, a person who would go to the market would put on the shoes and, after returning, would put the shoes in a certain place, and each person would wear them in turn. This characterizes the extent of the poverty there was in our small town, but it also brought out the intimacy and spirit of togetherness of the Jews of Zalamanke Street.

In the winter, people had to heat their homes because of the cold weather, but in the summer, everyone wanted to save by burning as little wood as possible. For this reason, when one would see that the oven was burning in their neighbor's house, they would bring over a pot of food to cook. My wife, Chaya Bayla, of blessed memory, would welcome every person very courteously. She was the incarnation of politeness and kindness. She was also a good merchant as well. It was a great joy for her to have a guest for the Sabbath, and she considered it a *mitzvah*, performing a good deed. She seated the poor person in the best place and gave him or her the finest and best food.

My dear son Michel possessed the qualities of a diligent Jew. He knew the entire prayer service inside out. When he was eight years old, he would run to the earliest prayer service to be part of the quorum. My dear son Yudele would do likewise. He would always show everyone where Argentina was located on the map and where father was. My dear Tomele was also an exceptional child. The years I was in Argentina, my brother Binyamin, of blessed memory, could not stop praising her. The German beasts exterminated everyone.

My brother Binyamin, who was a good teacher in Novogrudek, was also murdered with the martyrs. My sister Sarah-Nechama was murdered with her children in Ivye. My sister Bashke was murdered with her children and grandchildren in Baranovitch. I thus remained an orphan and in sorrow for the rest of my life. May God punish the criminals for shedding the innocent blood of my brothers and sisters.

---

[Pages 129-133]

# Rebuilding Activity In Korelitz*

## Shalom Cohen

### Translated from the Yiddish by Harvey Spitzer

After the cease-fire agreement was concluded between the Germans and Russians and after the Germans moved eastward from the positions they had occupied since the end of September 1915, some of the several hundred Jewish families who had been expelled to Novogrudek by the Germans from the front area (including the small towns of Korelitz, Lubtch, Deliatitch and Neishtot) began to return to their former places. A committee was established for that purpose, and on May 17, 1918, it was approved by the German authorities. The committee was made up of 18 members, 17 of whom were representatives of the four above-mentioned small towns and the 18th, the chairman, was Rabbi Menachem Krakovski. Later, one representative from Horodishtch was added. The committee's rights were 1) to organize the return of the homeless to their former places, 2) to give financial support for rebuilding and renovating houses, 3) to organize community life in the above-mentioned small towns and to build synagogues and other institutions, 4) to maintain contact with the Central Support Committee in Vilna (Chairman, Rabbi Rubinstein), and 5) to serve as a body representing the homeless before the German military authorities.

Being from Korelitz, I was naturally more interested in my small town. My first task was to find families capable of working and possessing a little produce as well as a horse and cow. The area around Korelitz was a wasteland with uncultivated fields and communities in ruins (including Korelitz). Those who returned had to be ready to cultivate neglected ground and build homes in the ruins which remained in the small town. Our selection included about a dozen families who were in the villages around Novogrudek. In order to encourage them to move and also in order for them to receive various relief measures and easy conditions from the committee, another committee member and I went out to the villages. The relief which we requested consisted of the following: 1) to provide them with grain for three months in advance, 2) to permit them to take out their horses, cows and calves to graze, 3) to permit them to come at harvest time to reap the grain that had been sown the previous year and to dig up the potatoes that had been planted the same year (we visited them in 1918)

--------------------

* According to records of *Yekopa*, Province reports and reminiscences, p. 502-22.

and 4) to give them wagons at no cost to transport their household goods to Korelitz. The commander, Miechov, had a reputation in the whole district as a wicked person and murderer. We arrived very early at his "residence", a lovely nobleman's palace in the middle of an orchard. As soon as he saw us, he welcomed us into his consultation room, listened to us and took our written request. A month later, when a few of the families moved to Korelitz, it appeared that our mission had been successful.

In April 1918, I composed and sent a memorandum to the Central Support Committee in Vilna regarding the return of a number of homeless people to their former places and requested money for that purpose. The memorandum was forwarded to the 5th Ob-Ost Department (Director, Lieutenant Dr. Struk)

On May 30, 1918, the Central Committee sent us a communication from the head commander of the 10thArmy (dated May 27th) informing us that all the authoritative bodies had received instructions to supply building wood to the returning wanderers with which to build their houses. On May 11, 1918, we received DM 15,000 for those returning to Korelitz, Lubtch and Neishtot. Regarding the return of the homeless from Korelitz, there were obstacles on the part of the German commander. Rabbi Krakovski, myself and a representative from Korelitz received a certified order to come to an understanding with the commander. Already 12 km before one got to Korelitz, the devastation which the war years had caused was visible - a real wasteland. There was a sign hanging from a post on the side of the road 8km from Korelitz with writing in two languages – German and Russian: "Whoever crosses the line will be shot".

The "fire zone" started from that place. 3 km before we came to Korelitz, the first cement trenches began to appear, and the last 2 km, we went through a large number of wire fences. As we entered the small town, we were stopped by a soldier with a gun. He ordered us to go back to the quarter where the commander lived. Not finding the commander at home, we prevailed upon the writers in the "service house" to permit us, in the presence of a soldier, to look around the small town of Korelitz with its few remaining lonely ruins; with its market place overgrown with yard-high grass; with the " __ " little woods on the squares and yards; with the cemetery, open on all sides, in the middle of the synagogue quarter through which wild cats were wandering, and when frightened, running away and hiding in the cemetery mausoleums. Even the sidewalk from the synagogue quarter to the bath house which the Germans had laid down with the tombstones broken off from the graves - I was completely lost. Rabbi Krakovski consoled me and spoke about the rapid rebuilding of the small town - which has now, in about 6 years, become a reality. Only one ruin of a building remained on the long street leading to the front. The whole street and everything around it and further ahead created an impression of a wilderness, with trenches and holes and dug up bushes. The commander sent us to the district officer, who was stationed 6 km from Korelitz.

Before leaving the small town, I wanted to clarify another matter which concerned many residents of Korelitz. Before the war, our town had quite a number of students. They each had a lovely library of books (*Talmud, responsa* literature and books of sermons) which they didn't manage to take with them. Many other books (Hebrew and Russian) were also left behind in our small town.

On *Yom Kippur* 5677 (1917), there was a pastor among the German visitors in our synagogue. Several of the worshippers turned to the pastor concerning the fate of their books. On October 1, 1917, we received a letter from him which gave us hope that our books were preserved and protected from destruction. I showed the letter to the commander and he immediately handed over the keys to the oldest writer and ordered him to take me to the place where the books were kept. The writer took me to the Russian Orthodox church and we went inside. No trace of destruction.... What a contrast to the ruins of the remaining Jewish study halls (synagogues) with the doors and windows taken away, chopped up interior walls, floors and ceiling and sawed away balconies! The study halls themselves now served as stalls for horses, and two heaps of manure made entering very difficult. The books, which were supposed to be in the cases behind the altar, were instead a few thick books on "Slavic Churches". I still haven't found the Jewish books and surely they were used by the soldiers to heat the trenches or for worse purposes.

The district officer sent us to the district economy officer, Lange Bekmann. We visited him the following day, and he told us that we would receive an answer in a few days. The reply came, but I don't remember its precise content. All I remember is that it was very unclear. We understood the representatives of the German authorities better when they issued orders and not when they spoke unclearly and gave us vague answers in our negotiations with them. The Germans in the summer of 1918 were no longer the same as they were in the autumn of 1915. During those few years we were oppressed by the laws of occupation which were enforced without mercy. We now sensed a weakening in all directions. On *Shavuoth* (Feast of Weeks) 5678 (1918), the first 4 families from the villages returned to Korelitz and, by the autumn of 1918, there were already over 30 families. After May 31, 1918, however, we received a refusal from the German command to our request to allow more families to return. The introduction to the refusal was as follows: "All of the small towns lie in the zone of closure (between the first and second positions). The return of the homeless is completely forbidden."

The orders, however, were not carried out in real life. The officials, soldiers and officers were happy that people were settling in the devastated area. They hoped that the renewal of life in the district would make life easier for them as well. The soldiers and officers began selling wood and boards from the trenches to the returning homeless. The work involved in taking apart the trenches was remunerative for the Germans and beneficial for the returnees. For just a little money they obtained boards, bricks, iron, doors, windows, etc. The Germans also hired out their horses to the homeless so that they could till their fields. Others were able to get materials from the near-by forests using the horses.

At the same time, we had difficulties with the higher command. The economics bureau made life hard for the homeless. If, for example, a resident of Korelitz needed to go to Novogrudek, he had to be accompanied by an officer stationed 6km from Korelitz and then by an officer stationed 10km from the Korelitz-Novogrudek road.

On June 11, 1918, we received DM 25,000 from the Vilna Central Committee. On October 26, 1918, we received DM 2,000 from Herman Struk with which to teach children of poor homeless families. On December 2, 1918 (3 weeks before the German withdrawal and the seizure of our area by the Bolsheviks), we received the last DM 2,000 from the Central Committee. In addition, we received money from several individuals from Minsk (collected by Rabbi A. Abavitch and N. Bakaltshuk) and from several smaller towns from the State of Minsk (collected by Z. Kliatshkin and M.Yoselevitch). We received smaller amounts from Radon, Stutshin and Varanova (State of Vilna) and from the small town of Luna (State of Grodno).

The process of determining who should receive financial support and how to divide the money began on May 22, 1918. The largest amount of assistance was set at DM 200 and later at DM 300 paid in two installments. To cultivate a field or sow a garden, DM 40. Later, support was also given for buying a horse or other farm animals, to purchase agricultural machinery or work tools, to pay a teacher for teaching children, for renovation of synagogues and baths and for other town needs as well as for help in buying medicine. We received the last DM 20,000 from the Central Committee at the beginning of the winter. Before the arrival of the Bolsheviks, this money was distributed for the last two kinds of assistance during the winter and spring of 1919 until we received support from the *Yekopa* from Vilna.

There was one house with windows and doors in Korelitz at that time. This house served as a gathering point for all the homeless. There were two baking ovens. There was not a living soul nearly 15km all about. There wasn't a place to get even a kernel of grain. Bread was scarce. The houses were in ruin. Wolves played havoc in the trenches around the town and they carried off not one goat from a poor Jew...

A new front was in place in the summer of 1919. The bullets fired by the Bolsheviks reached right into our small town. The Bolshevik regime brought with it hunger and unemployment. The activity of *Yekopa* started at the beginning of the summer of 1919. When they became aware of our difficult situation, they sent us a sum of DM 10,000. At the beginning of the *Yekopa* work in our region, they focused their activity on the following: bread for the hungry and medicine for the sick. We are now beginning to receive - together with the money for renovation - sums of money for an elementary school, library, savings and loan fund and later for wood for construction.

---

*[Pages 134-135]*

# Between Two Wars

## Noach Gershenovsky - Givatayim

### Translated from the Hebrew by Ann Belinsky

At the beginning of the nineteen-twenties with the return of the inhabitants of Korelitz from the expulsion of the First World War - they found the town in ruins and ravaged. It was necessary to start "from the beginning". The people who returned were hungry, lacking clothes and elementary means of existence. The first question was: a roof over their heads, a place to lay their heads and among the first worries was also to find a drop of milk for the babies. The inhabitants began to solve the problem in an original manner - to buy a cow or goat to tend and get some milk from it for the baby. But quickly sources of relief and assistance were opened. The Jewish institutions began to give aid: the first organized aid came from the *Yekope*, a Jewish aid institution giving long-term loans and with low interest for the first steps of organization. After that, there was help from the "Joint", which sent necessities and clothes to the poor. Immediately a committee was organized which dealt with receiving the goods and fairly dividing them amongst those in need. The same committee began also to care for the many children not only for requirements of food, but also for education and culture and thus the Jewish school was started, where the children studied and also received a hot meal every day. Slowly the inhabitants began to arise from the ruins of the town, houses were built and shops were set up around the market. A pharmacy was opened managed by Mr Elliasberg, who also was an enthusiastic and devoted public figure who quickly became a central public personality in Korelitz. His house became the home of the committee and a center for public business in the town.

## Art and Cultural Clubs

New strengths that were added to our town gave a push to promote the artistic-cultural life in the place. Shabbtai Klatzki, the son-in-law of Moshe

Kaganovitch, who was gifted in the area of stage arts, began to organize the dramatic society. He was the founder, the organizer and the director of the club that proceeded well and indeed after a short time, succeeded in establishing a dramatic club that was well known in the whole area for its acting of works by Goldfadden, Shalom Aleichem, Gordon etc. At the same time a local orchestra was also organized. Here, the founder was Shimon Mollier, an excellent musician and himself a violin player. At present he is in the United States and is in keen contact with people from his town in Israel. He is the man who aroused the youth with his love for music of all instruments. He organized special lessons for learning musical notes under the direction of Mr. Weiner. Young and talented resources were discovered there, who dedicated themselves and succeeded well in the orchestra. There were many cases where whole families participated in the orchestra with much success. Among the families that excelled in playing various instruments, the Gershonovsky family and the Lipshitz family must be noted. Baruch Tzolkovitz was the conductor. At the beginning, the orchestra was an institution by itself but quickly it moved to the patronage of the fire brigade. Apart from the artistic organizations, other institutions were founded such as the local bank with Yitzhak Meir Klatski as the manager of accounts and a charity fund. One of the prominent and important institutions was the library with about 4000 books. There was a rich Yiddish library on all topics.

In 1929 the town was burnt down, and the library too went up in smoke, but when the town was rebuilt, a new library also arose quickly, with the active help of Alter Greenfeld. He was a man of the book and an author who dedicated himself especially to this enterprise.

---

*[Pages 135-136]*

# From The Distant And Close Past

## Mordecai Malkieli-Krolavetsky - Hod HaSharon

### Translated from the Hebrew by Ann Belinsky and Harvey Spitzer

I was born in Korelitz, however at the young age of seven, I was uprooted from there with all my family following the outbreak of the First World War. The town was conquered by the Germans and the inhabitants were expelled. My family moved to the nearby city Novogrudek and there we lived until things calmed down. With the conquest of the area by the Poles we returned to Korelitz, in 1921. Therefore I lived, again, in our town but my heart was already somewhere in Eretz-Israel; I was already completely brainwashed by Zionist idealism until I made *aliyah* in 1926. Here I want to tell about two episodes, types of chapters from the close and distant past.

## The tailor's strike in the 18th century

As I said, I made *aliyah* to Eretz-Israel in 1926, I was still relatively young and my *aliyah* was made possible only after I added a few years to my age in my documents. It is natural that the longings for my hometown and my friends were great and anything connected to Korelitz "bounced" me. How surprised I was, when at one of the workers assemblies in Petach Tikva where I lived, I heard from the speaker an interesting story about Korelitz in the context of the topic "The development of workers movements of the Jewish people in the Diaspora". The story told was that one of the first strikes in the 18th century in the Jewish community was in Korelitz, and goes as follows: On one of the Sabbaths, the tailors and their apprentices appeared in the synagogue of the town dressed in long coats of Shabbat from the same long coats that were sewn for the important householders in honor of Shabbat. The tailors walked up to the eastern wall near the Holy Ark and asked permission to pray together with the honorables of the town. Immediately the community leaders got up and expelled the tailors and their apprentices from the synagogue. In response, the tailors announced a strike and that they would no longer sew long coats for the honorables of the community until their right to pray with the honorables would be recognized, as they had tried to do. How the same strike ended I do not remember exactly, but I assume that the tailors won this war.

Later when I visited the town in 1935, I spoke on this matter with the person in charge of the *Pinkas Kehilah* (community record book), the ritual slaughterer R' Avraham Volpin, and he confirmed the truth of this story.

## Everything about the *Keren Kayemet* [Jewish National Fund]

And from that story taken from the past, to the closer period and this time it is about the Zionistic enthusiasm of the youth in our town. I have already told, at the beginning of my words, the story that my family returned to Korelitz in 1921 and I remained in the town 5 years, until 1926, the year of my *aliyah* to Eretz-Israel. During those five years I was completely immersed in the Zionist issues, one of the basic principles of Zionistic work was: collecting money for the *Keren Kayemet* (Jewish National Fund). We had a difficult problem: the town was poor and our enthusiasm to collect money was great. What to do: we decided that the teenagers would go to work and the money that we received would be transferred to the *Keren Kayemet*. But we Jewish youth couldn't even find work in those days and here came a good chance: at that time an elementary school was opened in the town and we offered our services to sweep the rooms and heat the stoves in the night for the pupils who came next morning to the school. Thus we got up, each according to his turn, in the night and washed floors, cut wood and worked in starting the stoves until the morning light appeared, returning home tired and happy: we received an income for the *Keren Kayemet*.

We also found another job for the *Keren Kayemet* in the Jewish community and that was to bake *matzot* for Passover. In the town there was a custom that immediately after Purim, the preparations for baking *matzot* for Passover began. We, the pioneering youth, took upon ourselves to do this work "*podriad*". In other words we were "contractors". The matter was quite complicated: we needed to overcome the opposition of the bakers; to get the Rabbinical *kashrut* and naturally the agreement of the important house owners. But we overcame all the obstacles and our happiness was great; we saved the honor of the town outwardly: we collected money for the *Keren Kayemet*. Indeed, the romantic Zionistic days - where are they, those fine days?

**The Jewish National Fund**
(*Keren Kayemet Leyisrael*)

# A Memorial Certificate

## To Mordechai Krolavetzky

### In Korelitz
--------------------

## For diligent participation in work
## For the Jewish National Fund

### In the year 1925

**The Jewish National Fund**
**National Polish Office**
----------------------

**Signatures**

*[Pages 137-139]*

# My Birthplace ...

## Y.A. Malkieli - Petach Tikva

### Translated from the Hebrew by Harvey Spitzer

Out of the ancient mists of childhood
Slumbering in somnolent meditations,
Between reality and illusion,
This is the little town - Korelitz.

Perhaps it's a dream or maybe what it really was_ _ _
Peeping at me through the lattices of time,
Do I remember it as it is
Or as a dream? - Will I awaken its charm? _ _ _

I was a four year old toddler when I left Korelitz with my parents and went into the wide world. I suckled my mother's milk within the walls of its tiny houses where I took my first steps of life. Since then, my life has flowed in new streams, and the days of my childhood and my youth passed by in various occupations without my paying any attention to the "rock whence I was hewn" (*Isaiah 51*). This period of childhood sank into my consciousness in darkness and was covered with new layers which came in turn and covered one another.

However, from time to time, at the earliest age, flashes of memories and blurred fragments of vision from the not too distant past lurked in the enclosures of my soul. With the passage of time, these memories also grew dim and vanished, leaving behind a deposit of sub-memories, that is to say, a faint trace of the old memories. Pictures of memory in their visual reality disappeared from the library of memory which the Creator of man fixed so wondrously in our brain and (these pictures) completely disappeared as though they had never existed.

And if I try to raise to consciousness some of these sub-memories, there is no doubt that fiction and illusion will grasp most of the picture. There may also be a crude mixture of words which were absorbed in my consciousness, not from my own memory but from stories and from fragments of words which reached my ears directly or indirectly in family conversations and perhaps even from reading and especially from my looking at the life of these small towns on winter days when I was at the Radin Yeshiva under the administration of the *Hafetz Haim* (Rabbi Yisrael Meir Kagan, 1838-1933), of blessed memory. At that same period, I also made a short visit to my hometown of Korelitz for the purpose of obtaining a passport for a trip to Eretz Yisrael, and I glimpsed the place through the eyes of a guest. I went there with my heart pounding, my emotions overwhelming me like rushing waters ahead of my meeting with my birthplace, the magical land. However, I didn't find an interpretation to my dreams as I conceived in my imagination which was far removed from the existing reality.

> ...Sometimes I see your residences,
> Wooden shacks providing little warmth;
> Inside, your faces are beaming,
> So delicate, soft, innocent_ _ _

How do I remember my small town in my somnolent memories hidden under piles and accumulations of existence and occurrences of time which have elapsed since then?

I see the small house made of thick wooden beams which were brought straight from the forest and still retained their fragrance. These beams were only slightly planed so that they could be joined to each other. I don't remember if they were plastered on the inside, or if they were whitewashed. There was no flooring. The tenants walked on tightly packed or loosened earth, on which they would sprinkle yellow sand in honor of the Sabbath or holiday. The sand was brought by a farmer in a wagon. As he made his way among the houses, he would call out his merchandise and housewives would buy a pailful of yellow sand for one *kopek* or more.

I remember the *Bet Midrash*, whose windows looked out onto a different world cloaked in mystery and fear. There were simple wooden tables and benches on which the children would jump and among which they would play hide and seek and show off their bravery in demonstrations of jumping and running. The shacks in the gardens were topped with straw and served as permanent homes for all kinds of fowl and four-legged animals. Between the "straw hat" of the house and the walls, lay thick beams which served various uses including that of a pantry for all kinds of spices and concoctions as well as a place for concealing different valuables, and there was also a full storehouse of stock of all kinds. I don't remember if they used closets then because the clothes were always hanging on the walls unguarded and uncovered.

I remember that my grandmother was always confined to her bed which she didn't leave until the day she died. Not far from the bed, in the middle of the room, stood a plain, rough, wooden table around which we youngsters sat, bent over all day long, and learned the alphabet and reading from the mouth of our grandfather, Rabbi Eliezer Reuven Marishinsky, of blessed memory, who was called, "Marishiner". He used to treat the children with tenderness and humility and never raised his hand or voice.

It seems that in the same house, opposite grandfather's room, there was an entrance way to the home of my Aunt Shifra, my mother's, of blessed memory, sister. In my remote memories, images have remained of those many colored biscuits and crackers, sometimes made in the shape of birds, which she baked and displayed in the window. I loved those baked goods and I remember that a few years after leaving Korelitz, I could still see them, and they demonstrated their magic before me whether I was awake or dreaming.

I remember a broad, open yard between houses – yards had no fences – in which we, boys and girls, played together. Was that the synagogue yard or my grandfather's yard or maybe a yard common to both? A girl scratched my face and I cried. I don't know who the girl was. Is she still alive and perhaps among us, or was she struck by cruel fate and killed together with her brothers and sisters and undoubtedly with her offspring as well in that same awful mass destruction of the Jewish People?

I don't have memories of my parents in this field of vision because, being with them all the years afterwards, traces have not remained from the past except for those abrupt experiences which have stayed in my memory from the period of my illness, my second illness, which claimed the lives of two children in our young family. In the delirium of my very high fever, I saw terrible sights on the wall, and my father, of blessed memory, wanted to calm me by hitting the wall with a rod and chasing away the demon who instilled his dread and fear in me.

When I returned to Korelitz in 1924 to obtain my birth certificate as I mentioned earlier, I found a world different from what I had imagined. Among my relatives, were my Uncle Kalman, my aunt and their daughter. I stayed at their home the day I arrived. My father's sister, Chana Layzorovitch, was also there. She was a "woman of valor", active in many areas, a person who endeavored to improve the lot of our people as much as possible, may her memory be for a blessing! Looking back now, it has become clear to me that my aunt had suffered many bitter experiences. Several years later she asked me to bring her son Yankel-Yudel and his family of many children who lived in Novogrudek to Israel, but it didn't work out. I was then busy bringing my parents, brothers and sister and other cousins to Israel and I didn't manage to devote time to her request. They were all subsequently killed in the Holocaust.

There was also another family that was related to our family in Korelitz. This was the Oberzhansky family. The father of the family was the one who helped me procure my birth certificate from the local authorities. Is there anyone from that family in our country (Israel) today?

My poor little hometown was destroyed in the smoke of death together with thousands of Jewish communities, large and small. How great is my pain and heartache knowing that I did not "remember the affection of your youth" (*Jeremiah, 2:2*) and I disparaged you on that winter day when I visited you 46 years ago! Who could have imagined that the end would come, the end of all your sons and daughters, men and women, old and young, that you would all be consumed by fire, the fire of the inferno, the torments of hell?

Where is the writer who will describe all the hundreds of days and nights, thousands of hours of hunger and distress, disgrace and humiliation, suffering and agony, when you were led from evil to evil and from death to death? My heart goes out to all of you, wretched in life and sold to death, for whom the sun, which rules in the world, withdrew its light and the moon its radiance, and you were all sent "like an abhorred offshoot" (*Isaiah,14:19*) to mass graves and were "dung upon the open fields." (*Jeremiah, 9:21*).

Are there reparations for the dread of these atrocities, for this eternal murder? Is there yet revenge in the world which can atone for these terrible things? "I see him (it), but not now; I behold him (it), but not nigh" (*Numbers 24:17*). "for hidden are the ways of Providence".

And together with Rabbi Kolonymus, son of Rabbi Yehudah, let us mourn the slain and lament their tragic deaths:

(Unrhymed translation)

"Oh that my head were waters and my eyes a fountain of tears
(*Jeremiah, 8:23*),
And that I might weep all the days of my life
For the slain - infants, young children, the elderly, my community.

And you answer: Woe unto me!
And weep with great wailing –
Over the Lord's people and over the House of Israel,
For they fell by the sword!"

---

*[Pages 140-143 -Hebrew]*

# Return To Korelitz

## Leah Kornfeld-Lubchansky -- Herzlia

### A.

Korelitz was situated in a valley. On the one side, it was closed off by Mount Zapoli, while on the other side, the Rutka River flowed. The other two sides were open to a way called "Napoleon's Tract". In the middle of the town was a market and shops. On the north side stood two Synagogues; the Old House of Learning and the New House of Learning. Behind the Old House of Learning was the *Chassidim Shtibel* and the well, which provided ample quantities of water. Not far from there was the Bath-house as well as the Cemetery. To the east of the Old House of Learning stood the Elementary School. This whole section was called *Schulhoif*, i.e. the Synagogue Square. On the north side stood the Rabbi's house and Kalman Marshinsky's house. To the west were the houses of my parents, Chaim and Chaya-Etta Lubchansky, my Uncle Eliyahu Chaim Osherowitz, my Aunt Shprinza and her husband Alter Friedman and my Aunt Bedna and her husband Tzvi Kivlevitz.

On an artificial hill in a central place in the town, there arose in great splendor and luxury the Pravoslavic House of Worship. Surrounding the church was a beautiful ornamental garden with shade-giving trees. The House of Worship's garden was a sort of extension of the Squire's wonderfully beautiful garden. At the other end of this garden, stood his palace. The road from the town to the palace was planted with an avenue of lilac bushes whose strong and pleasing fragrance filled the space of the town,

The land of Korelitz was fertile and was blessed with plenty of dew and rains.

**B.**

"How did the Jews of Korelitz earn a living?" my cousin asked me. He was born in Korelitz, left there at an early age and today lives in one of the richer countries. He remembered nothing of the way of life in the town. However, within the perspective of the Atomic Era, it is difficult to understand the concept of living in a small town at that time.

I asked myself the same question: How and from what did our ancestors in Korelitz live in those days, without the transportation networks, without raw materials; without planning and budgets; how did they nevertheless live without newspapers, without review or elections, without factories; how did they keep their food without food-colorings... and without cold-storage?

But they lived nevertheless...

Korelitz did not have any well-known industry -- it did not have any industry at all. There were, however, some things in Korelitz which had a far-and-wide reputation: the Yellow Cheese industry which caused the cheese to be called *Korelitzer Kezelach* (Korelitz Cheese). The youth considered this name as an insult.

The Korelitzian Cucumber was also highly regarded in the region. Since our town earned its living in part from agriculture, and since many of the town's inhabitants specialized in growing vegetables, they managed to develop a good variety of cucumber, which became popular in the whole region. The cucumber was the popular Jewish foodstuff at almost all levels of society, almost like the herring. The reason was simple: The cucumber was a cheap and easily available commodity. For the poor man, the cucumber with bread was a meal in itself. The cucumber was eaten fresh in summer and pickled in winter. It was pickled in large wooden barrels and remained faithful to its owner. It did not become spoiled or moldy, and was a tasty foodstuff during the entire winter until the new cucumbers arrived on the market in the new season.

From our distant perspective, the life in the town in those days seems like "living on air", as if they survived on miracles. However, as we try to approach the reality of life in the town, things become fleshed out. Everything lives before our eyes and we see and understand how each being in the town lived at that time, in the same way as we approach a multi-coloured picture and begin to understand the play of colors in all their hues.

The life of the town followed the conventional rules of a circuit -- the Rabbis, the ritual slaughterers, the teachers, the pharmacist, the doctor and all the services earned their living from the public. They did not, however, have a fixed salary as we understand it today, nor did they have social benefits or vacations. Of course, they did not have strikes either, but they did make a living somehow from the public as is customary in Jewish communities. We loved all our public officials, each for his own peculiar characteristics. There were two Rabbis in Korelitz. One was Rabbi Vernik, who had come from Slonim, and the other was Rabbi Moshe Oberzhansky, a local lad, and a lover of all creatures. We loved the ritual slaughterer, Moshe Avraham Volpin because of his Zionism and his holy love of all that was connected to the Land of Israel. The ritual slaughterer Alter Mordechovitz was loved because of his love of all his fellow creatures.

We had cattle dealers and grain dealers because our agricultural environment was rich in both products. These dealers used to buy their produce in the region and dispatched it to far-away Germany. Of course, the produce passed through the hands of many intermediaries and large traders before reaching their destinations. A large part of the townspeople were involved in trade and were the owners of small and tiny shops which depended mainly on the Gentile buyers from the nearby villages. These buyers came to town mainly on Market Days. They used to bring with them the produce of their fields or farms for sale. In return, they bought in the shops and brought these products home. If a Market Day was good and successful, then the whole week was successful. However, if there was no turnover on Market Day, there would be no income for the whole week.

Not only the shopkeepers were involved in the Market Day. The artisans were also involved in one way or another. It was then that the villagers used to order suits at the tailors or shoes at the shoemakers. We had some excellent tailors who used to make clothes for the gentry, and there were those who used to make the well-known *Peltselen*, which all the villagers used to wear.

This group of artisans and traders used to work busily day and night, in order to produce for the whole region and thus to make a living.

## C.

I was born not long before WW1, and while I was still a child, the war broke out. During the war years, when the town's inhabitants were exiled, we lived in a village near Darchin. In addition to worries about income, housing and health, my parents also had the burden of educating their brood of young children. My eldest brother Shaul, who today lives in South Africa, was sent far away from home to my Aunt Zelda. We, the little ones, were exempt from the burdens of Torah. There was a teacher of Russian in this village, and I was sent to him to learn a bit of knowledge. However, instead of learning, he taught me to cross myself in front of the Icon hanging in the left corner of the room. When I refused to cross myself, he threw me out.

My parents were among the first to return to Korelitz after the war. For the adults it was a return, but not so for us children. Everything was strange to us. We did not know one another. There was neither a school nor any other educational framework.

The returnees started to collect the remnants that remained. They started cleaning up the courtyards, which had been covered in thorns and thistles. They started rebuilding their houses, and we, the children, once more heard the moans of our parents regarding the problem of the children's education. Salvation came from Aaron Yaakov Aaronovitz, who opened the first *Cheider* after the war in his spacious house. This was one of the few houses which remained standing relatively undamaged after the war. The Rebbe, an aging man with a heavy body and a long gray beard, gathered together almost all the children of the town. At first, he taught each child separately, in order to establish each one's quality. He later organized us into groups of three students. My group partners were Shaul Zalmansky and Yisrael Shatskes. There were no books, and when our turn to study came, the Rebbe used to transfer to us the only page on which the Hebrew Alphabet was printed -- to us from a previous group and so on.

When we reached the level of being able to read, things were easier for us, because there was a *Siddur* (Jewish prayer book) in every Jewish home. After two study "periods" with the *Rebbe*, a school was opened, in which the languages of instruction were Yiddish and Hebrew. My group and I entered the school at the level of grade 3. These are the names of my teachers, the founders of the school and the promoters of education: The principal was Shalom Cohen, the son of the Rabbi. Moshe Eliyahu Shuster was the Nature Studies teacher. Yitschak Meyer Klatski was the Bible teacher -- he later became a bank manager in the town. *Itske der Melamed* [Itske the teacher] (I have forgotten his surname) - his given name was well known. The education of every person in the town measured according to the number of years that he studied under *Itske der Melamed*. Another teacher at the school was Dudy Tsvi Kiblevitz, who taught Torah on a full-time basis until the day he died.

*[Page 142]*

**Teachers at the Elementary School**
**From right:**
Yitzchak Meyer Klatski, Shalom Cohen, Gershon Eliasberg, Moshe Shuster, Yosef Portnoy

## D.

As previously mentioned, our house was near the House of Study. It was a spacious and organized house, and was always filled with gaiety and life. I almost did not know what it was to return to a locked house. The rare occasions on which I found a locked house, I remember to this day. These occasions leave a memory of sadness. I was always happy to return home, because I knew that my mother's kindly eyes would greet me, as well as the gaiety and laughs of my brothers and sisters. I also remember the serious face of my father who worked hard to sustain his family with honour.

Since my parents were busy and occupied during all six weekdays in making a living, the day of rest was very strongly felt. On the Sabbath, the house was especially clean. A white tablecloth was spread over the table on which the candles burned. We wore our Sabbath clothes. Our joyous parents were released from the worries of earning a living on the Sabbath. All these factors inspired in us a festive state of mind. Until this day, I remember the Sabbath in our house as a wonderful revelation of splendor and majesty. The intimacy and "the sitting of brothers together" were the source of the Sabbath happiness. This family discipline was especially kept at the Sabbath meal.

My mother, like all the other Jewish mothers in the town, used to work during the whole week in house matters. However, she always found time to help others. She did this not only in faithfulness, but also with a care and a holy awe which were special. I remember an example: In the house of our neighbors, Malka Riva and Kalman Marashiner, there lived an old woman, by the name of Chana. She was ill with tuberculosis. Her only son had died, and she became bed-ridden from her heavy grief. Malka Riva and my mother turned to an old-aged home in Novogrodok and organized a place for her there. However, until she was transferred there, many days passed. In the meantime, she had to be cared for and her needs handled. Of course, most of the burden fell on Malka Riva, but my mother was also harnessed for the burden. She used to send food for the ill woman by my hands. Until this day, the words of my mother still ring in my ears when she directed me regarding my behavior with the old woman. "Enter quietly", she told me, "Don't close the door loudly. Gather the utensils from the previous meal, and take care that you don't drop the plates, which would disturb our neighbour Malka-Riva". Finally, when I was finally outside, my mother used to run after me and, almost in shame, added: "And try not to come too close to her bed..."

---

*[Pages 144-146 - Hebrew]*

# Portrait of a Town

## Raya Schneur Kaplan

Korelitz was one of those towns in Northern Poland which were not indicated on the map. It was a "*Shtetl*", but a breathing volcanic *Shtetl* in its own way; the way of the little places in Poland of that period, with large Jewish populations.

Its wooden houses and its unplanned streets seemed as if they came down from heaven at the Time of Creation. Even the daily routines of life appeared to be forever unchanged. The water drawer used to carry his pails of water from the well on his poles. The laundry was washed by hand and hung on the rooftops for a few days until it dried.

My town, however, did have its requirements, which it needed for its existence in its own way. There were two elementary schools, two synagogues, a Rabbi, two ritual slaughterers, a cemetery, a kindergarten, a high school, a culture house, and a cinema. There were also one doctor, a pharmacy, a dental clinic and one factory. The parents were immersed in their work from morning to evening and, because there was generally little income, the people used to work harder. The artisans were also immersed in their work the whole day. Among these were tailors, shoemakers and blacksmiths. A professional man's workshop was very small, but this was the little world in which all of them lived. The shopkeepers (most of them female) kept their shifts. The women were not content with standing in their shops and waiting for customers. They stood at the entrance of their shops, advertising their wares to the passers- by, so that they should enter and purchase the "inexpensive and high quality" merchandise. At home, the housewives did crushing work. These women stood excitedly by the oven and the stove, raising fire from the damp wood-chips, baking, cooking and frying, and trying to gladden the hearts of their households with special foods, especially made by mother.

The youth of the town wandered around aimlessly. They were the ones who felt the futility and the lack of purpose of the shriveled and meager town. Many of them did their utmost to help their parents. Many assisted in the workshops and followed their parents' trade. Most however, used to wander astray in their lifestyles, unemployed and immersed in their thoughts and their daydreams.

Nevertheless, when we look back, there always arise strong yearnings for the town. Are these just yearnings for the days of our youth? Or are these yearnings for those who lived there and are no more?

Undoubtedly, the main reason for the yearning was in the life of purity and belief which surrounded the town. The Jews of all types, artisans and shopkeepers, were traditional Jews, most of whom dreamed of Zion and Jerusalem. These were innocent, but wise Jews, who were content with what they had, and did not aspire to riches and ease. Our mothers did not dream of or need the luxurious kitchen accessories to which we have become accustomed in modern times. They did not aspire to baking ovens and washing machines. Their thoughts were about raising their children to be healthy and to get satisfaction from them. Our parents were full of love, love for others, love for the source of their origins, and a love for their national values. These Jews always had a place for a wandering Jew to stay, they gave of their food to a poor man, and never complained. It is difficult not to remember and not to love this town, with all its Jews, its houses and its way of life. Because of this, there is a strong feeling of affinity for all those who came from this town and for all memories of those days.

**On Market Day**

On one day of the week, on "Market Day" on Wednesdays in Korelitz, the town woke up from its depression and turned in to a noisy, stormy and colorful town.

Who among us does not remember Wednesdays, which were wholly dedicated to the market? The shopkeepers would get up early, open their shops and prepare their merchandise for sale.

They stood waiting for the farmers who came from the whole region, from the nearby towns and villages, to buy goods for the whole week. They bought cloths, clothes, work- implements and household goods. But they came mainly to sell their own merchandise: the produce of their farms, their fields and their gardens.

The market was flooded with men and women of all types and of all ages, dressed in a variegated manner. Carts loaded with merchandise and harnessed to horses, streamed from dawn onwards to the Town Square. Each shopkeeper occupied his market stall on which he would display his wares.

Horses neigh, cows moo and farmers loudly proclaim and praise their wares. Others go immediately to the bars "to dampen their throats" while still others turn to the shops and don't miss the opportunity to take whatever is available surreptitiously, under cover of the crowds and the noise.

The excited and perspiring shopkeepers happily and vigorously sell their merchandise, while counting the coins with satisfaction.

The little children come to help their parents. If they cannot sell, they are able to watch over the Gentiles so that they won't steal, G-d Forbid!

We tried as much as we could to help our parents, but we did not always manage to do so. The temptation of the road was very big. How is it possible to stand in one place and look at the gentile while everything around you calls you: Come and see! Feel the merchandise, buy it, meet young people! Look what your friends and acquaintances are doing! Who are they meeting and what are they talking about?? Leave the shop! Nonsense, there is no reason to supervise, no one will take anything!

And why not pass between the stalls, which are loaded with good things: pullets, fowls, ducks, geese, turkeys, calves, cows, foals, horses, and even pigs. Look there at the choice fruit of all types! Their smell is aromatic, and their taste is the taste of heaven!

Well, people are leaving (*men lazet zich vag arien*).

And here, you are not alone: here are all the young girls who have already stopped dressing up and preening, and they are all touring among the carts and hunting their quarry.

There were those that succeeded immediately at their first try, and they were already with a boy or a group of boys. Others were pressed, their eyes wide open, casting their bright eyes around them, searching and searching..."

The young boys who were busy at work, stopped working for a moment and went out to the market. They are only flesh-and-blood and their souls are not raisins (*zayer iz niet kein rozinke*). They tour around in groups, with their eyes turning in all directions to look for the fair sex.

Towards evening, the noise calms down. The market starts emptying. The farmers return to their homes. The shops start emptying of people, the youths return to their homes, and the shopkeepers sigh with relief. Today was a successful market day. While the head is heavy and hurts from all the tension, work and noise, the pocket is full, and that is the main thing...

Here and there, a few salt herrings and white bread are bought and sold, and are eaten with great appetite and enjoyment.

After the shops are closed, each shopkeeper goes home with his cash-box, tired and weary, and in his heart one thought only -- to rest after a day of hard work and to gather strength for the next market day on Wednesday.

---

*[Pages 147-148 - Hebrew]*

# When a Visitor Came to Korelitz

## Esther Shkolnik-Horowitz - Jerusalem

Korelitz was known as a very hospitable town. A visitor who came to our town was not left alone and lonely. He was taken care of and his needs were met.

Like all the towns in Poland and Lithuania, the town was pleasant and popular among those poor Jews who wandered around from town to town. The first destination of these Jews was, as usual, the synagogue. These people used to come there and, as usual, salvation was not late in coming. When a stranger was seen in the House of Learning, a local resident immediately approached him and, after a few standard questions such as: "*Shalom Aleichem,* where are you from? How long have you been on your way?", he used to invite him to his home to eat his fill, so that a Jew shouldn't go hungry, G-d forbid! The housewives were used to these occurrences and didn't ask questions. It had been the custom for many generations that a Jew would come home from the synagogue, accompanied by a "guest". There were "Weekday guests" and "Sabbath guests". The housewife who prepared the meals for the family did not scrimp in her preparations. There was always place for another person at the table.

Another sort of "guest" were the *Yeshiva Bochers.* These were youths who came from far away to study to study Torah, either with a famous *Melamed* (teacher), or merely to devote himself to the study of Torah at the town's the House of Learning. These youths arrived without concern for sustenance, since it was customary to eat at the homes of local residents This type of arrangement was called, in Yiddish, *Essen Tog,* i.e., on each day the young man would eat at a different home. These days were arranged on a permanent basis. A householder who took upon himself to feed a *Yeshiva Bocher* on a certain day had to feed him during the whole year on the same day every week. The well known song by Avraham Reizen was based on this concept of "*Yeshiva Bocher* days" from that period: "*Essen tog shlingen trerren*" [** translator's note: *Eating days to swallow the tears* **]. These young men came from good Jewish homes, and they were not accustomed to eating in the homes of strangers, even though they were well fed and their hosts tried to ease their longings for their mothers' homes. These hosts tried to turn them into independent adults who knew how to look after themselves.

Apart from the things which were customary in all Jewish towns and cities, Korelitz was known for its more modern hospitality. This was hospitality for educated young men who came to the town for varying periods of time. In Korelitz, various societies were formed, bearing the names of those who organized them; for example, the "society" for meetings and recreation which are common in Israel today. Thus, there were the groups of Zlatke Beigin, Leah Kaplan, Menucha Abramowich, Riva Trivetsky, Liba Nisselevitz and others.

People coming to the town could easily find place at one of these societies, each to his taste end level of education. It was also an experience for the local society to receive a new guest from the outside, who used to add his characteristics to the ongoing lifestyle of the town. People used to take interest in such a young man who was received into the society, and who was in town for some purpose or other. He was never left alone. They organized a home for him in which to eat and drink and even organized some suitable company for him. In the nearby towns, you could hear all sorts of stories about the good food that was eaten at the Sabbath meal in Korelitz -- Gefilte Fish, the traditional Cholent, the Oil with Bulbetchkes, the Bebelach, the Kneidlach, the stuffed Kishke, the aromatic Tsimmes, the sweet Pie and, of course, the tasty Compote.

Even this was not enough. The guest who came to our town, used to leave not only with good impressions, a full stomach, and pleasant experiences, but also with an additional name, i.e. a nickname.

The nickname was generally given to the guest immediately on his appearance in the town. For this purpose, there was a "Bunch of Clowns", as it was generally called. They used to meditate about the characteristics of a new guest immediately on his arrival, in an almost official style... A messenger of the society came to the place where the visitor was staying and tried to judge his qualities. Was he tall or short, fat or thin, intelligent or stupid? Finally, after consultations with the society, a temporary nickname was found. However, during the man's sojourn, his permanent nickname was invented, based on his "Topography".

Thus, every guest used to go out happy and joyful with a nickname which stayed with him for life...

---

[Pages 149-158 –Yiddish- Below]
[Pages XV-XVI –English abridged – **See also page 356**]

# Occupations Of The Jews In Korelitz

## Yaacov Abramowich - Neveh Oz

### Translated from the Yiddish by Harvey Spitzer

Korelitz was a small town of many Hassidim and craftsmen. All the residents had a source of income. Some made a living by growing vegetables in small gardens. During the season, Jewish children would also work in the gardens. Cucumbers from Korelitz were sent to Vilna, Warsaw and other places.

The peasants from the surrounding villages used to bring wool on market days. Jewish tradesmen would buy it and the wool would be processed by machine in the small town.

The orchard keepers would lease orchards from Gentile men of leisure. Jewish boys would also work picking fruit which would be sent to the big cities.

Jews also had dairy concessions. They processed Dutch-type cheese in cellars especially made for that purpose, where the cheese was regularly checked and assorted. Cheese of the best quality was transported to the big cities. Dutch-type cheese from Korelitz was renowned and had a good name in the area.

There was a row of all kinds of stores in the center of the town. Wares of all kinds were displayed in big markets on Mondays and Wednesdays. Christians from the surrounding villages would travel to Korelitz to sell a variety of products. They would then spend their money in the Jewish stores.

The grain merchants did their business for the most part before the Christians came into town. The merchants would buy up their grain before the Christians arrived in town.

Butchers, besides having meat markets and living off the patronage of the town residents, also made a living by buying live cattle. The animals were displayed in the large markets in Korelitz, and many merchants would travel to Korelitz from distant places.

There were also carpenters' workshops. Some carpenters would go out to the nearest villages for an entire week. They returned home on Friday in order to be together with their family on the Sabbath. They would bring home the best of everything: butter, chickens, eggs, bread, potatoes, etc. They also brought peddlers.

Blacksmiths worked there too. Hammers and anvils rang out mainly at the time of the grain harvest. Many Christians would go to Korelitz to sharpen their sickles and scythes. Lines of farmers stood at the blacksmiths' at that season.

Tailors, shoemakers and cap makers worked feverishly mostly before the holidays when the residents of the town were expected to dress up in new suits of clothes, new shoes and new hats... Whenever people met in the street, they would ask one another: "Who sewed for you?" and they would wish each other a "Wear it well!"

Michael Shuster's lumber yard permeated the town with the fragrance of pine boards. Those living at the other end of the town enjoyed the healthy scent of pinewood coming from the lumber yard which Eliahu Seilovitzki made beyond the town limits. However, he wasn't successful and went into the grain business instead.

The residents of the town lived like one family. People would help each other. A saying went around, "One pair of shoes for the entire Zalamanke Street."

[Page 150]

**A Section of Mill Street**

Steam mills - On one side, Yitzchak Stoler and his partners; on the other side, Alex Srebrenik and Yossel Bernstein. The mills were steam operated. The water mill, which belonged to Yisrael-Michel Slotzky and his partner Ezra Pomerchik, worked on less power. Many peasants with fully packed bags of grain would stand around the mills, waiting in turn to have their cereals ground. How we miss our beloved little town of Korelitz with its dear fellow Jews!

*English* – see also page 374
## The Fire Brigade – Volunteer Firemen in Korelitz

My father, Layzer, of blessed memory, was a house economy officer in the fire brigade. When the officers grew old and died, there were new officers.

I remember the new officers: chairman – **Eliasberg**, druggist; chief – **Dovid Slutzky**; deputy chief – **Savelia Klatzka;**   adjutant - **Mordechai Benin;** managers – **Gertz Namiat**, **Reuven Perevolotsky**; commander of first unit - **Yisrael Izrealit**; commander of second group – **Chaim Abramowich**; commander of third unit – water manager, **Baruch Tsalkovich**; band leader (formerly **Shimon Miller**).

[Page 151]
**Fire Brigade Members**
**From right to left:** Leibel Perevolotsky, Avraham Kaplan, Eliezer Abramowich, Ozer Kaplan, Getzel Yelin, Eliahu Meites

Whenever there was a rehearsal, I would come to listen. They wouldn't accept me in the fire brigade because I was still too young. I was envious of the other firemen when I saw them in their uniforms with their shiny buttons and red-rimmed navy blue cuffs. I would always stand and watch their drills as they pulled themselves up the ropes, climbed up the ladders and worked with the water pumps.

And so time went by. People got older. The chief, Dovid Slutzky, called me over and said, "Yankel, you will take over the position of house economy commander and be responsible for the brigade's inventory".

My work consisted of the following tasks: to see to it that the hose didn't leak, the wagons were in good condition, the wheels were painted, the axels were greased, the barrels on both wheels were always filled with water and that the water pumps were always in good condition. What I could fix myself - fine! What I couldn't, I should get a worker to make the repairs. In case of a real fire, all the tools should be ready for the work of extinguishing the blaze.

"This is an inheritance from your father," he added.

I told him that everything would be carried out properly. Thereupon, he gave me my first order: to go into a store and get cloth for a uniform and a cap. I immediately got material and shiny buttons which I brought to Shlomke Kabat, the tailor. As for the cap, I brought the cloth to Moshe-Hillel Kirzshner for him to make. My joy was indescribable.

I was in the fire brigade more than I was at home. I painted the wagons and wheels, greased the axels, saw to it that the barrels were always filled with water, kept the hoses in good repair so they wouldn't leak, saw to it that the ladders were always in good condition, that the axels weren't broken and would hold firmly to their wooden shaft and that the water pumps were working properly.

I had a good teacher. He was Noach Gershnovsky. His house was opposite the fire brigade and he had the key. He would always come and look around. He taught me what I had to do and also lent a hand.

Fire drills and rehearsals were always held on Sundays. Sunday morning, Yoshe Gershnovsky would give a signal on his instrument. He would go from street to street, reminding people to attend the drills. When he got older, his job was taken over by his brother Yudke, Dovid Lifschitz and also Leibe Izachovsky. All the fire brigade members would gather together with the officers in the fire brigade yard which was on Toibe Street.

**The Parade Through the Streets**
Reuven Benin, the adjutant, was first to stand in full fire brigade uniform. He would sometimes ride on his bicycle. The band director, Baruch Tzelkovitch, walked about two meters away, followed by the fire brigade band which had a very good name.

Moshe Gershnovsky – clarinet; Noach Gershnovsky- trombone; Yoshe -cornet; Gedaliahu the Shoemaker's four sons also belonged to the band. The fifth son, Yankel, was in the Ladasvinkas Company. Their father, Gedaliahu, was devoted heart and soul to the fire brigade.

The other members of the band were Aharon Lifschitz's four sons: Yitzchak - ; Berl – clarinet; Dovid - tenor sax; Dan-Yeshayahu Gershnovsky, Markel Gershnovsky, Avrahomel Lipchon - drums; Ozerovsky and Idl Savitzky - cymbals.

The officers walked behind the band. Behind the officers was the commander of the Ladasvinkas group, R. Perevolotsky, followed by his group who were the first workers at a fire. All of them were robust fire brigade members with their brass helmets and axes hanging from the leather bands around their waist on the left side.

The second group *botchnikes* – i.e. those who worked with the water pumps. The first – Yisrael Izraelit, and behind him was his group wearing uniforms.

The third group – water suppliers, commander - Ch. Abramowich followed by his group.

The band would play and then march through the streets keeping in time to the beat. Our dear residents of Korelitz would welcome us with applause.

## Drills
After marching through the streets of the small town, they came back to the fire brigade. They would connect the four-wheeled wagon [to the ____ ] behind the groups. On the wagon were loaded big ladders, hooks, hoses and then fire brigade tools: water pumps, several iron barrels, several wooden barrels painted red and decorated with white on two wheels. They would go to the river and conduct drills so that they would know how to manage when there was a fire. Each division with its leaders would perform the drills diligently.

The fire brigade was maintained for the most part by the residents of Korelitz, who paid monthly taxes. The Korelitz administration also helped. The town judge, Suchozsheivski, belonged to the authorities as well. There were cases involving residents who were unwilling to pay their taxes.

When there was a practice, they would place a big ladder against the house of a resident who refused to pay his taxes. They would drag out the hoses with the nozzle on the roof and put them directly down the chimney. The water pump was ready to deliver water. The "patient" would see that he had no choice: there would soon be water in his house. He had to pay for all the time he was in arrears.

*[Page 154]*

**FIREFIGHTERS AND THE BAND**

Bottom – from right to left –
**(First row,** sitting**):** Moshe Lifschitz, Moshe Gershnovsky, Berl Lifschitz, Baruch Tzalkovitch, Yoshe Gershnovsky, Henech Yoselovich, …….. , Noach Gershnovsky.
**(Second row):** Avraham Lifchin, Markel Gershnovsky, Yona Yelin, ………, Abramovich, Moshe Stoler, Motel Levin, Chaim Dushkin, Alter Greenfeld.
**(Third row):** Yisrael Izraelit, Mordechai, Reuven Begin, Chaya-Leah Kaplan (Shereshevsky), Leah Trayevitzsky, Reuven Perevolotsky, Savelia Klatzka.
**(Fourth row):** Gershovitz, Mordechai Mordchovich, Shmuel Yankelevitch, Yitzchak Stoler, Anshel Abramovich, Shlomo Gertzovski, Moshe Lifchin, Avraham Berman, ……….. , Shaul Lubchansky, Yehuda, Motel Mordchovich, Choneh (?), Lifchin, Abramovich, Yaakov Gershnovsky, ……….., Yosef Lifchin, Bragel (Christian).
**(Fifth row):** Chaim Berkovitch, Yeshayahu Gershnovsky, Yitzchak Stoler, Benzion Gulkowich, Yoel Meyerovitch, Motel Izechovski, Alter Abramovich.

# Theatres

Artists passing through Korelitz would perform with the fire brigade. All the musical instruments would be taken out. There was a stage especially made for theatrical productions. The fire brigade would receive payment for their services.

There was a dramatics club in Korelitz which would put on shows. The money taken in would go to the fire brigade. Alter Boyarsky was the first manager. When he left for Argentina, Savelia Klatzka became the manager.

There were markets twice a week in Korelitz. Christians would sometimes get drunk and start behaving wildly. A tumult would ensue. Some of the Jews would close their shops and run off. An alarm would suddenly be sounded and all the firemen would be on the scene at once. When there was an alarm, the firemen had the right to seize horses belonging to the peasants in the market wherever they could, and they immediately went into the market with water pumps and barrels of water. When the order was given, they would begin pouring water until the Christians left the market and things calmed down.

Our fire brigade also received a mechanical pump from the security department and was then on equal footing with the larger fire departments. Our fire brigade would go out on calls to fight fires in other small towns. Our firemen would push their way into the burning house with axes, iron bars and hooks. They would tear apart the house and pour water on the flames until the fire was quenched.

Our beloved Yisrael-Yudel Efroimski, chairman of the workers' union, would sit in the ticket office at the fire brigade house whenever there was a show. He would sell the tickets with great devotion. When there were a lot of people in attendance, he would say, "The audience was quite large and so was the cashier's box."

*[English abridged –Page XXXVII –* **Page 376***]*

## Sports Groups in Korelitz

There was a soccer team in Korelitz called "Maccabi". The playing area was at the Poplava fields. People played even when there was only a little time. They also kicked the ball around in the market place. One group of players stood on one side of the shops, and another group stood on the other side. This is how they practiced kicking the ball to one another.

The team's inventory of items was kept at Yeshayahu Bolotnitzky's shop in the center of the market place. The uniform consisted of white shirts and short pants. Inscribed on the shirt was a Star of David and "Maccabi"- Korelitz. The Jewish flag was blue and white.

They used to go to Novogrudek and Turetz to play. There was also a Christian soccer team in Korelitz under the direction of Tadek Yozkevitch, the nobleman's son. The Jewish team would compete with them, too.

I recall an incident: It was a Sunday. Mordechai Krolavetzky (today Malkieli) came to Korelitz as a guest from Israel. As it happened, there was a game with the local Christians. Mordechai also took part in the game. Both teams met on the field. The Jewish team in blue and white outfits; those on the other team wore red and white clothing.

They began playing. It was a relentless struggle. Both teams wanted to beat the other. Our team won after a hard game. The Christians didn't like losing, and a fight broke out. Mordecai Malkieli (Krolavetzky) broke the bones of a player on the other team. But the winners were the Jews!!

A volley ball team was formed at my initiative. We collected money and purchased a ball. My brother Gavriel, Shaul Zalmansky and I knitted a net. Other players were also eager to help.

We made two light posts having iron tips at the bottom and two hooks on the top. One of the team members, Berl Lubchansky, did the iron work free of charge. The volley ball team's inventory of items was kept in my house. The players gathered together near my house.

The male team members would take the nets; the female members would carry the lighter things. We would all go together to the playing site on Zapol Hill where there were markets for cattle, sheep, horses, etc. Naturally, the place wasn't clean. We cleaned it up right away and made marks, boundaries and a place for the center. We stuck the poles into the ground with the iron tips, spread out the net and everyone took their place. The game started when the whistle was blown.

There were six players on each team. Everyone played enthusiastically. Many spectators would come to the game. Later, a team of younger players was formed. We played whenever we had free time.

Each of the team members had a job to do. Whoever came first saw to it that the place was clean and that it was even marked out with chalk.

We used to go out to contests in the near-by towns, such as Turetz, Neishtat and Lubtch. I remember that one Sabbath day, a team from Korelitz including myself went to Turetz to play. When the Jews in Turetz saw us, they began shouting, "Gentiles! Will you play on the Sabbath?!!"

They started throwing stones at us. We had to leave Turetz, but I never lost the spirit to play.

There was also a team of Christian players in the Polish public school. Mr. Delenbe was the school principal. We, the Jewish older team, often competed against them in the public school yard where there was a place to play. We would beat them quite often. There were good players on our team. Players from the high school in Novogrudek came to the Polish public school. The principal of the public school, Mr. Delenbe, would send for a few of the better players on our team such as myself, Gitel Kivelevitch, Motke Poluzhsky, Gavriel Abramowich and would ask us to play with their players. The more we took part, the more they would come out the winners. They were so happy, they didn't know what they could do for us.

The number of members of that section of players grew from day to day. The police chief's wife began to play ball with us and became a steady player. Thanks to that, we were able to take advantage of the influence of having the police chief's wife on our team. And that was very useful to us on more than one occasion.

The games were mainly played on the Sabbath. This, of course, came to the rabbi's attention. The town rabbi, Rabbi Vernik, of blessed memory, called in a few of the team members and said that while sport was actually very good for one's health, we should nevertheless avoid playing on the Sabbath. We followed his advice somewhat, but it was hard for us to carry out his request. On the Sabbath, we would play behind the town on the Poplav fields.

It is worth noting that the Christian players liked me because I played well. When the Germans occupied our section, the Christian players were asked to draw up a list of the Jewish players. This was done so the Germans could take them out of Korelitz first to be murdered. The Christian players did not include me and my brother in the list. And thanks to that, I had the opportunity to run away and remain alive.

---

[Page 158]                    **Winter Sport**

*[Pages 159-160]*

# A Drill In Town
## Michael Beigin – Jerusalem
### Translated from the Yiddish by Harvey Spitzer

It's a hot, summer, Sunday market day in town. The few Gentiles who came to the market are going home. The woman shopkeepers are seated next to their closed stores, counting their day's earnings. They exchange a little gossip. Everyone in town is busy at work. The youngsters, however, go to the little river behind the town for a little swim and to cool off after the hot summer day. In the distance, one can see Kalman the Marashina swimming on his back, his white beard sliding over the shallow water no longer visible. A few boys are playing "_____", chasing one another and trying to catch up with one another.

The atmosphere on the shore is joyful and boisterous. The women's section is a little further off. Among the girls bathing there are Chaya-Leahke with her blond hair, Lola and others. Some of the boys like Kalman, Yona and others are rascals and are bold enough to cover their faces with mud and start swimming over to the women, thinking that no one will recognize them. But, all of a sudden, there's a scream and a shriek. The boys turn around from fright and swim back to the shore, terrified.

Suddenly, a signal is heard. Yoshinke, Gedalia's son, holding his clarinet (cornet) goes by, dressed up in a pair of lovely, shiny boots. His blond hair is combed very smoothly and he calls the members of the fire brigade for a rehearsal. He gives the first signal near his home on Toib Street. Everyone has already heard him. He goes on further towards the right to the market place and gives his familiar signal. From the market place he goes to Zalamanke Street. Children run after him from all sides and Yoshinke is beaming with joy. Who is equal to him? He raises his cornet and doesn't stop blowing until he turns subtly around with his trumpet and skillfully plays a melody which he composed himself. He finally gives another loud signal and when he is already convinced that everyone has heard him, goes on his way.

All of the firemen are now gathering for the drill. Decked out in shiny, brass helmets, they take out the barrels of water and the fire extinguishers from the station, and are ready for further orders from the authorities.

Itche the Mute comes running up out of breath like a chief officer. He begins to busy himself with the long, canvas hose which he lays out on the street and checks to see that everything is all right. Then he rolls the hose up so that it is ready for use. The "general staff" arrives – Shefke Klatchke, accompanied by

Mordechai Raube. The firemen stand in two rows like soldiers. They show proper respect for the commanders especially for the top general, H. Eliasberg.

The drill begins under the direction of Baruch Pines. The parade starts out, led by the band, followed by the "generals". A little further away march the firemen, keeping in step with the music like soldiers. Children run after them from all sides and women holding children are among the large crowd which accompanies the fire brigade. All are thrilled to be at the festive parade on a weekday in the small town.

They soon put up the big ladders against one of the town roofs and deliver water. Quick as a cat, one of the firemen climbs up the ladder and, in a hoarse voice, keeps on giving an order - *vada* (water)! He sprinkles water in every direction and also sprinkles the crowd with cold water "by mistake". Again a shout with a hubbub.

When it already grew dark quite late at night, when the fire was already put out and the drill came to an end, an order is given to bring the apparatus back in proper condition. The firemen line up in rows and the band plays one of its familiar marches. The fire brigade then marches back to the station, keeping to the beat of the music, and the rehearsal is over.

Dear town of Korelitz, you were once alive but no more. Your people, institutions, characters and personalities are no more. Your "common people" and sacred objects are no more, but you will always remain in our memory.

---

[Page 161- Hebrew]

# On the Main Road

## Arye Shalit-Karolevsky - Raanana

Korelitz is situated on the main road from Novogrodok to Minsk. As a result, the town was an important way station for all the *Magidim*, the "Emissaries" and all the paupers of the whole region. In Korelitz, there was a scholar by the name of Reb Aaron Yaakov Davidovitz, who used to take care that all those passing through the town would find board and lodgings. On Sabbath eves, he used to ensure at the synagogue that each guest would find a householder who would take him home for the Sabbath meal. When there were many guests, and if he did not find enough householders for them all, he used to take those remaining to his own home. His wife and children were already used to this situation and did not complain. They shared their food with them and accepted matters with joy.

**Mutual Aid**

The characteristic lines of Korelitz are Mutual Aid. Mutual Aid was expressed in the life of the town in many areas, and this was what gave the color of "All

Israel are guarantors for one another" in tangible manner. One man's devotion to his friend was expressed in mutual aid. This impressed itself also on the younger generation in the future. The pioneer youth, which arose in Korelitz, were devoted heart and soul to the Zionist Ideal. They were among the first to emigrate to Palestine.

Korelitz was not a rich town, but the Jews lived in dignity, and those who were poverty-stricken were honorably assisted. There were those who took care that no Jewish house would lack the essentials for the Sabbath and that the children would not lack clothes, food or education. They were also supplied with *matzos* and wine for the Passover, and potatoes and firewood in winter.

**The Law and Zionism**

At that time, the authorities did not approve of Zionist activities in our region. Their anger, however, was most aroused against Moshe Avraham the ritual slaughterer. He was a Zionist zealot, a sermonizer and an unlimited activist. The Regional Governor came especially to the town and stayed at our place. He invited the only policeman in the place and gave him the job of investigating who was this Jew who was openly propagandizing. When the Governor left, the policeman asked my father what Zionism was. And what was this Jew doing, the one who was preaching so hard for Zionism? My father told him that this was a poor Jew who was collecting money for himself so that he could go and see the holy places in the Holy Land. "If so", said the policeman, "I am also a Zionist, because I also wish to visit the Holy Places". He abandoned the whole matter of investigating Moshe Avraham the Zionist.

---

*[Page 162 -Hebrew]*

# Cucumbers

## Gutke Nohomovski-Gantzevitz

People in Korelitz were also active in agriculture. I remember that my father had a few hectares of land. He used to cultivate it devotedly and faithfully. I especially remember the enthusiasm for growing cucumbers, so much so that our town was famous for its pleasant cucumbers. Not only did they find their way onto the tables of the local Jews, but were also exported overseas and to many places in Poland. The reputation of Korelitz cucumbers rose so high that many Jews who grew cucumbers set up marketing "partnerships". I remember an incident which aroused the innocent Jews. In the common warehouse where the good small cucumbers were kept, large yellow cucumbers were found. Apparently, one of the partners had smuggled them in, hoping to get rid of them in this way. The Jewish "farmers" could not forgive the one who had threatened to the high reputation of our cucumbers.

We, the children, were faithful partners in the cucumber operations. Firstly, the work in the fields captivated us, mainly during the harvest. The days of harvest were truly like a holiday to us. On those beautiful summer days, the cucumbers ripened, and we put our hands between the large leaves to check whether the fruit was ripe and ready to pick. Of course, we were not connoisseurs, and many young cucumbers found themselves directly in our mouths... without washing or blessing...

---

*[Pages 162 -164]*

# My Visit To Korelitz In 1937

## Vital Arieli – Netanya

### Translated from the Yiddish by Harvey Spitzer

Five years have already gone by since I left my small town of Korelitz. It wasn't easy for me to part with my family, all my friends and beloved and dear people. It was even harder, however, to adjust to the new country, to our living conditions, to foreign people, to another language and other customs. The whole time I lived and breathed with the past, with the small town of Korelitz. Standing before my eyes was the small town, its majestic landscape, the people, houses and lanes.

In 1937 I had the opportunity to travel to Poland on a small ship, the *Har Zion*. I took my small son, packed the necessary things and gifts and started out on my way. The trip lasted 8 days. The closer I got to Korelitz, the more impatient I grew to see those near to me.

And there I was in Warsaw – another kind of air, other people, another language. My brother-in-law and my sister Merke were waiting for me in Novoyelnia. Our meeting was heartfelt and touching. We spent the night at our Aunt Shayna's with her son and daughter. Although I was very tired from the long trip, we stayed up all night, talking non-stop until the morning, when we left for Novogrudek. It just happened that it was a Thursday market day. Devorah Poluzhsky knew of my coming. She left her business and was waiting for me at the bus stop. We went to her house, waiting for the bus from Korelitz. We met acquaintances from Korelitz on the bus: Feivel Nisselevitz and other good friends. We chatted so much that we didn't realize that the trip was over so quickly. From time to time, my child asked me in Hebrew: "What are they talking about? Where are we? What is this place?" As we were entering Korelitz, he noticed pigs in the yards of the Gentiles. He was very surprised and said, "How many dogs are here?" When I translated what he said to the passengers on the bus, they all laughed a lot. And there we were in Korelitz. I felt like a guest the first few days, but little by little, I got into the normal routine of small town life. I only spoke Hebrew with my son and with my cousin, Moshe Perevolotsky.

I told everyone about our small and lovely country- about its mountains and valleys, kibbutzim and moshavim (collective settlements), about Jordan and Jerusalem, about the new towns and settlements which were being built up everywhere. Everyone listened attentively to what I had to say about the Land of Israel, which was both near and far away.

They prepared the best food the first Sabbath I was there. All my relatives and acquaintances gathered in the house, and anyone who had relatives in the Land of Israel came to get or send a greeting. I remember that among the guests were my Uncle Leibe with Elka and their children. Reuven Perevolotsky with his family, Gershon Poluzhsky and Esther, the Levitt family, Dovid Nisselevitz and Saraka, Koltzitzky and family, Lipke Beigin and Zlatka, Rabbi Alter Mordechovitch the ritual slaughterer, with his wife, Rabbi Moshe Avraham Volfin the ritual slaughterer. I treated the men to cigarettes from the Land of Israel and they were very happy with them.

I would sit and chat a lot with Dushke Abramowich every day. I also used to chat a lot with Mushke Shuster, Shlomke Oberzhansky, the Efroimski family and others. I think there wasn't a single acquaintance in the town with whom I didn't chat then. My former friends - boys and girls - would come over and we would go out for a walk together. Many of my acquaintances made special receptions for me. Among these were Gittel Kaplan and Feigel Kaganovitch. Lola Trayevetzky came especially from Baronovitch to see me. Merka Izraelit came especially from Mir.

I told them about the new Jewish cities and towns which were being built and especially about Jerusalem and Tel Aviv. Each one imagined that the Jewish country was nothing less than a paradise, and many of them dreamed of moving to Israel and envied me because I already lived there.

My family was overly happy with my coming to visit. They looked at my child as if he were an angel speaking Hebrew. My little boy quickly made friends with the Korelitz children and had even begun speaking Yiddish.

The time went by quickly and, unfortunately, we had to get ready to go back. I naturally promised everyone that I would come again as a guest. I couldn't imagine that that would be my last visit to Korelitz and that I would never again see my dear people, my family, and that I was parting with them forever.

The Holocaust came and destroyed our small town together with its dear Jews. Only my father and a few acquaintances managed to escape and come to our country. My father lived in Israel for 18 years, but his thoughts were always there in Korelitz. Even before his death, he still spoke about Korelitz.

Everything went up in flames. Only their memory has remained for us to cherish.

---

*[Pages 165-166]*

# There Where I Was Born – Grows A Tree

## Leah Kornfeld-Lubchansky - Herzliya

### Translated from the Yiddish by Harvey Spitzer

Not far from the open road to the small town of Mir, several tens of meters from Perevolotsky's house, stand three trees, two of which reach up to the sky, with many branches and fresh, green leaves aglow from the golden rays of the sun. Many such trees grow there in that section. There were times when I even bore a hatred to them.

The first in a row of standing, hunchbacked trees is mine. It belongs to my feelings. I took care of it with my own hands.

I remember one day when we assembled in the large hall of the Povshechne synagogue, each class in its place standing in rows. The school principal, Mr. Zolmbe, comes out of the office and says, "Children, tomorrow you have a day off from school. Tomorrow we're going to plant trees on the border of the streets in Korelitz. Those of you who want to take part in planting trees should come tomorrow afternoon with planting tools. And so we set out, loaded down with spades and axes via Ogrodnik to the Pritzonevitch small woods. And on the way, I was chatting with Nechama Meyerovitch, and when we got to the little woods, we saw the last of our group vanish, just as if the woods had swallowed them up. We were afraid to go any deeper into the woods and went back. We returned over the road which connected Ogrodnik with Korelitz, passing by Yisrael Slutzky's mill and through the miller's inclined street. The frolicking sounds of children playing have remained in my memory to this very day as they slid down the hill on their little sleds on frosty, wintery evenings.

But this time, going through Vilner Street, there was no joy in my heart. Due to my own carelessness, I missed the opportunity to decorate the naked streets of Korelitz with trees. There was no reason to be sorry, however, because the pupils from the lower grades went out to plant trees the next day, and my friend Chayke Dushkin and I joined them in planting trees.

The sapling we planted didn't live very long. A cruel hand tore it out of the ground. We planted another sapling, carefully tying the branches around with little ropes and securing it to the ground with stones. We carried water for it from the river more than once to quench its thirst so that it would not dry out. We hoped that when the tree grew and put on fresh, green leaves, we would come and sit under the tree to protect ourselves from the burning sun.

Once, when we passed by, we noticed our little tree standing bare. There were no more ropes by which it was tied to the ground. But, as if on spite, it grew high, with great audacity, to heaven. Is our tree still standing there? Don't say it's not there.

[Page 166]

**Teachers and Pupils in the Hebrew School, 1929**

**Sitting from the right**
(**First row**): Chaim Bolotnitzky, Malka Rabinovitz, ..........., Elka Mordchovitz, Shifra Rakovitzky, Gutel Mordchovitz, Yitzchak-Berl Gantzevitz;
(**Second row**): Moshe Kuznietz, Yarka Yelin, Elka Kuznietz, Solomon ( teacher), Raisel Nissilevitz, Berl Lubchansky, ............ ;
(**Third row**): Yosef Portnoy (teacher), Grisha, Yaakov Abramowich, Rivka Yelin, Menucha Abramowich, Shlomo Davidovsky (teacher), Yehudit Karelitzky (Gulkowich), Chaya Niegnievitzky, Goldberg (teacher).

*[Pages 167-172 –Hebrew- below]*
*[Page XXXIII – English, abridged –* **see also page 373***]*

# The Bank And Benevolent Fund In Korelitz

## Fruma Gulkowich-Berger - New York

### Translated from the Yiddish by Harvey Spitzer

Despite the many years that have gone by since the Holocaust, time has not erased our love for the way of life that once characterized our small town. We were all one big family.

Korelitz Jews were not especially wealthy, but they had a good reputation as people who were always concerned about one another. They empathized with someone's sorrow or trouble, and they rejoiced together on happy occasions. The quality of helping someone in need was always developed among the Jews in Korelitz.

In order to ease the difficult material situation of the needy, a people's bank and benevolent fund were created in the small town. Both of these charity institutions were very important for many Jews of Korelitz. The bank was created from subsidies received from the *Yakopa* organization, whose main committee was in Vilna. Thanks to the energetic efforts of certain activists who were concerned about the welfare of the needy, the doors of the bank were always open for those in need of loans.

Here we should mention the manager and bookkeeper of the bank, Yitzchak-Meyer Klatzkis, a former Jewish teacher, an intelligent, conscientious person who performed his work with love and devotion. The management of the bank was responsible for supervising the bank's work which involved many technical things. For the most part, the bank's administration was made up of three or four officers. I don't remember exactly who they were, but I think the following people belonged to the directorate: G. Namiot (druggist), Getzl Relien (merchant) and T. Koltzitzki (Klecici) – a merchant.

Whoever needed a bank loan had to have two guarantors considered trustworthy. The guarantors naturally had to sign. Interest was charged for the borrowed money, but if the borrower was, God forbid, unable to pay back the loan, the co-signers were responsible for covering the debt.

The bank's conditions were often too strict for many poor people, and so a benevolent fund was set up in the town. The fund actually belonged to the handworkers' union. One could take out a short-term, interest free loan, and craftsmen and those belonging to the poorer layer of the population especially enjoyed the benefits of the charity fund.

The benevolent fund was created thanks to money sent from America and from money raised in the town itself for that purpose through various funds and enterprises.  Our dramatics club, for example, put on plays, and the proceeds were entirely reserved for the benevolent fund.

The following persons belonged to the management of the fund: Berl Busel, Yaakov Gershenovsky, Yisrael Rudel, Efroimski and Berl Poluzhsky. The above-mentioned people accomplished a lot and were very active in the area of creating money funds for the benevolent fund charity and managed its operation.

The directorate would often change, of course, and therefore, anyone who was interested and capable of working in the fund would be able to do so. Both institutions - the people's bank and the charity fund – were very important for the Jewish population of Korelitz, both for the businessman and craftsman who often needed loans. The Korelitz Jews knew that there was a place to turn in time of trouble.

This is now all destroyed. No more Jews on the streets of the town - no more Jewish institutions.

*[Page XXXIV –English abridged – **see page 373]***

# The Dramatics Club

With these lines, I will eternalize the amateur theatrical performers from Korelitz and, at the same time, show the creative powers and the contributions of the Korelitz dramatics club for the development of Jewish culture in our small town.

Our small town was on a high cultural level. We had talented and intelligent young people who strove to create something. There were youth organizations bustling with activity in their meeting places. One of the most important and respectable youth groups was the dramatics club, which brought together amateur theatrical performers of the Yiddish stage.

*[Page 169]*

**Dramatics Club and the Band**

**(Bottom, from right)**
**First row** Chaim Stoler, Noach Gershenovsky, Avraham Nissilevitz, Yosef Gershenovsky, Yehuda Gershenovsky, Berl Lifschitz, Motel Levin, Grinfeld.
**Second row**: Avraham Lifchin, Moshe Gershenovsky, Yitzchak Lifschitz, Bracha Kaplan, Namiot, Eliasberg, Baruch Tzelekovitz, Berl Poluzhsky, ........, Moshe Shuster, Gitel Londin.
**Third row**: Yitzchak Gershenovitz, Chaim Dushkin, Dovid Lifschitz, Chaim Abramowich, Teibel Dvortzky(Trotzky), Manya Kaganovitch, Alter Boyarski, Savelia Klatzky, Pessia Efroimsky, Kalman Mordchovitz, ......., Zalman Nissilevitz, Yaakov Gershenovsky, Sheindel Perevolotsky (Kuznietz).

I was the youngest of the third generation of performers in that ensemble. We used to put on Yiddish plays, which brought joy and festivity to young and old alike in our small town. This was the only entertainment of its kind because a troupe of professional actors seldom came to us. There were no movies either. The intake of our ensemble was used for important aims.

Our dramatics club would perform plays and dramas by classical Yiddish playwrights and dramatists.

Many very talented performers who could be compared to professional actors grew up in our dramatics club. Among these were the following:

**Berl Poluzhsky** who starred in *Koldunia* in the role of the witch. Although I was still too young at the time, the picture of the witch as performed by Berl still moves before my eyes today. And together with him, the whole ensemble held the audience spellbound.

**Sheppe Klatchka**, a precious personality in the art of theatre. He was the director and, at the same time, played some of the most difficult roles. He influenced and held the whole ensemble together. We all listened to his remarks and directions with the utmost respect.

**Chaim Bosel**, a teacher at the Jewish school who would also find time to act in the Yiddish theatre. Many of us remember him in the role of "Batiushka Prokop" in the play *Chasia the Orphan*.

**Berl Abrinsky** – one of the rare artists on the stage. I can still see him in the role of *Nevalah*. With what passion he played in *Yosha Kalb*! – an unforgettable talent.

The **Gershenovsky** brothers, from the oldest to the youngest, all performed in the theatre – Yankel, Moishel, Yashe and Rutshke. My friend **Yashe** always acted well and was well suited to his role. **Yankel** and **Moishel** especially excelled in various roles. I performed with Moishel in "Jewish King Lear", playing the part of his daughter, Teibele. I also performed together with **Rutshke** in *Groisen Gevins*. These were talents in whom one could take pride.

The **Lifschitz** brothers Berl and Dovid played various instruments, sang and danced. They were capable of doing everything.

**The Women in the Ensemble:**
The "comédienne", **Rivke Yelin** – we called her Esther-Rachel Kaminski - was blessed with a great talent for acting. As soon as she appeared on the stage, she captivated the audience. She brought a lot of joy and laughter to the spectators, who thanked her with long, sustained applause.

Our dramatics club possessed very beautiful women including **Menucha Abramowich** (she lives in Israel), **Shefia Levitt**, **Chaya-Leahke Shereshevski** and others. If we needed someone for a smaller part, there was no problem. One became an artist overnight.

The leading roles - prima donna - were, for the most part, played by **Menucha Abramowich**. **Manya Kaganovitch** (also living in Israel) was also one of the most important actresses.

Several of the former members of the Korelitz Dramatics Club live in America. Two of them are **Chayke Dushkin** and **Bentshe Gulkowich**, my brother. I remember that when I would come to rehearsals, they would also talk about Sheindel, Peshe and Roza as "big stars". Unfortunately, I didn't know them personally. They emigrated abroad, but no one in the town wanted to forget them. (**Sheindel Kuznietz** lives in Israel).

We would prepare a presentation for every holiday, and every show would turn into a great cultural event in our small town. The dramatics club would also go out into the "provinces" to perform in the surrounding small towns and would also bring the local Jews much joy.

[Page 171]
**Dramatics Club**

**Bottom**: Yehuda Gershenovsky.
**Second row (from right):** Chaim Bussel, Chaya Leah Kaplan, Alter Grinfeld, Shifra Levitt, Berl Poluzhsky, Fania Lifschitz, Menucha Abramowich, Rivke Yellin.
**Third row:** Berl Lifschitz, Manya Kaganovich, Yaakov Gershenovsky, Zalman Nissilevitz, Ben-Zion Gulkowich, Savelia Klatzki, Avraham Gorodiski, Yaakov Oberzhansky, Moshe Gershenovsky.

Our theatre was located in the firemen's station house or, as we used to joke, our actors were performing on the "pumps" in the fire brigade. We performed a repertoire of plays from the Yiddish theatre, which gave us spiritual pleasure. Each new production would bring much life to the town. Wherever the townspeople would go, they would talk about the play, the actors and imitate their movements and sing the new little songs.

The last play our ensemble performed was *Gott, Mentsh un Teivel* (God, Man and the Devil). The "Devil" - Hitler – destroyed everything. No more Korelitz, no more dramatics club. No one would believe that all of this "was once". And today? Nothing remains but desolation and the longing for such a beloved and unforgettable past.

[Pages 172-174]

# Theatre And Orchestra

## Raya Shneor

### Translated from the Hebrew by Ann Belinsky

What didn't we have in Korelitz? Even theatre, naturally an amateur theatre, where dramas, tragedies and comedies were enthusiastically acted. The preparations for the show went on a long time, but no more than one performance of the show was presented. Not, God forbid, because the play was not good, but simply: there was no-one to play to, because already at the first show, all the potential theatrical crowd were present. On the other hand, nobody raised the idea or possibility that the troupe would present the play outside of Korelitz - in another town.

Our dramatic club was called for short *Drampar*, which was a sort of comparison to the name of the orchestra and the fire-station which were called *Pozharna- Komanda* (fire brigade command). The dramatics club began several decades before my time. The initiator, founder and director was Shefa Klatzki, who was gifted in his talent for acting. The actors were of different ages and of different levels -all amateurs. The plays took place in the school until the big fire in 1929. In this school they would open up a wall between two classes and a sort of relatively large hall was made. The rehearsals took place in different private houses. The audience was a "good audience". They were not passively listening to what was being said on the stage, but an audience which reacted, encouraging the actors. The audience tried to prove to the actors that the effort invested in the performance was worthwhile. They mainly presented Gordon: "Chassia the Orphan", "God, Man and the Devil", "Broken Hearts" as well as "The Witch" and "Shulamit" by Goldfaden and "The Jewish King Lear". The stage settings were not of the highest quality and more than once the audience recognized the dresses and accessories that they had loaned the actors before the play. The tickets were not sold at high prices but generally the proceeds managed to cover the expenses and there was even some money left over for philanthropic aims.

Among the more prominent actors we can mention Sheindel Kuznietz who is with us in Israel, who is gifted with a pleasant soprano voice and acting ability. She was the "Prima-donna". Pessia excelled in acting to hit the mark (?). Amongst the male actors Klatzko, who always played the main role, and the comedian Berl Poluzhsky were prominent. Who amongst us does not remember him in his roles in "Baba Yachna" in "The Witch"? There was always a lack of male actors. And here I remember an oddity when 3 young women appeared in male roles in the play "3 Agents". When they appeared on stage, the three of them started giggling joyfully. Naturally the audience identified them immediately and laughed with them. Over the years new talents joined the troupe, including Menucha Abramowich and Fruma Gulkowich. Both were prominent in their pleasant appearance and good acting.

*[Page 173]*
**The Youth Orchestra with the teacher Kalpetzky**
**Below, 1ˢᵗ row - from the right:** ----, Sarah Meirovitz, ----, Leah Namiat, Chaya Kovensky, Duba Niegnievitzky, ----.
**2ⁿᵈ Row:** (----): Perevolotsky, ----, Luba Gantzewitz, Hava Vernik, Levitzky, Kalpetzky, ----, Sonia Pshenitzy (Gorodisky).
**3ʳᵈ Row:** (----): Y. Yellin, Chana Lipshitz, Miriam Klatzko, Gutkeh Gantzevitz.
**4ᵗʰ Row:** (----): Chava Leah Yankelevitz, ----, Breina Kagan, Rakovitzki, Gavriel Abramowich, Aharon Kivilevitz, ----, Aharon Bernstein, ----.

In parallel to the *Drampar* Dramatics Club, an orchestra was founded which, over the years, developed and grew to be an important factor in the entertainment and performances in the town. The orchestra appeared as "solo" and also took part in various events of the town. From the founders of the orchestra I will mention here Molier Shenigan the violinist, and the initiator Viener, who played the flute. An honorable participant in the orchestra was also my father, may he live long. As if in a hazy dream I remember the successive evenings of rehearsals in our house with Moshe Gershonovsky and Baruch Tzelkovitz (who over time became the conductor of the orchestra), and my father would assist them. He became especially devoted to the clarinet, for this was an instrument which he played in his youth. The majority of the orchestra players were members of two families: the Gershonovsky family and one of their sons is with us here; and the Lipshitz family. The people originating from Karelitz are proud of their orchestra up to this very day.

And finally, if we are talking about the artistic strengths let us remember the fire-brigade, the "*Pozharna- Komanda*", which was a faithful accompaniment to the artistic strengths in the town. Not one of us will forget the *Pozharna's* exercises on Sundays and especially the "parades" which were accompanied by the orchestra. The whole town was on its feet when the fire brigade appeared in the parade in the streets and at its head were Klatzko, David Slutzky and Mordechai Reuven Begin. The last was really flying as he marched along in his beautiful uniform and white gloves.

This was not a theatre or orchestra in today's terms, but in those days these institutions brought with them warmth and infused rays of light into the grey life of the town.

[Page 174]

**The Executive Board of *HeChalutz***

**Standing from right:** Chaim Bolutnitzky, Tziril Abramowich, Miriam Shkolnik, Sirka Yosselovitz (Dushkin).
**Sitting from right:** Gittel Londin, Mordecai Malkieli (Krolavetsky), Shifra Levitt, Moshe Eliyahu Shuster, Chassia Oberzhansky (Turtel)

**On the placard:**
*HeChalutz* Youth Committee
In Karelitz
5685 (1925)

---

*[Pages 175-180 – Hebrew - below]*
*[Pages XXXVIII-XL – English -* **See also page 377***]*

# A History of *HeChalutz*
# and *Hashomer Hatsa'ir* in our Town

## Kalman Osherowitz - Raanana

The period of the Zionist pioneer youth started towards the end of WW1; in other words, about 50 years ago. This youth produced devoted and faithful pioneers. If we look at them today, we are concerned with various settlements in Israel where people from our town put down their roots, places where they played an important role in building our land. After all the hardship suffered by our youth, we are very proud of their achievements especially after they went through a long route full of alternating sacrifices, hopes and disappointments. These youths went through a glorious period, were educated on the lessons of Tel Chai, went through *HeChalutz* and *Hashomer Hatsa'ir*, the conquest of work and defense. They played a large part in the establishment of the State of Israel. Our town of Korelitz symbolizes the way of this youth.

When the battles of WW1 were waning, the town was destroyed and deserted because, during the war, when the Germans occupied the region, the war front was formed on the eastern side of our town and all the town's inhabitants were expelled, and they scattered in all directions. The Jews bought a landholding in the Grodno area and many of them settled temporarily in Novogrodok and its environs. At the end of the war, the Jews returned to the destroyed town and began rebuilding it. Many houses had disappeared from view because the Germans had used their materials to build bunkers on the front. Like good Jews, the inhabitants gave first priority to public institutions. The Synagogue, which had been partially destroyed, was rebuilt, and they started looking for a place for a school. Most of the inhabitants worked in agriculture in those days. Despite the fact that they did not have their own land, the inhabitants covered the empty plots and cultivated them, since these plots had no owners. The artisans returned to their occupations and the shopkeepers started reorganizing their business premises.

In the meanwhile, before they managed to recover from the troubles of the war, the town became involved in the war of the Bolsheviks against the Poles. The Russians entered the town and set up the new regime which was unpopular with the local population. After a while, this war was also forgotten, the town stayed under Polish rule, and life started to return to its normal routine. The Jews once more continued where they had previously stopped: a house was built for the Rabbi, and a school and synagogues were established. Shalom Cohen, the rabbi's son was appointed as principal of the school. The school was under the supervision of the *Tarbut* schools network. Some of the future *HeChalutz* members studied at this school.

**Between *Bund* and Zionism**

WW1 caused agitation not only among the nations of Europe, but also among the Jews. In this period, an organization by the name of the *Bund* became active among the Jews. This was an organization of Jewish workers, which was active in raising the standards of Jewish workers and the improvement of their situation. Mainly, it strove for the equality of rights for Jewish workers among the Poles. Our town, which had a Jewish identity, found itself on one side of the barricades - that of Zionism. In this period, just after the Balfour Declaration and the Zionist Wave, the *HeChalutz* movement arose, first in Russia, and later in the cities and towns of Poland.

The first "Swallow" of *HeChalutz* in Korelitz was Mordechai Karolevsky (known in Israel as Mordechai Malkieli). The Karolevsky family returned at that time from Novogrodok to Korelitz, and the son, Mordechai, was the man who started to organize the *HeChalutz Hatsa'ir* movement. I remember that once, when I wandered near the market, Yosef Portnoy came up to me and told me that we had a guest lecture, Comrade Bilopolsky from Warsaw. We gathered at the Synagogue and the lecturer read us a brochure about the happenings at Tel-Chai. He ended with the words of Trumpeldor; "It is good to die for our country".

Mordechai Karolevsky organized the *HeChalutz Hatsa'ir*, assisted by Hassia Oberzhansky and others. An older group of members became organized in the *Hechalutz*. The heads of this group were Moshe-Eli Shuster, Nissan Zalmanovsky and Yosef Portnoy (May he have a long life!).

The first lecturers to appear on the subject of *HeChalutz* were Yosef Bankover (living today in Ramat Hakovesh) and Bilopolsky. They explained the principles and ideas of the *HeChalutz* movement to us. I remember a lecture by Bilopolsky in the Korelitz *Bet Midrash*. The school janitor (we called him "Peter Zecks"), who used to be the prayer crier for the synagogue ("*Yidden in Shul arein*!" - "Jews, come to the synagogue!"), went out and announced an important speech to be given by a visitor from Warsaw on Saturday afternoon. Indeed, the audience responded. Youngsters and older people appeared. Thus, systematically, we encircled the town with ideas of the *HeChalutz*, and we set up a framework of cultural action, classes, information, and practical activities. Brcina, the Rabbi's daughter, taught Hebrew while Moshe-Eli Shuster taught knowledge of the Land of Israel. We organized literary trials and published a "live" newspaper every week, which was read collectively every Friday evening. The editor of the newspaper was Alter Rozovsky. The newspaper reflected the ideas of the *Hechalutz* and promoted its ways. Most of the inhabitants participated in reading the paper at parties of members.

**Ups and Downs**

When the suspense of enthusiasm arose and the organizational work flourished, something happened which stopped everything, and we had to start all over. This is what happened: The *HeChalutz* Headquarters rewarded our work and, in order to show its appreciation of us, it allocated us a "certificate" for *aliya* to Palestine, to one member of *HeChalutz*. This member, who had been awarded the certificate, was heavily involved in business matters and could not "release himself" for *aliya* to Palestine. This caused laxity in our work, and others even left the movement. The nucleus, however, was already too strong to break up. We started rebuilding *HeChalutz* anew. We ordered reading material from Palestine and started to inculcate the study of occupations among the members in order to prepare them for *aliya*.

## Firing Stoves

We decided that we had to introduce the members to the atmosphere of working for the Land of Israel, and to accustom them to sacrifice and action for the Concept. So, it was that we began to teach trades. We started teaching the boys carpentry, and the girls sewing. We went out to fire the stoves of the schools on winter nights and we cleaned out the classrooms. Wages were dedicated to the JNF and to the Palestine workers' fund. We leased the bakery from Alter the baker in order to bake *matzos* for Passover. The specialist was Noah Gershenovsky and, in this case as well, revenues were donated to funds in the Land of Israel. At that time, I was conscripted to the Polish Army, so I only learned what was happening in the town through letters from friends.

In 1925-6 we received a number of *aliya* "certificates" The first to go on *aliya* were Leime Polchak (who now lives in Ramat Hasharon), Yosef Portnoy (who is in Kfar Saba), Gittel Londin (Kfar Saba), Bracha Kaplan (Kibbutz Hakovesh), Sheindel Perevolotsky (now Kuznietz - in Tel Aviv), Pessia Ephroimsky (Gorfinkel - in Mishmar Hashloshah), Mordechai Karolevsky (Malkieli - in Hod Hasharon), and Stoliar (returned to Europe and died in the Holocaust). All those who made *aliya* went to Kibbutz *Hakovaysh*, but in the course of time, they relocated to various places in Israel.

[Page 177]

**Committee of the *Histadrut HeChalutz* in Korelitz,**
**From right**: David Portnoy, Bracha Kaplan, Pessia Ephroimsky, Moshe Shuster, Yosef Portnoy, Gittel Londin

The tension rose and morale was high in Korelitz at that time. A training group arrived in our town from Vilna. This group worked at digging fishponds. This was heavy work. Many members of this training group made *aliya*, and are living on Kibbutz Ramat Hakovesh.

It happened again that there was a drop in tension. The 1927 crisis in Palestine caused a spiritual laxity. We also in Korelitz "gained" two people who returned to our town from Palestine, and membership dropped once more.

We, the veteran group, decided to continue running *HeChalutz* in Korelitz. Comrade Leah Kaplan (now living on Kibbutz Giv'at Chaim), who kept faith with the movement, "maintained standards", at least with respect to headquarters. In her reports to Headquarters, there appeared more members than there really were. We even paid membership dues for these "members" from our own pockets, in order to "maintain the firm" in the eyes of the outside world.

*[Page 178]*

**The *HeChalutz* Organization in Korelitz**

**Standing from Right, 1ˢᵗ Row**: Chaim Abramowich, Chaim Kalmanovsky, Layma Polchik, Abramowich, Yaakov Mazurtzky, Mordechai Krolavetsky (Malchieli), Chassia Oberzhansky (Turtel), Leah Kaplan, Berl Gurevitz, Chaim Bolotnitzky, Yitzhak Lipshitz.

**2ⁿᵈ Row**: Alter Rozovsky, Alter Greenfeld, Mordechovitz, Michael Beigin, Malka Mordechovitz (Avny), Kalman Mordechovitz, Sheindel Kuznietz (Perevolotsky), ----, Dvorah Yossilevitz

**3ʳᵈ Row:** Moshe Stoller, Leybel Kopernik, Chaim Stoller, Avraham Lipchin, Yehudit Berkovitz, Noach Gershnovsky, Yitzhak Stoller, Itay Lipshitz, Yossef Portnoy

**4ᵗʰ Row:** Tzvi Shuster, Chaya-Leah Kaplan Sharshevsky, Sonia Rabinovitz (Kaplan), Chaim Kaplan.

(**Sign** - The *HeChalutz* Organization in Korelitz)

## Hashomer Hatsa'ir

At that time, there appeared an intelligent and lively fellow, by the name of Chaim Bussel. He was a graduate of *HaShomer Hatsa'ir* and suggested organizing a cell of the movement. The remnants of *HeChalutz* were opposed, but the crises and disappointments had their effect. The *HaShomer Hatsa'ir* cell arose from the remnants of *HeChalutz,* and covered most of the youth in the town. There were also graduates who joined. Chaim Bussel proved himself an excellent organizer and he knew how to bridge between various ideas. He tried to draw in those who felt uneasy within the new framework. He divided the cell on the basis of age, and organized groups named *Yehuda.* The older people tried to inculcate pioneer education into the youth so that, when the time came, they would be ready and able to make Aliya to Eretz Israel.

[Page 179]

**1st Row - Standing from right:** Berl Abrinsky, Bayla Kuznietz, Menucha Abramowich (Itzkowitz), Riva Yellin, Berl Kaplan
**2nd Row - from right:** Yosef-Chaim Osherowitz, David Meirovitz, Chaim Berkowitz, ----, Yeshayahu Bolotintzky
**3rd Row - from right:** Berchi Yellin, Merka Yellin, Chaya Slutzky (Meirovitz) Shraga Nissilevitz

[Page 180]

**The *HaShomer HaTsa'ir* Council in Korelitz**
**From right Standing - 1ˢᵗ Row:** Alter Greenfeld, Yona Oberzhansky, Yaakov Oberzhansky, Chaim Bussel, Michael Yellin, Malka Mordechovitz (Avny), Kalman Bezalel Osherowitz
**2ⁿᵈ Row:** Leah Kaplan, Shifra Levitt, Chaya-Leah Kaplan, ----,----.

We carried out cultural, sport and entertainment activities. On *Lag Ba'Omer*, we organized a big camp in one of the forests in the area. I remember how we sang with awe "We are Rising", and *Techezakna* [translator's note: a famous poem/song written/composed by Chaim Nachman Bialik).

In the summer of 1928, we organized a regional convention in Korelitz in the festive atmosphere of a mass movement.

Once more, however, disasters fell upon us. The town was totally burned down in a fire which broke out. The bloody events in Palestine in 1929 added to this by bringing an end to the *HaShomer Hatsa'ir* movement in Korelitz.

In 1930, I made *aliya* with my wife Sarah. When in Palestine, we heard that Korelitz had been rebuilt upon its previous ruins.

Times changed. The yearning for the Land of Israel increased and strengthened in Poland. There was a shortage of Certificates and the many demands of the youth to make *aliya* could not be met. The training Kibbutzim in Poland filled up, and the cream of young men and young women who wanted to make *aliya* were stuck there for years. The illegal immigration to Palestine started to be organized - the young people of Israel started travelling the seas, often endangering their lives. Some of them managed to reach safe havens in Palestine, where they were considered by the British authorities to be "illegal immigrants". Nevertheless, they organized themselves in Palestine and found their places. The majority, however, stayed there... they are no more, because they were destroyed by the Oppressors of Israel.

Our work in Israel, the sacrifice and the heroism of the Youth of Israel are a magnificent monument to the idealistic Zionist Youth that was and is no more.

*[Page 181]*

The *HeChalutz* Organization in Korelitz - Succot 5691 (1930)

**The *HeChalutz* Committee**
**From right:** Yaakov Mazurtzky, Berl Gurevitz, Sonia Kaplan, Leah Kaplan, Leah Trayevitsky,
Kalman Mordechovitz, Yitzhak Stoller
**Standing:** Mordechai Malkieli (Krolavetsky), Tzvi Shuster

*[Page 182]*

# HaShomer HaTsa'ir

## Malka Poluzhsky-Pomerchik - Kfar Saba

The *Hashomer HaTsa'ir* cell was established in Korelitz in the years 1927-30 by Chaim Bussel, an energetic young man with an amazing organizational ability. He came to us with his family from the town of Klutzk. He brought with him both the concept and the organizational ability. He succeeded in gathering around him the youth and the children of the school where he worked as a teacher and as an instructor. His impressive appearance, formal dress and his red ties - all these, together with the trumpet parades, charmed the youth who united within the movement. As long as Chaim Bussel was active, the cell thrived and developed. A few years passed, however, and Chaim grew older. He entered regular civilian life. Members began leaving the movement, which started to slacken.

This situation was exploited by the leaders of *Betar* -- the Gantzevitz brothers, Gertel Mordechovitz, Yehoshua Kalmanovitz and others. They increased their numbers at the expense of the *Hashomer HaTsa'ir*. The youth were thirsty for activities and, without *Hashomer HaTsa'ir* activities, many joined *Betar*.

When I completed my studies in Novogrodek and returned home in 1934, I found the *Hashomer Hatsa'ir* movement in a state of torpor. I was happy to find the remnants of the movement: Mordechai Shimshelevitz, Tanchum Kaplan, Gutel Kivlevitz and David Lipshitz. These serious people were loyal to the ideals of the movement. We started to revive the glorious past of *HaShomer HaTsa'ir* in Korelitz. When we first started these steps, we had no resources; I offered our private house in order to begin operations. This was made possible, thanks to my parents, who were adherents of Zionism and progress, and who understood our spirit.

In a short time, we started attracting many of the youth to our movement, mainly from the two schools as well as from among the older youth. We started working on cultural and promotional activities. With the growth in the number of members, there was a corresponding growth in means. We rented a clubhouse from Alter Nachumovsky (Alter *der Soifer*). Every evening, the house was filled with the joyous and fresh voices of the cell's children. The movement once more became a prominent and recognizable in the town. Parades were once more held and the sounds of drums and bugles were once more heard. There were *Tu B'Shvat* celebrations and trips to far places and to the nearby woods in order to study nature. Our members took an active part in the Zionist activities of the town, such as emptying the JNF boxes, etc. I especially remember an important and educational project in our cell. We organized an exhibition of handwork of the young members of the movement. The children put their hearts and souls into the assignment, each one in his own hobby and area of interest. The exhibition succeeded to such an extent that it attracted people of all ages, and all of them talked about it enthusiastically. We contacted the movement's headquarters in Warsaw, who sent us emissaries and lecturers. There was singing every evening in the cell.

Apart from our cultural activities, we also had a political struggle with the *Beitarists* who were entrenched in the house of Dvoshke Gantzevitz (the house was called *Die Broine Hoiz*). The members of *Betar* were embarrassed, because most of their members returned one by one to their origins, to *HaShomer HaTsa'ir*. Even older members joined: Esther Shkolnik (Horowitz), Masha Kaplan, Sarah Mina Meyerovitz, Libke Sharshevsky, Aaron Perevolotsky, Gisha Stoliar, and others. Even today, a pleasant quivering passes through me when I remember that exciting and interesting period.

The graduates of *HaShomer HaTsa'ir* were automatically also members of *HeChalutz* when lively new blood was needed, or energetic and lively youngsters were required. We were like that in those days.

*[Page 183]*

**HaShomer HaTsa'ir Leadership in 1934**

**Seated from right**: Esther Shkolnik-Horowitz, David Lifschitz, Masha Kaplan.
**Standing from right**: Tanchum Kaplan, Mordechai Shimshelevitz, Malka Poluzhsky (Pomerchik), Aharon Nissilevitz, Moshe Kuznietz.

---

*[Pages 184-185]*

# *Hashomer HaTsa'ir* (The Young Guard)

## Malka Poluzhsky – Pomerchik, Kfar Saba

### Translated from the Yiddish by Harvey Spitzer

The town of Korelitz lies on the Rutka River, between Novogrudek and Turetz, 21km from Novogrudek and 14km from Turetz. The town is small – just like all the small towns in the area of White Russia. The streets are paved and lined with stores. The entire center of the town was owned by Jews. There were only a few Christian homes on the street. In fact, the Christian population of the town itself was very small. They comprised just a small percentage of the town's residents. However, the parts of the town surrounding the central area were Christian, and Christians lived in the villages. Korelitz was almost exclusively a Jewish town. Before coming to Korelitz, I lived in the small town of Yeremich where the Jewish and Christian population was mixed. I simply didn't recognize any difference. When I moved to Korelitz, however, I noticed a big contrast. The Jews and Christians lived so much apart that there was no connection between them.

The specific sources of livelihood in the town were the following: small businesses. The market was bordered on both sides by a row of stores. There were about 60 stores in the town. Besides being storekeepers, a large part of the population made their living from farming. They mainly planted cucumbers which were sold in the large cities. And a large part of the residents were craftsmen and handworkers. There were small machines for cleaning wool.

A certain portion of our young people went to schools in the larger city of Novogrudek. Naturally, there was close contact between the youth of Novogrudek and Korelitz. They tried to bring everything they saw and considered progressive in Novogrudek and copy it in Korelitz. Our girls who studied in Novogrudek were members of *HaShomer HaTsa'ir*. Coming home, they themselves began to be very active in organizing a *HaShomer HaTsa'ir* chapter in Korelitz. The culture of the big city had an influence on the cultural level of our small town.

I studied at the "Adam Mickiewicz" public high school. I graduated in 1934. I came back to Korelitz and then went to Grodno to participate in a training program under the auspices of *HaShomer HaTsa'ir* for the purpose of immigrating to the Land of Israel. I was in the training program for nine months. Then I returned to Korelitz because I had the opportunity of going to the Land of Israel in the *HeChalutz* organization. We arranged seminars in which all the teachers of the town's Hebrew School participated. The seminars lasted a week and sometimes two. We used to put out lively newspapers. The Jewish National Fund encouraged and supported our endeavors and tradition.

---

*[Page 185]*

**HaShomer HaTsa'ir Leadership in 1935**
**A group of young HaShomer HaTsa'ir graduates**

**Front, from right:** Yosel Berkowitz, Gishe Stoler, Nissin Shimshelevitz, Sarah Beigin, Libke Shereshevsky.
**Second row, from right:** Sarah-Minia Meyerovitz, Gutel Kivelevitz, Tanchum Kaplan, Shifra Rakovitzky, Minia Lifschitz, Aharon Perevolotsky

[Page 186]

*HaShomer HaTza'ir* in 1930

The Lion Cubs *Yehudit* Battalion - *HaShomer HaTza'ir*

*[Pages 187-188 – Hebrew - below*
*[Page XL – English* **– see also page 379** *]*

# BETAR

## Gutka Nohumovski-Ganczewicz (Gantzevitz)
*[This chapter is similar to the English transcription, with the addition of the 2 photos below - AB]*

The *Betar* Youth Movement in Korelitz came into being as a result of the enthusiasm engendered by Zeev Jabotinsky's visit in Poland. Its founding was opposed by the already existing *Hashomer Hatsa'ir* and *Hechalutz*, but with the help of veteran adult members of the Revisionist movement, the Club proceeded with its work. As the opposing groups increased their activities, the town was overcome by an avalanche of debates and disputations.

It was real pioneering work: we worked day and night organizing, with rallies and with cooperation of lecturers and external guests. The *HaShomer HaTsa'ir* and *HeChalutz* members had no part in the success: they organized opposing activities and propaganda against cooperation with *Betar*. The strife was part of daily life of the whole town in those days, which had never known stormy discussions and arguments, like that when the *Betar* group was being formed. But the stubborn fight brought welcome results and eventually *Betar* members received their uniforms, started organizing routine activities. The first *Betar* commander of Korelitz made his aliya and in the town a rousing farewell was organised. Members of *Betar* and *HaZohar* (Union of Zionists-Revisionists) were those who called day and night to the local population not to be deluded, and make *aliya*, following the call of the leader of *Betar*, Zeev Jabotinsky, who forecast the destruction of Jewry in Europe many years previous to the catastrophe. Unfortunately, not enough heed was paid to the call, and thus we remained in mourning for those good dedicated Zionists who remained in the Diaspora and were annihilated in the Destruction. Only a very few succeeded in leaving the fields of death in time.

*[Page 187]*

**Left Placard**:
Before the *aliyah* of our brother Mordechovitz to *Eretz [Israel]* 15 VIII 1935
**Right Placard**:
The *Brit Trumpeldor* [*Betar* youth group] in Poland. The Korelitz *Ken* [local group, cell]

*[Page 188]*
**Right:** The home of Faygel -Tzirus Kaganovitz
**Left:** The home of Shabbtai Klatchko

*[Pages 189-190 Yiddish]*
*[Page XLIV - English – abridged:* **see also page 383***]*

# Yitzhak Katzenelson In His Hometown, Korelitz*

### Translated from the Yiddish by Harvey Spitzer

Yitzhak began his journey as a writer across the small towns and cites of Lithuania in his birthplace, Korelitz. Kith and kin prepared to greet him. The welcome at the station was a demonstration of the people's love and admiration. They took him to the home of the rabbi, his grandfather, Rabbi Yitzchak Yechiel Benin, where he stayed during his visit. There they showed him his very own cradle which was preserved as a keepsake of their famous fellow-townsman.

Yitzhak remembered that as a child of six he had thrown a ball onto the attic of a house and he now wanted to find it. And so it was. They began walking along the little streets until Yitzhak recognized an old, dilapidated small house. They made a ladder and one of the boys climbed up to the attic and, following Yitzchak's instructions, found the ball. Many years later Yitzchak wove this incident into his dramatic comedy, "Fatima".

During the several days he spent in Korelitz, he would walk with the young people along the roadway and all the surrounding places. Yitzchak sang them Yiddish and Hebrew songs, told them Yiddish stories and spoke about the present day Land of Israel (which he never visited). Once he turned to the young people and said, "Dear Jewish daughters and sons, your place is in the Land of Israel. Go there and you will build a new, Jewish life."

This is how Yitzhak described a walk in his hometown:

"........ and I'm already walking on the roadway, and it's very joyful. Every living person has left the town and has gone onto the roadway. And the roadway is very long. They say that it extends as far as Kabrin..... And Kabrin is very far away. The sky ends and a new sky spreads out over the town of Kabrin.

--------------------------------

* **Yitzhak Katzenelson** – *Zein Leben un Shafen* (His Life and Creative Work) - by Zippora Katzenelson – Nachumov, Chapter 22, Pg. 150.

And here is a description of the roadway on Friday afternoon before the Sabbath:

> At the roadway, in the avenues
> Your bride sits under a tree,
> On the roadway, in the avenues
> Jewish girls are taking a walk –
> Slender pine trees, red roses –
> Sparkling Jewish daughters.
> The dark, charming girls
> In their Sabbath clothes,
> Their hair is somewhat unkempt.
> Jewish daughters are modest –
> Won't comb their hair on the Sabbath.
> And the ribbons and kerchiefs
> Tied around their neck –
> They won't wear on the Sabbath.
> "Come my beloved to greet the bride."
> At the roadway, on the avenues
> Sits a sun-drenched girl,
> Sits under a green oak
> Sits and waits for you, the groom,
> "Come my beloved to greet the bride."

A group of boys passed by. A boy wearing a red shirt is leading them. A red shirt – and in the town. It seems that they knew I was a "new face" in town because, as soon as they noticed me, they began singing, "Oh, poor workers". Socialist rebels ...... and in the town.

A few minutes later, another group of boys passed by. A boy wearing a blue shirt was leading them. A blue shirt – and in the town. The boys looked me over and went on. And a minute later, I heard someone say, "A home for the Jewish worker."
Supporters of the Zionist Workers Party....... and in the town.

I looked up – in the distance I saw the two groups going on ahead to the dark forest. Each of the groups went separately, but the area between them was so small that it was easy for them to meld into one group.
More sounds of a song reach my ear. One can no longer tell the words apart. I think it's one song – the two songs become one... Without at all intending to, I glanced into the forest – an argument..... and in the town.

---

*[Page 191]*

# PERSONALITIES AND FIGURES

*[Page 192 -Yiddish]*
*[Page XLIV - English – abridged:* **see also page 383***]*

# Yaakov Binyamin Katzenelson

### Translated from the Yiddish by Harvey Spitzer

Yaakov Binyamin Katzenelson was born in Kapulia in 1859 and studied at the *yeshivot* (rabbinic seminaries) in Volozhin and Kovna. He was the author of *"Ol'lot Efraim"* ("Gleaning of Efraim", 1889), a poem which drew attention to the *"Maskilim"* ("intellectuals") at a time of negative relations to the followers of the "Enlightenment" movement whom Katzenelson describes unsympathetically as career opportunists [and whom he compares] to the beloved and idealized heroes, the enlightened *yeshiva* students with their desire for education. "Ben Yemini" (Katzenelson) then lived in Warsaw and was a collaborator on the Hebrew encyclopedia, *"Eshkol"*. At that time, his wife lived in Korelitz, at the home of her mother, the widow of the rabbi of Korelitz, Rabbi Yitzchak Yechiel Davidson and there, in Korelitz, their son, Yitzchak Katzenelson, was born (*Tammuz* 1886).

*Lexicon of Yiddish Literature, Zalman Rajzen, Vol. III. Vilna, 1929.*


Rich in achievements, the elderly Hebrew writer, "Ben Yemini" (Yaakov Binyamin Katzenelson), has passed away. He lived and breathed totally with love for the Hebrew language and the Jewish People. His erudition in the field of Judaism was immense. He was especially well-versed in Jewish history. He wanted to continue where the Enlightenment poet, Weisel, left off. This work remained in manuscript.

He was active for decades as an educator and raised a generation of pupils of whom he was proud. His son, the poet Yitzchak Katzenelson, grew up under his supervision; Yaakov Cohen learned his masterly Hebrew from him. The engineer, Shmuel Shwartz, who discovered the *anusim* (Jews compelled to convert to Christianity) in Portugal, was his pupil. Hundreds of his pupils may be found around the world. To the last day of his life, he took an interest in all the latest works that appeared in Hebrew and Yiddish. He was the initiator of and collaborator on the first Hebrew encyclopedia, *HaEshkol*.

*Friday edition, "Haynt" 5 Kislev 5691 (Nov. 28. 1931), Issue 272*

---

*[Page 193]*

# Moshe Avraham Volpin
## Raya Schneur (Rishe Kaplan)

**Translated from the Yiddish by Harvey Spitzer**

If we are talking about the Zionist Korelitz, I recall the noble and delicate figure of Reb Moshe Avraham, the ritual slaughterer, and the JNF representative in our town. Dressed in a black *capote* and with a cane in his hand, he used to rush to business concerning the Land of Israel. From the day of his arrival in our town to his last day, he had within his heart a burning love for the Zionist Ideal. His arrival in Korelitz aroused a scandal because of his Zionism. When he arrived in our town from Odessa, many inhabitants opposed him at first, because of his well- known opinions on Zionism. He quickly organized the Zionists in the town, and these held a heavy campaign on his behalf. A strike was called, and the meat of the other slaughterers was boycotted until his opponents stopped their war against him and he was accepted as a ritual slaughterer. From the moment that he started his duty, his life devoted to the Zionist ideal. He took part in strenuous work and activities, which raised his status among the youth of Korelitz as a symbol and an example of action and devotion.

He himself had a hard life. His family life was surrounded by troubles and suffering, He was a widower, and the daughters that his late wife had given him, lived with him in his house. One of his daughters was married with many children, and some of these children were brought up by their grandfather. None of the problems in his house clouded his vision of Zion or of anything connected with Zionism: he organized, explained, convinced, and collected funds. He was a permanent citizen in all the town's houses, which he visited in order to organize pairs of youths for emptying the JNF boxes. Eventually, when a large part of the youth made *aliya*, and others avoided jobs of this kind, he used to go to all the houses to empty the boxes. He did this in order to keep the operation going and to keep in touch with the contributors.

He himself did not have the courage to make *aliya*, but he wholeheartedly assisted those who aspired to make *aliya*. I remember that one of the girls' *aliya* was delayed (she now lives in Kfar Saba). He immediately turned to the Palestine office to discover the reasons for the delay, and labored to speed up her *aliya*. Every time that the pioneers going on *aliya* traveled to Novogrodek on their way to Palestine, he used to travel the long way to Novogrodek with them. Reading the articles of S. Pitrushka on Fridays in the *Heint* newspaper, *Vos Hert Zich in Eretz Yisroel?* ("What's new in Palestine?") was, for him, like a *mitzva* or the pleasure of prayer with a religious man. He used to thirstily drink in each line on what was happening in Palestine. When it happened that Pitrushka's usual article was not published on a Friday, Moshe Avraham used to write a letter to the *Heint* newspaper, "Why didn't you publish Pitrushka's article on Palestine?" How was it possible to read a Friday newspaper without an article on the Land of Israel, he asked. Mrs. Vittal Shkolnik-Arieli, who visited Korelitz in 1937, told me that Reb Moshe Avraham used to visit her at her home every day in order to hear some living words about the Land of Israel.

There was no initiative within our activities in which he did not participate. I remember in the market - the bazaar, when we started organizing in aid of the JNF. To our joy, the public responded to this enterprise, and the revenues were larger than expected. Reb Moshe Aaron was happy with this new enterprise which we had discovered and with our modesty in such great success. A short while after the bazaar, Moshe Avraham came to our house and told me that he had a present for me for my distinction and my success in this bazaar. I told him, "It's not necessary!" and I said that I considered the success itself as a prize and a source of happiness. He, however, was adamant and, a few days later, he brought me a small album published by the JNF to mark the inauguration of the Hebrew University in Jerusalem. The album contained his own dedication: words of love of Zion and longing for the land of our fathers.

To this day, when I participate in a market-bazaar of the Working-Mothers' Association, the memory "Zionist market" in Korelitz stands before me and energizes me in memory of the innocent and distinguished Zionist, which does not leave me.

My father told me about the same matter that Reb Moshe Avraham used to correspond with various Zionist functionaries. It happened that letters of his were found on Behr Borochov. The police, who were looking for Zionist activists, went out to search for him and to find him. At first, they searched for him in Novogrodek, but they eventually found him in Korelitz. They arrested him *davke* on a Saturday and held him in jail for a month. Thanks only to the efforts of Reb Nachum Ayzik Beigin the *Shochet*, he managed to raise a sum of money, and was thus released. My father also noted that that Reb Nachum Ayzik Beigin was also an honorable Jew and a good Zionist.

---

*[Page 194 – Hebrew]*
*[Page XLV – English –abridged:* **See also page 384***]*

# Moshe Avraham, son of Reb Shaul Naftali Osherowitz

## Kalman Osherowitz -- Raanana

### Translated from the Yiddish by Harvey Spitzer

**Moshe Avraham Osherowitz**

My grandfather was one of the biggest grain merchants and one of the owners of a flourmill in the Vilna region. He was a learned man and a successful businessman, and carried on the business dealings of his father, Reb Idel-Asher (this was the source of the family name - Osherowitz). He worked in the supply and transfer of produce on the Minsk-Vilna line and was blessed in his work. With the foundation of the railway line in this region, he lost his financial base and lived in poverty. He wanted to teach his eldest son to do clean and easy work. He chose for him the profession of writing Holy Books. Indeed, my father succeeded in his profession as a highly talented artist. He excelled in making "houses" for Phylacteries from one skin. He did not, however make a good living, since, in his time, there was little demand for his products. The simple people did not understand this subject, while the pedants did not have the money to buy high quality Phylacteries. On the other hand, the work was hard and exhausting, and required a high degree of exactitude. My father therefore expanded his business and also dealt with the processing of leather for Torah parchment and for Phylactery straps. He also manufactured tombstones with a high degree of artistry.

He also fulfilled the task of Attendant in the court of our town's Rabbi, as well as Attendant at the old house of learning. He served well known Rabbis such as, for example, the late Rabbi Mordechle Slonimer, who served in our town before he came to Slonim. When Rabbi Avraham Cohen was ill and bed-ridden in his last years, he passed on to my father the task of handling weddings. My father fulfilled this task all his life, with the rabbis who came after the passing away of Rabbi Avraham Cohen. In our town, people used to say: A wedding without Klezmers is still possible but, without Reb Moshe-Avraham, it is impossible. He instructed young rabbis with his advice, and they took his opinions into account. He was popular among both young and old, and many people asked for his advice.

In those days, a young woman who gave birth to a son would not turn to a doctor, but rather to Reb Moshe- Avraham. He was the circumsciser, and he was the expert who decided whether the child was ready to enter the covenant of Abraham our Father. After the *Brit* he used to visit the newborn child a number of times, until the wound had completely healed up. He even used to advise the mother how to take care of the child.

He was renowned for his hospitality. An "emissary" who came to the town, a wandering preacher, or any other passer-by - they all found a place in his house to lodge and to rest. This was how my grandfather used to serve the public in a variegated manner. When he used to sit down to the work from which he made his living - he could not always sit peacefully and do his work. Public affairs disturbed him all the time, while he earned almost nothing from public affairs. He was a member of all the societies which existed in Korelitz at the time. Among these, he was one of the members of the *Chevra Kadisha*, and managed the cemetery list all his life. Without him, nothing was done. He was a member of the "Psalms Society" and the "*Mishna* Society". He himself handled a *Mishna* study group for members of the "*Amcha* Society". He had a wonderful talent for explanation.

My mother Leachika died young, and I never got to know her. My father remained a widower for most of his life. As the youngest child, I used to accompany him to his lessons, celebrations and festivities. I remember his beautiful stories and the enthusiasm of his listeners. Often, when I remember the days of my youth, I regret that I did not learn by heart his words and proverbs in order to set them down in print.

My father was a dedicated and faithful Zionist. He used to buy the Zionist Shekel every year. When the Zionist Bank was established, he was one of the first to buy a share.

His dream was to go to Palestine and to settle there. We helped him to fulfill this vision. When I made *aliya*, I started to take care of his *aliya*. We finally brought him when he was 78 years old. I remember his joy when we traveled to Jaffa to get Palestinian Citizenship from the British Mandatory Authorities.

He was happy from the honour which he received from his son and grandchildren. In order to realize his dream of settlement, we bought him a plot of land in Herzlia. This plot he later bequeathed to his grandchildren who survived the Holocaust. He died of old age, at the age of 88, on the 9th November 1943.

---

*[Page 196 - Hebrew]*
*[Pages XLV-XLVI English – Abridged-* **See also Page 384***]*

# Pesach Kaplan

## Hassia Turtel-Oberzhansky

### Translated from the Hebrew by Harvey Spitzer

Reb Pesach, son of Yeshayahu Baruch the Cohen, Kaplan, was more than 90 years old when he died. He was one of the senior householders in Korelitz. He managed to live in the Land of Israel for a few decades, and was buried next to his wife Hinda-Faygel in Karkur. He had lived there from his arrival in Palestine until he was widowed. His was a personality of Torah, tradition, love of others, common sense, humor and hilarity, and a deep understanding of the problems of his time and of the youth. He was involved in the life of the community and he played a significant part in its ongoing daily problems, such as making a living, public worries, educating the younger generation, negotiations with the hostile authorities, whether the Czar's government, or whether the Anti-Semitic Polish Republic. He fulfilled his public duties in a warm and sensitive manner, without expecting to be rewarded. He spent a few years wandering around the USA. On his return to Korelitz at the beginning of the 20th century, he knew enough English to be able to write letters for inhabitants of Korelitz to their relatives in America. Three generations of Korelitzers benefited from this public service. Reb Pesach showed a high talent in musicianship and *Chazanut*. He was a scripture-reader and prayer leader on Sabbaths and high holidays at the new Synagogue. His house was used for public meetings. He educated his four daughters and only son in the spirit of Zionist pioneering. All of them made *aliya*. His children inherited his musical talents from him, as well as his righteousness, his faithfulness and perseverance in fulfilling his functions responsibly. His house in Korelitz became the focus of the youth who were organized in the pioneering movements. Reb Pesach managed to make *aliya* with his wife Hinda Faygel, to his children in the land of Israel. He underwent all the absorption problems as a pioneer. In his final years, he was a member of a Kibbutz, together with his daughters. He bestowed a great heritage to us Korelitzers, who went out from the town to pave roads in the wide world. Each of these roads brought us thither.

---

*[Page 197]*

# Pesach Kaplan

## Y. Ch. Bielsky

**Translated from the Hebrew by Harvey Spitzer**

**The Jewish Community Executive Board
in the year 5695 (1935)**
**(R-L) Seated:** Berl Bussel, Pesach Kaplan
**Standing:** Getzel Yellin, Leibel Perevolutsky

He was old when he was gathered to his people. He was the scion of the race of powerful Hebrews in his body and in his spirit. He was born in Korelitz, from where he gathered his family thirty-five years ago and went to *Eretz Israel*. He knew that his religious beliefs did not clash with the secular life of his daughters who were living on the following Kibbutzim: Einat, Givat Chaim, Yagur (home of his daughter Raya), and the town of his son, Netanya. As long as he had the strength to do so, he supported himself by working as a bookkeeper in Karkur, where he was an honored citizen, and loved by everyone. It also happened, when he spent the last period of his life with his daughter on Kibbutz Givat Chaim or with his daughter on Kibbutz Yagur, that he was a loved visitor on the Kibbutzim. He was involved in their lives, and followed their lifestyles. He enlivened their parties with his pleasant voice and lively humor. Before the young members he often rolled chapters of life with hilarity, spiced with sayings, proverbs, jokes and wisdom. These were all drawn from his rich popular reservoir. He lived within his beliefs, while honoring his children's beliefs. They also honored him and were proud of his nobility. At every family gathering, he used to carry with him a heart full of love for children, and brought with him a fresh breeze. Pesach Kaplan held within himself the best and most superior of his generation, as well as a mature and wise knowledge which was aware of his family who were saddened by his passing. His Jewish Melody will flow forever in the life of his extended family, as well as in the life of his friends from Korelitz and other friends.

---

*[Pages 198-199 – Yiddish - below]*
*[Page XLVI English – Abridged*: **see also page 385***]*

# Gershon Eliasberg

### Translated from the Yiddish by Harvey Spitzer

**Coordinator's note:** The **Yiddish text** is similar to the English text, but **includes additional information**

He was born in Novohorodek in 1876. He was a descendant of the famous Harkavi family. He learnt in the *heder*, then completed State municipal school. He chose his father's career - pharmacy, and became a pharmacy student in Dvinsk [Latvia]. In 1900 he received his pharmacy degree (called in Russian - *Provizor*) from the University of Yurev [?Tartu, Estonia - AB]. As a pharmacist he worked in St Petersburg and in Novogrudek and in 1912 he became the manager of the pharmacy in Korelitz. The owner was Avraham Abramowich (who was the nephew of Mendeleh Mocher Sfarim). In 1915 Eliasberg was deported to St Petersburg. From there he went to Uralsk [a city in northwestern Kazakhstan - AB]. In 1919 he visited the medical faculty of Saratov University and in 1921 he returned to Korelitz, where he remained a pharmacist for a long time.

From his earliest years he was involved in community social work. In Novogrudek he was active in the *Shokedey Malacha* group. Besides endeavoring to improve school education, he helped organize clubs for the local youth. In the Pskov Governorate (*Gubernia*) he was involved in social-democratic circles and became very active as a member of these groups. In Lower Uralsk he was chairman of the Pharmacists Society and was very active in this organization. When he returned to Korelitz he devoted himself to the rehabilitation of the families which had undergone economic ruin, and formed ties to the *Yekope* aid association, later becoming a member of its board. He became the delegate from Korelitz to the Second and Third Area Committee of the *Yekope* and was also a member of its plenum. In Korelitz he became the chairman of local institutions such as the People's Cooperative Bank and the Rebuilding Commission, Free Loan Society and various general welfare societies of the town, gaining the respect and gratitude of all its inhabitants.

---

*[Page 199 - Yiddish]*
*[Page XLVI – English- abridged: See also* **page 385***]*

# Shalom Cohen

### Translated from the Yiddish by Harvey Spitzer

**Coordinator's note:** The **Yiddish text** is similar to the English text, but **includes additional information**

Born into a rabbinic family in Korelitz in 1880, Shalom Cohen received his first education in the traditional *cheder* and *yeshiva*. He subsequently graduated from a Russian public school and was a pupil for a short time in Cohen's 6-grade Gymnasium (secondary school) in Vilna.

From age 18 until the outbreak of the First World War, he held positions as bookkeeper and cashier in various places. When he was deported from Korelitz by the Germans, he moved in with his father's family in Novogrudek. There he gave private lessons and was involved in social activities. Prior to that, he had gained experience working on a relief committee which distributed money contributed by Jews from Berlin to support the needy and homeless and victims of the war who were then living in Novogrudek.

From the summer of 1918 to the summer of 1919, he served as secretary of the "Supervisory Building and Relief Committee" in Novogrudek and from the summer of 1919 to the end of 1920, he served as secretary of the Jewish committee and later as secretary of the first democratically elected community council in Novogrudek. He was one of the founders and builders of the Novogrudek public school, in which he worked as a teacher for 4 years. He worked for 3 years as a teacher and administrator in the Korelitz public school which he also helped establish and build. Shalom Cohen was one of the first members of the regional reconstruction company *Yekopa* in the Novogrudek area and was a delegate at its conferences. In 1929 he was active in undertaking a review of 70 benevolent societies conducted by *Yekopa* and was a colleague of the *Yekopa* journal.

*Yekopa* **Journal, Vilna 1930**

---

[Pages 200-201, Hebrew]
[Page XLVII, English – abridged: see also **page 385** ]

# Rina Grabelsky*
## Hassia Turtel-Oberzhansky

Rina Grabelsky, nee Mordechovitz - the last representative of our parents' generation - was born in 1891. She was born into a lower class working family. In Korelitz, she diligently studied everything that could be studied through private teachers and at the *Cheder*. The Bible, Hebrew, Russian, Arithmetic, etc. At the age of 16 or 17, she emigrated to the USA, to study and to be educated. After arriving in New York, she succeeded in finding a post in the Hebrew department of the local National Library. While she was working, she attended evening lessons, studied English, and even attended lectures at the City College until after her marriage. The National and Zionist heritage was imbedded in Rina's blood. Thus, in 1920, she emigrated to Palestine, together with her nine-year-old daughter, and went to Mikve-Yisrael to work in Agriculture. Rina also spent a period of pioneering in Kibbutz Ein-Harod. She experienced many changes in her life; she returned to the USA, returned one more to Palestine - and in 1930, she came with her husband, the Author Moshe Stavy-Stavesky for a visit to her town of birth, Korelitz. For the pioneering youth of Korelitz, her visit was an unforgettable experience.

**Seated from right:** Alter Greenfeld, the author Moshe Stavy (Stavesky), Chaim Bussel.
**Standing from right:** M. Mordechovitz, Hassia Oberzhansky (Turtel), Rina Stavesky (Grabelsky), Elka Mordechovitz, Falkeh Mordechovitz.

Thirty years later, we met again in Jerusalem, at one of the parties of the "Working Mothers' Organization". Rina's alert social sense found its expression in extensive and dedicated activities: with the Working Mothers' Organization, with the Hebrew Language Administration during the period of mass immigration, and in recent years with the "Committee for Soldiers". She did not miss one lecture of the State's Ministers and even regularly attended the Bible Circle at the State President's residence until her last moments.

In the last weeks of her life, she planned to visit her daughter and granddaughter in the USA. During my last visit to her, after her heart attack, two days before she passed away, I saw a photograph of her on her table. She had just brought this photograph from the photographer. I said to Rina, "Please give it to me". She took a pen and wrote a dedication. When I told her the general date, she replied that she wanted the Hebrew date. She wrote while saying out loud, "17th *Av*, 5729".

Her memory is blessed as one of one of the dearest and distinguished people of our town, Korelitz.

*Coordinator's note:** The **Hebrew text** is similar to the English text, but **includes additional information**

---

[Pages 201-202 – Yiddish - below]
[Page XLVII – English abridged:**see also page 386**]

# Alter Greenfeld

### Translated from the Yiddish by Harvey Spitzer

**Coordinator's note:** The **Yiddish text** is similar to the English text, but **includes additional information**

Alter Greenfeld was born in Korelitz in 1908. He attended the traditional *cheder* and was also taught by private teachers. With the outbreak of the First World War, when the Jews of Korelitz were deported from the town, he lived with his family in Svislach (Svislats) and in Novogrudek. When his father was taken into forced labor and his mother fell ill, Greenfeld supported the family by raising chickens for a German officer and helping French war prisoners to fell timber in the forest around Bialovezsher. In the evenings, he studied German and Bible with the help of a Jewish prisoner of war. In 1919, he studied other subjects in Russian evening courses and later in the Yiddish-Hebrew public school in Novogrudek. He worked as a quilter and became socially active in his hometown, where he opened a children's club and library and later organized and led the local branch of the *HeChalutz* organization. In 1929, he was elected to serve on the board of the *Galilee* chapter of *HeChalutz*.

He travelled around the province giving lectures on political and literary topics. He edited newspapers and wrote poetry and articles.

In 1934, he joined the staff of the *Novogrudek Leben* periodical, in which he published articles under the name of A. Gad. In 1936, the Korelitz library published his collection of poems, *Mir iz Gut* (I Have It Made). Greenfeld also prepared a work for publication entitled *Di Yugent oif der Provintz* and a second book of poetry. In 1937, he submitted his application to work on the YIVO "*Aspirantor*" youth research series" in Vilna. In 1939, when the Red Army entered Poland, Greenfeld crossed over into Russia and his fate is unknown.

**Literarishe-Bletter, Warsaw, Aug. 28, 1936 (Leizer Ran) and**
**Lexicon of New Yiddish Literature, Vol. II, New York, 1958**

---

*[Page 202 – Hebrew- below]*
*[Pages XLVII-XLVIII – English-abridged:* **see also page 386***]*

# Yossel der Zalamanker

## Leah Lubchansky-Kornfeld

I wish to set up a monument to the many Korelitzers, among whom I grew up. Together with them, I toured the streets; I rejoiced in their joys and I suffered with them in their sorrows. Among them were extended families of which, no remnant or fugitive remained. I chose one figure, who was etched in my memory more than any others. His name was Yossel der Zalamanker, Yossel der Geller. What was his surname? It is doubtful whether I ever really knew. It is even doubtful whether he ever used it, except for official purposes, of course. Why should I have chosen him especially? Maybe it was because I was a witness to a consultation between him and my uncle Eliyahu-Chaim regarding the establishment of an *Eyn-Yaakov* study group, on which my uncle was counting. Or maybe it was because I loved to watch people when they were walking to the *Bet Midrash* (House-of-Study). I do not know whether this man died a natural death and had a grave of his own, which the town's residents accompanied him in sorrow at his funeral, or whether he died in one of the strange killings, together with those with whom he had lived, and above whose graves were heard the sounds of wild exultation.

He had no children, and all his property was the goodness of his heart and his honesty. He was short, his face was covered by a yellow beard, and his blue eyes were very calming. He paced slowly and comfortably on his way to the *Bet Midrash*, looking left and right, in case he should encounter someone with whom he could hold a conversation. However, things were different on Wednesdays, Market day, when he made his weekly living as a trader in eggs.

Fearing that he would be late for the *Mincha* prayer, he would make haste. He used to run straight, and would leave behind everyone that he met on the way. He was hot in his coat, his jacket was open, and he undid the buttons of his shirt while he was running. He huffed and he puffed as he ran. When he approached the *Bet Midrash* and met people whose destination was the same as his, a grin broke out on his weary face, and he started gleaming all over. It sometimes happened, however, that he used to arrive when the *Bet Midrash* was empty. He then went outside and walked around the building. Maybe a *minyan* could be gathered. Every so often, he would look at the sky to see whether it wasn't too late for prayer.

---

*[Page 203 – Yiddish]*
*[Page XLVIII –English – below,* **as on Page 387***]*

# A. Feivel Nisselevitz
## Yaacov Abramowich
*[English text version]*

He was the postman of the town, along with his being a coachman. Everyone who needed transportation to Novogrudek (21 kilometers) wanted to ride with Feivel. His tunes and anecdotes were much to the liking of his passengers, although he did ask them to walk up the steep inclines on the way to make it easier for the horses. The police at the Novohorodok checkpoint knew him well and waved him through without inspection.

His family was wiped out by the Nazis, except for one daughter, who left for Eretz-Israel before the war and settled in Tel Yosef.

**Coordinator's note:**
The **Yiddish text** is similar to the English text, but **includes additional information** as follows:
### (Notes by Harvey Spitzer)
The only genealogical information not included in the English translation is the name of Feivel's only surviving child: Feigel (Faygl) (see last sentence). The rest of the Yiddish text deals with his lame horse (which he refused to replace although it took twice as long to get to Novogrudek and back) and about a Russian peasant in the town of Radun (half way) who offered Feivel a glass of milk every time he passed by. Feivel, in turn, brought the peasant gifts such as a comb, handkerchief or a pair of socks.

---

*[Page 204 - Yiddish]*
*[Page XLVIII –English – below,* **as on page 387***]*

# B. The PORUSH, Kalman Marashiner
## Yaacov Abramowich
### [English text version]

He used to come to our school just before dismissal time, then take the boys with him to the *Bet-Hamidrash* and had them recite Psalms, in return for which he gave them gifts - a pencil, notebook and other small items of this kind.

He spent his entire day in the *Bet-Hamidrash*. Malkah, his wife, would bring his meals to him, and instead of sleeping he would lie on the wooden bench and take a brief nap, despite the sound of study around him.

In time he and his wife joined their children in Eretz-Israel.

## Coordinator's note:
The **Yiddish text** is similar to the English text, but **includes additional information** as follows:

### (Translated by Harvey Spitzer)
[In Israel] they lived with their son, Aharon, in Kfar Ma'as. Kalman resumed his life of study in the *Beit Midrash* in a hut in Kfar Ma'as, and later in the synagogue in nearby Gat Rimon. He also visited their daughter, Shifra, in Givatayim, where she lived with her family. (Shifra was subsequently killed in a car accident, leaving behind her husband and children.)

In 1947 I met with Kalman and his wife in Kfar Ma'as, near Petach Tikvah. They would often visit my sister Menucha with her husband Haim Itzkovitz and family.

Kalman passed away on 10 *Av* 5711 (1951). His wife, Malka, died on 25 *Tishrei* 5713 (1953).

---

*[Page 205]*

# DESTRUCTION AND HEROISM

**Memorial Stone**

## In Memory of the Martyrs of

## NOVOHORODEK AND THE ENVIRONS
(=Novogrudek)

**(L-R): Selib**          **Lubtch**          **Karelitz**
(Vyselub)                (Lyubcha)           (Korelichi)

*[Pages 206-207 -Yiddish]*

# I AM THE LAST

## Fruma Gulkowich-Berger

**As translated from the Yiddish in her book
"With Courage Shall We Fight"**

I am the only one left to remember.
My thoughts torment me at night.
The fires of the huge number blaze
as the anguish in my heart
grows deeper and deeper.

Drifting before me:
how fresh the graves are!
The terror of my murdered
brothers and sister.
Smoke rising from the earth.
Now silence all around.
And nothing is left of the little children
but a number.

I look back and see that day, that hour,
So majestically beautiful.
And suddenly there's war!
Disorder erupts in the town.
This one runs. That one weeps.
Everyone is packing to go.

We have barely made it through
the terrifying dark night
when a new day breaks, uncaring,
Under a new command.
Domination by villains, a regime of robbers.
And the town has utterly mutated.

The Jews are driven out of their homes.
The Gentiles, our neighbors, dance with anticipation.
They seize all of our belongings
and pay us with spit in our faces, obscenely insulting us.

And before you know it, the Gestapo is there,
With their edict:

"You must wear a yellow patch"
Every day, some new decree from the SS.

Can this "performance" be forgotten?
When they led Alter Strebenik by a rope,
Dragged him like a dog,
and "marched" him through the streets.

I cannot forget that horrifying moment
When the screams of "FIRE!" reached us.
The holy book, the Torah scrolls, in flames.
Two grenades are thrown into the Aron Kodesh at once.

Now, all of us are standing in rows
in the marketplace.
Driven from the town,
we set off on our final march.

I am the last to remember
where my house was,
The last to remember those I loved so well.
Where are my sisters, my brothers, my friends?
Where are my mother and father today?

                                   ---

*[Page 207 - Yiddish]*

# JEWISH PARTISANS
## Fruma Gulkowich-Berger

### As translated from the Yiddish in her book
### "With Courage Shall We Fight"

*[Coordinator's comment - This poem is the first part of a trilogy of poems appearing under the title of "Jewish Partisans" in the book "With Courage Shall We Fight". The other parts appear in this book under the title of "A Partisan" on page 257. A.B.]*

At the very time of black despair's grim chance
A brilliant thought shone forth: resistance!
The dense forests into barracks changed will be.
And to the lofty trees we'll swear our loyalty.

The gloomy night will our protector be,
It's not strife of equal partners that we'll see,

Not warriors here shall our power mete,
But death with dignity is also triumph great!

The heart is sad but the body is with comfort filled,
For 'tis the day when vengeance's hour will be fulfilled.
Also the hour of fate, uncertain I must say,
Whither the angry storm our lives will bear away.


For it is not a struggle of equals, justice fair,
But against the slaughterer a lamb's struggle in despair,
Yet suddenly lamb as lion transformed we see
Fight with pistol in its hands for a better morning, free!

---

*[Pages 208-9 -Yiddish]*
*[Page XLIX-English – below,* **as on page 388***]*

# THE ROAD OF SUFFERING
## Malka Pomerchik - Kfar Saba [English text version]

The Russians entered Korelitz, at the outbreak of the German-Polish fighting, and began operating in Soviet style. First they "nationalized" the large buildings, then closed down the stores and set up one large shopping center. Immediately a shortage of commodities occurred, and long lines queued up for supplies. Everyone was put to work in cooperatives. I became a teacher in a Russian school, teaching German and working with the Fourth Grade. My prominent position in the town placed me in danger, and I left at the first opportunity for Russia, along with my husband, sister and brother-in-law, and one brother.

On the way, we became separated but managed to reunite and reach Tashkent, where we spent the war years. Returning to Korelitz we found there but a handful of Jews - too tired to move away. We went on to Austria, hoping to proceed to *Eretz-Israel* with *Aliya Bet* (illegal immigration), but our child was too young. We had to wait until after the War of Liberation. Eventually we settled in Kfar Saba.

## Coordinator's note:
The **Yiddish text** is similar to the English text, but **includes additional information** as follows:
### (Translated by Harvey Spitzer)
Among the Jews who survived and remained in Korelitz were Sadieh the leather worker, Motel with his son, Zelda with her husband and Michael – just 8 Jews. They didn't want to move away and I couldn't convince them to leave. I

went to Turetz to stay with my uncles, who remained alive and fought with the partisans. We stayed there until I gave birth. Two weeks later we left for Poland in order to continue on our way to the Land of Israel. I succeeded in convincing my uncles to go along with us.

We arrived in the country on May 31, 1949. En route, we stopped in Austria, thinking that we could go to Israel sooner illegally. However, because my child was so young, we were unable to travel to Israel illegally. We had to wait until the War of Independence was over. Then the borders were open and we came to Israel and settled in Kfar Saba.

**The elementary school in Korelitz**

[Pages 210-212]

# In Peace And In Days Of War

## Dov Cohen (Berel Kagan)

### Translated from the Hebrew by Ann Belinsky

Despite the fact that I am not a townsman of Korelitz, but from Novogrudek - I was connected to Korelitz by strong family ties, because my grandmother's house (on my mother's side) was there. The house of my grandmother, Hana-Gittel Gurevitz, stood on the banks of the river, some distance from the center of the town, on the way leading to Mir. My mother, Shoshka Kagan, was born Gurevitz, so she was from Korelitz and many of her family were from there and among them are etched in my memory: my Uncle Yoskeh Gurevitz with his wife Breina Feigel (nee Londin); my Aunt Malka Kapuchevsky. I did not know my grandfather, Dov Gurevitz, as he died before I was born. A big photo of him always hung in our house and in my mind's eye I always had a vision of his image as that of Dr Herzl, with his imposing figure and honor.

During my youth I would travel a lot to my grandmother in Korelitz and every trip was an adventure in my mind, which left me with pleasant feelings in my heart, youthful impressions - for many days.

Travel from Novogrudek was always with the wagon-driver Hillel, whose wagon was carefully padded with sweet-smelling fresh straw. A grey-white mare was always tethered to the wagon, and she also was always brushed and clean, an intelligent horse who knew and understood the soul of the wagon driver. One word from Hillel was enough to move or stop the horse or make any other movement. And thus I sit on the wagon making its way via the gentile villages so well known to the driver, who would vary his journey with jokes and clever stories. In order to show me "Who is Hillel the Wagon-driver"; the farmers working in the fields receive the blessing of Hillel - *Pomahi-Buch* (God be with you), which are faultily expressed from his mouth (on purpose, in Yiddish) *ein broch* (a plague upon your head!) and the farmer answers *Spazebo* (thank you) and Hillel laughs wholeheartedly. My grandmother's house was an old house and appeared quite wretched from the outside, a low and crooked house with a straw roof that was changed at the end of its days to a tiled roof. But the inside of the house was warm and clean. Part of the house was even without flooring. Surrounding the house was a large vegetable garden of five dunams. From this garden my grandmother made her living.

In my grandmother's house was an attic that did not have regular steps leading to it, but rather an old shaky ladder that stood there. A story comes to mind that connects the attic to my Uncle Yoskeh. The story was familiar in my grandmother's house about my Uncle Yoskeh's courage: it happened in the days of the First World War. Uncle Yoskeh was a youth who hid in the attic out of fear of the work enlistment by the Cossacks who were in the town. And here it happened that a Cossack came to look for people to work and in his search he came to the attic and tried to climb the rickety steps of the ladder to the attic. Yoskeh, who sat above and saw that all hope was lost, made a courageous decision: when the Cossack reached the top rung, he pushed the ladder, causing it to fall with the Cossack. The man was frightened and didn't understand what had happened. The people in the house told him that there had always been demons and ghosts in the attic and none of them ever entered it. This influenced him and he left. And thus Yoskeh was saved from the work enlistment and from the hands of the Cossack.

When I grew up a little, I tried to understand Uncle Yoskeh, to get details of this nice story and its veracity, but he always brushed me away with a movement of his hands, as if he didn't put much importance on these things.

Stories of this kind which I heard in Korelitz during my visits there, added double charm to my love of Korelitz and the stories remained with me as something special and mischievous from the spirit of youth in this place.

The Faivelevitz family lived next door to my grandmother. Because they were such good neighbors, they felt as part of the family to me. We only knew the nickname of the head of the family - "Mika"; with a short beard and a short, busy wife whom he was afraid of. Mika had two sons, one - Ezra - was a big youth who would feed me with strange stories and even tell me secret love stories, but I was still young and didn't understand much about these matters.

* *
*

The second period in my life connected to Korelitz was the terrible period of the Second World War, the time of destruction caused by the war whose dimensions we could not estimate at its outbreak. I had grown up and was already a man and with the outbreak of the war every man and every Jewish family began to make an account of the situation - where to escape? - where to hide "until the danger is past"? But the danger did not pass until almost everything was destroyed. In our family in Novogrudek we began to make secret plans and think - Where would it be safer? In a small place or in a large city? And thus it was decided in our family to send a delegation to Korelitz: My uncle Yankel Kagan, my cousin Idel Kagan and I made our way by foot via winding paths to Korelitz. We arrived at my grandmother's house after a terrible night of walking and evading the German guards. And the next day we were taken out by the Germans, together with all the Jews of the place, to the market square. The square was full of the German Gestapo troops and the SS and their assistants - people from the local police who, with blows and abuse, placed the Jews in close-packed rows. Youth, women and old people whose faces all expressed fear and helplessness. And here the Germans now also bring the local Rabbi. His intelligent face was shining opposite the large assembly, as if to imbue them with hope, belief and courage. When I looked at the proud Rabbi with his majestic appearance, I understood his look, as if he were giving a fiery speech to the bewildered and wretched audience; his face reminded me of the many years of history of the Jewish people, years sown with torture and persecution and...hope. I was stopped in thought-reading by one of the town notables at the order of the Germans. He read a prepared list of the town notables who were ordered to leave the rows and move to a special place which was assigned to them, and no-one knew where it was safer: between the rows of people who were ordered to go to the assigned place, or in the tightly-packed rows that remained as they were. The Nazi troops do not stop at this: after reading the list, they move among the close-packed rows with kicks and abuse, pull out more people and push them towards the people who had just been moved, and now the Rabbi joins them. After this satanic show is over, the Germans disperse the rest of the crowd with blows and shouts.

All these people who were removed from the rows according to the list were transferred overnight to imprisonment in the cellar of the synagogue of the town, and the next day moved to Novogrudek. There they were shot and executed the same day, near the forest.

We left Korelitz the next day and returned to Novogrudek and I never returned to see Korelitz again.

I met up during the war years with townspeople of Korelitz in the forests of the partisans in our struggle against the Germans and all excelled in their courage in the bloody war with the Nazis and in their determination to avenge the spilled blood of their brothers and families.

---

*[Pages 212-225 -Yiddish]*
*[Pages XLIX-L – English, abridged:* **see also page 388***]*

# On The Brink Of Destruction

## Ben –Ir
*[This is a pen name ="A son of the town" HS]*
*(It relates to Yaacov Abramowich - AB)*

### Translated from the Yiddish by Harvey Spitzer

When the Soviets came into our small town, they took away the merchants. Since we had a hardware store, where I worked, I quickly went into painting. The wealthier merchants were taken away.

There were few house painters in Korelitz, and as I had begun working as a painter, I was needed and was kept employed till the last minute. That is how I was saved and wasn't taken away to Russia.

When the Soviet-German war broke out, the Soviets ran off. Things were chaotic in the town, like in a time of war.

We heard that the Germans were getting closer to our section. There was a panic. Each person was thinking of a way to save himself. Many people ran off towards Russia, including my brother Gavriel and myself. On the road between Mir and Stolptzi, we met many people in vehicles or on foot. There were many wounded and killed. The Germans pursued us. We were told that they were burning bridges and destroying the roads so that we wouldn't be able to return to Korelitz or reach Russia either. We decided to go back.

The Germans came into Korelitz at the end of June 1941. For a few days there was no law and order. The Christians would come with bags and wagons and rob and beat Jews. It didn't matter what we gave them. They robbed Jewish property and everything we had toiled for.

The Germans set up headquarters in Yosef Bernstein's house. The commander of the station was Kasperovitch, a Christian from Korelitz. Later he was replaced by Strashke and after Strashke was Drutshke. They supported the German armed forces. The names of the Germans were Birkhoff and Ehrhardt. The SS people were stationed in a second brick house under the command of Hentshike. He was a bloodsucker. I don't remember the names of the others. They beat Jews with murderous blows.

They quickly ordered the Jews to form a Jewish Council. The Jewish Council was in the rabbi's house. Rabbi Vernik was forced to be the head of the

Council. He had the cooperation of Shimon Zelaviansky, Moshke Kivelevitch and Baruch Shimshelevitch. The secretary was Lipke, a refugee.

The Jewish Council received orders. The first – a contribution: gold and other valuables were to be delivered to them. In case these items were not furnished, everyone would be killed. Jews brought whatever they had. This was repeated several times. When the SS men would come for the contributions, they would beat the rabbi.

A ghetto was set up in a short time. The remaining Jews in Korelitz were all concentrated in a two-storey house which belonged to Lifschitz. There were several more houses near that house. It was very packed. We slept on the floor or in a bunk bed, one over the other.

Several families from surrounding villages such as Paluzsheh, Maytshet (Molchad), Palinoi , Shepetnitze and Mondzin were brought to our ghetto.
People were not allowed to bring any food with them. They were starving, yet they shared whatever they had with one another. They began to get used to this life.

A short time later, all the men were ordered to assemble at the market place. Many men escaped the blows of the Germans by working in nearby places like Prizhnevitch or by working in small villages without pay – which was better than being beaten.

The day the men were ordered to go to the market place (in July or August), I was in Prizhnevitch, a small village, 3 km from Korelitz. As I was working, I suddenly heard that a woman had come and had fallen. This was Dvashke Ganzevitz.  She said: "Children, men, run quickly to town, to the marketplace because if one man is missing, all the men will be shot." Her children, Moshe-Dovid and Itze-Berl, were also working with us. All of us who were working in Prizhnevitch, ran quickly back to town. All the men standing in the marketplace were lined up against the stores. Germans and policemen with guns were standing all over. We were also put into the lines.

About 10 to 15 minutes later, a German SS man began reading from a note which the Christian boys had handed him. He said that the men whose names he would call out were useful Jews who were needed and that they would remain alive. All of those who were called out by name were seated on vehicles.

I remember that Michel Shuster, a wigmaker, whose son Reuven was a young boy, was not included in the list and, as the 105 men whose names were called out would remain alive, the father begged the German to have pity and also take his son for work because he was capable and useful. The German answered that he didn't need him because he was still young.

The 105 men were taken to the *Bet Midrash*. The others who remained standing in the market place were beaten and dispersed.

The 105 men were then removed from the *Bet Midrash* and taken to Novogrudek, where they were murdered.

When the 105 men were still in the *Bet Midrash*, Henke, Velvel's daughter, wanted to look at her husband through the window and say good-bye to him for the last time. She was shot at and wounded. Rivke Slutzky was also wounded.

Christians would come to the Jews in Korelitz and bring regards from the Jews who had been taken away. They told the Jews in Korelitz that these Jews had nothing to eat and were asking their family and friends to send them food and other things. The Jews in Korelitz collected the little they had and sent it to their husbands and children. This, however, was a lie. The Christians would steal the food and other things for themselves because, as we found out, the 105 men had been shot at once near the barracks.

Besides causing unbearable hardships and giving beatings, the Germans also organized several transports. Three transports of Jews were sent to the camp in Dvoretz. This was a "T.A.D.T." (German firm) camp where people worked.

In addition, Jews were also transported to the ghetto in Novogrudek.

Exactly how many Jews lived in the ghetto, I can't say. I think there were about 300. The ghetto was surrounded by a barbwire fence. Policemen under the supervision of the Germans served as guards. These were White Russian policemen wearing German uniforms.

I remember one instance: 2 refugees who came to Korelitz asked the Germans whether they could travel to the "third realm", i.e. to Bialystok. They were taken for spies and brought to the study hall. The rabbi was brought in and the two were shot. Then their bodies were placed on a bed sheet and buried together. The Rabbi asked the Germans to place the man separately and the woman separately, but precisely because the rabbi requested this, the two were laid to rest together. This was either at the end of 1941 or the beginning of 1942.

In November or December 1942, the final transport of Jews was carried out and Korelitz became cleansed of Jews, *Jüdenrein*. This last transport was also taken to the ghetto in Novogrudek.

I want to add to the barbarism of the Germans. When the two Jews were shot in the study hall in the presence of the rabbi, the Torah scrolls, tables and benches were also taken outside. They grabbed the rabbi, pulled him by his beard, beat him and burned everything. Then the rabbi was taken to the synagogue yard, where there was a well. The water was drawn with a chain. The rabbi was ordered to draw water with a bucket. Then they tormented him by spilling water over him until he fell down.

Finally, the rabbi was accused of being a communist and was taken with a group of "communists" to Novogrudek and shot with the group near the barracks.

Little remained of the Jews' possessions. Individual, familiar Christians would come to the wire fence and bring a small loaf of bread, an egg and take the last of what the Jews had. I was working as master painter outside the ghetto. What I earned, I managed to bring into the ghetto, and one person shared with another the food which he could obtain through indirect ways.

I ran away from Korelitz to the camp in Dvoretz a few days before Korelitz became *Jüdenrein*. I did so because I heard that one could escape from the camp in Dvoretz and join the partisans.

It wasn't so easy for me to get into the Dvoretz camp. I came to a forest in the daytime. The camp was guarded by policemen, so I couldn't get into the camp during the day. Suddenly, I saw a couple of boys from afar. I recognized one of them: Yitzchak Stoler's son, who was a carpenter and worked in Dvoretz. I called the boys over with my hand. They came closer and I asked the boy I knew to transmit a few words to his father from me. The boy ran off at once. I waited and looked through the trees. From afar, I noticed Yitzchak Stoler walking with an axe and a saw. When he came over to me, we both wept. I told him what troubles I had experienced and how I had gotten there.

We both cut down a tree and together carried the tree into the camp on our shoulders. This was proof that we were both returning from work. He was familiar with the Dvoretz camp. As soon as I was inside the camp, I was locked up among all the other workers. Yitzchak Stoler took me around and registered me in his group of carpenters so that I would get a little more groats and a piece of bread.

I was in the Dvoretz camp several months. Exactly how many Jews were in the camp, I can't say because I was there only a short time and escaped to Novogrudek in the summer of 1942.

In Novogrudek I worked as a master painter. I was taken to work under guard. I remember that I worked in a church and the priest would give us a piece of bread, a few eggs, a small chicken. He helped us in whatever way he could. This kept us alive: me, my brother Gavriel and our mother.

When we had been in Novogrudek a short time, mother said to us: "Children, try to escape. Maybe one of you will survive so that a memory of our family might remain. I'm sick and can't go with you."

We escaped to the ghetto in Pereshke (Peresica). One day we went with a group in search of water. Coming to a place of water, we hid among the bushes. When everyone left, we stayed there thinking of how to escape.

We escaped and reached some Christians near Novogrudek. We wandered through villages, asking for a small piece of bread. While doing so, I was wounded by a German airplane and also by some policemen.

One day, as we were wandering about, I met some young fellows from Korelitz who were partisans in Bielski's unit. They were Bentshe Gulkowich and Chaim Abramowich. Seeing them, a new world opened up before me. They took us with them to Bielski. There, Dr. Itler treated my wounds for the first time and I slowly regained my strength.

I was put into the ranks of the scouts. In time I was ordered to be the commander of the scouts. I myself wasn't capable of giving any orders. I would always carry out the mission myself.

Bielski called me over and said he didn't want me to go out on missions alone, but I told him I didn't want to be a commander. I refused to be a commander but stayed in the ranks of the scouts.

We carried out all kinds of missions. Once, we even went around Korelitz.

The unit numbered 1,200 people, all Jews. There was little to eat and there were also few armed men because most of the armed men were placed in Ordzhenikidze's unit. The majority were women, older men. There were in all 120-150 partisans with guns. We were in the Nalibok forest where there were many units. It was very hard to get food. Besides, we weren't allowed to take anything around our section. We had to go to outlying places, closer to the Germans.

We went into Ogrodnik (a village) one or one and a half km from Korelitz. We immediately noticed the priest and the veterinarian. Our men, who were standing outside, didn't think anything was wrong. They took wagons and loaded them up with whatever they could. As we left with 10 wagons full, the police in the yard began shooting at us. We hardly escaped alive, and we left everything there.

On the way back, we went into villages because we were ashamed to return to our unit empty handed. We brought back a great wealth of provisions. When we got back, we told Bielski what had happened. He admired our heroism and was glad that we managed to get away safely.

----- Besides partisans, there were also White Poles in the Nalibok forest.

The Germans set up a blockade and I received an order from Bielsky to go and see who was in the area. We were always in contact with Christians who would give us news. I went out with Chaim Kravetz and Barke Rubizhevski. We rode slowly and came to a Christian. Before entering a village, we would stop at the first house and find out whether there were any Germans in the village. The Christian told us that everything was quiet in the village and that there were no Germans. We went in further and we were suddenly caught in a storm of bullets. This killed the White Poles.

I remember an instance when Bielski called the group of scouts which I was leading and said that there was a peasant in the village of Izveh who was informing the Germans where Jews and partisans were hiding. Our task was to wipe out the whole family.

We went there. Our group consisted of the Lubavitch brothers, Ben-Zion Gulkowich and Yisrael Salanter (as he was called among the partisans). I knocked on the Christian's door. The Christian's wife opened the door. We left our horses in the forest. The Christian woman and her two children were the only ones in the house. She said that her husband wasn't home. We told her that we were good friends and that if she needed anything she couldn't get because of the war, we would bring everything for her. She replied that they wanted to build on, and that if we could bring a saw, she would give us whatever we wanted. When we bring the saw, she said, her husband would also be there and we'd have a good drink.

We said goodbye and promised to bring what she needed. We went back to the forest, got on our horses and rode to Stankevitch, to the home of a Christian. We asked him for a saw and promised to return it. He gave it to us. We got back on our horses and left.

We returned to the Gentile woman and I again knocked on the door and knocked on the windowsill with the saw. When you hit something with a saw, it makes a ringing sound. When the Gentile woman heard the sound of the saw, she quickly opened the door. Again, the woman with her two children were the only ones at home.

Two of our group of partisans remained standing on the street as guards to make sure the Germans would not attack us. Four of the partisans came into the house: the Lubavitch brothers, Yisrael Salanter and myself. We told her that everything was perfectly fine, but that we'd like to talk to her husband. Seeing that everything was ready, that we brought the saw which we had promised, she opened the window and called her husband.

Each person in our group was assigned a task in advance so that we each knew what we had to do. Yisrael Salanter was to kill her husband. Michl Lubavtich was to kill his wife; I - one daughter and Zalman Lubavitch, the other daughter.

The husband came in. Yisrael Salanter went for his gun. The man was healthy and strong and began wrestling with Yisrael. They both fell down in the middle of the house. Seeing what was happening, I wanted to shoot him with my gun, but I was afraid I might kill Yisrael instead. I turned the gun over and hit him over the head with the wooden part. The wood broke. He let go of Yisrael who took out his pistol and shot him.

The woman begged us not to kill her. She would give us everything she had, but money meant nothing to us. Michl shot her. I shot one daughter who was hiding in bed, and Zalman Lubavitch shot the other daughter.

When we went out of the house, we let the horses and cows out of the stable. Then we set fire to the house and stable. We left a note: "A person who collaborates with the Germans deserves to die like this." We got on our horses and went back to our unit. Our act of revenge against that family caused a great panic in the villages. Christians were afraid to inform the Germans where the partisans were moving around. It was a little better for us; it was easier to be in the forest.

Bielski sent out a group of partisans with good guns to perform an operation, and the group carried out what they had to do. This was done during the day and they couldn't go back to their base during the day because the Germans were moving about on the roads. They (the partisans) came to a peasant's hut. His last name was Bielorus and was known to the group. This was a group of the best men in the unit. They left their wagon in the yard. The Christian gave them a fine welcome. The group was exhausted and they lay down to rest.

The Christian's daughter asked to go out to milk the cows. They let her leave. After all, they knew the Christian and she went out. Novogrudek wasn't far away and she informed the Germans.

Germans arrived, surrounded the entire hut and killed everyone. A miracle occurred when Polanski hid in the henhouse. (Christians had big ovens, beneath which was the henhouse). Seeing that everything had become quiet, he crawled out of the henhouse and called out to the White Russian, who was standing there alarmed, seeing everyone lying there dead.
----- "What do you think? We'll keep quiet about your part in this?"
As soon as he said this, the Gentile took an axe and killed him, too, the last of the group of Jewish partisans.

Not far away was Vishnievski's group, which found out about this. Bielski called together the unit and announced that we shouldn't move about in the villages.

One of Vishnievski's group came and said that he knew where the group was killed. There were the two Bielorus brothers who informed on the Jews and, on account of them, the group of partisans was killed.

The Bielorus family knew that we wouldn't keep quiet, so they moved to Novogrudek and their hut remained empty. Later, Bielorus returned to his hut, seeing that the partisans were no longer coming into the area (due to Bielski's order) and fearing that their crops would die if their fields weren't cultivated because it was now summer.

Vishnievski's group found out when he came back and warned us. A group of 25 men was selected including myself. Pesach Friedberg and our commissary were in our group. Bielski's brother Asael was the leader of the group. The group had to take revenge.

On our way to the Bielorus house, we found out that a boy from Korelitz was killed when a Christian informed on him. The boy was running through the villages and stole a bucket from that Christian. The Gentile went to the ghetto in Novogrudek. They lined up the Jews and the Gentile had to identify the boy. He in fact recognized him (I don't remember the family name, but I knew they came from Korelitz) and the Germans shot him. We received an order from Asael to burn down the house and kill the Gentiles. We carried out the task before going to the Bielorus house.

When we came to the Bielorus house, Bielski gave an order as to who was to go into the house and who was to keep watch to make sure that no one would attack us.

I was among those who were to keep guard on the street. When our men knocked on the door, no one answered. They forced the door open and found Bielorus. In his pocket was a letter of commendation, praising him for informing on a Jew for which he was entitled to receive a certain sum of money from the district commissary of Novogrudek. They took the letter and wrote a protocol as to why they had come and were carrying out the sentence. Then they shot the whole family and let the cows and horses out of stable before setting the house on fire.

On the way back, we left notes on all the posts explaining why we carried out the act of revenge against the two Bielorus brothers and their families. They were being paid back for having turned the group of partisans over to the Germans. The Christians for the surrounding places were now frightened. We instilled fear in them.

When the Germans began running away from the Baranovitch - Lida roads, Bielski sent out a group of 12 spies who were to blow up the highways. Yudel

Levin, Alek Pshenitze, Bentshe Gulkowich, the two Lubavitch brothers, Niame Berkovitch and others. I also belonged to the group. Yudel was the mine layer.

We did our job and wanted to return to our base. We rode in single file, one behind the other. I was the first. When the road was already in sight, we heard: "*Stoi! Kto yedzhie?* (Stay there! Who is going?) Password!" We didn't have a password. We thought they were Christian partisans, but they were White Russians who worked together with the Germans. We didn't even manage to speak out when they opened fire with a hail of bullets.

Yehosha fell off his horse at once and I also fell off. The others who were behind us managed to turn their horses around and ride off.

I couldn't see where I was. I slowly began dragging myself on the ground and how surprised and happy I was when I noticed the group which had gone about half a kilometer ahead. Having noticed that I was missing, they were waiting for me. They put me on a horse and we rode further on.

We came to Victor Pantchenko's unit. This was a group which had originally worked together with Bielski's unit when they had begun to organize. We stayed with them. They would take our horses and ride around. They told us that the day of liberation was getting closer.

We didn't plan to stay with them much longer. Yudel Levin told me that there was only one way out: to ride closer to Novogrudek.

Once in Novogrudek, we went up to the cemetery. Yudel himself was from Novogrudek and was a photographer by trade. He called to me:
---- "I don't know if I'll have another opportunity, so I'd like to take a look at my house and see who's living there." There was a Christian in the house who was also a photographer. Yudel asked him if he knew who he was. Yudel then introduced himself and said he was the owner.

---- "You know what? Take our picture!" The Gentile took out his camera and took our picture in the yard. I still have the photo. Then the Christian invited us into the house and asked if we would like to eat. He told us: "Children, run away because Germans are moving around the streets, if you want to live."

We believed him. We got on our horses and rode off. We reached the forest, where we heard from the partisans that these were the final hours of the occupation. We would soon be liberated. We rode on further to our unit. I was first and Yudel was behind me. I had a Russian rifle which I carried across my chest. My horse was small. It was a summer day. We were riding along the sands in the forest. In the distance, I noticed a line of Germans moving along. Yudel wouldn't believe me. He said there were no Germans in the forest.

*[Page 223]*                          **Jews from Korelitz in Italy**
L-R: Ben-Zion Gulkowich, Yaacov Abramowich, -------, Shmuel Zalman Leibowitz

This was actually a group of Germans walking one behind the other, 3-5 meters apart. When I got closer to the Germans, one of them aimed his rifle at me and wanted to shoot me. Out of great fear, I sat on the *strumianes* which one rides on a horse (?) and, with a movement of my finger, I said in Russian, "Don't dare shoot!"

I don't know whether it was my luck, but the German put down his gun. Yudel and I quickly jumped off our horses. The German remained there and the others went on ahead. I shot at the German but my gun jammed and wouldn't shoot. Seeing this, the German ran into the forest.

We, Yudel and I, stood there thinking what to do. I didn't want to go ahead. I didn't want to be hit by a German bullet. We went back and on the way we met many Christian partisans. We stopped them and told them that Germans were moving around and that they shouldn't go any further. We selected a group of 40-50 men. We then decided to go and capture the Germans because we were now a stronger group, but we didn't meet up with any.

We returned happily to our unit, but a misfortune occurred. When the Germans were running through the forest, the partisans were ordered to go and chase after them. A battle ensued during which 10 partisans lost their lives.

----- We were liberated in June, 1944. We gathered together and Bielsky spoke to us. Our joy was indescribable. Russian soldiers were already in the forest.

As was said, our unit (Bielski's) numbered 1,200 men and women who remained alive, in fact, thanks to Tuvia Bielsky and his brothers. Jews who had escaped from a ghetto came to a camp which had an address, a place to come. It was very important for them. Christian partisans used to capture Jews who were fleeing and shoot them. When Bielski's unit was formed, however, things were different. You had to settle accounts with him.

We came to Novogrudek. Bielski called together all the partisans and said we could go wherever we wanted to. All the Christian partisans who remained alive were sent further on the front. When Bielski was asked where the partisans from his unit were, he answered that they should have asked him that question earlier because he had disbanded the unit and each of his men went on his way and he didn't know where they were.

After the liberation, I began to think what I should do next. I went to Korelitz to take a look at the place where I was born and where my family had lived. I found Christians who had come from Russia living in my house. I introduced myself as the owner of the house. They explained to me that they weren't at fault. They were settled there. I was there together with Gulkowich.

I couldn't stay in the house any longer. After all, my mother and little brother had lived in that house. I didn't meet anyone. I left the house. The Christians gave us a small loaf of bread for the way and more food. I met a Christian lady in Korelitz who recognized us. I asked her if there were any Jews still in Korelitz. She answered that there were a few: Zelde Stoler, Sadia Gertzovski ("*der rimer*"), Motl Ushechovski and Michael Kogan (the fur coat maker). These were all that were left in Korelitz. We met with them and had a good cry. We regretted the fact that hardly but a few individual Jews remained alive out of such a population in Korelitz.

We said goodbye to Korelitz and returned to Novogrudek, where I sought ways to escape.

I went to Lodz. It took time but I found ways to go to pre-state Israel. I went from Lodz to Germany, from Germany to Austria, from Austria to Italy, where I met former partisans. I met with Kavenski, who wanted to transfer his work-place over to me. I created the first "*kibbutz*" (group) of partisans in Aqua Santa - later Anzio Nettuno. I served on the committee. I maintained contact with the "Joint" and provided food for the group.

In 1947 I was sent to Germany. I travelled together with Yashke Mazavietski and David Palotnik. In Germany, we had to organize groups of Jews who were to go to Israel while the war was going on. I worked in the so-called "illegal immigration" to Israel.

When I returned to my "*kibbutz*" in Italy, I no longer found my group there. In 1947, I was sent to pre-state Israel.

I went to my sister's home. I immediately began looking for work.

---

*[Page 226]*

# THE GHETTO

## Fruma Gulkowich-Berger

**As translated from the Yiddish in her book
"With Courage Shall We Fight"**

Hitler-Nazis seized our neighborhoods,
And immediately started to rule with brutal edicts,
Built ghettos with high walls for Jews,
Tortured, murdered, burnt in the ovens.

A high wall, with barbed wire.
Like a prison, it was forbidden to leave.
Guards above, guards all around ---
And those in the middle - are to be destroyed.

The Nazis drove everyone between the ghetto-walls:
Old, young, brides and grooms in love,
The suffering is horrible behind the wall
The rulers of Hitler-land have no compassion.

What kind of work? What kind of certificate?
They misled us into "school".
Jews are dying of hunger, from pain and filth.
Everyday there are corpses - by the dozen.

The flames of blind hatred took prisoners.
All were murdered in an appalling manner:
fathers, mothers, tiny children.
They were forced, under rifles,
to the mass graves to undress.
The ground quickly disappeared under the naked corpses.

And the world was blind and deaf,
It did not see how man turned his fellow man
To ash and dust.
It did not hear the children crying and screaming
Or the sighing and the quiet moaning of the elderly...

No vestige remained of the Jews in the ghetto
Not of the victims nor wagonload
after wagonload of their belongings.
The Nazi murderer, with gun and flame,
Eradicated the stock of our generations to the very root.

Our homes are desolate - empty under their roofs.
Now, only the black holes of death remain
And over them the skies without pity, empty and void.
All that can help is to shed another tear...

---

*[Pages 226-227]*

# BREAD IN THE GHETTO

## Fruma Gulkowich-Berger

### As translated from the Yiddish in her book
### "With Courage Shall We Fight"

Why is it so- tell me, World,
That a morsel of bread is worth more than gold?
A slice of bread to quiet the hunger
A loaf of bread, looked upon as a wonder.

"Bread, bread, I am so hungry - it's gnawing my heart away"
I hear the little girl to her mother say.
"Oh, my child, in the ghetto there is no bread to eat.
Tomorrow will perhaps be better - meanwhile we must forget, my sweet."

Ah, bread! Today you are the dream that stokes my life's fire.
A piece of bread to eat- my dearest desire.
Once, before day's dawning hour,
I managed to get hold of a little flour.
But carrying the sack so that the policeman might not see -
You cannot fathom what sacrifice that required of me!
For a potato, more than one smuggler lay dead!
What punishment would the murderers mete out for bread?

It was my day, the policeman looked away!
My father is standing with his Psalms, to pray.
My sisters are waiting, the kneading trough prepared,
We couldn't imagine the approaching hour when no one would be spared.

The dough already kneaded, the oven getting warm,
Rising in the trough, the loaves about to form.
But suddenly pleading and screaming reach our ears,
The ghetto is surrounded by murderers - the worst of our fears.

The flames in the oven are but barely glowing,
From trough and from oven, the dough is overflowing.
There are no more hands to bake the bread
In their pitiless graves lies everyone - dead.

The bread in the trough, abandoned on the sideboard it stands,
As inevitable as its overflow, our delivery into "their" hands.
So tell me, world, can you feel this pain as I do?
You destroyed my people. Tell me. What happened to you?

---

*[Pages 228 - 231]*

# MEMORIES OF THE GHETTO
## Fruma Gulkowich-Berger

### Translated from the Yiddish by Harvey Spitzer

**Fruma Gulkowich-Berger**

This happened in the small Jewish town of Korelitz, between Novogrudek and Mir. Dear, warm-hearted Jews with a long and distinguished pedigree lived there.

When the Second World War broke out in September 1939, Korelitz was occupied by the Soviet government. Everything in Jewish life changed at once; it was no longer the same as before. But Jews adjusted to the new conditions. We went on living with hope and confidence.

Suddenly, this, too, was destroyed. That was on June 22, 1941, when Hitler unexpectedly attacked Soviet Russia. A hell on earth began for the Jews in Korelitz as it did for Jews in other places as well.

From the start, we were driven into a ghetto in Korelitz. I was there with my mother, father, my three sisters and a brother. Our misery was great. There was no limit to our suffering and pain. In that same year, 1941, local Nazi collaborators headed by Britchkovski beat up my mother and she died from her wounds. I will never forget this...

*

In May 1942, when a bright spring day arose over God's world, all the Jews were driven out onto the market place in Korelitz. I was standing in the first row with my sisters: Grunia, Feigel and Brina. My father, Shlomo, was standing next to them. He could hardly stand on his swollen feet.

All at once, the Nazi murderers with their local "helpers" began driving the Jews onto the road. The "march" was accompanied by beatings and insults, with (soldiers) standing around with guns fixed at us, ready to shoot. The day dragged on like an eternity for the Jews.

"At night, we finally came to Novogrudek. Tortured, exhausted, hungry and thirsty, we were driven like animals into the stables of the Pereshike (Peresica) ghetto, where there were also Jews from Novogrudek and other small towns: Lubtch, Ivenitz, Nalibok, Selib and others. A long chain of endless suffering and pain began there for every one of us."

Thursday morning, August 6, 1942, we pushed and shoved our way to the gate to go to work. (We already had the feeling that the ghetto would be surrounded by Nazis in the coming days.) My 6 year old niece asked to be taken along. I managed to do so only because the policeman pretended not to notice. For some reason, this day at work was a little freer. But don't rejoice, foolish person. A minute before dark becomes easier...

All of a sudden, there was a commotion. We started to run. We didn't know where we were running. News reached us that the ghetto was already surrounded. My brother's wife and I began running to the barracks because the others were running there. I didn't see my sisters any more. There we underwent a "sorting" – this one to the right, this one to the left – to life or to death.

Those selected for death were driven back to the Pereshike ghetto. It had already started getting dark. The ghetto was already full of Nazis. I was back in "our" stable. My father was standing beside his bunk bed, wrapped in his prayer shawl, reciting psalms. My God! How did one bullet kill an honest and devout Jew? I will never forget how he looked at me...

My sisters were hiding somewhere in an attic. Yehudit, my sister-in-law, pulled me by the hand, "Come, let's go and look somewhere for a hiding place." I myself was strangely motionless, like a stone. We went out of the stable. Where could we find a hole to crawl into? After all, we were strangers there. The ground would just not open for us and hide us! We passed by a few people who had been killed. I knew one of them, a girl from Korelitz, Merke Yellin. She had the courage to spit in the face of a German.

We passed by the large outhouse which stood in the middle of the ghetto. Without a minute to think, we went inside, and that became our hiding place. We dropped down into the filth which came up to our chests. Two women were already lying there: Esther Menaker and Mashe Rabinovitch. We sat in all four corners because, in case someone heard our breathing, we wouldn't all be seen at the same time...

The night passed quietly. On Friday, August 7 (24 Av), we heard the sound of cars. The murderous beasts were coming for their victims. The cries of little children still ring in my ears today.

"Daddy, mommy, where are you? Why have you left us?" The children were locked in the cars at once. The sound of the cars diminished as they drove further away. Soon shooting was heard and then it was quiet. Four thousand lives were cut down.

Music was heard in the ghetto. The resounding voice of a Nazi was speaking. He said they were carrying out a sacred task which they must complete – searching for the remaining Jews in their hiding places.

Suddenly, we heard steps of human beasts and dogs.

The dogs began barking and it became clear to them that Jews were there. They began shooting at us. The first bullet hit Esther Menaker. She didn't even let out a sigh. A bullet tore off a piece of my dress and slightly grazed my right hand. The Nazis apparently didn't see the other two women on the opposite side. I heard the murderers say to one another that if they're still alive there, they'll die anyway. And they went further on, looking for hiding places.

We lay in the filth of the toilet six days without eating or drinking. Worms were eating our bodies voraciously, and whenever someone entered, our hearts stopped beating out of fright. I still have a weak heart to this very day.

On the seventh day, the surviving Jews were brought back from the barracks, and among them was also my brother Ben-Zion. The ghetto was made smaller and, that being the case, the outhouse in which we were hiding was now outside the ghetto.

When my brother found out about us, he dragged us out of the cesspool. It was then that we saw the great disaster. There were so few of us left, you could count us on the fingers of your hand.

We began escaping from the ghetto in groups. My brother was the first to run away with a group. He quickly came and took us out of the ghetto with 25 people. We became partisans. We fought against the Nazis for two and a half years and lived to see the liberation as proud Jews.

*[Pages 231-234]*

# Under The Yoke Of The Nazis

## Ben-Zion Gulkowich

### Translated from the Yiddish by Harvey Spitzer

Every Jew who lived through the German occupation has very much to relate about the sufferings and frightful days when one's life was constantly in danger. To this very day I cannot understand the miracle of my survival.

Right after the Germans came into Korelitz in the summer of 1941, they began to issue decrees: they confiscated Jewish property, drove the Jews out of their homes and sent them to perform slave labor. None of us could believe that our small town would become *Jüdenrein*, cleansed of all Jews. Who could imagine that Jews who had lived in the cities and towns for hundreds of years would be uprooted from their homes and killed in the cruelest way.

The first decree began when the Germans ordered all the men to line up in the market place. They selected 105 men, especially young people, according to a list which the Christians drew up. The Germans said that they were taking these people to work, but the Gentiles later told us that they were all shot to death not far from Novogrudek. My name also appeared on the list, but I ran away from the town just in time before the police came to get me. They searched in all the corners of the house while, at the same time, stealing whatever they liked. I was then saved from a certain death.

Among the 105 victims was my father-in-law, Avraham Karelitzer, the first victim from our family. Whenever the SS men came to look for Jewish victims, the local "bandits" would point me out, but I managed to elude them.

In the summer of 1942, the Germans drove all the Jews out of Korelitz and herded us into the Pereshike ghetto in Novogrudek. It was then that we realized that this would be the end of our suffering and torment. We felt that our situation was hopeless. We were despondent and waited for the end to come, but the impulse to live was great, and each of us had to take revenge on the enemy of the Jewish people. Many young men carried this idea around in the ghetto. I spoke to a group of friends about escaping into the forest around Nalibok because news reached us that there were partisans in that area. I no longer remember the names of each one in the group, but Dovid Lifshitz from Korelitz and Bentshe Movshovitch were among them.

I don't know who revealed to the Jewish council that I was organizing people to escape from the ghetto and that I was the leader of the group. They watched my every step. At night they took away my boots so that I couldn't go out with the group. As a result, the fellows escaped without me. The group did, in fact, reach the Nalibok forest and met up with the partisans from Stalin's unit, who were called the *Stalintses*. A Jewish group was organized in that unit under the direction of a Jewish lieutenant, Smolenski. The commander of the *Stalintses* promised that if the Jewish partisans excelled in combat, they would be taken into his unit.

Meanwhile, many Germans with their collaborators came to Nalibok and gave chase to the partisans. The commander of Stalinsk unit ordered the Jewish group, which numbered 20 partisans, to go into the church, make an ambush and put up resistance to the Germans. A bitter fight ensued. The Jewish partisans fought heroically to the last bullet, but they didn't receive the help that was promised them. Dovid Lifshitz, of blessed memory, from Korelitz was among the heroes who fell in battle. (Later, when I was a partisan around Nalibok, I heard this from the *Stalintses*.) This sad news reached the Jews in the Novogrudek ghetto. The watch was strengthened. The second slaughter of the Jews in the ghetto took place soon after, on August 7, 1942. This was the first and last slaughter for the Jews of Korelitz because nearly all of them were killed then.

On the sixth day after the slaughter when I was brought back to the Peresheke ghetto from the orchard, I saw the great disaster. When I found out that there were no open _____ in the ghetto, I ran in search of them, hoping that someone of my family was saved. It is hard for me to report how many dead, suffocated persons I dragged out of the pits, but I didn't find anyone from my family. I suddenly heard that someone was asking about Ben-Zion Gulkowich. It was a Jew from Lubtch who told me that my wife Yehudit and my sister Fruma were lying in the filth in the toilets. I immediately jumped over the ghetto fence and ran to save them before the police found them. I dragged them out with much effort. They were living skeletons – and we were the only remnants of our large family. My sorrow is three-fold: the sorrow of a father who lost a child, Chayele, my dear, little daughter who was hardly three years old; the sorrow of a son and brother who lost his parents and sisters; and the great sorrow of a Jew of whose people, thousands of souls were murdered. In that slaughter alone, thousands of Jews were killed.

Seeing what awaited us – those of us who were still alive – I again began looking for a way to escape from the ghetto and take revenge on the enemy of the Jewish people.

At that time, a group of people got out of the ghetto and reached the forests around Mokretz. A few days later, another group got out and I went along with them. Yehudit and Fruma remained the ghetto meanwhile. When I reached the forest, I found a group of Jews consisting of about 40 people. This was actually the beginning of a Jewish partisan unit which eventually grew to 1,200. Most were Jews, escapees from the ghettos: Novogrudek, Lida, Dvoretz and others. This was the Jewish unit of the heroic commander, Tuvia Bielski.

When I had been in the unit a few weeks, we were given guns to make an ambush on the Germans on the highway. Later, I went to Novogrudek to take my wife and sister out of the ghetto as well as a few more Jews who wanted to go along. My partner was Yitzchak Reznik from Novogrudek, who was very familiar with the roads. I took out a group of 25 people from the ghetto. It's easy to imagine how difficult it was for us to get into the ghetto and later to get out. Several people in the group were left hanging on the electric wires or left dead by the fence as the Nazis were shooting.

I remember that it was hard for me to talk Yoel Mayerovitch into going along with us. We had to actually drag him out of the ghetto. He had become so apathetic and dependent.

I was a *razviedchik* (spy) in the unit. My task was to find out where the enemy was located and to report back to the command. All partisans from Korelitz took an active part in all assignments. Many women would stay at the posts. We often waged difficult battles with the Germans and the White Russian police. At every turn we avenged the innocent blood that was shed of our murdered families. We seldom spent the night in the same place where we had been during the day. The young partisans who served in the combat group also had to provide food, clothing and weapons for the unit. I won't expand on the time I spent in Bielski's unit as these things are already well known and much has already been written about the partisans' activities by other comrades.

---

*[Pages 235-244]*

# The Experiences I Went Through In World War II

## Mordechai Mayerovitch

### Translated from the Yiddish by Harvey Spitzer

Prior to the Second World War, I lived in the small town of Ruzhanke for many years. When war broke out between Russia and Germany on June 21, 1941, there was a great panic in the town. Many Jews ran away from the town in order to go further east. I, too, left with my two older sons. On the way, a Russian truck driver let us sit up on his truck, but when he ran out of gas, my sons went back home on foot and I continued on towards the small town of Mir. My third son, who was then a pupil at a trade school, also returned home.

On the first day of the war, the Soviets captured 7 German parachutists as they made their descent. They were shot and then hanged. A few days later, when the Germans came into Ruzhanke, the local Gentiles told the Germans that the Jews had shown the Russians where the German parachutists had landed and one of the Gentiles, a Polish woman, a big anti-Semite, informed the Germans that many Jewish communists lived in the town and that the Jewish communists had taken part in the murder of the German parachutists. The Germans thereupon selected 72 Jews, young and old. They were taken out behind the town, severely tortured and then shot. The Germans shot both my sons at that time – one was 20 years old and the other - 18.

The Germans tied up my father-in-law, Yona the Tailor, an 85 year old Jew who could no longer walk, and pulled him over the ground to the pit. Then, at the time of the slaughter, the Germans drove all the Jews in the town to the market place. The Germans went into the Jewish homes and took whatever they liked. A few days later, the Germans again shot several Jews whom the Gentiles indicated as being active on behalf of the Soviets.

In the autumn of 1941, the Germans drove out all the Jews in the town to Shtutchin, and on May 6, 1942, a great slaughter took place in Shtutchin in which the Jews were killed. My wife and youngest son were murdered in that slaughter.

As I mentioned earlier, I separated from my two older sons forever and with great difficulty trudged to Mir on June 26, 1941. The roads were filled with Jews carrying bags and little children in their arms. German planes flew low over their heads, shooting at them with machine guns. There were many dead and wounded. People wore out their feet from walking and were left stuck on the road. They were hungry and thirsty. They couldn't get any bread and could hardly drag themselves to a well on account of the very hot weather for a drink of cold water. People would collapse, exhausted, unable to go any further. The Germans came quickly and shot those lying on the ground right on the spot.

When the Germans came into Mir, Russian soldiers were still in the town. Both sides began shooting at one another. The Germans threw incendiary bombs and many wooden houses caught on fire. In panic, people ran into the fields naked. Many Jews were left without a roof over their heads. Many Soviet soldiers were killed while retreating and a large number were taken captive.

A few days after the Germans came into Mir, a local police force was organized and the Gentiles began settling accounts with the Jews. I saw that nothing good awaited me in Mir, so I decided to go to Korelitz, my native town. On the way, however, the Germans captured me and brought me to a camp where there were many Soviet prisoners of war. People soon realized that I was Jewish, and the Gentiles began tormenting me. They began to hit me over the head and I collapsed in pain. They spilled cold water on me and stood next to me and laughed. I suffered a lot at their hands. Later the camp was liquidated and I managed to get to Korelitz in great distress.

The hooligans were already behaving wildly in Korelitz. Every night the local Gentiles would enter Jewish homes and rob Jewish property. There were several robust Jewish boys who got together and offered resistance. There was a lot of fighting. Later, when the Gentile young men became town policemen, they did whatever they wanted to the Jews. They would hit them and rob them.

Once they came into the home of Dovid Nisselevitch, the tailor and beat him up severely. They threw him down on ground and forcefully tore out his gold teeth. He fainted from the intense pain. They spilled cold water over him and carried out all the valuable items from his house. Afterwards, they went into Yoel Mayerovitch's house on Zamliankar Street in the middle of the night. They gave him a severe beating and he was ill a long time afterwards. Only thanks to the fact that he was physically in good shape was he able to endure what he went through. Yoel Mayerovitch later ran away and joined the partisans. He survived the war and now lives in America.

Every day the Germans forced the Jews out to work. They had to collect in one place all the broken machinery that was lying on the roads. And when they would come home exhausted after their hard work, various hooligans would come into their houses. They would beat and rob them. One of those in particular, Bratchkovsky, behaved wildly in Korelitz. The Jews suffered terribly from him.

At the end of 1941, Germans from Novogrudek came into Korelitz and ordered the rabbi and several other Jews to form a Jewish Council. Then we were ordered to wear a yellow patch on our chest and shoulders. The Germans threatened to shoot us if we didn't obey this order. The Jewish Council was forced to carry out all the orders from the German authorities. Every day there were new troubles: the Germans ordered the Jews to hand over all the gold items they had in their possession. The Jews were threatened with the death penalty for not carrying out the order. The Germans took and sent away to Novogrudek everything the Jews handed over.

A few days later, SS men came and ordered all the men – young and old – to assemble on the market place. The Germans selected 100 men from those assembled. The ill and elderly were locked up in the study hall. A large number of policemen guarded them and no one was allowed to give those locked up anything to eat. When a woman approached a policeman she knew with a little package of food, he shot her legs and she was left a cripple.

The next morning, vehicles came and took away the 100 men in an unknown direction. Later, familiar Gentiles came to Korelitz and related that they saw the Jews working and that the Jews asked their relatives to send them money and quilts because they were dying of hunger and sleeping on the streets. Naturally, everyone sent whatever they could with the Gentiles. This was repeated several times. The Gentiles would come and trick the Jews into giving them money and things. When the Jews in Korelitz asked the Gentiles to bring some kind of little letter from their relatives, they answered that the Jews were afraid to write. That was, of course, a big lie. The truth was that the 100 Jews were soon shot and we didn't even know where they were buried.

Familiar peasants from the area would often come to the Jews in Korelitz and suggest that the Jews hide various valuables – money, gold, merchandise, household items – with them. "Anyway", the Gentiles claimed, "when the Germans kill you, rather than having your possessions remain with the Germans, you should give it to us". "Besides", the Gentiles said, "if you manage to survive the war, you can take back your possessions."

On August 15, 1941, many Germans drove through Korelitz and stopped in the town. They immediately went into Jewish houses, pretending to be looking for guns, but stole the best things during their search. Using the pretext that they were looking for guns, they stole Jewish property. A woman from the town of Lotz, whose name was Chcnke, went to the Germans and asked whether one could go to Lotz. She was with a man and an 8 year old boy. The Germans threw them into a cellar where they were kept a half a day and then shot. The same Germans ordered the Jewish Council to send for the town rabbi, Rabbi Yisrael Viernik, and 10 more men. When the rabbi and the 10 men came, the Germans ordered them to carry out to the street all the Torah scrolls, prayer shawls, prayer books and the furniture from the synagogue.

The Germans then set all of this on fire. They also wanted the rabbi to lie on a bonfire to be burned, but they realized that this would take too long. There was a well not far from that place. They wanted to throw the rabbi into the well, but since the well was not deep and the rabbi was tall, they didn't throw him in. Therefore, they tormented him immensely. The Germans tore out his beard together with his flesh. He was bleeding profusely. Besides, they played a game: they threw his beard into the fire. They said that if the beard remained lying on the fire, they would also lay the rabbi on the fire and burn him, and if the wind blew the beard away, they would free the rabbi. The wind blew the rabbi's beard out of the fire, and the Germans freed the rabbi.

The Jews carried the rabbi, who was all covered with blood, home. Then the Germans brought a group of Jews who had been locked up in a cellar to the fire and wanted to burn them. As they were being led to the fire, however, the Jews managed to run into the synagogue. The Germans caught them in the synagogue and shot them on the spot. The next morning the Germans took the rabbi away and brought him to Novogrudek, where they tortured him in jail and then shot him.

No synagogues remained in Korelitz. The Torah scrolls and books were burned. The Jews would assemble in homes and pray in secret.

I saw that nothing good awaited me in Korelitz and that the town was on the point of death, so I decided to go to Novogrudek, a bigger town where more Jews lived. I walked only at night because I was afraid to be seen during the day and besides it was forbidden for Jews to go from one place to another. If a Jew was caught on the way, he would be shot at once. I reached Novogrudek with great fear. It was Friday, August 29. The city was burned. I went into Shlomo Glezer's home. He let me spend the Sabbath with him. Just that Sabbath morning the town was in panic. All the Jews were ordered to assemble in the market place. The Gentiles selected about 50 men, ordered them to dance and while they were dancing, the Gentiles shot them. Gestapo SS men were standing by, playing harmonicas and laughing while watching the Jews performing their death dance.

I realized that I wouldn't be able to arrange my life in Novogrudek either, and since there was no place for me there, I went back to Korelitz. On the way, I met a Gentile who asked me if I was Jewish. I told him my situation. He introduced himself as a Russian major by the name Kuznietsov Mikhael Mikhailovitch. He was staying in the village with many Russian prisoners of war. They were working with the peasants and were organizing a unit of partisans. He took me to a village called Kriniak, gave me a false document attesting that I was a Russian by the name Aleshkevitch Aleksai Vasilevitch, born in Vitebsk, a mute, and a tailor by profession. He arranged for me to work for the village elder's wife who was also a seamstress and who was also from Vitebsk. She told everyone that I was her mute brother. I told the major everything I heard and saw about the Germans. He lived in another village, Slaboda, with the partisans' staff. The major would often come to see me and I would give him information. And so I pretended to be a mute Gentile tailor.

I was once called to the Russian partisans' staff where there were big anti-Semites. They took away my false documents and told me that I could no longer live in the village and that I had to back to Korelitz, where there were Jews. They told me I should make weapons and organize a group of Jews who would be ready to go out to the partisans in the forests.

I went back to Korelitz, to the home of the chairman of the Jewish Council, Shimon Zalivansky. He was a very good person. He wanted to register me, but Lipkan, the secretary, in no way wanted me to be registered. I told the chairman what my goal was in returning to Korelitz and that, in case of a massacre, I would be able to be very helpful thanks to the partisans. The chairman gave a gold watch to the registrar of the administration and I was finally registered and given a document. Work was arranged for me as a tailor with Velvele Kozak. Of course, I was in contact with the partisans. They used to come to see me and I would transmit information to them.

We organized a small group in Korelitz and we wanted to leave and join the partisans. We did our best to make weapons. It wasn't hard to get out of the ghetto, but we took into account the fact that if we escaped from the ghetto, the Germans would kill all the Jews because the Germans had applied a law of collective responsibility regarding the Jews. If one Jew escaped, they would all be punished. These are the people who belonged to the group besides myself: Moshe Shiling, Dovid Lifshitz, Bentshe Gulkowich, Itche Hilert, Helena Kalita, a woman, and also another Dovid Lifshitz, who was free. Partisans would come to him and we were thus in contact with them.

There were only two Germans in Korelitz: the commander and another German. The police, however, caused the Jews much distress. In the town there was a Jew from Lodz, a refugee, named Liebhaber. He spoke German very well. He served as an interpreter for the commander and had a great influence on him. The German commander did not allow the Korelitz police (which consisted solely of local Christians) to behave wildly. The policemen realized that the Jewish interpreter was informing on them to the commander. One night in November 1941, a policeman woke him from his sleep and said that the commander was calling him. When Liebhaber got dressed and went to the commander, the policeman shot him on the way. The policeman's name was Britzkovski.

A young Gentile fellow, Yuzhik, worked for the shoemaker, Avromel Balitnitzky. Yuzhik was a policeman. He once came and arrested the shoemaker's daughter whom he brought to the police station, where she was tortured and violated. She was later shot to death in Novogrudek.

There was a miller in Korelitz, Alter Serebrenik (Saravenik), who was hiding in a village at the home of a Gentile. The police conducted a search and found him. They tied him to the back of a horse with a rope and drove the horse through the town, dragging Alter on the ground. This was in December, 1941. Then they took him to the river, chopped a hole in the ice and pushed him into the water tied to a rope. They submerged him in the freezing water several time. Later he was again dragged through the streets, covered with blood. He was thrown into a stable with horses where he lay unconscious all night long until he was nearly frozen. The Gestapo men came in the morning and were happy with the way the police had dealt with Alter Serebrenik.

There was a 20 year old man, Mordechai Dushkin, in the town. He was healthy and robust, a butcher's son. Whenever the Gentiles would go around robbing Jewish property, he stood up against them and they were afraid of him. Now the Gentiles availed themselves of the opportunity to get revenge and they took him behind the town together with Alter Serebrenik and shot them both. Alter was already anyway a frozen piece of wood. The police took a boy, Yosef Chalib, and told him to dig a hole and ordered him to throw Alter Serebrenik and Mordechai Dushkin into the hole and cover them with dirt. The boy refused. A policeman hit him over the head. Then the boy struck the policeman over the head with the spade and cried out: "Your end will be the same as ours!" Thereupon, the policeman shot him.

The Germans forced us to do the hardest work. They ordered us to load a big truck up with hay in a half an hour and if not, they threatened to shoot us. We loaded the truck and then they ordered us to pull the truck by ourselves, but we in no way could move the truck. Thereupon, the Germans with the Gentiles began beating us with sticks and pushing us, but we still couldn't move the truck. And thus they tormented and beat us the whole time.

At the beginning of December 1941, they already began making the surrounding small towns *Jüdenrein*, cleansed of all Jews. In Turetz, for example, they took half the town's Jews away to the cemetery and ordered them to dig their own graves and shot them. One woman managed to run away from there. She came and told us what had happened.

At the end of 1941, the Germans went away with the police for a few days. No one knew where they had gone. Later we found out from the Gentiles that very many Jews had been killed in Novogrudek. Many Jews in Korelitz had relatives and acquaintances there. We wanted to know what happened in Novogrudek, so we paid a Gentile and asked him to go there and find out the truth about the situation because Jews were not allowed to travel from one town to another. The Gentile came back and brought a letter from a Jew in which he wrote the truth about what had taken place in Novogrudek. We found out that the Jews were driven out of their homes into the street. A selection was conducted. Those with a trade were taken to the former Polish justice building, and the others were shot behind the town. Heartrending scenes were played out at the selection. Children were separated from their parents, husbands from wives: one to live and one to die.

In February 1942, the Germans ordered the Jews to make a ghetto. They had to leave the main streets and move into a few houses. Many families were crowded into each house, and each person could take only what he or she could carry. Up to 50 people lived in each house. They slept in beds with three levels, one person above the other with a 40 cm entrance. They lived in tight conditions and in hunger. Children would ask why the Gentile children were free to go around while they were locked up. The Gentile children would go by the ghetto and tease the Jewish children. They would say that the Jews would be shot anyway. People wept at first, but they slowly got used to their troubles.

Workshops were set up for all craftsmen outside the ghetto. Gentiles would bring a ticket from the administration and the craftsmen had to do everything without money. Other Gentiles, however, would throw in a piece of bread, a potato or something else before going to work. We suffered great distress. We were forced to go out in the intense cold to pull cars which got stuck on the roads. We were beaten with sticks while doing this. When we had already dragged out the cars, the police ordered us to bring water in our hats and wash the tires. Next we had to lick the tires with our tongues and then we had to lick their boots with our tongues. On the way back to the ghetto, the Germans ordered us to undress to our shirt and sing Russian songs. But we sang instead: "When will the redemption come?" and "May the Messiah come already!" This is how we returned and worked again. Many people fell ill. I myself lay in bed four weeks with pneumonia.

## The Liquidation of the Korelitz Ghetto
In May 1942, the Germans summoned the members of the Jewish Council and ordered them to draw up a list of workers who would be sent to work in Novogrudek, women and children as well. We realized that they weren't sending us to work but rather to be killed. People stubbornly refused to go. We were already organized at that time and had some weapons and we made preparations to go to the partisans. However, every morning and every evening they would count the people and if one was missing, everyone was threatened with death. We therefore refused to run away to the partisans out of fear that all the Jews in the ghetto would have to suffer on account of us. There were good people in the Jewish Council and in the Jewish police, and meanwhile they hadn't drawn up the lists.

Several weeks went by and the Germans again summoned the Jewish Council and ordered them to make Korelitz *Jüdenrein* in three days. And if the Jews refused to leave willingly, they would all be shot. There was no other choice. We packed our belongings and started out. At the same time, the Gentiles from the villages were informed that the Jews of Korelitz were going to be taken away to Novogrudek. The Gentiles hurried to Korelitz like locusts and began to trade with the Jews. They exchanged things. The Gentiles loaded their wagons full with Jewish possessions and went home.

The place of assembly was at the market place. Every man was ordered to stand in line, together with wives and children, each next to his family. The children asked where they were being taken and wept. Many Gentiles were standing there, laughing. They were happy about the misfortune of the Jews. The Jews had the feeling that they were parting forever with their beloved town of Korelitz. No one had any illusion that this was the final hour of the Korelitz community.

The elderly and ill that lay in bed and couldn't go to the market place were shot in their homes. We had to carry the dead to the cemetery and bury them. After the fresh victims were laid to rest, the order came to leave Korelitz. Darkness descended on the little town. People wept and some even fainted. They said goodbye to their little town where they were born and raised, to the small town where they had lived their whole life and were now leaving forever.

When the mass of people started to move, some tried to return, but the police pushed them back and threatened to shoot.

Thus we were the living witnesses to the destruction and end of the glorious, old Korelitz community. This was at the end of May 1942.

We walked a whole day in very hot weather 21km to Novogrudek. It was already night when we arrived there. We were taken to the ghetto in Pereshke. It was dark. We could hardly see one another. It was pouring and we were soaked to the bones.

We stood in the street like this for a long time. Then we were taken into the stables.

*[Pages 245-247]*

# Memories Of The Holocaust Period

## Chaya Niegnievitsky – Atlanta, Georgia

### Translated from the Yiddish by Harvey Spitzer

Our family was comprised of 8 persons: our parents and 6 children. It was my fate to be the only one of my unforgettable family to survive.

My parents were honest, hard-working people who made every effort to give their children a good education. We, the younger children, were influenced by our older sister Eshket, who was a very gifted and intelligent girl, and we always wanted to follow her example. She was killed with her husband and two children in the small town of Mir.

When the Germans led away the Korelitz Jews to Novogrudek in the spring of 1942, I was with my family. In the Novogrudek ghetto, we already felt that the Germans were bringing in Jews from surrounding towns to kill them there.

In June 1942, when the *aktion* (slaughter) took place in the Novogrudek ghetto, my sister Rivka and I were in town and the remaining family members were in the orchard buildings, and so we remained alive. Rivka and I, along with some other Jews were designated to go into the barracks and, as we believed, the Jews in the barracks were destined to live. When we got there, however, our places had been taken by other Jews. It was chaotic and the Germans took us back to the Pereshke ghetto. I realized that the ghetto was a trap and that we had to escape. Taking advantage of the opportunity that presented itself in our being led past the work bureau, opposite the jail, Rivka and I broke away from the column of Jews without being noticed and we went up into the attic. I decided to hide there because I worked there with the Molares and I knew every little corner.

I realized that the Molares would not be killed because they were professional people and that they would return to work after the *aktion* and that I would find out more about the situation from them and whether we could leave our hiding place. We lay a long time under the gravel, broken bricks and sand - for 5 whole days without bread or water. When the Molares returned, we became aware of the extent of the tragedy. Many Jews were no longer among the living.

We couldn't stay in hiding any longer. We were tortured by hunger and thirst. I told my sister that I would go out to look for a place of rescue and in case I was unable to give her a sign that I was alive – this meant that she should try to save herself as best she could.

[Page 246]          **Esther Niegnievitsky**     **Dobe Niegnievitsky**

When I got out into the street about to collapse, some Christian children noticed me and knew I was Jewish. They informed a policeman who immediately arrested me and was taking me to the police station. I realized that it was the way to death. With tears in my eyes and with courage, I begged the policeman not to take me to the police station and to give me a chance to save myself. Apparently, my tears and pleading had an effect on him and instead of conducting me to the police station, he took me to the Jews who had remained alive after the *aktion*. He even agreed to bring my sister Rivka from her hiding place and brought her to me. Later, however, she was tragically killed together with my dear parents and brother, Avraham.

I remained alive together with my two younger sisters, Dobe and Gittele, in the Pereshke ghetto, alone, in hunger and need. We had the feeling that our lives were coming to an end and that we had to find a way to save ourselves. At that time, many Jews were already running away from the Novogrudek ghetto to join the partisans in the forests. We already knew that the escapees were with Bielski's unit.

Death lurked all around us. It was imperative that at least a trace of our many-branched family should survive. On March 15, 1943, when the sun had already gotten a little warmer and the snow was beginning to melt, the urge to stay alive also grew stronger. It was then that we decided to escape from the Novogrudek ghetto individually. Our goal was to meet at a certain point near Korelitz.

We quickly got through the barbwire fence surrounding the ghetto, each one separately. We hoped that familiar Christians in Korelitz would help us. Unfortunately, however, Dobe and Gittele were caught around Korelitz and were murdered. And so I lost them forever.

Thus, after escaping from the Novogrudek ghetto, I didn't meet up with my sisters at the arranged point. I trudged around the villages, on the roads and in the forests for two weeks. With the last of my strength, I made my way to a forest where Jews who had escaped from the ghetto after the slaughters were in hiding. We would leave our hiding place at night to look for something to eat. We would go begging from house to house and I often regretted that I had remained alive. We never spent the night in the same place we were during the day. Some hidden Jews were murdered by the Germans as well as by armed partisans. It was a great miracle that I managed to save myself from their murderous hands.

In October 1943, our group of Jews united with Bielski's unit in the Nalibok forest. We were no longer alone in the unit and were protected. I carried out my duties as a partisan: standing on guard and performing other tasks. While in the unit, I got married to my husband, who was a good partisan.

In the summer of 1943, when we were liberated and left the forests, I returned to our former, dear small town of Korelitz. My heart was pained to see how the town had become an orphan. There were no more Jews, the houses had been taken over by local Gentiles, every Jewish house seemed to be weeping and in sorrow. There was no purpose in my staying in Korelitz and after waiting for my husband to return from the Red Army after the war, we both ran away from the cursed ground that was soaked with Jewish blood. That was in September 1945. It took another 4 years until we managed to make our way to America, where we set up home in Atlanta, Georgia.

---

*[Pages 248-249]*

# In The Shadow Of Death

## Chaim-Leib Dvoretsky

### Translated from the Yiddish by Harvey Spitzer

I originally came from Ivyeh and married Teibel Tratsky from Korelitz. My father-in-law, R' Moshe-Shmuel Tratsky, died while still young. He was known in Korelitz as a kind-hearted, good Jew, learned in Torah, who loved to do a favor. He was a lumber merchant and had a good reputation in our small town and in the area. My mother-in-law, Bayle, and her children, Motke and Basha, had fine names in Korelitz and gave charity to the needy. They were murdered in Novogrudek during the great slaughter.

I was in the ghetto in Ivyeh with my family, which consisted of 23 people. I shall never forget the sad day – 9th of *Av* in Ivyeh - the beginning of our great distress. On that day, the Germans assembled men on the market place. These were 200 of the dearest, finest Jews of the town, especially the intelligentsia: rabbis, ritual slaughters, religious judges, teachers and members of other free professions. My dear brother, Shmuel (Molieh), was also taken away from us on that sad day.

Later, the Jews from all the smaller towns of the area were gathered together in Ivyeh, including Jews from Lifnishak, Subotnik, Baksht, Trab, Borisevke, as well as Jewish farmers from the surrounding villages, and on May, 12, 1942, the Germans carried out the most terrible mass slaughter.

During the "selection", others believed that the craftsmen would at least remain alive. Therefore, a family from Ivyeh entrusted their son to a blacksmith from Trab, hoping that he at least would remain alive so that one member of the family would at least survive. The child and the blacksmith, however, were destined to be killed while the parents were left alive and are now in Israel.

The remaining Jews were locked up in a small ghetto which was surrounded by barbwire. We lived in crowded conditions, in hunger and cold, and subject to beatings.

In January 1943, the German regional commander in Lida issued an order requiring that Ivyeh be made *Jüdenrein*, cleansed of all Jews. The Jews were driven out of the ghetto on foot in the bitter cold to the Gavish train station, where formations of freight cars were standing ready and waiting. Some of the Jews were sent to a work camp in Borisov and others to the workshops in Lida. We were among those sent to Lida.

The situation in the Lida ghetto was very difficult at that time. We all knew that we wouldn't remain alive for long, but we had no way out. Teenage boys and girls tried to make contact with partisans. A few actually managed to escape from the ghetto and a few, after escaping, fell into the hands of the anti-Semitic partisans. It was much harder for families with children to escape. We took stock of the situation: Who would accept us with small children? We actually lost hope of being able to save our lives.

One day, as we were awaiting death, a messenger from Bielski's unit came into the Lida ghetto and brought us a letter from Yaacov*. He wrote that we shouldn't wait any longer and escape as quickly as possible and join them in Bielski's unit. He added that, if possible, we should bring a gun; if not, we should come without one. He promised that he would see to it that we would be accepted into the unit.

Here I must note that this letter from Yaacov brought us much hope and courage, and we decided to try to escape from the ghetto. And so, one evening, our family along with another group of Jews broke through the barbwire fence surrounding the ghetto and wandered through the forests, covering a distance of 40km. Thus, hungry and exhausted, we made our way to Bielsky's unit. The first to welcome us were Yaacov and Yoel Mayerovitch. Other Jews from Korelitz were also very friendly to us.

Yaacov would often come to our tent and bring us food and even a pat of butter for the children. He would always come with a smile and comfort us with warm words, reminding us that we would now be able to avenge the spilled, innocent blood of our family members who were tragically and cruelly murdered, and assuring us that we would live to see the liberation.

* Probably Yaacov Abramowich

---

*[Pages 250-254]*
*[Pages LV-LVI –English –abridged:* **see also page 394***]*

# Idel Kagan

## *Michael Walzer-Fass* - Hod Hasharon

### Translated from the Hebrew by Ann Belinsky

An autumn Shabbat evening. A typical Israeli in the "Hilton" Hotel in Tel Aviv. The beginning of November 1970. In the company of Yaacov Abramowich, one of the prominent activists of the "Korelitz Book" committee, I sat at the table with Idel Kagan - one of the biggest business men in England, who had been invited by the government of Israel in the framework of meetings with rich Jews from overseas who have strong attachments with the State of Israel, caring for its fate and willing to put their shoulder to the wheel to help the state with guidance and actions in economic matters.

I did not know Idel Kagan previously, I had only heard his name: a Jewish youth from Novogrudek, who had spent much time in Korelitz before the war with his uncles and grandfather, passed as a youth the "seven departments of hell" in the Novogrudek-Korelitz Ghetto, was with the partisans; and after the war went to England and rose very high in the economic hierarchy. He rose but did not forget his beginnings, and was strongly attached to his partisan friends and with the State. The meeting was organized for me in the framework of the book that people from Korelitz are publishing in remembrance of their town and its good townspeople. This is the same youth Idel Kagan whose feet froze in the icy river water during one of the escapes to the partisans, who returned illegally to the ghetto and was primitively "operated" on with a kitchen knife; this is the same youth who escaped with people of the ghetto via a tunnel and remained alive after the Germans killed most of the escapees. Idel Kagan speaks of those days, on the eve of the war, the few days of happiness in the bosom of his family and the relatives in Novogrudek and Korelitz; of the first days of the war and the selections, the death of his father, mother, sister, uncle and his family; of Berel Kagan his cousin, the partisan who is now in Israel, who also was the only one of his family to remain alive; of the attempts to invest in Israel, of his first days in England, his rise in life, his marriage and building of a family and of his decision to come here forever...

There I was present, looking on the illuminated Jewish face of the man sitting opposite me and telling his story. I knew that the man sitting opposite me - visited Israel no less that fourteen times, and I thought to myself, what is the enormous strength inside this man? What strengthened that youth in those terrible days when he stared death in the face so many times, standing opposite a German firing squad, and would he be able to overcome all these things? What is the strength that helped him to surmount while seeing his beloved ones falling one after other - his father who remained alive after many selections and was killed when he was escaping from the Koldichevo concentration camp, his mother who was murdered with her daughter in one of the selections in the ghetto, while Idel, still recovering from his foot "operation" was miraculously saved while lying on a bed of wooden boards under a pile of rags and pillows, which the murderers had thrown there, not discovering his presence.

What made it possible for him, after all this, to continue, to move around Germany, Russia and Poland and to try his luck here and there and to begin a new life in England, to succeed and remain loyal to his destiny - to his people, to his friends and to his dear ones?

A common saying is that when Fate invites a man to meeting at a certain place, the man will cross all the obstacles to arrive at the meeting place and meet his fate. Idel's fate waited for him in London - there he started on the road to his destination which is not yet final; for because of his many journeys to Israel - it seems, that Idel Kagan can expect a rosy future in the State of Israel.
The cup of tea on my table has cooled a long time ago, time passes as if instinctively for the guest, and I have no desire to turn to the cup and sip from it - but to listen, more and more about what happened to this man. And Idel Kagan speaks as if he is drawing you a living picture from the valley of death, from the ghetto and its environs; and on the other hand - his struggle for life after the war from his struggle and the beginnings of his steps in Great Britain. The names of his dear and loved ones that he mentions seem engraved on the board of his heart forever; Berel Kagan the partisan, his

cousin who is older by several years and is sitting here with us in the hotel - to whom the youth Idel strived to meet in the forests to the partisans.

You hear again about the terrible horrors of the Nazis, their monstrous actions against the Jews, actions that still no-one has been able to get up and explain their meaning: Why? How could this thing happen?

In Poland they were used to seeing the Jewish *Litvaks* (Lithuanians) who dwelled in the cities and towns around the Russian border - proud courageous Jews with their clear and practical (way of) thinking and indeed this Judaism extracted from it famous and glorious names in literature, philosophy, medicine, technology and economics all over the world. In front of me sat such a practical *Litvak*, who always does what is necessary without getting overly excited or vocal.

***

Idel Kagan grew up in an ideal family in the city of Novogrudek, his father Yaacov and his uncle Moshe married two sisters Dvorah and Shoshana Gurevitz from Korelitz. The two families each had two children and they lived together with real friendliness and devotion. Idel's father had a shoe and sandal factory and shop. The youth Idel therefore grew up in a pleasant family atmosphere. He would come to Korelitz, as the way his older cousin Berel came, to his maternal grandmother and to his uncles. His friends from Korelitz speak about the handsome and always neat youth who would come every year to Korelitz, who loved its people and thirstily drank up the stories of the youth and adults. Many stories that Korelitz was always blessed with.

When the war broke out and the Jews in the towns and cities of Poland saw the poisoned German arrows were mainly aimed at destroying them - they began to seek a way to escape, to hide: every town thought that they would be able to exist in another town. When a deputation of the Kagan family was sent to the Korelitz family in order to check the situation, Idel Kagan together with his older cousin Berel Kagan, was with the group which passed the German guards on foot and arrived with their lives in danger to Korelitz, only to see and to be in a sclection that already was done there the next morning and to be saved from death by a miracle. They quickly returned on foot to Novogrudek in order to pass on the bad news that the ring of destruction had encircled everything. Everything.

In the first period of the war, when he is only 12 years old, Idel Kagan works collecting stones of destroyed houses and in other types of work. His father and brothers change their shoe factory to something more useful - harness-making. And among other things - they make saddles that the German army needs for their horses. But even this craft does not help for too long. The uncle Moshe Kagan, his wife Shoshka and their son Eliezer are executed in one of the first selections. From all the family, only Berel Kagan remains alive, thanks to his work as a locksmith in the barracks of the German army. After the selection he remains with Idel Kagan's family in the Novogrudek ghetto.

Beatings and abuse are the only tunes accompanying the work and every moment their lives are hanging on a thread. In one of the selections he is brought in front of a firing squad and waits to be shot. Idel tries to turn his back in order not to look death in the face. But the German turns him back again with his white-gloved hand to face the rifle barrels. Another miracle: the execution is postponed because in the eyes of the executors it seems to be too normal a death, and they decide to add them to the next selection which will take place in the next few days. In the meanwhile he stands to be executed in another selection: a selection of children and youth. Idel puts on his father's clothes in order to look older, and somehow passes this selection and remains alive.

The area of Novogrudek-Korelitz was well known in Poland for its large ancient forests. In these forests during the war years, Jewish partisans as well as Polish and Russian partisans organized themselves into groups, and likewise bands of robbers in various dress organized into groups with the aim of stealing and looting and especially stealing from and murdering Jews. In order to save their lives, the Jewish partisans in Poland more than once had to fight against those seeking their death amongst the Polish partisans and others who saw as a good deed and right to kill a Jew or to inform on him and hand him over to the Germans. The Jewish partisans were exposed to the danger of death from the various Gentile partisans and they had to be careful of bandit groups or of any Gentiles, but many of the Jewish youth sought flight from this (time of) great distress by escaping to the thick forests that the Germans were afraid to penetrate: the actual feeling of holding firearms gave security to the Jewish partisans, knowing that here at least if they fell - they would fall in battle with weapons in their hands and would not be led like sheep to their deaths. When this awareness of the partisans matured in some of the Jewish youth, his cousin was one of the first who joined the partisans in the forest. The youth Idel also began to search for a way to the partisans and to his cousin. The story of his attempt to join the partisans, an attempt that ended with frozen feet, is written in the Novogrudek Yizkor Book by Idel Kagan himself. The failed attempt to escape led to his being considered an invalid in the ghetto and even to be "illegal" as he was no longer registered in the ghetto.

Returning to the ghetto after the first escape, he was comforted at least that he had returned to his family and relations, but the Germans did not let this illusion remain for long. The "selections" came one after the other and in each, whole parts of the ghetto were exterminated in violent deaths. After his mother and sister were killed by the Germans, Idel thought he would hold his father's hand and pass the rest of the way with him. In days of despair his father planned to commit suicide with his son, but his father was sent abruptly to another camp. There he was killed during an attempted escape.

***

**The Tunnel***

The tunnel that the people of the Novogrudek-Korelitz ghetto and others from the area dug is one of the biggest and most daring that was planned in the most modern way. Several hundred people surreptitiously overcame the Germans, the informers and the collaborators, and found a way to maintain discipline in the weak-characters and the pessimists. Over several months they dug a tunnel of several hundred meters and finally all left via it to freedom, which unfortunately only part of them achieved in the end, for the Germans sensed their escape when they were on their way out and killed many, while others were killed while running away. Idel, who had tried already once to escape alone in this way and failed, made a short cut together with his friend. In his escape he discovered the partisans and these brought him quickly to his cousin.

***

The war finished when Idel Kagan was 15. Satiated with suffering, but with improved health. With the end of the war, he underwent a series of surgeries on his feet because of the frozen toes and thus began to return to his strength. His hometown no longer existed; Poland is a blood-saturated country and it is not suitable to remain there. Idel decides to emigrate to England to a family relative. After a short time of staying in England, he tries to come to Israel. In Israel he finds his friends from the struggle and suffering and hopes, but the time is the Period of Austerity which does not encourage the *aliyah* of young people, and Idel returns to England.

He begins to work as an independent, as a wage-earner. The period is one of economic growth in all of the Western world: free enterprise and prosperity

---------------------------------------------

* see the research of Mr Yizhak Alperovitz, Yad VaShem

join hands and very many who are talented and blessed with good luck succeed and rise very high. Factory after factory is built and Idel Kagan also begins to think about himself. He resurrects the Kagan family. He marries Barbara Steinfeld and they have three children: Michael (after his uncle Moshe), Jeffery (the father - Yaacov) and Dvorah (his mother).

*[Page 253]* **Idel Kagan and his wife Barbara (Steinfeld) - Tel Aviv, November 1970**

But the road has not yet ended.

Idel Kagan sitting in front of us in the Hilton hotel in Tel Aviv on an autumn Shabbat evening - his eyes and heart are both given to the memories of those days and to the future. His many visits in Israel only strengthen and connect him to his friends and to the land. "I will come" he says, I will come forever. And I am certain that it will happen.

---

[Pages 255-262]

# The First Partisan From Korelitz

## Ben-Ir
### [This is a pen name ="A son of the town" - HS]
### (Pen name of Yaacov Abramowich - AB)

### Translated from the Yiddish by Harvey Spitzer

Dovid Lifshitz, son of Aharon and Sarah-Rachel, graduated from the Polish public grade school. Since he came from a large family and they could hardly make a living, David stopped studying and went to work with his brother Berel in a hairdresser's establishment (wig makers), which enabled him to help his family. He was a member of *Hashomer Hatsa'ir* youth movement and belonged to the town band. He was always happy and full of life.

Little by little, his family emigrated abroad. The majority, including his parents, went to pre-state Israel. Dovid remained in Korelitz all alone because he had to go into the Polish army.

In 1942, a ghetto was set up in Korelitz. Their big house became part of the ghetto. Our family was moved into their house. Jews from surrounding communities and from the small town of Tsirn were also settled in their house. They made bunk beds and people even slept on the floor.

The situation went from bad to worse. The SS people and their leader Henzike would issue all kinds of decrees and would beat the Jews mercilessly. The Germans from the local headquarters and armed forces, Birkritz, Ehrhardt and others, forced the Jews to make all kinds of "contributions". The Jews did everything possible to pay the ransom and stay alive. If you didn't obey the order, you paid with your life.

Dovid and I (I was very young then) would very often have a talk in the evening. We mainly discussed the question: What can we do? Dovid let me in on a secret: He met with Moshke Funt from Ivenitz (Yisrael Slonimsky's cousin) and Moshke promised him that he would soon come and take him and enroll him in a group of partisans. I asked him not to forget about me and my brother Gavriel. He promised me that if the plan succeeded, he would think about other young men from Korelitz, including us.

A short time went by and Dovid was no longer seen in the ghetto. He carried out his plan. I hoped and waited for him to keep his promise, but it was in vain.

Dovid joined a group of partisans and carried out various operations against the Germans. His name became famous: a good Jewish partisan.

A group of Christian and Jewish partisans, including Dovid and his friend Moshke Funt from Ivenitz, marched into the small town of Nalibok. Their task was to take over the police station. The Germans from Ivenitz, however, unexpectedly found out about the plan, and a large force of German soldiers arrived in Nalibok from Ivenitz. The partisans fortified themselves in a church in Nalibok. The Germans surrounded the church and, using a loud speaker, ordered the partisans to surrender voluntarily. The heroic partisans, however, did not give themselves up alive into the hands of the Germans. They kept shooting at the Germans until their last bullet. The whole group of partisans was murdered. Among them were also our first partisan, Dovid Lifshitz, and his friend Moshke.

His sister Chana and brother Moshke live in Israel and another sister lives abroad.

---

*[Pages 256-258 - Yiddish]*
*[Page LI – English – abridged:* **page 389***]*

# The Heroism Of The Korelitz Young Men

## Reuben Dushkin

*Ben-Ir* **(Yaacov Abramowich) – English text**

Reuben Dushkin, a meat dealer by occupation, was a quiet, honest, hard-working man with a large family. His eldest daughter, Sara, married Shlomo Navitsky, and the two men operated one meat market.

In 1941, as the Nazis drew near, the peasants and townspeople of Korelitz set about pillaging Jewish homes, going from one house to the next and dragging out furniture and other household goods.

A band of hooligans came to Reuben's home, sacks ready to be filled. But Reuben and his sons - Yankl, Motel and Hayyim - and son-in-law beat them back. The hooligans bided their time until the Germans came into Korelitz. But the Jews knew what was coming, and those who managed to flee and join the partisans gave a good account of themselves.

**Coordinator's note:**
The **Yiddish text** is similar to the English text, but **includes additional information** as follows:

**(Translated by Harvey Spitzer)**
His wife, Munia, helped him in his work as a butcher.

When the Germans came into Korelitz and they and their collaborators began rounding up and tormenting Jews, Reuben's daughter, Chaykeh, managed to warn her brother, Yankel and her brother-in-law Shlomo to escape to the forests. She was unable, however, to warn another brother, Motel, who worked in a steam mill in another part of town. He was tortured to death by the local hooligans.

Yankel, Chaykeh and two children survived. They joined the partisans and left for America after the war.

---

# The Korelitz Partisan Yaacov Slutzky
## *Ben-Ir* (Yaacov Abramowich) – English text

Yaacov Slutsky was a young farmer, but when he had to flee from Korelitz and joined the partisans he undertook an important task - to procure weapons. He went about the countryside, picking up discarded rifles and bits of metal, which he then fashioned into crude but serviceable firearms, mines and bombs, which he later used to blow up German communication lines.

**Coordinator's note:**
The **Yiddish text** is similar to the English text, but **includes additional information** as follows:
### (Translated by Harvey Spitzer)
He was born in Korelitz in 1914. His parents were Yitzchak and Tcherna Slutzky. His father was a leather tanner, but he also had a wagon and would bring merchandise from Baranovitch for the shopkeepers in Korelitz.

Yaacov attended a Polish public school and also had private instruction in Hebrew and Yiddish. He loved to read.

**Yaacov Slutzky**

*[Page 258]*

He escaped from the ghetto in 1943 and joined the Bielsky partisans. He and several of the partisans were killed when one of the mines he himself had prepared and planted under the railway exploded prematurely.

He carried out many acts of revenge and was highly respected by the Christian partisans.

*(The English text says he was a farmer, but that is not mentioned in the Yiddish text)*

**[Page 259 - A Drill in the Town by Michael Beigin- NOTE: This is actually a copy of Page 159 and appears here by mistake -H.S.**

---

## The Heroism Of The Korelitz Young Men, Ctd.

[Page 260-1-Yiddish]
[Page LI - English]
# Hershel  Shkolnik ( Hershel the Carpenter)
*Ben-Ir* (Yaacov Abramowich) – English text

 Hershl the Carpenter (the best in Korelitz) was taken to the Novohorodek concentration camp in 1942 and put to work in his craft. But he also succeeded in fashioning an escape tunnel from the ghetto, and succeeded in getting to the partisan camps, where he fashioned stocks for rifles. After the war he made his way to Israel and joined his daughter Vital in Jerusalem, where he continued with his craft.

**Coordinator's note:**
The **Yiddish text** is similar to the English text, but **includes additional information** as follows:

**(Translated by Harvey Spitzer)**
His wife, Sonia, died shortly before the holocaust. She had a store in Korelitz which her daughters, Vital and Merke, managed when she got older. Another daughter, Ester, was still in school at that time.

Vital went to live in the Land of Israel and encouraged her sister Ester to join her there. Merke got married and she and her husband managed the store in Korelitz. They and their children were murdered by the Germans.

Hershl was kept alive thanks to his skill as a carpenter.

---

*[Pages 261-262]*

# Yoel Mayerovitch

### *Ben-Ir* (Yaacov Abramowich)
### Translated from the Yiddish by Harvey Spitzer

We called Yoel Mayerovitch Yoel Moshkes (Moshke's son). He was of average height, broad shouldered and well-built. He and his brothers and sister managed the dry goods store in Korelitz. His sisters sewed articles of clothing for the business. They also cultivated their fields.

Their mother died. His sister Chaya got married and also operated a dry goods store in Korelitz. Her husband, Hershel Slutzky, came from a fine, respectable family in Tsirn. They led a fine and respectable life.

When the Germans marched into Korelitz, his brothers were among the 105 men who were led out to their death. Yoel and his sisters, Nechama, Sarah and Minieh, and their aunt Kreine moved into our house because it was too dangerous to live in the center of town. The Germans and police used to rob and beat everyone without pity and their first victims were those who lived in the center of town.

A few weeks later, the police took Yoel away. They beat him mercilessly at the police station. They broke his hand and tortured him. Then they threw him out into the yard almost on the verge of collapse. Yoel, the strong fellow, came to, ran through the woods and came to our yard. We heard someone falling in the yard near the door. I opened the door and found Yoel there almost in a faint. With all my strength, I brought him into the house and revived him because he had fainted from his serious wounds. When he came to, he told us that they asked him for money and items at the police station. When he refused to give them these things, they beat him until he lost consciousness.

We began to think how we could help him. Yoel was weeping. He said that the thugs had broken his bones and asked us to save him because he couldn't endure the pain.

His sister Nechama and I went through the fields to Dr. Livitzky, who wrote a note that Yoel had fallen and broken a hand (He was afraid to write that the police had done this) and sent him to a surgeon in Novogrudek.

We immediately hired a wagon and his sisters, Sarah and Minieh, went along with him.

At seven o'clock in the morning there was a knock on the door. The police were looking for Yoel.

----- "Where is he?"

------"You took him away", I answered, "and didn't bring him back."

Later we found out that the police had dug a pit and wanted to shoot him. That's how he was saved from death.

When the Korelitz ghetto was liquidated, the sisters met with Yoel. We were together in the Novogrudek ghetto.

Yoel was the only one from his large family to remain alive. We met in the forests. After the war, Yoel was drafted into the Red Army. He was wounded and came on a visit to Novogrudek. We wouldn't let him return to the army. We included him in our list of family members, and he went with us. We reached Italy and stayed together the whole time. We were in a *kibbutz* (group) near Rome.

We wanted to take him to pre-state Israel with us, but his family in America sent for him. He naturally wanted to meet some members of his family, so we said goodbye in 1947.

He went to America, got married, adjusted, worked and made a living. He kept up a correspondence with us the whole time. He promised to come see us in Israel, but the heroic, good Yoel suddenly died on January 29, 1967, 20 Tevet 5728.

---

[Pages 263-264]

# The Death Of Korelitz Boys

## Yaacov Abramowich

### Translated from the Yiddish by Harvey Spitzer

| Binyamin Shatzky | Leibish Bernstein | Gavriel Abramowich |

Groups of Jews from Korelitz were taken away to the T.A.D.T. [German firm] work camp in Dvoretz during the German occupation. In a small, broken-down house that was hardly big enough for one family, bunk beds were made-one above the other. And 30-40 men even slept on the floor if there was room. People were infested with lice and covered with scabs. There was no food.

One day, people were standing in small groups. Something was in the air, the Germans were preparing something. The camp director summoned the president, Novik, and the vice president of the Jewish council and told them that the work at the Dvoretz camp had ended, but since the Jews in the camp were useful, he was sending all the workers to another place to work. The first group was to consist solely of carpenters who had to prepare barracks for the workers in the new place. In addition, he said, if one of the carpenters was missing, they would all pay with their lives.

My brother Gavriel and Binyamin Shatzky, who were both quilt makers by profession, were called into the Jewish council. They were told to prepare bootlegs from canvas hoses. The carpenters were ordered to prepare small blocks as shoes for barefooted Jews because many were walking barefoot. Who knows where they would be taken? At least they should have shoes!

The work and preparations for leaving the camp went on at a fast tempo. It didn't take long, however. In the winter of 1943, the camp was surrounded by machine guns. Many vehicles with German murderers came for that purpose.

They began to lead away the unfortunate Jews. They led them straight to the ditches which had been dug not far from Dvoretz. The Jews were then thrown alive into the ditches. Some of the Jews in the camp prepared hide-outs. Some ran through the camp confused, not knowing what to do, looking for ways to stay alive.

My brother Gavriel, Binyamin Shatsky and Leibish Bernstein hid in a small house which was on a side near a fence. Gavriel and Binyamin were in the attic – Leibish under a bed. When the thugs were finished with their cruel work in the camp and they didn't see any more Jews - they left Dvoretz. Only a few walked around with guns.

Then the peasants made a dash into the camp to rob the remaining Jewish possessions. When a peasant came into the house where the three boys were hiding and had remained alive - he found my brother and his friend. They gave him a present and he promised he wouldn't tell anyone about them. He told them that when it got dark, they should climb over the wire fence and go on further. Leibish Bernstein, who was lying under the bed, stayed there miraculously. He had a desire to drink and was very thirsty. Finding a bottle containing a fluid, he took a good drink. It was brandy. He overheard what the peasant said to his friends.

The peasant reported this to a few workers, one of whom was called Korileh. Korileh went up into the attic and brought down the two terrified boys who were shot. Their bodies were then burned.

Leibish stayed under the bed and heard everything. When it got dark, he went out of the camp. He met some more friends who also managed to be saved from death. He told them about everything. Wandering over the roads in freezing weather, Leibish's toes became frostbitten and he couldn't walk any further. He died on the way.

I met the group on the way and they told me about it.

---

*[Page 265]*

# Shaul Kopilovitz

## Bezalel-Kalman Osherovitz

### Translated from the Hebrew by Ann Belinsky

Shaul, the son of Yaacov and Haya Bedana Kopilovitz, died in Israel. He was the son of a respected, observant family. He was involved in the Jewish social life in the area. Before the Second World War, Shaul lived in Novogrudek. When the city was conquered by the Nazis, his family was annihilated and he was sent to a work camp. Since he was an excellent motor mechanic, the Germans wanted to exploit his specialized talents for their own diabolical aims, as they did with many skilled Jews, who were left alive all for the time they were of use. However Kopilovitz did not acquiesce in this situation, and once, when fixing a car, he managed to evade the eyes of the Nazi guards and escape to the Naliboki Forest, there he joined Bielski's partisan regiments.

During his movements from one place to another, he caught a severe chill with a bad cough, which could be heard from a distance and could have caused his fighting friends to be captured by the enemy. In order to prevent this danger he distanced himself from his friends and lived a solitary life in difficult conditions and without any medical attention. His health deteriorated until he developed tuberculosis, and when the area was liberated by the Russian Army, Kopilovitz returned to Novogrudek, in a critical and almost terminally ill condition. Thanks to the devoted and dedicated treatment of his second wife, he slowly improved until he was totally cured. However his health remained unstable -he suffered from chronic asthma all his life. When he made *aliyah* to Israel with his wife in 1951, there was no limit to his happiness and joy. Here it was as if his youth was renewed and he was aware of all that was going on in Israel, especially with regard to security matters. He was wondrous of all that he saw here, loved everything and everyone, especially the young generation of builders and fighters. Despite his very social character in the Diaspora, here he preferred to isolate himself at home and was not outstanding in society.

When Shaul Kopilovitz died, the last remnant of this dear and honorable family disappeared.

---

[Pages 266-267]

# THE HERO – EPHRAIM

## Fruma Gulkowich-Berger

**Dedicated to my cousin, Ephraim Gulkowich, who fell in battle (May, 1944), serving in the Tchkalovske partisan unit.**

**As translated from the Yiddish in her book
"With Courage Shall We Fight"**

"Why? Why? If there is any sense in death,
I will take revenge for you" swears Ephraim, the Partisan.
Yesterday, still suffering in the ghetto, with a bowed back,
Having seen that there were no miracles today
He searched for an idea.

A quiet voice called in the black night.
It came from the big, mass grave, from the deepest pit.
"I see the vision of light and hear the whisper from my bride,
'Remember, you must take revenge for all of us.'"

"Now I see their final look, from their last hour,
The shudders of the final agony of mothers and fathers.
And so many little hands are calling me now.
'You must take revenge for every slaughtered child.'"

"I will not forgive the murderers.
Revenge for you is my purpose in life,
I will demand blood for blood.
To destroy the enemy, I will fight with courage."

Forward, forward he races on his white horse,
Nimble as a hare, he does not touch the ground.
The automatic rifle on his shoulder,
the automatic pistol in his hand.
He carries fire to the enemy, wherever he goes.

Like a flaming bird, as an eagle he flies,
With pride he wants to carry the name "Jew".
The first in the fight, as a tiger, a beast,
He brings the enemy new destruction.

But he fell in the battle,
The Partisan Ephraim,
Even the gentiles mourned for him.
There by the mound, near the tall tree,
Lies a proud "Jew," hardly twenty years old.

He left the world a testament, a pledge,
To carry the spirit of the Hasmoneans of long ago,
To take revenge for all those who were so early destroyed
By the murderers, and taken away from the world.

---

*[Page 267]* - <u>Coordinator's note:</u> In the original Korelitz Yizkor book, there was a continuation here, of the poem "The Ghetto" on *page 226* (original). In this book, the poem "The Ghetto" appears in its entirety on **pages 221-222. A.B.**

---

*[Pages 268-269]*

# A PARTISAN

## Fruma Gulkowich-Berger

### As translated from the Yiddish in her book
### "With Courage Shall We Fight"

*[Coordinator's comment - This poem is the second and third part of a trilogy of poems appearing under the title of "Jewish Partisans" in the book "With Courage Shall We Fight". The first part appears in this book under the title of "Jewish partisans" on **page 203**. A.B.]*

The hour has struck, 'tis time to take a stand.
A call to battle! Quickly take the gun in hand!
The ash of murdered ones the wind has blown.
With blood of millions is my courage sown.

I stand here on guard - a shot rends the air,
For vengeance it calls! For the mission I bear.
My struggle is just, this in my soul I feel,
The enemy to destroy   that is my goal.

The camp is aroused, to their arms they go,
The bullets are flying to and fro,
With earnest piety, sacred as prayer,
To strife called "guerilla" into battle we dare.

The night is descending, take stock of the dead,

Death stalks our path, but for this we're prepared!
Over dense forests now onward I bend,
With gun at my shoulder, with pistol in hand.

And if this is our fate, since the world has us betrayed.
With courage shall we fight, with gun and with grenade!
The bright days pass, 'fore me dark shadows rise.
My comrade fell today, gloom grips me in its vise.

I stand like a guard at the hour I'm free,
At my sigh the trees seem to mourn with me,
Lines of misfortune still etched in my face,
Stone and victim cry out, the loss to replace!


I can still feel the tremor, the horror, the rage
Through blood-soaked whips of my holocaust-age,
From mountains of corpses goes my wandering soul,
With gun on my shoulder through dense forests I roam.

Sole survivor am I, no place need I hasten,
For miles and miles death its grim toll has taken...
Victory...how can I with triumphant tread
Join the nations that march, while I mourn for these dead?

Many an image appears 'fore my eyes,
Time like an arrow from its bow can fly,
But forget shall I never that season's black day
Of blood and of flame that has shadowed my way.

*[Page 269]*

**A Group of Partisans**

**Standing from right to left:** Herzl Nohimovksi, ---, Fruma Gulkowich-Berger, Tuvia Bielski, --

[Pages 270 – 272 –Yiddish, below]
[Pages LVII-LVIII – English, abridged: **see also page 395**]

# The Visit To Korelitz After The War

## Yaacov Abramowich

### Translated from the Yiddish by Harvey Spitzer

Ben-Zion and I travelled from Novogrudek to Korelitz in a wagon. As we got closer to Korelitz, having covered 21 km, our hearts began to beat strongly and our faces changed color. We looked at each other without talking, but we understood and knew what was awaiting us.

When we got closer to the steam mill which had belonged to Reuven Begin and Tartak, we met many Christians with wagons filled with grain, waiting for their turn at the mill. Glancing around, we looked for a Jew, a partner of the mill. Unfortunately, no one. Where is the happy, cheerful Begin, who would always be at the place? Everything is destroyed, as if no one had ever been there....

The mill is in operation. We go on further. We are both quiet, carrying the same pain in our broken hearts. We came closer to the Zalamenke spring which used to give the Korelitz Jews fresh, clean water. Once, many women, men and children would stand on line and there was always enough water. Now no one is seen there....

We're approaching the center of the blacksmith shops – to the left, the Zapale Hill. Every day the sounds of hammer and anvil would ring out here. Yudke the smith, Yaakov Slutzky, Avraham Lifchin with his children, Alter Abramovitch and many more who worked here. ... Today it's quiet. Everything is closed.

In Feigel-Tsire's hotel – everything is quiet, no one is here. You don't see a single Jew here.

Here is Yankel Zalemanski, the egg dealer's, house. Yankel, with his red beard, would stop the Christians who came into the town from the villages of Zapalie, Liesok, Kalzenoi, etc, and would take them to sell grain and chickens. He would then bring them to his yard and buy products from them. It was really very noisy there. No there's no one! Quiet.

We get closer to our house. Our hearts begin to pound. We stop and go into the house. We started crying. We found peasants living in the house. I told them that I was the former owner. I was born there and lived there many years with my family until the Germans came in and drove us all away.

The peasants welcomed us, gave us food and told us that they were from Russia and were allotted the house. They said that they were not responsible for the misfortune that had befallen us. As we left, they also gave us a small loaf of bread, a small piece of butter and few eggs.

With a pain in my heart and with tears in my eyes, I said goodbye to my house. My beloved mother, my brother are no longer there - everything lost!

We go by the large house which belonged to Shlomke Oberzhansky, the town elder. There would always be a lot of noise in his house. People would drink beer and buy cigarettes there. There were always a lot of customers. It was always merry and gay there. Now there's no one.

We don't meet any Jews. The whole town is empty. You don't see anyone. Where are you, my dear Korelitz Jews?

We're at the synagogue yard. We see our community synagogue which was always happy and cheerful with the voices of Jewish children – Shlomeles, Yankeles, Dovidels. And of our warm-hearted teacher. Now it's quiet. Everything is lost!

And we see both study halls. Not one Jewish word is heard. Here is Rabbi Viernik's house from which we used to hear words of Torah. People would go to the rabbi for an answer to their questions and for a decision on a matter relating to Jewish law. Now it's quiet, empty as if no Jews had ever been or lived there.

We come to the cemetery, but you can't tell that there was once a cemetery here. Something of a stone sticks out – this means a gravestone. Everything is broken, desolate and destroyed.

We go down to Mill Street. Here I see my Uncle Ezra Pomerchik's house, where we spent our childhood years. This was a house for everyone. We were a group called the "big ones". We used to gather all together: my uncle, my aunt and the whole family. We spent a lot of time together and joked. Every Saturday night my Aunt Liebe used to cook for all the company – sometimes oat grits with chicken fat and potato pancakes, too; sometimes, lentil soup and a bun for everyone; sometimes potatoes with herring. We would all sit together at the table, eat and have a good time. My aunt and uncle were not like old people, but like our friends. They used to take part in our discussions and show an interest in and about everyone and everything. We loved them and had a lot of respect for them.

In their house we now find a Korelitz peasant who has his own house, but this house is bigger, better and nicer and cost him nothing – Jewish toil in vain. He just took it without asking anyone. I ask him:

"Where are the owners, my good, smart Aunt Liebe, my Uncle Ezra, Berel? Where are they?" - No one answers.

I see the lovely orchard behind the house which the children had planted by themselves. Everything is in place, but the people are no longer here.

We meet a Christian woman from Mill Street, Todoretchke. She recognized us and asked how we were and what we were doing there.

____ "You're still alive?" !!, she wonders in surprise.

____ "Yes", I answer. "We're still alive and we'll outlive you. We're looking for Jews from Korelitz", we say.

_____"Yes, There is Zelde Mashke, the carpenter's daughter", she answers. "Sadzhie the saddle-maker, Michael Kagan, Motel the saddlemaker and his son Leibe."

____ "Where are they?", we ask.

_____"You'll find them", she answers.

We go on looking for the few individuals who are in the town, a trace of the hundreds of Korelitz Jews.

We go past Ben-Zion's house, but we don't go in. We already knew what to expect...

We met with the few remaining Jews and we wept together. Each of us knew the same news.

With broken hearts, we returned to Novogrudek. We had taken a good look at our beloved little town and said goodbye to it. Who knows if we'll ever again be in Korelitz, the Korelitz of this world below?

*[Page 273]*

# THE FALLEN

*[Pages 273-274]*

**SHLOMO STOLER**

**(ANONYMOUS - BEN IR)**

**Notes on the Hebrew text by Ann Belinsky**

Most of the information appears in the Yiddish translation on **pages 264-5**. **The following additional information appears in Hebrew (below):**

He was born in 1926.
After the war he was in displaced persons camps in Italy for several years and came from Italy to Palestine [AB - on the ship "Dov Hoz" in 1946].
When the War of Independence broke out he came to Israel and lived in the house of his uncle Moshe Stoler.
Shlomo fell in the battle near Latrun, on the 4th of *Iyar*, 5708. (13th May, 1948) [AB - his place of burial is unknown. His memory is marked by a plaque at the Mt Herzl military cemetery in Jerusalem]

[Pages 274-275]

# Shlomo Stoler (The Little *Keiderel*)

## *BEN-IR*

### Translated from the Yiddish by Harvey Spitzer

He was born in Korelitz. His father Zelig and his mother Toibe were quiet, calm parents. His father was always content with what he had.

Zelig worked in construction. When construction work was unavailable, however, he had a horse and would go around in the villages with all kinds of merchandise and sell his wares to the peasants or barter with old clothes.

His son Shlomo completed public school and helped his father feed the family. Together with his father, he would go around the villages all week long. They would come home for the Sabbath with their earnings: money and provisions of food.

This is what he did until the war. In 1942, the Korelitz Jews were transferred to the ghetto in Novogrudek. In August 1942, when the Korelitz Jews were murdered in a great massacre, a small number miraculously saved themselves, including Shlomo and his brother. For months they went around the villages around Korelitz along with other teenagers from Korelitz. Shlomo was familiar with the area from earlier times when he used to go around with his father. They went around like this until the winter. Some Christians would give them a small loaf of bread, a bottle of milk. Sometimes they slept in a barn or in a storage pit for potatoes. They spent the day in the woods or in the bushes.

There were no more Jews there. Christians were afraid to let a Jew into their houses on account of the Germans or were just unwilling to save any Jews. As he was wandering about like this, Shlomo found out that there was a group of partisans under the direction of the Jewish commander, Tuvia Bielski and his brothers.

With great effort, he reached the group led by Chaim Abramovich, a young man from Korelitz. Chaim took him into his group. From the start, Shlomo's devotion and courage were in evidence.

His abilities were revealed when Bielski's group was sent to the Nalibok forest. The whole area was full of partisans. Bielski's unit alone numbered about 1,200 members. Food was naturally a problem. Shlomo was made a group leader by an order from Commander Bielski. They went to the area around

Korelitz, into the villages which were under the nose of the Germans. "Bring back a lot of food: grain, meat, etc." The partisans who went with him were amazed how capable and proud he was. They liked him a lot. He was modest.

After the liberation, Shlomo left the forests and went to Italy and from Italy he came to Israel. He learned a trade and supported his family honorably. He often visited my family. He asked me, "How can I help you?" He asked if I needed any money, or if I wanted him to teach me his trade, which was a way to earn a lot of money.

He was drafted into the Israel Defense Forces and fell in battle near Latrun, defending the newly proclaimed State.

May his memory be honored!
**(See additional information on Page 263)**

*[Page 275]*

# Yaacov Oberzhansky

### Translated from the Hebrew by Ann Belinsky

Yaacov ben Leibe Hirsh Oberzhansky was born in Korelitz in 1908. He went to the *cheder*, the *yeshiva*, and spent three years in the Hebrew Teachers Seminar *Tarbut* (1925-1928). He went to the training farm (*hachshara*) in Vilna and was head of the *kibbutz* there. He came to *Eretz Israel* in 1938 and joined Kibbutz Ramat Rachel. In 1939 he moved to Kibbutz Yagur. He was an excellent dairyman.

He participated in the War of Independence and fell in the Negev area, 1st *Heshvan* 5709 (1949). He was buried in the military cemetery in Jerusalem.

[Pages 276-277]

# Tzvi (Tzvika) Malkieli*
**Translated from the Hebrew by Ann Belinsky**

The son of Mordechai and Chassida. He was born on 27th *Sivan* 5706 (26.6.1946) in Raanana. After finishing his studies with distinction at the elementary school in Hod HaSharon, he studied and finished his high school studies in Kfar Saba, at the Berl Katznelson School. In his spare time he was devoted to collecting Israeli stamps solely and was interested in sport. In his childhood he won first prize in table-tennis at the *HaPoel* Ramatayim Club. Afterwards he was a sports instructor for *Maccabi*. In his youth he also won first place in a champion competition of chess between youth from the Southern Sharon area that took place in the Amateur Chess Club in Kfar Saba. In August 1964 he was eligible to be drafted into the army but because he was an outstanding pupil, he was accepted into the academic reserve and studied at the Hebrew Technion in Haifa.

In this framework he participated in a section commander's course for officers of the academic reserve and was about to finish his third year of studies in the Faculty of Mechanics. On finishing his studies at the Technion he would have gone on to do full military service. Because of his pleasant character traits, he attracted many friends. The love of life pulsated strongly within him. He did not offend anyone, nor did he insult any of his acquaintances.

------------------------------

\* *Yizkor...Gimel'* **The Israel Government Publishers, edited by Reuven Avinoam, Page 228 Aleph**.

Despite his success and excellence, he behaved with modesty and did not "show off". He was about to marry in July 1967. But in the meanwhile the Six Day War broke out, and on the second day of battle, 27 *Iyar* 5727 (6.6.1967) he fell in battle at Shveika in the Samaria area, displaying devotion and endurance. He was brought to eternal rest in the Kiryat Shaul Army Cemetery. In the courtyard of the Berl Katznelson School there is a marble memorial stone in his memory. Also on the way to Shechem (Nablus) by Kalkliya there is a memorial stone with his name engraved on it. In Raanana, a special room was opened in his memory. In the Hebrew Technion in Haifa, a prize of a memorial trophy cup in his name is given to the Chess Champion. His name is memorialized in the newspaper of the Raanana Local Council. His name appears in the pamphlet that was published by the municipality of Netanya in memory of the fallen. In the album "The Sharon Military Division in the 6 Day War" published by the headquarters of his brigade, his name is memorialized with his photograph. The book, containing chapters from the history of his life and his legacy was published by his parents.

*[Page 277]*

# Two Who Fell

## Kalman Osherovitz

### Translated from the Hebrew by Ann Belinsky

I wish to draw a picture of the memory of two Korelitzers, who fell in the War of Independence and were not privileged to arrive with us thus far and see our state become established and enlarged.

### Yaacov Oberzhansky

I met Yaacov Oberzhansky at Kibbutz Yagur and the days were towards the end of World War Two. These were the days of the revolt against the British in *Eretz-Israel*, revolt against the hunters of the illegal immigrants, revolt against the closure of the gates of *Eretz-Isruel* to the rcfugees from the Holocaust and who were knocking on our doors. The British announced from time to time on a curfew on the roads, and because of a curfew I was delayed at Yagur and thus spent a number of hours in a friendly conversation with Yaacov. Yaacov still didn't believe then that European Jewry had been annihilated and overpowered. He spoke of the Jews from Korelitz who would come to Erctz Israel. He was well absorbed into the kibbutz and satisfied with his work. He was a member of the *Hagana* and fell in the battles in the Negev.

### Shlomo Stoler

Shlomo, son of Zelig Stoler from a family of craftsmen in Korelitz, went through the horrors of the Second World War in the battlefields of the Jewish youth in the Polish forests. He was in the town when the Germans took it over, escaped to the surrounding forests and joined the partisans, was annexed to the partisan regiment and was outstanding as a scout. He arrived to *Eretz-Israel* with the first illegal immigrants, was absorbed well and was well-liked by his friends and all his acquaintances. At the beginning of the War of Independence he volunteered to the *Hagana* and fell in the area of Jerusalem.

May his memory be remembered and engraved on our hearts together with the memories of the dear holy martyrs who were destroyed by the Nazis in the exile in Poland.

*[Pages 278-279]*

# The Poem Of The Annihilated Jewish People
## (Unrhymed translation)

## Yitzchak Katzenelson

### Translated from the Yiddish by Harvey Spitzer

"Sing, sing! Raise aloud your pained and broken voice,
Search! Search for Him up there, above, if He is still here –
And sing to Him.... Sing to Him the last song of the last Jews,
Lived, died, not buried and no more..."

---- How can I sing - since the world is desolate for me?
How can I play with broken hands?
Where are my dead ones? I'm looking for my dead ones, God, in every pile of rubbish,
In every mound of ashes: Oh! - Tell me where you are!

Shout out from every pile of sand, from every stone,
Shout out from the all the dust, flames, smoke –
It's your blood and sap, it's the marrow of your bone,
It's your body and life! Shout out, shout aloud!

Oh, show yourself to me my people, show yourself, extend your hand
Out of the pits, deep and miles long, thickly packed,
Layer under layer, poured over with lime and burned,
Up! Up! Rise up from the lowest, deepest layer!

Come all of you from Treblinka, from Sobibor, from Auschwitz,
From Bergen-Belsen, come from Ponary and from more, more and more!
With eyes torn open, a frozen shout, "Oh, Lord, enough already!" and voiceless!
Come from swamps, from mud deeply sunken, from decayed moss.

Come dried up, crushed, rubbed to pieces, come, present yourselves
In a round dance, a large circle around me, a large ring –
Grandfathers, grandmothers, mothers with little children on their laps –
Come, Jewish bones from powders, from pieces of soap.

Show yourselves to me, all of you show yourselves to me, come all, come.
I want to see you all, I want to look at you, I want
To have a look at my annihilated people, mute, silenced.
And I will sing... Yes.... Here the harp - I play.

*[Page 279]*

**Yitzchak Katzenelson, Chana Katzenelson \* and their son Zvi Katzenelson \*\***

אֲנִי צְבִי
אֲנִי צְבִי, כְּלוֹמַר: צְבִי בֶּן יִצְחָק

**Caption under photo:**
To my Uncle Avraham Katzenelson

**I, Zvi**, that is to say: **Z**vi **b**en**Y**itzchak,
am sending you, Uncle, my picture.
A little boy cared for with love and devotion –
This is my signature:
Zvi Katzenelson

\*Chana (Andzha) Katzenelson, wife of Yitzchak Katzenelson, sister of physician, Dr. Rosenberg from Lodz. She was born in 1900 and was murdered together with her two sons: Ben-Zion and Binyamin, summer 1942.
\*\* Zvi Katzenelson, older son of Yitzchak Katzenelson. In the first year of the German occupation, he was a student at the high school of the underground established by the *Dror* (freedom) movement; in the summer of 1942, he worked with his father in the factory of the German, A.G. Shultz. He came to Vital with his father and from here was sent back to Poland for annihilation at the age of 18.
 **(see Last Writings – Yitzchak Katzenelson)**

[Page 280]

From right: **Morris Effner, Meyer Rotkoff, Morris Kessler, Chaim Abrahams, Albert Patikoff, Hyman Itzkowitz, Max Zussman, Pollack**

From right: **Chiena Caspi, Malka Poluzhsky, Yaacov Abramowich, Michael Walter-Fass (the editor) Fruma Berger-Gulkowich, Guttel Simon, (guests from the USA), Leah Lubchansky-Kornfeld**

*[Page 281]*

# THE KORELITZER SOCIETIES IN ISRAEL AND THE WORLD

**The Korelitz Pioneering Division at work, 10<sup>th</sup> June, 1925**

*[Pages 282-289]*

# The Korelitzer Society in Israel

## Michael Beigin

### Translated from the Hebrew by Ann Belinsky

Our town of Korelitz lives now only in our hearts: in the hearts of a small group of townspeople now in Israel, in the United States, in South Africa and in every place where there is a person who ever lived and breathed in the same little town, warm, direct and honest. At each meeting of the ex-Korelitzers, this town rises and lives and from every meeting or mention of its name on a day of mourning or a day of joyfulness, it rises again from the mists, rises and becomes more and more clear. And when this book will appear and is published, the name of Korelitz will be memorialized - Korelitz of above; for the real, suffering, fighting Korelitz - that is lost and is no more. It may be that after some generations - with all the commemoration that is being done, -they will tell about this town - once upon a time there was Korelitz.....

...Once upon a time came the day of the Great World War when the Germans took control of Poland and the methodical extermination began. In the same way as was done to all the cities and towns in Poland, at the beginning - the townspeople were humiliated and removed from all law and order and from that - several massacres took place. In fast continuation of the events, the townspeople were expelled in February 1942 to the Novogrudek Ghetto. In the big slaughter in Novogrudek on the 3rd of August 1942 almost all the Jews of Korelitz were annihilated.

Several dozens of the townspeople succeeded in escaping and spread out to different places: amongst the partisans and in hiding places. Some remained alive. Most of them headed towards *Eretz Israel* and began to rebuild their lives among the refugees from the great destruction who arrived in the country after the annihilation.

Once the storm of the war had subsided, refugees of the destruction, together with veterans in Israel who had come from Europe, began to work on memorializing their loved ones and remembering their towns and cities. The people of Korelitz in Israel, although few, succeeded on the initiative of Kalman Avrahami-Mordechovitz, to establish the "Korelitzer Society" in Israel, numbering 100 members.

The aim of the Korelitzer society was: not to forget our dear town and to remember and memorialize it in all possible ways.

The beginning was modest: the Korelitzers in Israel are scattered in all places in Israel, in agricultural settlements and in kibbutzim. A memorial date was set: 23rd 24th of *Av*. On that day Korelitzers from all over Israel gather together for a reunion of friends in order to honor the memory of the martyrs with a traditional ceremony: public reciting of *Kaddish, Yizkor* and suitable Psalms.

*[Page 283]*

**Sitting from right**: Yitzchak Lipshitz, Pessia Ephroimsky, Tova Londin-Rogovin, Haim Kaplan, Yosef Portnoy.
**Standing**: Shoshana Lipshitz, Abraham Kuznietz, Sheindel Perevolotsky, Bracha Kaplan, Leyma Polchuk.

**From right**: Berl Horvitz, Mordechai Malkieli (Krulovzky), Yosef Portnoy, Aharon Mor (Maroshinsky), Tzvi Shuster.

In continuation of the activity, contacts for commemoration were made with townspeople in other parts of the world and, as with other commemoration societies, we set up a memorial stone in the Holocaust Cellar on Mt. Zion in Jerusalem.

In the first years of the Society none of us dared to dream of our own Yizkor Book; all our initiative was to appear in a book being prepared by Novogrudek townspeople; the discussion on this subject was long but our efforts were successful. We made sure to provide "A historical survey of our town" in the book that was published by the Association of Jews from Poland: "*Landsmanschaften* in Israel" (page 185).

While being involved in this activity and learning the ways, we began to think of publishing our own book: "The Book of Korelitz", for during these meetings we noted that as well as the love steeping our hearts for our martyrs and departed dear ones, Korelitz has something to say to our youth and to the new generation which is building and creating in Israel.

With the collection of the material it became apparent how much light and warmth were buried in our little town: how many dear scholars grew up within it: poets, dreamers and fighters: audacious pioneers and those of great deeds. There are no words to express our admiration and tribute to those who invested so much in the ideas around the book: and those who took pains and wrote the pleasant things which enwrap within them the multi-variegated face of our town.

Let me detail the names of my friends, active today and who were the motivators for this undertaking:
Michael Beigin - Chairman; Chiena Caspi - Secretary; Yaacov Abramowich, Malka and Yaacov Poluzhsky, Malka Avni (Mordechovitz), Noah Gershenovsky, Abraham Kuznietz, Mordecai Malkieli and Leah Kornfeld.

I was chosen as Chairman of the Society in 1957. The first problems that kept us busy were about the memorialization of our town. We carried out discussions with the publishers of "The Encyclopedia of the Galuyot/Diaspora", had contact with the Association of Jews from Poland and participated in their conferences.

In 1960 we had a festive meeting with visiting overseas guests: Markol Gershenovsky from South Africa and Yerechmiel Gershenovsky from the USA. The meeting took place in the home of Chiena and Yonatan Caspi. There was a sort of "housewarming" following their moving into their new home; Committee members came with their wives and other townspeople not on the committee were also invited. It was a festive meeting with sorrowful memories. We spoke about the town and what could be done to perpetuate its memory forever.

Many meetings took place with representatives of *Yad Vashem*.We were invited to participate in 2 central conventions of *Yad VaShem* in Jerusalem and in Tel Aviv. Sarah and Michael Beigin participated in Jerusalem and Chiena Caspi, Malka and Yaacov Poluzhsky in Tel Aviv.

At the committee meeting of 28th April 1960 it was decided to participate in the Novogrudek Yizkor book which was to be published. In September we received a contract regarding the book of societies which was going to appear under the auspices of the Association of Jews from Poland .The survey was prepared with the active help of Hassia Turtel (Oberzhansky).

In 1960 Yaacov Abramowich visited the USA and participated in a meeting of the Society dealing with publishing the book.

There was a meeting with Mr Gutel Simon from the USA who told us about the activities of the Society there. The possibility of financial support from the Korelitzer Society in America was discussed. Gutel Simon himself has remained our friend to this day in his strong desire to bind ties between the two societies and continues his visits to Israel and the connection between the two organizations.

In the middle of 1961, Zelda and her husband Yaacov visited us from South Africa; Rivka Broida -also from Africa, and Ethel Lipshitz (Aron) from South America .We received the first donations which, although modest, were used as a lever for action and encouragement. These contributions increased in 1962 in a meeting of the committee with guests from America: Shlomo Londin, Zlata Lubchansky, Broida, Aharon Bernshtein, Yudel and Sonia Pollack. Mordechai Slutsky, Guttel Simon, Mina Abramowich and Atta Eizen. Also amongst the first donors were: Yossef Wolpin, Noach Gershenovsky, Malka Avni, Yaacov Abramowich, Chiena Caspi, Yaacov Poluzhsky, Rivka Shuster, Beigin, Vital Shkolnik and Kalman Osherovitz.

The warm response and the donations gave the first initiators the encouragement to think about organizing special Memorial Evenings for Korelitzers, because at first we were partners to Novogrudek Memorial Evenings. With time we felt that we needed to do something for ourselves and to be concerned for ourselves. The following members were added to the Committee: Yaacov Abramowich, Yehuda Shapira, Malka and Yaacov Poluzhsky, and Mordechai Meyerovitz. Our association entered into its orderly course with our memorial assembly - amongst our townspeople, with a different atmosphere and a different mood.

At the beginning of 1963 several impressive activities of the Association of Jews from Poland and *Yad VaShem* took place – in which we also participated. In January the Council of Organizations discussed preparations for marking 20 years since the Warsaw Ghetto uprising; the problem of compensation from

Germany, publishing Yizkor books etc. In April there was an opening assembly of Holocaust and Heroism Day on the occasion of 20 years of the ghetto revolt. This assembly took place in the *Hechal Hatarbut* Auditorium in Tel Aviv with our participation.

In April 1963 we had a meeting in one of the coffee shops in Tel Aviv in honor of the guests from overseas, Polack Yudel and his wife Sonia, Yaacov Lipka and his wife from Africa and Mordechai Slutzky from Canada . We gave a report to the guests about our activities, the guests promised full help in all our activities. Ideas were raised for commemoration: a book about Korelitz, setting up *Gimilat Chesed* and planting trees in the "Martyrs Forest". The guests from overseas agreed to be our representatives overseas for shared activities of our associations. Later in the year Yeshayahu Gershenovsky from the USA visited us.

In August 1965 the annual memorial service of our town was held. A regular religious ceremony was held and with broken hearts we remembered those who had died: Aharon Lipshitz, Tzvi Shkolnik, Rivka Shuster, Tzvi Arieli and Chimbalist.

In 1966, a festive meeting in honor of our guest Sonia Greenberg was held. Already then we were seriously talking about publishing a book on Korelitz. We were informed that in the account there was an amount of almost three thousand IL (Israeli *lira*).

Alter Boyarsky and his Family

**From right, sitting**: Alter Boyarsky, Michael (his grandson), Rivka, Masha (their daughter)
**Standing from right**: Yehoshua, Hirshel, Moshe (his sons), Akiva Moses (his son-in-law).

August: the traditional memorial evening. The guest Alter Boyarsky and his wife were also present. Alter spoke about the need to install the consciousness of the past in our youth and to tell them about what Korelitz was and the life there before the destruction.

Towards the end of 1966 the idea of the book began to take shape. At the meeting in November an action plan was prepared: First of all - to begin collecting material to give content to the book. In these cases of commemoration, once you decide to act you must do so quickly, because it is about the past, which distances itself from day to day; yesterday you could have spoken to another person who remembers such and such, and today - the person is gone. At this meeting it was decided to whom to turn, how to turn to them, what to write and about what to write. It was decided to turn to elderly people from Korelitz who live in Israel and receive material and photos of Korelitz. To turn to Pesach Kaplan who was involved in the life of the town and knew it closely. We decided to travel to Kibbutz Yagur where he was a member and talk to him and request him to write his memoirs. It was decided to turn to all townspeople to write about things close to their hearts in the town. Thus we would receive and build the complete mosaic of Korelitz. We turned to Hassia Turtel-Oberzhansky, to collect the historical material. The committee took upon itself to be active in commemorating the town in a book worthy of its name and of our town. Thus the committee began to discuss the financial problems involved in publishing a book like this and the help that we could expect from the Korelitzer Society in the United States. Several fundamental decisions made in these early discussions were: To turn in writing to all who could write about the town - that they would do so as soon as possible; to request from all townspeople in the Diaspora to donate money and to send in their impressions of the town. It was decided to turn to well-known people who could help in collecting information and material about our town. At the beginning of 1967 the work of the book committee continued at full speed. An editing committee was chosen: Chiena Caspi, Malka Poluzhsky, Yaacov Abramowich, Abraham Kuznietz, Noach Gershenovsky, Mordechai Malkieli, and Michael Beigin. From this group, secretaries were chosen: Malka Poluzhsky, Yaacov Abramowich and Mordecai Malkieli, who took upon themselves especial devotion to this undertaking of publishing the book and all the technical problems involved.

In the middle of 1967 at a meeting at the house of Yaacov Poluzhsky in Kfar Saba we already dealt with the memories connected to the book. Characters and educators from the town were mentioned; Shalom Cohen, Benyamin Ovsivitz, Tzvi Kivilevitz, Yitzhak Meir Klatzky, Haim Bussel, Moshe-Eli Shuster and prominent personalities who were born in Korelitz; the poet Yitzhak Katzenelson, David Einhorn, Prof. Shaul Aharon Adler. Also, memorial evenings were already influenced by the widespread activity around the book. Memorial assemblies became more varied. In anticipation of the memorial evening of the 30th August 1967, a detailed plan was prepared in the spirit of those evenings commonly accepted in the State: lighting of a 6 candle candelabra in remembrance of the six million murdered in Europe; a list of those missing in Israel was prepared. The agenda of the memorial evening was: Opening - by the Chairman Michael Beigin; In Memory of the Missing Ones; "Hospitality in Korelitz" written and read by Esther Shkolnik; Memories of Yaacov Abramowich, read by Michael Beigin; a poem by Fruma Gulkowich in memory of Korelitz, read by Malka Poluzhsky; Chana Garabalsky read about "A Visit to the Town"; Yizkor and publicly recited Kaddish.

A party was organized at the home of Yaacov Abramowich in honor of the guests from London: Idel Kagan and his wife Barbara.

On the 15th January 1967 at a meeting in the house of Malka Avni (Mordechowitz) there was a report from Malka Avni about her visit to the United States; a report from Yaacov Abramowich; a report from Malka Poluzhsky about the book; and candidates for the conference at *Yad Vashem* were chosen.

In a meeting at the beginning of 1968 at a meeting held at the home of Sheindel and Avraham Kuznietz there was a discussion concerning the monument for the memory of Jews from Novogrudek which they were going to erect without specifically mentioning the name of Korelitz. We demanded that the name Korelitz be written next to Novogrudek, for the people of Korelitz were annihilated in the Novogrudek ghetto and one can't come to terms with the disappearance of our town in this case. A special group of delegates was chosen - Yaacov Abramowich and Noach Gershenovsky - to carry out negotiations with the Novogrudek activists.

The negotiations with the people of Novogrudek took a long time. The name of Korelitz appears on the Novogrudek monument.

At a Gala meeting which took place in April 1968 at the home of Malka Avni, there was a welcome for our friends from America, Moshe (Morris) Kessler and his wife Miriam. Mr. Kessler passed on interesting details about the type of activities of the American Korelitzer Society. Each country has its own problems. The type of activity there is completely different. Mr. Kessler brought with him a donation for publishing the book, but he told us that in the account of the society there is a sum of about ten thousand dollars which is not being touched. Usually, the custom there is for the Society to pay for the funeral arrangements of a member who dies. Also a certain amount is given to the widow.

[Page 288]

**A Reception for Miriam and Moshe Kessler**
**From right:** Malka Poluzhsky, Yaakov Poluzhsky, Yocheved Abramovich, Miriam (Minnie) Kessler, Yaacov Abramowich, Chiena Caspi, Sarah Beigin, Michael Beigin, --- Gershenovsky, Malka Avni. **In front, from right**: Noach Avni, Merkel Gershenovsky

In January 1969 there was a festive meeting in honor of the guests Shaul Lubchanzsky and his wife from South Africa, Berl Horwitz and his wife, Chaim Berkovitz, Berl and Yossel Borovsky. The meeting took place in the house of Chiena Caspi. Those present gave their donations towards the book publication.

In May of the same year we decided to contact Mr. Michael Walzer-Fass to edit the book. Mr. Michael Walzer-Fass is known as a person who deals with editing and publishing these types of books with great success. He puts his whole heart and soul into commemorating the destroyed Jewish towns – and he does so solely for the sake of perpetuating the memory of these towns and villages.

In July there was a meeting with the committee at the house of the Poluzhsky family in Kfar Saba in the presence of the book editor Mr. Michael Walzer-Fass.

At a meeting in honor of the guest Mr Guttel Simon who was visiting Israel for the fourth time, Mr Michael Walzer-Fass gave details about the book, its form and content. He noted that the book would be in three languages: Hebrew, Yiddish and English.

At a committee meeting at the home of Yaffa and Abraham Kuznietz in Tel Aviv, our guest Hayyim Abramowitz, President of the Korelitzer Society in America was present. The guest gave details of the discussions of the society there. Among other matters, he said that in the Six Day war he suggested withdrawing all the money in the bank account of the society, a total of seventeen thousand dollars, and donating it to Israel to buy a cannon or some other weapon. The Society worked for commemorating the name of the town on a monument in America. Mr. Hayyim Abramowitz was pleased to meet the members of the Society here in Israel and passed on warm regards from our brothers in America.

At meetings that took place we discussed speeding up publication of the book. We are eager to see the fruits of our labor and the investment and the dreams of the townspeople. According to the details that we received from the editor, we expect that indeed there will be a book with much content which will glorify the name of our town forever.

*[Page 289]*

**A Reception for Gutel Simon (Shimonovitz)**
**From right:**Yaakov Poluzhsky, Noach Gershenovsky, ---, Michael Beigin, Malka Avni, Yaacov Abramowich, Gutel Simon (Shimonovitz), Malka Poluzhsky, Avraham Kuznietz, Chiena Caspi.

[Pages 290-291]

# Good Friends Meet

## Yaacov Abramowich

### Translated from the Yiddish by Harvey Spitzer

Among the guests who used to come to visit Korelitz, I remember Idel Kagan. He was a young boy of 7 or 8, nicely dressed, handsome, clean and elegant. He would come to his uncle, Yashke Gurevitch, and family. His father's name was Ya(n)kel; his mother's, Devorkeh. She was Yashke's sister.

Yashke's house was opposite our store in the market place. Yashke also had a store not far from ours.

Idel would always visit me and we would spend time together. He would tell me that he liked Korelitz with its dear and warm-hearted people. That's why he came to Korelitz every year. I remember promising to take him for a ride in my car if he were a good boy. He was still a child and believed me. Once he asked me, "So when are we going for a ride?" I answered that my car was in the garage. I didn't have a car.

The years went by in this way until the dark war broke out. We met again in the forests where he was hiding with his cousin Berel. He always had courage and hope. We said goodbye to one another after the liberation. Each of us sought a little corner, a nest, in which to build his future. It wasn't easy to go back to our homeland, where nothing remained but ruins and graves. We had lost our closest and dearest relatives and friends.

Idel is no longer a boy. He's married to a fine woman, has lovely, fine children and leads a Jewish life. He has begun to visit Israel where he has two cousins: Berel Kagan and Layzer Senderovsky and their families.

We again meet together. We take an interest in one another and inquire about each other separately. He visited me and my family. At get-togethers at my house, there were friends with whom we went through the worst times together.

As we're talking, I tell him about the Korelitz committee. We, the few survivors, would like to create some kind of memorial for our dearest and most beloved who were murdered. Many cities and towns have already done this.

He asked me about this and showed much interest in what we want to create. Idel didn't have to think too long and offered a donation for the Korelitz committee's work. He added that I should write to him and not be ashamed to ask for more and that he would gladly help us.

He visits Israel every year. He meets with his family and friends. He comes to the Yizkor meetings in memory of the martyrs of Novogrudek. He makes a contribution to help Jews from Novogrudek as well as from Korelitz and others who are in need.

**Memorial meeting in the USA**
**From right to left:** Y. Gutel Simon, Hayyim Avramowitz, Albert Paticoff, Jack Pollak, Morris Kessler, Fruma Gulkowich-Berger, Hyman Itzkowitz

*[Pages 292-295 - Yiddish]*
*[Page LIX – English, below, as on* **page 397***, with an addition from the Yiddish text*

# Society Of Fellow Countrymen From Korelitz In America
## (The Korelitzer Society of America Inc.)

## Morris Kessler
## Gutel Simon

***Coordinator's Note:*** *This text is the same as the English Section text, but* **in** **addition***, the Constitution Committee names and roles and Constitution of the Society are given* **(pages 286-288***) and there are different photographs from those in the English Section.*

In New York there is an organization which bears the name "Korelitzer Society". The organization was formed on April 4, 1904, by a group of individuals born in Korelitz, at the home of Benjamin and Golda (Rochel Zlatess) Horwitz.

Early in the twentieth century, the decrees, oppression and pogroms perpetuated against the Jews by Czarist Russia set into motion a large-scale immigration to America. The situation of Russia's Jews was very bad. Many Jews were being persecuted because of political activity - particularly the young people who belonged to revolutionary organizations. Jews living within the pale of settlement were impoverished, and the vision of "Golden America" attracted masses of them to the New World. But when they did arrive in America, they found themselves in difficult circumstances. The native tongue was foreign to them; the customs were alien, and work in the sweatshops was hard. The entire country was then in the process of development, but jobs did not come so readily, and the pay was poor.

Depressed and confused in the tumult of New York, they clung to each other and to their friends. Most of the immigrants were men who had left their families behind in the Old World and were expected to send them sustenance, until they were able to bring them to America, and a few of them were single. Those who had relatives in America moved in with them, sleeping wherever there was room - on the floor, on a cot, and living as cheaply as possible, since every American dollar meant two rubles.

The difficult circumstances and the loneliness of the newly-arrived immigrants were bound to bring about organization into landsmannschaften, such as the Korelitzer *landsmannschaft* in New York. The organization was named *Chevra B'nai Yitzhak-Yechiel Anshel Korelitz*: a place was rented in which the Chevra established its own Synagogue. It was named for Rabbi Yitzhak-Yehiel, for many years the illustrious rabbi of Korelitz (and grandfather of the martyred Hebrew poet Yitzhak Katznelson).

The following attended the founding meeting of the Society: Nissan Rabinowich o.b.m. (the first President); Isaac David Itzkowitz; Joseph Chessler; Gedalyahu Becker; Abraham-Samuel Shimenowitz; Yaacov-Joseph Pomerantz; Alter Shimenowitz; Leibe-Itche Kaplan; Yitzhak-Yona Itzkowitz; Tevel Hurewitz; Feivel Polusky, and Harry Barrish.

The first aim of the Korelitzer Society was mutual aid and a sick fund. Each member paid membership dues. The income was used for various purposes - the acquisition of a cemetery plot for any Korelitzer who passed away, the rental of a hall for the semi-monthly meetings, and similar purposes.

[Page 293]

**Korelitzers in America**

**Right to left:** Miriam Kessler, Hayyim Itzkowitz, Morris Afner, Yaacov Pollack, Zussman, Yudel Pollack, Mrs Pollack, Shlomo Mordecowitz, Pollack, Mrs Zussman, Mayer Rotkoff, (?Max) Florentz, Max Zussman

The carpenters among the Korelitzer donated an Ark, bought a Scroll of the Torah for the Korelitzer synagogue; on Sabbaths, holidays, and even weekdays the synagogue was packed with worshippers. The synagogue was the only place where the Korelitzer met regularly. As was the custom among the Jews in Korelitz itself, Torah honors (*aliyot*) were apportioned. The custom was in effect for many years.

In the Second World War the situation changed completely. Many people came up from the South to New York, adding to the congestion. Living quarters became scarce. Until then the Korelitzer lived in the poorer sections of New York, and the newcomers kept penetrating more and more deeply into the Jewish sections. The large influx of the population forced a move to the surrounding towns.

The financial situation of the new immigrants began to improve, and many among the Korelitzer began moving out of New York. The meetings were not well attended.

The organization was then re-chartered under the laws of the State of New York and renamed "The Korelitzer Society". The religious coloration of the society also underwent change. The meeting date was shifted from Saturday night to Sunday afternoon and the meetings were held once monthly. Since 1970 it has been meeting four times a year.

The Korelitzer Society presently numbers 150 members, of which 40 are widows.

The following are the Presidents who served the society since its formation: Nissan Rabinowitz, Tevel Hurewitz, Gedalya Becker, Mendel Tobias, Note Levine, Feivel Polusky, Jacob Pomerantz, Gutel Shimenowitz (Simon). Louis Simenowitz, Joseph Chessler, Harry Barrish, Meyer Itzkowitz, Joseph Mendelson, Sender Mendelson, Max Zussman, Meyer Rotkoff, Hayyim Abramowitz, Hyman Itzkowitz, the current president Morris Kessler, Moshe-Kopel Abramowich, Louis Cohen, Isaac Geshvisky. Some also served as Vice-Presidents, and Moshe-Kopel Abramowich also served as Protocol Secretary.

---

*[Pages 294-295]*

**Translated from the Yiddish by Harvey Spitzer**

# CONSTITUTION COMMITTEE

Max Zussman....................................Chairman
Mendel Tobias ...................................Secretary
Feivel Polusky
Jake Pomerantz
Yosef Chessler
Meyer Itzkowitz
Max Florentz
Harry Barrish

Gutel Shimenovitch
Isaac Neshwisky

### ENDOWNMENT FUND TRUSTEES

Meyer Itzkowitz and Mendel Tobias

### OLD AGE TRUSTEES

Yosef Chessler and Feivel Polusky

### BENEVOLENT FUND TRUSTEES

Max Florentz, Feivel Polusky

### SOCIETY TRUSTEES
From savings account

Jake Pomerantz, Max Zussman

### BENEVOLENT FUND CHECKING ACCOUNT

Jake Pomerantz, Chairman
Hymie Kraus, Secretary

# CONSTITUTION OF THE KORELITZ SOCIETY

Founded April 4, 1904 at the home of Mr. Binyamin Horwitz
77 Norfolk Street, New York
Amended and Approved 1934

### Ex-Presidents

Nissan Rabinovitch, of blessed memory
Tevel Horwitz, of blessed memory
Gedaliahu Becker
Mendel Tobias
Neta Levin
Feivel Polusky
Yaakov Pomerantz
Gutel Shimenovitch
Louie Simenoff
Harry Barrish

### Officials

Yosef Chessler ............................................ President
Harry Barrish .............................................Vice president

[Page 295]

Y.Gutel Simon (Shimonovitch)

Morris and Miriam Kessler

*[Page 296]*

# A Memorial Candle
## Aharon Marshinsky (Mor)
### Translated from the Hebrew by Ann Belinsky

Who am I to erect a monument in your memory?
I did not stand close to you during your Holocaust, I did not see you when you rolled in your blood. In front of my eyes I still see how your sons and daughter, women and children, old men and women, newborn and infants, are being brought to the Field of Slaughter and are murdered in cold blood and terrible torture.

The history of the Jews is rich in Jewish blood, in all their wanderings and all over the world.
But Babylon and Assyria, Antiochus, Titus, Haman, Torquemada and Petlura, all of these together do not reach the ankles of the terrible German oppressor and his assistants - the people of "culture" of the 20th century who destroyed by all sorts of torture that the devil could not even invent, a third of the Jewish people.
In truth, in their bodies our martyrs were murdered, suffocated and burnt, but the hand of the oppressor could not reach or wound their souls.

The holy and pure souls hover above their graves in the European diaspora, wherever the tainted feet of the oppressor only managed to walk - and (their souls) participate with the Jewish People in the pure prayer read on Sabbaths and Festivals after the Shacharit prayers: Father of Mercy.......in His powerful compassion, may He recall with compassion the devout, the upright, and the perfect ones, the holy congregations who gave their lives for the Sanctification of the Name..... May our God remember them for good with the other righteous of the world. May He, before our eyes, exact retribution for the spilled blood of His servants.

Where is the revenge?

**A group of Jews who survived, at the grave of their brethren**

*[Page 297]*

While the defiled was covered with your blood,
Clean and holy blood, the blood of atonement,
We shall carve with the blood of our hearts, your names
In the scroll of fasting and in the book of suffering.

Chaim Nachman Bialik

# And These are the Names...

Let us remember

The names of the holy ones of the Korelitz community,
let us carry their memories

with love in our afflicted hearts, and let us not forget
them forever.

Let these pages be a candle of remembrance.

*[Page 298]*

## Alef א

Abramowich Eliezer
Abramowich Breine
Abramowich Alter
Abramowich Chaim
Abramowich Yehoshua
Abramowich Rachel
Abramowich Yehoshua-Leib
Abramowich Yehuda
Abramowich Merke
Abrazhansky Moshe-Shmuel
Abrazhansky Yentel and 2 children
Abrinsky Berl
Ovsivitz Michael
Ovsivitz Binyamin
Ozhkovsky Chaya-Sarah
Olirt Chaya-Leah
Atlasky Fruma
Atlasky Rachel
Izralit Chanya
Epstein Feivel
Osherowitz Eli Chaim
Ephroimsky Chana
Ephroimsky Yisrael
Itzkowitz Sonia
Archonovsky Yitschak -- shochet
Itzkowitz Yaakov
Osherowitz Shaul-Nachum
Osherowitz Blume

Abramowich Doshke
Abramowich Osnat
Abramowich and her three children
Abramowich Shosha-Leah
Abramowich his wife
Abramowich Yisrael
Abramowich his wife and 2 children
Abramowich Moshe
Abrazhansky Shlomo
Abrazhansky Hirsh- Leib
Abrazhansky Shimon
Abrinsky Duba
Ovsivitz Chaya-Bayle
Ovsivitz Tamar
Ozhkovsky Eliezer
Ozhkovsky Alka
Atlasky Yosef
Izralit Yisrael
Izralit Merke
Epstein Doshke
Osherowitz Nashko
Ephroimsky Faygel
Itzkowitz Zissel
Itzkowitz Yitschak
Archonovsky Esther
Itzkowitz Chana
Osherowitz Faygel
Osherowitz Leah- Dayche

Abramowich Gabriel
Abramowich Riva and children
Abramowich Zilca
Abramowich Genasia
Abramowich Tsire and son
Abramowich Chaya- Dvora and 3 children
Abramowich Leah-Rachel
Abramowich Chaya and children
Abrazhansky Ettel
Abrazhansky Miriam
Abrinsky Chisha and child
Abrinsky Sarah
Ovsivitz Yehuda
Ozhkovsky Yossel
Ozhkovsky Moshe
Atlasky Nissan
Atlasky Baruch
Izralit Hinda
Epstein David
Osherowitz Yosef-Chaim
Ephroimsky Herzl
Ephroimsky Esther
Itzkowitz Moshe
Itzkowitz Yelda [** daughter???**]
Archonovsky David
Itzkowitz Zushke
Osherowitz Shmuel Isser

## Bet ב

Begin Mordechai Reuven
Begin Yosef
Bolutnitzky Grunia
Bolutnitzky Minia
Bussel Berl
Bussel child
Beigin Libke
Beigin Tzirl

Begin Gittel
Begin Tzippe and children
Bolutnitzky Rayzel
Bussel Chaim
Bussel Pesach
Bussel Blume
Beigin Zlatte
Beigin Nachum Aizik

Begin Kayle
Bolutnitzky Avraham
Bolutnitzky Masha
Bussel Golda and son
Bussel Sonia
Borovsky Shifra
Beigin Eliyahu
Beigin Sarah

Butansky Esther-Bashe
Butansky Rachel
Bernstein Leibush
Becker Nachum-Yitzchak
Breslin Avraham
Berkowitz Gedalia
Berkowitz China and 2 children
Berkowitz Zelte
Berkowitz Velvel
Berkowitz Elke
Berman Shayndel

Butansky Rayze-Rachel
Bernstein Yosef
Bernstein Sinai
Breslin Shamai
Breslin Solye
Berkowitz Dodzha
Berkowitz Miriam
Berkowitz Chana-Chaya
Berkowitz Mussia
Berkowitz Yosef

Butansky Yosef
Bernstein Rachel
Becker Yosef
Breslin Faygel
Breslin Chaya
Berkowitz Chana
Berkowitz Moshe
Berkowitz Yehudit and husband
Berkowitz Esther- Rachel
Berman Avraham

## Gimel ℷ

Gurevitz Falke
Gurevitz Yosef
Gurevitz Chasia
Gitlin Chaim
Gitlin Dishke
Gershovitz Nechama
Gintzberg Yudel
Galwitzky Yaakov
Gorodinsky Fridel
Gorodinsky Nishke
Gorodinsky Avraham
Gorodinsky, 2 children
Golkowitz Faygel
Greenberg Taibel
Greenberg Rizel
Greenfeld Alter
Greenfeld David
Gershovitz Masha
Gershonovsky Musia
Gershonovsky Yosef
Gershonovsky Michla
Gershonovsky Liba
Gershonovsky Sarah Rachel
Gershonovsky Brina
Gershonovsky Aliza
Gershonovsky Shlomo
Gershonovsky Leah
Gentzwitz Dvoshke
Gentzwitz Yehuda
Gartsovsky, his wife and daughter
Gartsovsky Rachel
Goldshmid Moshe Reuven
Goldshmid Gutka
Garshovitz Moshe
Gutsicks Shim'on

Gurevitz Esther-Rachel
Gurevitz Brina-Faygel
Gitlin Yaakov
Gitlin Rachel
Gershovitz Laybel
Gershovitz Hadassa
Gintzberg Gishe
Galwitzky Leah
Gorodinsky, child
Gorodinsky Fraydel
Gorodinsky Hinde-Bayle
Golkowitz Shlomo
Golkowitz Brine
Greenberg Yehuda
Greenfeld Chine
Greenfeld Rayzel
Gershovitz Aaron
Gershovitz Mordechai
Gershonovsky Moshe
Gershonovsky Rachel
Gershonovsky Yocheved
Gershonovsky Chaya-Bila
Gershonovsky, girl
Gershonovsky Shlomo
Gershonovsky Gedalya
Gershonovsky Sarah
Gershonovsky Ziske
Gentzwitz Yitzchak Berl
Gentzwitz Liova
Gartsovsky Chasia
Gartsovsky Leah
Goldshmid Basia
Garshovitz Noach
Garshovitz Batsheva
Gutsichs Nacha

Gurevitz Dvora
Gurevitz Nechama
Gitlin Chika
Gitlin Gittel
Gershovitz Minia
Gershovitz Yitzchak
Gintzberg Rayzel
Galwitzky Mordechai
Gorodinsky Berl
Gorodinsky Benzion
Gorodinsky Moshe
Golkowitz Rachel
Greenberg Messel
Greenberg Gisha
Greenfeld Shim'on
Gurevitz Chava-Gittel
Gershovitz Bunia
Gershonovsky Yosef
Gershonovsky Gedaliahu
Gershonovsky Malka-Riva
Gershonovsky Chaim
Gershonovsky Yaakov
Gershonovsky Yehuda
Gershonovsky Rayzke
Gershonovsky Rayzke
Gershonovsky Bashke
Gentzwitz Zelig
Gentzwitz Moshe David
Gartsovsky Shlomo
Gartsovsky Sa'adia
Gartsovsky Shlomo, wife and son
Goldshmid Rachel
Garshovitz Mira
Gutsiks Gudel and wife Nacha

## Daled ד

| | | |
|---|---|---|
| Dushkin Eliyahu | Dushkin Avraham | Dushkin Chaim |
| Dushkin Finkel and son | Dushkin Reuben | Dushkin Minye |
| Dushkin Mordechai | Dushkin Chaim | Dushkin Zissel |
| Dameshek Berl | Dameshek Buza | Dameshek Yehudit |
| Dameshek Sulia | | |

## Hey ה

| | |
|---|---|
| Hordus Moshe | Hordus Gittel |

## Vav ו

| | | |
|---|---|---|
| Vernik the Rabbi and his wife | Vernik Chaim | Vernik Sender |
| Vernik Miriam | Vernik Riva | Volpin Moshe Avraham the Shochet |
| Volpin Yocheved | Wiener Kalman | Wiener Chaya |
| Wiener Yosef | Wiener Aaron | Weintroib Gronia and daughter |
| Weintroib Miriam | | |

## Zayin ז

| | | |
|---|---|---|
| Zalmansky Pia | Zalmansky Aydele | Zalmansky Nissan |
| Zalmansky Doshka | Zalmansky Moshe | Zalmansky Moshe |
| Zalmansky Yaakov | Zalmansky Finkel | Zalmansky Sarah |
| Zalmansky Rayzel | Zalmansky Nissan, his wife and son | Zalmansky Shaul |
| Zalmansky Hirsh | Zalmansky Reuven | Zalmansky Aaron |
| Zalmansky Masha | Zussman Hertz | Zussman Rayzel and 2 children |
| Zamushchick Avraham | Zamushchik Chaya and 3 children | Zelivansky Shim'on |
| Zelivansky Rivka Raske | Zelivansky Leah and 2 children | Zelivansky Mordechai (Momo) |
| Zelivansky Nioma | Zelivansky Layb | |

## Het ח

| | |
|---|---|
| Chabakuk Yosef | Chabakuk Sarah Fayga |

## Tet ט

| | | |
|---|---|---|
| Trotsky Mordechai | Trotsky Bayle | Trotsky Batya |
| Trinkman Getzel | Trinkman Elka | Treievitsky Layb |
| Treievitsky Gusha Leah | Treievitsky Liole | Trovovitz Mottel |
| Trovovitz Gittel | Trovovitz Miriam | Trovovitz Meyer |

## Yod י

| | | |
|---|---|---|
| Yellin Getsel | Yellin Shina Figel | Yellin Yona |
| Yellin Esther Rachel | Yellin Berchi | Yellin Riva |
| Yossilewitz Henech | Yellin Michael | Yellin Bluma |
| Yellin Miriam | Yossilevitz Shira and two children | Yossilevitz Asher Moshe |
| Yossilevitz Ettel | Yossilevitz Orchy | Yossilevitz Lova |
| Yossilevitz Simcha | Yossilevitz Rachel | Yossilevitz Yosef |

Yossilevitz Ozer and his wife
Yossilevitz Dvora
Yankelevitz Alter
Yankelevitz Bashka
Yankelevitz Moshe
Yankelevsky David
Yankelevsky Chaim
Yosselivitz Chaya-Sarah
Yosselivitz Yenta

Yossilevitz Chaim and his wife
Yankelevitz Hinda
Yankelevitz Yehoshua- Yaakov
Yankelevitz Eliyahu
Yankelevitz Ritsa
Yankelevsky Bila
Yosselivitz Moshe
Yosselivitz Henya
Yosselivitz Sonia

Yossilevitz Shlomo
Yankelevitz Shmerl
Yankelevitz, his wife
Yankelevitz Dvora
Yankelevsky Tsira
Yankelevsky Lube
Yosselivitz Moshe, the Rabbi and wife
Yosselivitz Feivel
Yosselivitz Meyer

## Kaf כ

Kagan Yisrael
Kagan, a child
Kagan Itka
Kagan Shula

Kagan Esther
Kagan David
Kagan Reuven
Kagan, child

Kagan Chaya
Kagan, 2 children
Kagan Miriam
Katz (Simonovitz-Nisselevitz) Iddela-Shoshar

## Lamed ל

Lubchensky Yaakov Meyer
Lubchensky Chaya-Ette
Lubchensky Rachel
Lubchensky Bella
Lipkin Moshe Tsvi
Lipkin Zlote
Lipkin Henya
Lipkin David
Lipkin Rachel
Lipkin Moshe, wife and children
Lashchinsky Rivka
Levitt Yehuda
Levitt Liova
Lipko Henech (Chanoch)
Levin Sonia
Lipshitz David
Lev Faygel
Lev Hadassa
Leibovitz, girl

Lubchensky Nechama, 2 tchildren
Lubchensky Simcha
Lubchensky Yisrael
Lipkin Ortche
Lipkin Aaron
Lipkin Zhome
Lipkin Chaim
Lipkin Mordechai
Lipkin Zalman
Lipkin Sonia
Levitt Herzl
Levitt Shifra
Levitt Fraydel
Lipko Sonia and child
Levin Yachne
Lev Shalom
Lev Manos
Leibovitz Riva-Rayzel
Lasvin Chaskel

Lubchensky Chaim
Lubchensky Rayzel
Lubchensky Moshe
Lipkin Kunye Bayle
Lipkin Avraham-Shim'on
Lipkin Shifra and 4 children
Lipkin Bila
Lipkin Chana
Lipkin Eli-Chaim
Lashchinsky David
Levitt Itka
Levitt Yehudit
Lidsky Zissia
Levin Mordechai
Levin, 2 children
Lev Kyla
Lev Berke (Shkolnik)
Leibovitz David

## Mem מ

Mordechovi tz Chana-Leah
Mordechovitz Ethel
Mordechovitz Chaim-Itzie
Meirovitz Yehuda
Meirovitz Nechama
Mordechovitz Avraham Yltzchak - shochet
Mordechovitz Chasia
Mishkin Leah

Mordechovitz Elka
Mordechovitz Chaya
Mirsky Nechemia
Meirovitz Rachel
Meirovitz Sarah- Minia
Mordechovitz Falke

Mordechovitz Tova
Mishkin Chaim

Mordechovitz Mordechai
Mordechovitz Gudel
Mirsky Nechama
Meirovitz David
Mormordechovitz Sarah-Dvora
Mordechovitz Asher

Mordechovitz Chaim
Mishkin Michael

Mishkin Moshke                         Mishkin Rashke                         Mazorevitz Mordechai
Mazorewitz Frayzel (Kuznitz)

## Nun נ

Novitzky Shlomo                        Novitzky Sarah (Dushkin)               Novitzky Elka
Novitzky Yitschak                      Namyut Hertz                           Namyut Ethel
Namyut Leah                            Namyut Yaakov                          Namyut Rivka
Nignivitsky Yitzchak                   Nignivitsky Chana Sarah                Nignivitsky Eshka
Nignivitsky Duba                       Nignivitsky Riva                       Nignivitsky Avraham
Nignivitsky Gittel                     Nignivitsky Sarah                      Nisselevitz David
Nisselevitz Sarah                      Nisselevitz Abba                       Nisselevitz Sonye
Nisselevitz Luba                       Nisselevitz Faygel                     Nisselevitz Feivel
Nisselevitz Mashe                      Nisselevitz Aaron                      Nachumovsky Sonia

Nachumovsky Alter                      Nachumovsky Shlomo, wife and           Nachumovsky Shula
                                       children
Nachumovsky Laybel and child           Nisselevitz Zalman                     Nisselevitz Mussia
Nisselevitz Moshe                      Nisselevitz Baylka                     Nisselevitz Berl


## Samech ס

Stoller Yitschak                       Stoller Malka Rishe and child          Stoller Miriam
Slubotsky Feivel                       Slubotsky Eshka                        Slubotsky Rachel
Slubotsky Velvel                       Slubotsky Sharka                       Slutsky Yaakov-Layb
Slutsky Miriam                         Slutsky Chana                          Slutsky Yitschak
Slutsky Yehudit                        Slutsky Yaakov                         Slutsky Yoel
Slutsky David                          Slutsky David                          Slutsky Karina
Slutsky Shura                          Slutsky Yosef                          Slutsky Rivka
Slutsky Lippa                          Slutsky Hersh                          Slutsky Chaya
Slutsky Ben-Zion                       Solovitzky Eliyahu                     Solovitzky Rachel
Solovitzky David-Feitel                Solovitzky, 2 children                 Switsky Yitschak
Switsky Bilka                          Switsky Idel                           Switsky Chaim
Switsky Laybel                         Stoller Yitschak                       Stoller Leah
Stoller Yehuda                         Stoller Musia                          Stoller Yosef
Stoller Nioma                          Stoller Mira                           Stoller Moshe
Stoller Kayle                          Stoller Hirsh                          Stoller Gisha
Stoller Yitschak                       Stoller Leah                           Stoller Chaim
Stoller Luba                           Stoller Gittcl                         Stoller Zelig
Stoller Shlomo                         Stoller Fraydel                        Solodoche Aydele
Solodoche Yachke                       Saravenik Alter                        Saravenik Leah
Saravenik Rayzel                       Saravenik Mordechai                    Saravenik Sarah
Saravenik Isaac                        Saravenik Sonia                        Saravenik Raphael
Saravenik Golda                        Saravenik Yoel                         Skorochod Tsvia
Skorochod Baylka and child             Skorochod Sonia                        Slonimsky Alter
Slonimsky Aydle- Faye


## Peh פ

Polozhesky Chasia                      Polozhesky Merke                       Polozhesky Bracha
Polozhesky Gershon                     Polozhesky Esther                      Polozhesky Moshe
Polozhesky Chaya                       Polozhesky Berl                        Polozhesky Feivel

Friedman Riva Rayzel
Friedman Gittel
Portnoy David
Portnoy Chaim
Popko, child
Perevolotsky Bracha
Perevolotsky Shayna
Perevolotsky Mendel
Fivelevitz, his wife
Fivelevitz Eliyahu
Fivelevitz Hirshel
Fivelevitz Chaim
Fivelevitz Zaydel
Fivelevitz Etke
Fivelovitz Taibe
Fivelovitz Chana
Pomerchik Luba
Friedman Chaya
Friedman Tsirel

Friedman Alter
Portnoy Moshe-Hillel
Portnoy Zalman
Persky Yehudit
Perevolotsky Layb
Perevolotsky Chasia
Perevolotsky Hadassa
Fivelevitz Shimke
Fivelevitz Shlomo
Fivelevitz Sarah-Faygel
Fivelevitz Etka
Fivelevitz Zaydel
Fivelevitz Nachum
Fivelovitz Alter
Fivelovitz Rivka
Fivelovitz Yenta
Pomerchik Berl
Friedman Yosef
Friedman Moshe-David

Friedman Shprintsa
Portnoy, his wife
Portnoy Dvorah
Popko Aaron
Perevolotsky Elke
Perevolotsky Reuven
Perevolotsky Rachel
Fivelevitz Berchi
Fivelevitz Henia and child
Fivelevitz, 2 children
Fivelevitz Avraham
Fivelevitz Tsippa
Fivelevitz Sonia
Fivelovitz Chana Yenta
Fivelovitz Hillel
Pomerchik Ezra
Friedman Yehoshua Berl
Friedman Leah
Perelman Velvel

## Tsadik צ

Tsalkovitz Pinchas
Tsalkovitz Zlotta-Vilda

Tsalkovitz Zussia
Tsaflobodky Yudel

Tsalkovitz Baruch
Tsaflobodky Mina and children

## Koof ק

Kaposhavsky Sarah-Golda
Kivlevitz Badna
Kabak Moshe-Leib
Kabak Rayzel
Kopelovitz Avraham
Kalmanovsky Shmuel-Hirsh
Kalmanovsky Hadassa
Klutsky Chaya-Tsipa
Klutsky Yaakov
Krolavetsky Pessia
Krolavetsky Nachum
Kessler Mayrim
Kessler Arye
Kessler Tamar
Kalmanovitz Yitschak
Kaplan Levik
Kaplan Chaya-Leah
Kaplan Chana
Kaplan Gittel (Hordus)
Kaplan Ozer
Kaplan Vetsye
Kazanovitz Yosef
Koifman Idela

Kaposhavsky Alte
Kabak Shlomo
Kabak Chaim
Kabak Moshe and child
Kopelovitz Reuven
Kalmanovsky Chava- Elke
Kupernick Artsia
Klutsky Leah
Krolavetsky Grunia
Krolavetsky Tamar
Krolavetsky Avraham
Koltsitsky Tuvia
Kessler Esther
Kalmanovitz Yosef
Kalmanovitz Breina
Kaplan Bayle
Kaplan Shoshana
Kaplan Yosef
Kaplan Mashe
Kaplan Riva
Kaganovitz Moshe
Kazanovitz Rivka
Koifman Luba

Kaposhavsky Chaim, wife and children
Kabak Duba
Kabak Eliezer
Kopelovitz Gittel
Kopelovitz Shaul
Kalmanovsky Reuven
Klutsky Yitschak Meyer
Klutsky Noach
Krolavetsky Hirsh-Tsvi
Krolavetsky Aaron
Krolavetsky Yenta
Koltsitsky Chasia
Kessler Miriam
Kalmanovitz Bila
Kaplan Moshe
Kaplan Chaim
Kaplan Meyer
Kaplan Lipa
Kaplan Faygel
Kaplan Chana
Kaganovitz Faygel
Kazanovitz Riva
Koifman Yocheved

Kalmanovitz Shmuel
Kalmanovitz Yossel
Kovensky Tamar
Kibelevitz Moshe
Kibelevitz Aaron
Kliachko Miriam
Kuznitz Rachel
Kuznitz Alka
Kuznitz Rivka

Kalmanovitz Tova
Kovensky Shim'on
Kibelevitz Tsvi
Kibelevitz Eshke
Klachko Sovele
Klachko Yitschak
Kuznitz Moshe
Kuznitz Sarah (Beigin)
Kuznitz Pessia and children

Kalmanovitz Shina
Kovensky Yenta
Kibelevitz Bodone
Kibelevitz Gutel
Klachko Chaya-Sarah
Kuznitz Yehuda
Kuznitz Baylka
Kuznitz Asher
Kuznitz, children

## Reish ר

Rozovsky Yitschak
Rozovsky Tsirel (Mordechovitz)
Rozovsky Rivka
Rabinowitz Yaakov and child
Rakovitsky Shifra
Rakovitsky Shlomo
Ragshanitsky Frume

Rozovsky Shprintza
Rozovsky Shabtai
Raninovitz Shalom
Rakovitsky Nissan
Rakovitsky Bayle
Rabinovitz Lubche
Rappaport Shimke (Berkovitz)

Rozovsky Alter
Rozovsky Masha
Rabinovitz Sonia
Rakovitsky Chana
Rakovitsky Hirsh
Rabinovitz Noach

## Shin ש

Shatzky Malka
Shmulevitz Pinchas
Shimshelevitz Baruch
Shimshelevitz Mordechai
Shneider Shlomo
Sharushevsky Breina-Faygel
Sharushevsky Breina Gittel
Shimonovitz Shalom
Shimonovitz Baylka
Shimonovitz Ben-Zion
Shuster Moshe-Eli
Shuster Henia
Shuster David-Feitel
Shuster David-Feitel
Shkolnik Hirsh

Shatzky Yisrael
Shmulevitz Fruma and two children
Shimshelevitz Chana
Shimshelevitz Nissan
Shneider Milke (Gershunovsky) & kids
Sharushevsky Libka
Shlimovitz Sonia
Shimonovitz Elta
Shimonovitz Yehuda
Shuster Mussia
Shuster Chedva
Shuster Faygel
Shuster Moshe
Shuster Riva
Shkolnik Sonye

Shatzky Binyamin
Shmulevitz Yentel and children
Shimshelevitz Leah
Shimshelevitz Gershon
Sharushevsky Yechiel
Sharshevsky Yekutiel
Shlimovitz Yehuda
Shimonovitz Hirsh
Shimonovitz Minya
Shimonovitz Itta
Shuster Michael
Shuster Reuven
Shuster Baylke
Shuster Chasia

[Page 311]

## TRANSLATION OF THE MEMORIAL STONE:

**Pillar of Remembrance
On Mount Zion in Jerusalem
To the Saints of the Community of**

# Korelitz

**Near Novogrudok (Vilna Province)
Who were Murdered and Exterminated for the Sake of God
by the Nazis (May They be Damned)
During the Years of the Holocaust (1939-1945)**

**May Their Souls be Written in the Scroll of God**

**Remembrance Day on 3rd Av 5702 - 23.8.1942
Commemorators are the Organization of Korelitz Survivors in
Israel**

*On the left appear the words: "Scroll of Destruction"*

*[Page 312]*

# YAHRTZEIT CANDLES

## Fruma Gulkowich-Berger

**As translated from the Yiddish in her book
"With Courage Shall We Fight"**

I look up the dates in calendars of black days past.
And when I light memorial candles for the martyrs
I see the demon of evil spirits
who slaughtered and annihilated my people.

The first candle, I light for you, my mother.
You remained alone in your grave, among the first.
The suffering was dark and cold
when your soul expired.

Your only son had to prepare your grave,
But all of your children accompanied you to eternity.
Although everyone stifled their grief and tears,
They envied your early death.

Now, after the great destruction of six million,
The fires still glow under the ashes provoking, demanding.
I ask you, Mankind: "How many candles should I light?"
My exhausted brain cannot conceive it.

When the final calculations come into my thoughts,
There were such large extended families, young and old...
There are six candles burning - for everyone, together.
For brothers and sisters, for fathers and mothers.

In the dark fog, images surfaces
Of the outrageous injustice that the world had hidden.
So much tragedy in every shadow,
The blood is still flowing,
Its demands interwoven with "muteness".

If they could recount, if they could speak -
The flames of the candles that bear the sorrow -
The world should take notice, and remember,
Never to allow another executioner to rise.

[Page 313]

# IN MEMORIAM

*[Page 314]*

# Rabbi Moshe Hurewitz
# Ho-Romoh

## by Aharon Leib Oshman, New York, (nephew)

## Translated from the Hebrew by Harvey Spitzer

Rabbi Moshe Hurewitz, called by his acronym, *Ho-Romoh,* was born in Korelitz on the holiday of *Shavuoth* (Feast of Weeks), in the year 5631 (1871). His father, Rabbi Aharon-Yehuda, son of Rabbi Avraham, died in the prime of his life at the age of 39 and his mother, Chaya-Golda, daughter of Rabbi Nissan, remained a young widow for years. After her husband's death, she devoted her life to the love of her orphaned children, and the *Romoh* emphasizes in his book, *The Romoh's Outlook,* that all his Torah knowledge was her shadow. After his marriage to Grunia, daughter of Rabbi Yitzchak-Ze'ev from Eishishok, near Vilna, he left Korelitz and served for 18 years in the rabbinate in Lithuania, in the town of Legum in the district of Kovno. This was prior to the First World War when Judaism flourished in all its beauty and glory. It was at that time that his first two books appeared: "*The Romoh's Sermons*" and *The Romoh's Visions,* containing general sermons, sermons for the Holidays and for all the Sabbaths of the year, all bearing the national seal, all of them drawn from life and built on the words of our Sages. His third book, *The Romoh's Logic*, printed by the Tefillah Publishing Company in Warsaw in the year 5690 (1930) and his fourth book, *The Romoh's Outlook*, published in the year 5694 (1934) with his coming to New York, were the fruit of his observations of the terrors of the First World War and the terrors of the Russian Revolution. He served for 16 years in the rabbinate in the town of Roslav in the district of Smolensk, where he saw Russian Jewry in its tranquility, in its fighting a heroic war for its existence and in its heroic death.

His book, *The Romoh's Outlook*, includes observations on everything that had occurred during the last 25 years, years which confounded the world and people's minds. This book stands out to a great extent with its sound logic. With his clear outlook, the *Romoh* transmits his view as to what happened with the world in general and with our people in particular. His fifth (and final) book, *The Romoh's Observations*, was published in New York in the year 5699 (1939) - the fruit of his observations during the five years of his life in the USA. At a time when American Jewry had not yet managed to assume the form worthy of it, he was one of the first to cry out, "How long will you waver between two opinions", and he called out to the Jews of the USA to rise to the challenge of helping our people at a time of distress, when the existence of our people in the Land of Israel and in the Diaspora was in danger.

The *Romoh* was one of the most famous rabbis of his generation, one of the most well-known preachers of his time. He was a poet of Judaism, which he considered the most important thing in life. He dreamed the dream of the final redemption, and his love for our land brought him much closer to its free builders - in opinions. His books and sermons had a great influence on all those who read or heard them. In his lifetime, the *Romoh* became a symbol of honor to the Torah, a symbol of the Angel of Peace, a symbol of devotion to our land and the martyrs of our people.

He passed away in New York in the year 5706 (1946) at the age of 75.

*[Page 315]*

RABBI MOSES HUREWITZ

Formerly Rabbi of Raslav, Russia, and previously
of the city of Legum

Author of
"Droshos Horomoh," "Chozyonos Horomoh,"
"Hegyonos Horomoh" and "Hashkofos Horomoh"

303 MADISON STREET
NEW YORK CITY

הרב משה הורוויץ

רב דראסלאוו רוסיא ומלפנים בעיר ליגום

מחבר הספרים

„דרשות הרמה", „חזיונות הרמה", „הגיונות הרמה"
ו„השקפות הרמה"

253 רחוב מידיסון

ניו יורק

ב"ה 23 אקטאבר - 46

*handwritten Hebrew text*

---

**RABBI MOSES HUREVITZ**
**Formerly Rabbi of Roslav, Russia, and previously**
**of the city of Legum**

**Author of**
***Droshos Horomoh, Chozyonos Horomoh,***
***Hegyonos Haromoh* and *Hashkofos Haromoh***

**253 MADISON STREET**
**NEW YORK CITY**

*With God's help, October 23, 1946*

*To my dear nephew, my sister's son, Aharon Leib and his enlightened
wife Sarah and their little son, may he become great! Shalom Rav!*

*[Page 316]*

# Rabbi Avraham Hirshovitz

## Painfully submitted by Sarah Osherovitz - Ra'anana

Rivka Hirshovitz            Rabbi Avraham Hirshovitz

My father and teacher, Rabbi Avraham Hirshovitz, son of Rabbi Yona Hirshovitz from Korelitz, who was called Yona Zalamanker, was great in Torah knowledge, a leader, an orator and a lobbyist for the benefit of his co-religionists. He was a Zionist and took part in rabbinic conferences on behalf of Zionism. He served in the rabbinate in the towns of Kamai, Rovinishok and Skidel. He died on the 5th day of *Tishrei* 5675 (1915).

My mother and teacher, Mrs. Rivka Hirshovitz, was modest and honest. Her heart and hands were always open to the needy and oppressed. She passed away on the first day of *Chanukah* 5685 (1925).

[Page 317]

# My father Leib Londin

### by Tova Londin-Rogovin

### Translated from the Hebrew by Ann Belinsky

He was born in the village of Zessolia near Minsk. His father Mendeli was a God-fearing Jew and great in the Torah. In their old age his parents travelled to the Holy Land and are buried in Jerusalem on the Mount of Olives. My father had a wide-branching family, four brothers and two sisters, all of whom were engaged in Torah study. One of them was a Rabbi in Niesviezh. Most of them are not alive. Some of the remnants of the family live in America. When my father set up his family in Korelitz, he had been authorized for the Rabbinate, but did not agree to work in the Rabbinate, for his own reasons. He decided his place was in the *Bet Midrash* (house of study). My mother died in her youth. She left behind two sons and two daughters: Shlomo-Haim in London and Avraham-Eliyahu in Paris, Breyna-Feigel and her family were murdered in the Holocaust and Gitel is in Israel. It was hard for my father to carry this heavy blow and with no way out he left the children with my mother's parents and returned to Minsk, where his sister lived with her family. He lived the rest of his life in Persepha (a suburb of Minsk), and was the right-hand man of the local Rabbi. He taught *Gemara* to many pupils. He lived in poverty and bore his suffering in silence. During the Bolshevik period I was with him for eight months and got to know him; he was a believer, straightforward and well-liked. He read the newspaper every day and enthusiastically followed what was going on in the world. He loved *Eretz Yisrael* with all his heart and wanted to come to live here, but didn't make it. He died a martyr's death.

[Page 318]

# Shlomo Londin

## by Yaacov Abramovich

### Translated from the Yiddish by Harvey Spitzer

Shlomo Londin, a former resident of Korelitz, lived in London. He was involved with his fellow countrymen from Korelitz until his death.

I was among the few Korelitz survivors who were saved from that horrible war. We were in a *kibbutz* (collective group) in Italy in 1946 and I remember when we suddenly received a letter from a man who was looking for Jews from Korelitz. When we met with the man in Milan, we found out that Shlomo Londin had asked an acquaintance who went to Italy to look for Korelitz Jews and help them obtain whatever they might need. The man left us money in Shlomo Londin's name.

In 1962 Shlomo and his wife visited Israel, where he had a sister, Gitel. Several members of the Korelitz Committee met with him at that time. He was interested in everything. We informed him that we were dreaming of erecting a "monument" in memory of our dearest ones – parents, sisters and brothers, who were so cruelly murdered. In other words, we wanted to put out a Yizkor Book. We received £500 from him, the first donation for this fund. Shlomo corresponded with us until his death.

# Tzvi Kivilevitz

## By Michael Beigin

### Translated from the Hebrew by Ann Belinsky

Tzvi Kivilevitz, the teacher at the *Tarbut* Hebrew school, lived on Mount Zapoli. At the entrance to his house was a sign: "Welcome" and on the wall was written: "If God does not watch over the house - its builders have toiled in vain". During the big fire in the town in 1929, when half the town was burnt down and the flames reached his house, Kivilevitz's wooden house remained whole.

The house was one full of public activity; where meetings and assemblies were held and where the many ideas were born - all against the background of Eretz Israel. He was a modest man who didn't demand require much from life and on the other hand, was active and energetic for public interests. In his "live newspaper" he would accompany every person making *aliyah* (going to live in) to Eretz Israel with yearning and with great devotion as if all of us were participants in this individual's *aliyah*. I was amongst those to whom he dedicated a place in his "newspaper". He always believed with complete faith that the day would come and he himself would make *aliyah* to Eretz Israel. During the First World War he was in German captivity for three years. He published his impressions of the war and of his captivity in his "live newspaper" and thus tried to impart and pass on what he had gone through and learnt to his friends and acquaintances whom he so respected and loved. He hoped that the day would come and he would publish a book from the collections of his articles. But he never reached this day.

*[Page 319]*

# Alter Avraham-Yitzchak Mordechovitz

## by Leah Kornfeld-Lubshansky

## Translated from the Hebrew by Ann Belinsky

Among the figures that walked amongst us and determined the way of life in our town, is included Alter Mordechovitz, the ritual slaughterer. He was a learned man and well versed in the Torah. A genial smile hovered on his lips as if requesting to gladden the people around him. He lived with his family in modesty and when it was suggested to him to be the Rabbi in large cities he refused, in case others would be pushed aside. When R' Alter became sick, the people of the town wanted to repay him for his good heartedness, his spiritual assistance and good deeds, by giving help where there was sickness, calling for a doctor, or reading Psalms in the synagogue. He and his wife Sara-Dvorah led an exemplary life. They educated their children in their spirit.

*[Page 320]*

# Kalman Mordochovitz (Avrahami)
## By Michael Beigin

**Translated from the Yiddish by Harvey Spitzer**

Kalman was born in Korelitz in 1899, son of R' Alter, the ritual slaughterer. We know little about his childhood. Kalman was an active member of many institutions such as in the administration of *HeChalutz* Youth Movement and the Jewish National Fund. He was also an active member of the library, in the management of the fire department, etc.

While in Novogrudek during the First World War, he was secretary in the *Shokdei Melacha* trade school organization, in the management of the orphan home and in the management of the free kitchen which provided cocoa and small buns with sweet soup. In a word, he was a true community worker.

When Kalman came to this country, his home was always open to those who were hungry and to Korelitz Jews in particular. He would welcome each person with a smilc, a joke, and dispelled everyone's unhappy thoughts and bad mood.

Despite his poor health, he didn't rest until he helped each former Korelitz resident adjust and get started in their new country, and he observed the *yorzeit* of the great massacre. He was the first president of the *Yotzei Korelitz*, Korelitz Benevolent Society.

Kalman suffered for years. His voice became weaker at each memorial. His eyes grew dim, but his energy kept him on his feet.

He was a modest person and was careful never to insult anyone.

Kalman passed away on March 4, 1959 and left us forever.

*[Page 321]*

# Leah Kaplan

## Chasia Turtel Oberzhansky

### Translated from the Hebrew by Ann Belinsky

We called her Leah'keh - an expression for fondness and soul relationship; when we got older, we called her Leah Kaplan. My earliest hazy childhood memories stream by and are linked together with Leah'keh to the point that there is a blurring of bounds between us. We were both pupils in the *Heder Hametukan* ("Improved" elementary school) of Archkeh the *Melamed*. When we became the only girls in the town to join the boys studying *Gemara*, we were nicknamed "Half-boys". Leah'keh was prominent as a talented pupil, diligent and dedicated. With her honest, solid and consistent character she quickly rose to the rank of leadership in the *heder*. Before we are 12-13 years old, we are already given the job of rehabilitating the social and spiritual life of our town, which was almost destroyed in the First World War and Leah'keh is in the centre of activities and events. She has a hand in establishing the Children's Library, from which the public library developed with hundreds of volumes, organized the "Club" that was initiated by our friend Mordechai Karolevtzky (Malchieli), and it was Leah'keh who faithfully bothered to gather us together for weekly meetings - for discussions and shared reading.

When a local branch of *HeHalutz Hatzair* was set up in May 1924 in Korelitz by Bialopolsky, a *shaliach* (emissary) from the main branch in

Warsaw, Leah'keh was among the first ten boys and girls that came to the *Ezrat Nashim* (women's section) of the synagogue, where Bialopolsky established the branch - and she was also chosen as a member of the committee. From that very moment and until she made *aliyah* to Eretz Israel, all her life was dedicated to *HeChalutz HaTza'ir*. Afterwards, to *HeChalutz*, and to work for the National Fund organisations. Her entire personality was concentrated in one goal - emotional and spiritual preparation towards making *aliyah*. Leah'keh was blessed with all those dear and rare qualities which characterize the best of the Jewish-Russian intelligentsia from the days of the *Bilu* (first Russian pioneers, 1882) and up to the breaking forth of the young Russian Jews - a second and third generation from the October Revolution - to the beaches of the Homeland as a result of their aversion to the life in the Diaspora and its baseness on one hand, and longing for the life of redemption and a honor in *Eretz Israel* on the other. Leah'keh did not make do with her work in *HeChalutz* - she also did her proletarian duty - and went to acquire a profession in Vilna. On her return after receiving a diploma as a perfect dressmaker, with her practical talent, she dressed and decorated all the young girls in the town with all the latest models of dresses. Finally she left for the pioneering *hachshara* (training farm) in Stolin and from there to *Eretz-Israel* - to a life of pioneering fulfillment on a kibbutz. We admired Leah'keh for her original and pure integrity, her sharp, non-compromising logic, her loyalty to the aim of pioneering, her deep affinity for books, for her continual self enrichment.

Leah'keh was my friend and companion from the moment I learnt to recognize the environment, to think, to feel and look for ways of shaping personality and until the moment our ways parted when I left Poland. I always thought of her - in bringing up my town Korelitz in my mind's eye - in every place that fate brought me to - and a pleasurable, soft warmth came into my heart - when I remembered her. Our shared memories are engraved - preparing lessons, swimming in the river, playing games, shared reading, discussions, and dances, and above all the daily activity in *HeChalutz HaTza'ir*, in the reading room, the library and spending time in her parents' house, which was like my parents' home.

And here came death and took Leah'keh away forever. An important link was taken out of the organism of the "**I**" of Korelitz and is no more.

*[Page 322]*

# My brother Yona, son of Shlomo Oberzhansky
## Chasia Turtel-Oberzhansky

### Translated from the Hebrew by Ann Belinsky

In Norfolk in the State of Virginia a week before *Rosh Hashana* 5729 (1969), Yona ben Shlomo Oberzhansky died in his fifties. He was involved in the life of the conservative community in Norfolk, member of the local Zionist branch and a generous donor to the National Funds, and proud of the "Bonds" that he purchased towards the efforts on behalf of the building of the State of Israel.

In the second half of September 1969, after 12 days of a difficult fight with a heart attack, he returned his soul to the Creator. Yona was the scion of an old family in Korelitz that had planted roots in the town in the second half of the eighteenth century. On his father's side he was a great-grandson and grandson of landowners, learned scholars of the Torah, heads and leaders of the community. On his mother Itka's side, daughter of R' Moshe Shmuel Trotsky - a learned Torah scholar and a wealthy log merchant who was from the dynasty of the Luria family from the Minsk branch, which can be traced back to the *Ari Hakadosh*, Rabbi Yitzhak Luria of the Safed Kabbalists of the 16th century. The house of the grandfather R' Avraham Yitzhak and father Shlomo Oberzhansky was open to all who in need, and mother did her charitable deeds in modesty.

He made *aliyah* to *Eretz Israel* illegally, tried to find his place there, but in the spring of 1940 made his way to the United States, raised a family and had three boys to whom he gave a basic Jewish education. My grief is immeasurable - as the older sister, after the loss of my parents and murder of my younger brother Moshe Shmuel, he was cut down like a tree and died in the Diaspora and not on holy ground.

**My dearly loved ones, in memory**

Father: **Shlomo Oberzhansky**
Mother: **Itka**

Dedicated with sorrow by:
**Chasia Tutel-Oberzhansky**

[Page 324]

# An Eternal Light

**Aharon Abramowich** (grandfather)
**Sarah (Abramowich) Pinchuk**

**Eliezer Abramowich**

**Dushka Abramowich**

Dedicated in sorrow by:
**Menucha Itzkovitz (Abramowich)**
**Yaacov Abramowich**

---

# In Holy Remembrance
## Yisrael Berman

**Your memory is perpetuated in sorrow and grief**

By his wife:
**Raya Berman**

[Page 325]

# In Eternal Remembrance

**David Schultz**
**Reizel Schultz (Yasselevsky)**
**Yitzchak Meir Schultz** (their son)

Memorialized by:
**Lea Ackerman** - New York
**Shifra Ackerman** - New York

# In Holy Remembrance

**Nathan (Nissan) Ackerman**

Submitted in grief and sorrow:
His wife: **Lea Ackerman**
His daughters: **Sylvia Ackerman**
**Reizel Ackerman**

*[Page 326]*

# In Eternal Remembrance

From left: **Chaya-Bayle, Tama, Yudel Ovseyvitz**

**Binyamin Ovseyvitz**          **Michael Ovseyivitz**

Memorializing his wife, his brother and the children
**Reuven Ovseyvitz**

*[Page 327]*

# In Everlasting Remembrance

From right to left:

**Rachel Bernstein,** born 1898
**Yosef Bernstein,** born 1890
**Sinai Bernstein,** born 1930
**Aharon Bernstein** (may he be set apart for a long life!)
**Leibush Bernstein,** born 1925

**Moshe Kivelevitz**
**Eshke Kivelevitz,** born 1889
**Gutel Kivelevitz,** born 1917
**Aharon Kivelevitz,** born 1920

Submitted by:
**Dr. Aharon Bernstein** – New York

[Page 328]

# A Monument to the Souls of our Dear Ones

Father: **Moshe Berkowitz**
Mother: **Chana-Chava Berkowitz**
Sister: **Zalta Berkowvitz**
Sister: **Shimka Rappaport**
Brother-In Law: **Avraham Rappaport**
Their son: **Moshe Rappaport**
Sister: **Yehudit Fleisher**
Brother-in Law: **Mottel Fleisher**
Their daughter: **Masha Fleisher**

## Preserving their Memory Forever

Family: **Yosef (Berkowitz)**
**Kushneir**
**Haim Berkowitz**
**Yossel Berkowitz**
**Honey Berkowitz**

[Page 329]

# In Holy Remembrance

From right to left:
**Shmuel Issar Oshrovitz, Eliahu Chaim, Shaul Nachum,
Leah Deichah, Feigel (née Kivelevitz)**

Submitted in sorrow:
**Kalman Bezalel Oshrovitz**

# We Sanctify the Memory of Our Dear Ones

**Sonia Dovidovsky**       **Shlomo Dovidovsky**

Their memory is perpetuated in sorrow:
**Miriam Dovidovsky** – Argentina
**Zacharia Dovidovsky**
**Eliahu Dovidovsky**

*[Page 330]*

## In Memoriam

Photo within the Photo:
**Nachum Izik Beigin**

Sitting from Right:
**Tsirl Beigin, Libka** (mother, nee Gordon), **Sara-Leah Beigin**

Standing from Right:
**Michael Beigin** (may he be set apart for a long life), **Zlatka Beigin, Eliyahu Beigin**

Memorialized by
**Sara and Michael Beigin** - Jerusalem

## In Holy Remembrance

**Breina Gulkowitz     Grunia Gulkowitz (Weintraub)     Feigel Gulkowitz**

Their memory is perpetuated in sorrow:
**Fruma Gulkowitz-Berger, Benzion Gulkowitz** - New York

**\*Correct spelling of the family name: Gulkowich**

*[Page 331]*

# In Holy Remembrance

Sa'adia Gertzovsky

**In eternal sorrow we remember our unforgettable dear ones:**

Father: **Sa'adia Gertzovsky**
Mother: **Rachel Gertzovsky**
       **Leah Gertzovsky**
       **Shlomo Gertzovsky**
Aunt: **Chaske Gertzovsky**
Uncle: **Shlomo Gertzovsky**
Uncle: **Berel Gorodinsky**
Aunt: **Neshke Gorodinsky**
       **Chishe Gorodinsky**
       **Berel Gorodinsky**
       **Avraham Gorodinsky**
       **Benzion Gorodinsky**
Family: **Moshe Gorodinsky**

Their memory is perpetuated in sorrow:
**Sonia Greenberg (Gertzovsky) - Toronto**
**Perle Carson (Gertzovsky) - Toronto**

*[Page 332]*

# In Everlasting Memory

Sitting (from right): **Noach Gershonovsky** (may he be set apart for long life), **Avraham-Shmuel Gershonovsky** (may he be set apart for long life), **Herzl Ephroimsky, Yosef Gershonovsky**.
Standing (from right): **Moshe Berkowitz, Yaakov Gershonovsky, Leah Gershonovsky, Haim Gershonovsky, Mushia Gershonovsky, Gedaliahu Gershonovsky** (father), **Musha Perevolotsky, Aharon Perevolotsky** (child)


Perpetuating their memory in pain and sorrow
**Noach Gershonovsky** and his family

[Page 333]

## In Holy Remembrance

From left to right:
Shlomo Gershonovsky,
Bashke Gershonovksy,
Yashe Gershonovsky,
Soreleh Gershonovsky

From right to left (first row)
Moshel Gershonovsky,
Noach Gershonovsky
(may he be set apart for a long
life),
Moshia Gershonovsky

(second row)
Hertzl Efroimsky
Reuven Perevelusky

Their memory is perpetuated in sorrow:
Noach Gershonovsky

**Note: Perevelusky should be spelt Perevolotsky**

*[Page 334]*

## In Holy Remembrance

Seated from right:
**Yossel Gershonovsky, Malka Gershonovsky;**
Their son-in-law: **Mordechai-Reuven Begin**
Their sons: **Markol** (may he be separated for a long life!)
**Yeshayahu** (may he be separated for a long life!)

From right
**Yona Yellin, Yeshayahu Gershonovsky** (may he be separated for a long life!), **Avraham Gorodinsky**

Their memory is perpetuated in sorrow and grief:
**Yeshayahu Gershonovksy -** America, Lakewood, New Jersey
**Markol Gershonovsky –** South Africa, Capetown

[Page 335]

# In Memoriam

From right: **Shlomo Novitzky**
**Sara Novitzky (Dushkin)**
**Elka Novitzky (Dushkin)**
**Eliezer Novitzky** (may he be separated for a long life!)

Perpetuating their memory:
**Haya Zelbin (Dushkin)**
**Yaacov Dushkin**

# In Eternal Remembrance

**Haim Bussel**

**Rachel Meyerovitz (Bussel),
Ber Bussel, Pesach Bussel**

Memorializing:
**Yitzhak Trovovitz** (brother of one mother (*sic*))

*[Page 336]*

## An Eternal Light of Remembrance

**Haim, Chaya-Etya Lubchensky** and their son **Yisrael**

**Simcha and Rachel Lubchensky**

Memorializing:
**Shaul Lubotz (Lubchensky)**
**Leah Kornfeld (Lubchensky)**
**Berel Lubchensky**

**Note: the correct spelling is Lubchansky**

[Page 337]

# We Sanctify the Memory of Our Dear Ones

Grunia Krolavetsky          Shimon Krolavetsky

Preserving their memory in sorrow:
**Leah Dinai (Krolavetsky)**
**Mordechai Malchieli (Krolavetsky)**
**Arieh Shalit (Krolavetsky)**

# An Eternal Monument to my Parents

Avraham Kaplan              Rachel Kaplan

Dedicated by:
**Hana Kaplan-Kamin**

[Page 338]

# In Holy Remembrance

Grunia Krolavetsky          Meirim Kessler

**The Dearly Beloved whose Memory will be Kept Forever**

| | |
|---|---|
| **Tuvia Koltsitsky** | My father |
| **Chasia Koltsitsky** | My mother |
| **Pessia Krolavetsky** | My sister |
| **Tszvi Krolavetsky** | Her husband |
| **Grunia Krolavetsky Tamar Krolavetsky** | Their children |
| **Esther Kessler** | My sister |
| **Aryeh Kessler** | Her husband |
| **Meirim Kessler Tamar Kessler** | Their children |

Dedicated in sorrow and pain by:
**Hina Koltsitsky-Caspi**

*[Page 339]*

# In Eternal Remembrance

Binyamin and
Mordechai Zelivansky

Shimon and Rivka
Zelivansky (Krolavetsky)

From right sitting: **Leah** (may she be set apart for long life), **Sara, Shimon Ostchinsky**
(may he be set apart for long life), **Mordechai** (may he be set apart for long life), **Rivka.**
Standing: **Yosef Ostchinsky, Aharon, Tzvi, Aryeh** (may he be set apart for long life), **Nachum (Krolavetsky)**

Submitted by:
**Leah Dinai, Mordechai Malciel (Krolavetsky), Aryeh Shalit (Krolavetsky)**

*[Page 340]*

# In Eternal Remembrance

From Right: **Itche-Berel, Liova, Dvoshke, Zelig, Moshe David Genzwitz**

**Moshe David**          **Itche-Berel**          **Liova**

Perpetrating their memory:
**Tova Nachumovsky (Genzwitz) and her family**

**Note: the correct spelling is Nohomovski (Gantzevitz)**

[Page 341]

# In Eternal Remembrance

Sitting from right: **Rivka Yellin, Berchi Yellin, Shayna-Feigel Yellin, Getsel Yellin**
Standing from right: **Yona Yellin, Esther-Rachel Yellin**

Memorialised in sorrow:
**Leibel Bloch** - the State of Israel

# In Holy Remembrance

**Chana-Sorah Niegnievitzky**          **Yitzchak-Yosef Niegnievitzky**

Their memory is perpetuated in sorrow:
**Chaya Niegnievitzky**

*[Page 342]*

# We Will Always Remember

Golda Slutsky

David Slutsky

Mulik Slutsky

Liova Slutsky

*[Page 343]*

Grandfather — **Shlomo Slutsky**

Grandmother — **Chaya Sara Slutsky**

From left: **Leibel Slutsky, Taybel Slutsky**
Their children: **Avraham, Davidchik, Yaacov**

Perpetuating their memory:
**Motke Slutsky, Yocheved (Slutsky) Abramowitz,
Yehudit Slutsky, Tova (Genzwitz) Nachumovsky**

*[Page 344]*

# In Holy Remembrance

My father:
**Avraham-
Shmuel
Shimonovitz**

My mother:
**Eshke-Ita
Shimonovitz
(née Itzkovitz)**

My sister:
**Shayna-Gitel Moskovitz
(Shimonovitz)**

My sister:
**Chaya-Sorah
Shimonovitz**

My brother:
**Yosef-Nissan Shimonovitz**

Their memory is perpetuated in
sorrow:
**I. Gutel Simon (Shimonovitz)**
New York

[Page 345]

# In Memoriam

Sitting from left: **Luba Pomerchik, her husband Ezra Pomerchik, Henia Shuster (Pomerchik) Reuven Shuster, Dov Shuster**

Standing from left: **Hadassah Perlman (Pomerchik)** (may she be set apart for long life), **Gavriel Abramowitz, Berl Pomerchik, Leah Becker (Pomerchik), Yaacov Abramowitz** (may he be set apart for long life), **Feivel Pomerchik** (may he be set apart for long life), **Malka Polozhesky (Pomerchik)** (may she be set apart for long life), **Michael Shuster, Faygel Shuster**

Dedicated by
**Malka Polozhesky (Pomerchik), Leah Becker, Hadassah Perlman, Feivel Pomerchik**

*[Page 346]*

# In Holy Remembrance

**Etel Pomerchik
Moshe Pomerchik**

From right to left:
**Yisrael, Leah, Malka, Sorah-Mina Goldshmidt**

**Leah Pomerchik**

**Feivel and Galia
Pomerchik**

Their memory is perpetuated in sorrow:
**Yisrael Pomerchik and family** –America

*[Page 347]*

# In Eternal Remembrance

Standing: **Leah Lipkin, Chaim Stoller, Hirsch Stoller, Yitzchak Stoller, Zlote Lipkin, Shimon-Avraham Lipkin**
Sitting: **Gisha Lipkin, Bila Lipkin, Aharon Lipkin, Moshe-Hirschel Lipkin, a child, Shifra Lipkin**
From right, children: **Zalman, Moshe, Yosef Lipkin.**

**Shimon Avraham Lipkin**

Perpetuating their memory:
**Nacha Patrichavitch**

*[Page 348]*

# In Eternal Remembrance

**Mendel Perevolotsky**          **Simka-Freidel Perevolotsky**

## A Monument to the Souls of our Dear Ones

My parents **Menachem Mendel** and **Simka-Freidel Perevolotsky** were born and lived in Korelitz. My father was a tailor and from his work he made a livelihood for the family.

My parents had four children: **Leibel-Aryeh**, the oldest; the second son **Reuven**; I, **Sheindel** (I made *aliyah* to *Eretz-Israel* in 1926) and my sister **Musha**.

My parents came to *Eretz-Israel* in 1937, two years before the Second World War began. My brothers and sister remained in Korelitz. All, together with their many-branched families, were annihilated by the Germans. The parents lived with me and my husband Avraham Kuznietz in Tel Aviv.

My father **Menachem-Mendel** died in 1938, my mother **Simka-Freidel** died in 1943.

Preserving their memory forever
**Avraham and Sheindel Kuznietz** - Tel Aviv

*[Page 349]*

# We Hold Their Memory Sacred

Father: **Yaakov Kagan**   Mother: **Dvorah**

Their memory is perpetuated in grief:
**Idel Kagan and his wife Barbara (Steinfeld)**

*[Page 350]*

# In Everlasting Memory of Our Closest and Dearest

Standing (from left to right): **Shoske Kagan, Moshe Kagan, Dvorah Kagan, Gitel London** (née **Rogovin**) (may she be set apart for a long life!); **Moshe Kivelevitz.**
Seated (from right to left): **Berel Kagan** (may he be set apart for a long life!); **Yoshke Gurvitz, Breina-Feigel Gurvitz, Chaya-Gitel Gurvitz**

Submitted in sorrow by:
**Idel Kagan, Berel Kagan, Gitel (Londin) Rogovin and their families**

**\*Should be: Standing (from right to left):...**

# I Hold Sacred the Memory of My Nearest and Dearest

My father: **Zvi Hirsh (Irshel the Teacher)**
My mother: **Chaya Dvorah**
My sister: **Chana-Teibel,** with her two children

My brother-in-law: **Moshe Yankelevitz, May the Lord avenge his blood**

Their memory is perpetuated in sorrow:
**Moshe Yoel Kessler** – New York

# In Everlasting Remembrance

(from right to left): **Leah Kletzki, Yitzchak-Mayer Kletzki, Sarah Kletzki,** may she be set apart for a long life

Their memory is perpetuated in sorrow:
**Shlomo Kletzki, Chonia Kletzki, Dr. Sarah Kletzki,**
may she be set apart for a long life

*[Page 352]*

## In Remembrance

First row (standing from right to left): **Berel Damesek, Miriam Kletzko, Sovela Kletzko, Eliezer Ritz**

Second row (seated from right to left): **Boze Damesek (née Kagonovitz), Moshe Kagonovitz, Feigel-Tzires Kagonovitz, Chayke Kletzko (née Kaganovitz), Mania Ritz (née Kaganovitz)** (May she be set apart for a long life)

Third row (seated from right to left): **Soleh Damesek, Yehudit Damesek, Yitzchak Kletzko**

Their memory is perpetuated in sorrow:
**Yona Kagonovitz –America**
**Mania Ritz (Kagonovitz)**

*[Page 353]*

# A Memorial to the Souls of our Dear Ones

Sonye Shkolnik

Hirsh Shkolnik

From
left:     **Miriam Shkolnik (Lev)**
          **Monas Lev**
          **Chiena Finkelshtein**
          **(cousin)**

Their memory is perpetuated in
sorrow by:
**Vital Arieli (Shkolnik)**
**Esther Horwitz (Shkolnik)**

*[Page 354]*

## In Eternal Memory

My brother **Reuven Perevolotsky**

Dedicated in sorrow by: **Sheindel Kuznietz (Perevolotsky)**

------------------------------------------------------------------------------

## In Eternal Memory

**Moshe Poluzhsky**   **Esther Poluzhsky**   **Gershon Poluzhsky**

(Brother)       (Mother)       (Father)

Memorialized in Sorrow: **Yaacov & Mordechai Poluzhsky and their Families**

*[Page 355]*

An Assembly in the Town...

## In Eternal Memory
(Members of the Committee of the Society)

Rivka Reuveni-Shuster

Berl (Dov) Lipshitz

Dedicated in sorrow:
**The Committee of the Korelitzer Society in Israel**

[Page 356]

# Yizkor
## Fruma Gulkowich-Berger
### As translated from the Yiddish in her book
### "With Courage Shall We Fight"

It is *Yahrtzeit* today - my heart is sorrowful.
As I see the glowing embers and the black Swastika
That murdered my people - burned and roasted.
The angry whirlwind has scattered their ashes.

I say *Yizkor* for you, holy martyrs,
Sown and scattered, uncountable corpses.
Your fault was - only that one sin -
You carried the name "Jewish child".

I say *Yizkor*, and I light *Yahrtzeit* candles
For the millions tormented - fathers, mothers, and children.
For slaughtered brothers - I still feel their pain.
For sisters, raped - I still hear their screams.

I say *Yizkor* for you, the unknown hero
Who fell in battle on the blood-soaked ground
As a proud Jew, a courageous Partisan,
You showed the enemy that the spirit
Of the Maccabees still exists.

I say *Kaddish* for all the millions.
The *Yahrtzeit* candles burn to remind the world
Of the uneven battle of Evil against the helpless ghetto.
When the last one fell, the hour was already late.

The next generation asks, doubts, and wonders:
How could such brutality occur in the twentieth century?
Is this the land of Goethe, Nietzsche, and Heine
That annihilated six million of my brothers?

Maybe this was all a nightmare,
Only I alone know there was no savior!
When heads fell and were scattered all over
Heads shot, heads bloodied - in the deep, black pits.

I say *Yizkor* - it burns in my brain
And I see the executioner, Hitler, the murderer.
My head is bowed, my heart has tightened up -
And I ask the world: "How can it be that your faces reflect no shame?"

**Memorial to the Martyrs of Korelitz**
(Bet Moses Cemetery, West Bablylon, New York)

May their souls be bound to the souls of the living

*[not numbered = Page 358]*

# Sefer Korelitz Publication Committee

Iassia Turtel Oberzhansky

Michael Walzer-Fass,
Editor

Yaacov Abramowich

Malka Poluzhsky

Mordechai Malkieli

Chiena Caspi

*[not numbered = Page 359]*

# Committee of Korelitzer Society in Israel

Malka Avni (Mordechowitz)

Michael Beigin,
Committee Chairman

Leah Lubchansky-Kornfeld

Yaacov Poluzhsky

Abraham Kuznietz

Noah Gershenovsky

# PART II --- ENGLISH SECTION*

*Coordinator's Note: All the texts below were written and printed in **English** in the original Yizkor book. In the present book, they were either used in their entirety as the official translation, or because most were abridged versions, the translation from the original Hebrew/Yiddish texts were used, and differences between the two versions are noted in the texts. **Note** that not all of the articles in English appear in the Hebrew/Yiddish version (e.g. the Bielski brothers – page 391, and others).

------------------------------------

*[Pages VI-VIII English]*
*[Pages 13-14 - Hebrew]*
**(Identical to Page 1)**

# EDITOR'S FOREWARD

SEFER KORELITZ is intended to serve as a monument this old and elite Jewish community which, for centuries on end, was the center of vibrant and variegated Jewish life, a community of Diaspora Jews who bore the heritage of their people for many generations, struck root in alien soil, made steadfast their Jewish way of life, and maintained the continuity of their traditions.

The volume is meant to eternalize the memory of the dear ones who perished in the holocaust which overtook European Jewry during the Second World war, the memory of the town and its inhabitants, so that Jewish Korelitz may forever remain a star in the sky - a small shining star, someone's star.

SEFER KORELITZ will always be a fountain of inspiration to the men and women of Korelitz who were born there, were reared in the town, were part of its life and tribulations, and who, at an early age joined the Zionist chalutzim who went to the Land of Israel to rebuild its ruins. The volume will strengthen the townspeople who remained there until destruction stuck and escaped miraculously, after long and agonizing experiences. It will serve as a family album for those  former residents of Korelitz who left the town before the war and found their places in other countries on the face of the globe, struck root there and went on to live traditional lives, and for those who were saved from destruction but have not as yet come to Israel.

Editing a memorial volume involves many problems. Each passing day makes gathering the material more difficult; a townsman who passed on takes with him recollections which then become lost forever. Also, this material must be studied, edited and reworked, so as to achieve a certain balance, since the purpose of the editing is to project not only the life of the town as a whole but also to emphasize the role of the individuals who lived there, particularly if they contributed something unique to its cultural and social experience.

The volume is also a history of sorts of regular events. In history, as a rule, the farther one gets away from the period, the better equipped is he to write its annals. Here the situation is quite the opposite: the nearer one finds himself to the events, the more accurate and authentic is the compiled material. Pre-war Poland had about 2,800 Jewish towns and cities. Of these, about 600 have been memorialized in "Yizkor" volumes of one type or another. Each volume is in communion with its town and its dear ones. So is this volume. It brings us into communion with our dear ones and our town, for a twofold purpose: to perpetuate the memory of those who were taken from us by the most brutal destruction recorded in human history since the fall of the Temple, on the one hand, and to portray to the younger generation the images of its progenitors, whence they came, what brought them there, and who were their preceding generations. The young people in Israel and abroad should be told about this other life, more modest but intensely civilized, of dreamers and fighters, of pious and honest people whose were lives mirrored their creed.

In ordinary times, the Jews of Korelitz would not have thought of photographing their town and its personalities, for future generations. It would never have occurred to them that the history of the town should be written in order to preserve the elite reputation of the locality. There have been people who jotted down reports of events, particularly in times of distress (and these were not rare in the history of Poland's Jews), but these generally became lost. Even the records of the "Four Lands Committee" did not remain intact. However, it so happens that Korelitz maintained a written community record, part of which has survived and has served as a genuine source of information. An attempt to keep the record going and to preserve the information has been made by Hassia Turtel-Oberzhansky of Korelitz. Thus SEFER KORELITZ is able to present a broad tapestry of the town and constitute a worthy monument to its memory.

*

It is a pleasant duty for me to acknowledge the aid and assistance of those who were helpful in the compilation of this volume - particularly Moshe Cinowicz, Yitzhak Alperowicz, and Yad Vashem, and of Israel I. Taslitt, who abridged the material and translated it into English. My thanks to the Achdut Press, its managers and crew, for their fine work, to United Platemakers, and finally to the members of the publication committees in Israel and the U.S. and to all who once called Korelitz their home.

**Michael Walzer-Fass**

---

# LIFE AND HISTORY

*[Pages IX-XIII – English, slightly abridged, below]*
*[Pages 19-34 - Hebrew]*
**See also page 7**

# The History Of The Jews Of Korelitz

## Hassia Turtel -Oberzhansky (Jerusalem)

Like so many other localities near the Polish-Russian border, Korelitz (Korelicze) was alternately in the Polish County of Novohorodok and, in the days of the Czars, in Minsk County of White Russia.

Located on the Ruta River, on the main highway to Lithuania and the other crown lands of the old Polish dynasties, Korelitz was a strategic point in the structure of the kingdom. In 1505 it was looted by the Tartars, and in 1655 it was overrun by the invading Swedish army. In 1733, following the death of King August II, the Polish ruling circles gathered in Korelitz to choose his successor. In 1812 Napoleon's defeated forces straggled through Korelitz on their way back to France; this was after Korelitz had been annexed (in 1772) by Catherine II of Russia. For the next 142 years the town was in the northwestern Jewish pale of settlement allowed by the Czarist regime.

Jewish settlement in Korelitz dates back to the 17th century, but official community documents (mainly contracts between individual Jews and members of the Polish nobility, regarding commercial and trade concessions and leases) are from the 18th century. Under Polish rule, the community was subject to the authority of the Committee of the Four Lands, to which it paid a per capita tax; the record shows 336 such tax-payers. In its internal affairs Korelitz was guided by heads of the community, assisted by nine dignitaries who were rotated each month.

Like most of its sister communities, Korelitz maintained a pious Jewish life, both public and private, and it exercised measures of boycott and ostracism against "wrongdoers" (like the woman Batya, the daughter of R' Yitzhok Eizel, who was found guilty of having traveled in a cart with a peasant from Novohorodok to Korelitz - without a chaperone). The community also regulated the economic life of the individuals, forcing artisans to lower their prices when these were deemed to be too high.

Korelitz's Jews eked out their livelihoods from small business, peddling and crafts, for local consumption and the peasants in the area. Occupations were handed down from father to son, and no manual work was regarded as being below the dignity of the worker.

A major feature of Korelitz's community life was its communal institutions. Aside from its two synagogues and the Hassidic **kloiz**, where its Jews prayed, recited Psalms and studied the Talmud and religious writings, Korelitz also had a Bridal Society for marrying off girls without financial means, a Free Lodgings Society (for men and women), a Free Loan Fund (charity without embarrassment), a *Chevra Kadisha*, and a Ladies Aid Society (110 members) to help ailing women.

Much has been said, deservedly, about the rabbis and scholars who served the community, for such was the fame of Korelitz as a pious, law-abiding and Torah-loving town that many famous rabbis, down the generations, were proud to be its spiritual leaders.

The Jewish community of Korelitz was pious but not fanatic; the winds of enlightenment which swept European Jewry in the second half of the 19th century did not neglect Korelitz. In the summer of 1881, leaders of "The Disseminators of Enlightenment" opened a branch in Korelitz, along with a library. But the most vigorous stirring in the community came in the wake of the Zionist Movement. A branch of "The Lovers of Zion" was established in 1897, the year that saw the first Zionist Congress meet in Basel, and a year later the branch outstripped its counterparts in many of the larger communities.

The new era made its imprint on the education of the young. Talented boys were still sent to the famous *yeshivot* of Mir, Wolozhin and Slabodka, but the young people were also reading Hebrew and Russian literature. Girls were not left out of the picture; in 1902 public-spirited young people founded and operated a school for girls without means.

Close to the turn of the century (1897), according to the Czarist census, Korelitz had 2,559 inhabitants, of these 1,840 Jews. The growth of the Jewish population was dealt a severe setback in the fire that swept the town (1911) and burned 150 houses and public buildings down to the ground. Many Jews had to sleep in barns, until help came in response to an appeal sent out by Rabbi Avrohom Yitzhok Hakohen to the surrounding communities.

Among the famous personalities that Korelitz produced are the martyred poet Yitzhok Katzenelson (died in the Warsaw Ghetto); the poet David Einhorn; the bacteriologist Prof. Saul Aaron Adler (1895-1965, of the Hebrew University), and Architect Baruch Horowitz, who worked in St. Petersburg at the turn of the century and did a great deal to divert Jews into agriculture and the crafts.

## The Community in the First World War

Korelitz and its vicinity were at the front lines when the Kaiser's army broke through, and the populace was evacuated (the Jews found temporary shelter in Novohodorok). After the signing of the Treaty of Versailles, the Jews returned, to find their former homes in ruins; by a miracle the two synagogues were still left standing. The efforts of the Jews to rehabilitate themselves economically were hampered by the advent of a variety of commissars, who expropriated everything in order to avoid "speculation and the exploitation of the working class". The town was included in Poland by virtue of the agreement signed in Riga; its Jews numbered 535 souls.

For the next 18 years - until the Soviet invasion of the area in September of 1939 - the Jewish community looked to its spiritual continuity. Its children went to Hebrew schools and to the *Tarbut* Teachers School in Wilna. In the '20's, all of the youth groups in the Jewish world were represented in Korelitz: *Hechalutz, Hechalutz HaTza'ir, Hashomer HaTza'ir, Betar, Zukunft-Bund.* The young folks arranged literary evenings, social get-togethers, even a dramatic group for presentations in Hebrew and Yiddish. A constant stream of members of the Zionistic youth groups headed for the Land of Israel; once they reached its shores, they joined kibbutzim, worked on the roads and reforested the hills. They were the fortunate ones.

## The Second World War and the Destruction of the Community

At the outbreak of the Second World War, the Jewish community of Korelitz numbered some 1,300 souls. Its sorry economic state was alleviated to some extent by the help it received from relatives abroad. But its status in the country was threatened, first by veterans of Pilsudski's forces, who sought to oust the Jews from commerce and trade, and later by the announced policy of the Nazis to destroy the Jewish people. For a while the situation, though tense, was not alarming, but the beginning of the end came when the Nazi blitzkrieg hit White Russia, on June 21, 1941. The White Russian peasants inaugurated the assault by raiding and pillaging Jewish homes. Then they were given supervision of the town by the Germans, and they used their authority to make life unbearable for their former neighbors.

In July the Nazis ordered the heads of the community to set up a *Judenrat* to "govern" its affairs. Its first duty was to institute the yellow Magen David; later it was ordered to collect all the valuables that the Jews still had and hand them over to the Nazis. Later that month, the Nazis rounded up 105 of the town's foremost Jews, locked them in the synagogue and, on the next day, loaded them into trucks and carted them away - to be shot. Next the *Judenrat* was ordered to have the Rabbi and ten others burn the *Sifrei Torah, tallitot* and other religious articles. Jews who sought to put out the flames were shot. The aged Rabbi Viernik was taken to prison in Novohorodok, tortured and murdered.

Surreptitiously, young Jews began to organize. They obtained weapons and made contact with the partisans in the forests. For the time being they remained in town; the Nazis had announced that if a single Jew was not accounted for, the entire community would be slaughtered.

Then came the ghetto - 50 souls crowded into a single house, under horrible sanitary conditions, and hardly a chance to stay alive. On May 2, the expulsion of the Jews began, as peasants came to cart away the Jews - and take their belongings as booty. The sick were murdered in their beds. All this time the Polish populace looked on and jeered. The carts moved on slowly in the summer heat, and after a days journey (14 miles) arrived at the Novohodorok ghetto. They waited in a downpour four hours until they were allowed to go into the barns.

The young and the able-bodied were taken to work camps in the morning, and many took the first opportunity to escape into the forests, to join the partisans.

On August 8, on orders from the *Judenrat,* all the Jews in the Novohorodok ghetto gathered in the market place, ostensibly to be sent to camps in Russia. Trucks came and took them away - to freshly dug pits, where they were machine-gunned and buried.

In September, the only Jews remaining in the ghetto were the craftsmen, who were kept at work in the heavily-guarded town courthouse. The prisoners dug a tunnel under the courthouse, and several hundred escaped into the forests. (One of them, the cabinet maker Zvi Hirsh Shkolnik, eventually reached Eretz-Israel and lived there with his daughters).

Unfortunately, among the tunnel diggers was a demented young man who told the Nazi captain when the tunnel would be finished. At that moment, as the people in the tunnel began to emerge, they were greeted with a hail of bullets. Half of them were killed; the others scattered and managed to reach the forest, where they joined the partisans.

On May 7, 1943 the third and final massacre of the Jews in the ghetto was carried out and the last of Korelitz's Jews died with them. Thus, in blood and barbarism without precedent in human history, this marvelous White Russian *shtetl* came to an end.

---

[Pages XIV-XV-English - abridged]
[Pages 115-118 - Yiddish]
**See also page 112**

# Korelitz -
# The Idyllic Town Of Pre-World War One Days

## Alter Boyarsky

Several hundred years ago the (the exact date is unknown), a wealthy landowner name Korelitz decided to develop his estates in the area. He liked Jews and understood their economic importance. For the key figure of his project he selected a Jew from Minsk, who in turn brought his relatives to the spot, opened an inn and welcomed new settlers. Jews and non Jews came, and soon a town named for its patron, grew up there, located about 70 miles from Minsk, the country seat, on the road from Novohorodok to Turetz and Mir.

The Jewish presence in Korelitz developed, in time, to truly magnificent heights. The old "Cold" synagogue was a work of art; built of wood, it was adorned with fine wood carving, particularly on the Ark. Opposite this synagogue was the popular *Bet-Hamidrash*, the place of worship of the shopkeepers and craftsmen. Another *Bet-Midrash* was situated up toward the market place, opposite the Rabbi's quarters; here the congregants were members of the town's upper class - such as the grain and fabrics dealers. The Koidanover Hassidic *shtibl*, on the road to the cemetery, was frequented by Hassidim only. The public bath was between the *shtibl* and the cemetery fence.

The stalls in the paved market place belonged exclusively to Jews. Wednesday was market day; peasants from the surrounding areas came to buy commodities (salt, herring, soap, kerosene) and sell (grain, fowl, eggs, butter and cheese). This one day provided the livelihood for the entire week.

The town had several sources of water: the town well in the market place, which was always in need of repair and which never gave pure water; the well in the synagogue courtyard, which supplied clean, cold and fresh water, and a spring with good water located between the town's two inns. The inns also served as police quarters.

The Christian presence was marked by the single church in town, situated near the mansion of the Korelitz estate on Zalemanka Street.

All the traditional institutions of Jewish learning, from the beginners' *cheder* to the twixt-*Mincha*-and-*Maariv Talmud* study groups, held full sway in Korelitz until the decades before the Russian Revolution, when new ideologies penetrated the community - Socialism, Zionism, freedom, equality, brotherhood. A library was established and lectures were given on a variety of current themes. Former *yeshiva* students held forth on revival and revolution. The neighboring Raviner and Rutchiser Forest became the center of anti-Czarist meetings; other gatherings were held late Friday night - in the *Bet-Hamidrash*, unbeknown to the town fathers, but on Sabbath afternoons the same place and the same forest were thronged with Jews on the after-*cholent* stroll.

---

*[Pages XV-XVI]*
*[Pages 149-158 - Yiddish]*
**See also page 146**

# How They Made A Living

## Yaacov Abramowich

Korelitz's economy combined farming, trade and industry, and was thus an ideal example of regional economic development.

Farm work consisted mainly of picking fruit on the Korelitz estates which was later exported to the large cities. Many small enterprises manufactured Holland-style cheeses. Most of them operated on concessions granted by the estate.

Trade and commerce were constructed in the town market, except for grain. The Jewish grain dealers had their stalls just outside the town and the farmers disposed of their product before going on to the market to buy their commodities.

Cattle formed an important item in the commercial establishment. Many of the dealers also operated in the meat markets.

Carpentry and cabinetmaking also formed an important economic feature. Some carpenters moved about the region, visiting farmhouses to do repair jobs on furniture or sell furniture, and returning home for the Sabbath, laden with a variety of farm produce.

The blacksmiths were particularly busy around harvest time, sharpening scythes and sickles for the farms in the area. For the tailors, shoemakers and capmakers, the high season was before the holidays, especially Passover and

*Rosh Hashana*, when the entire home dressed up in honor of the festivals and "for the neighbors".

The fragrant scent of pine board in the center of town came from Michael Shuster's lumber yard (Eliyahu Seilovitzky had one outside the town, but it didn't do so well, and he eventually went into the grain business).

There were several mills in the town, one run by Isaac Stoller and his partners, and the other, on the opposite end of town, by Alter Shebrenik and Yossel Bernstein; both were powered by steam. The water mill, operated by Yisroel-Michael Slutzky and his partner Ezra Pomerchik, didn't do as well, but all the mills gave good service to the peasants and their wagon-loads of grain.

---

[Pages XVI-XVII]
[Pages 95-96, Hebrew]
**See also page 91**

# Education In Korelitz

## Yeheskel Zaks

Such was my little town of Korelitz - a small community in White Russia, with its little houses, narrow alleys, quaint people, as though depicted by an artist: the small-time grocer eagerly waiting for customers; the blacksmith at his anvil, barely eking out a living; the craftsman busy in his tiny workshop...everything on a small scale.

But from the confines of the *Bet-Hamidrash* the voices of the students rise and float out to the streets and alleys, and their message is that help comes not only from mundane sources; it must be sought in the upper spheres, as well.

Unlike the thorough schooling that the lads received, the girls fared less well. They merely learned how to read Yiddish at Moishe Shreiber's home (he was so named because he was the town's official writer of letters, and his calligraphy was indeed beautiful to behold). For "advanced studies" the girls went to Reuben Rotshetzer's; there they learned *Ivreh teitch* (reading the translations of the prayers into Yiddish). Both teachers had regular summer and winter semesters, and so did the years go by.

Then a sudden change came about. Moshe, the son of the Rabbi, came to town for a visit, from the big city where he was studying. In Korelitz this popular young man was known as a fine speaker and ardent Zionist. He persuaded his friend Alter-Herzl to take on the task of educating the girls. All at once we found ourselves learning the stories of the Torah and finding delight in them. The spirit of Zionism became part of our being. We looked forward to becoming members of the "Daughters of Zion" and listened eagerly to every word of news about the movement. Moshe helped our teacher in every way until it was time for him to return to the big city. We had a farewell party in his honor in a hall which we decorated with a picture of Dr. Theodor Herzl and Zionist banners.

I remember particularly an occasion when Moshe came back from a Zionist Congress which he had attended. He spoke to us, and we felt as though the immortal Theodor Herzl himself was standing before us.

I left the town and did not return until 1930, after a 23-year absence, for a day's visit. How things had changed! The young people were now receiving a complete Jewish education, and many of them were preparing to go to Eretz-Israel. I was sure that my town was on the threshold of a new, wonderful era. Little did I know that in another decade disaster would strike at European Jewry and destroy everything, almost everything.

---

*[Pages XVIII-XIX]*
*[Pages 97-99 –Hebrew]*
**See also page 93**

# This Is How We Studied

## Esther Shkolnik-Hurwitz

This was in the period between the two World Wars. Unlike other localities at the end of the First World War, Korelitz had no formal system of education. A child of three or four had to trust to luck for his education; his parents were too preoccupied with the problem of tomorrow's bread. He was left to his own playtime devices.

At the age of 6 -7 he was sent to *cheder*. I well remember mine, in the home of R' Aharon Yaakov Dovidovitz - a large room, long table, benches on either side. R' Aharon Yaakov had what was called an "advanced *cheder*"; he taught "reading, writing, as well as arithmetic" (the primary steps of addition and subtraction). We studied from morning till evening, reading and transcribing entire pages of the *Chumash*, after having learned their contents, word by word, in Yiddish translation. And woe was to the pupil who failed to remember! A male miscreant was placed in a corner with a dirty *shtreimel* dunce cap on his head. For girls, the usual punishment was to put their name on the blackboard and write a large zero filled with smaller zeros next to the name. On the other hand, a good student was rewarded with 5's next to her name.

The next *cheder* was R' Yitzhok's. He was well-versed in the Bible, Talmud and grammar, a martinet when to came to the boys but a fatherly sage with the girls. But one fine day a new school came into being, with expert teachers for every subject: Accountant Yitzhok Klatzki taught arithmetic, Poet Zvi Kivelevitz was invited to teach Hebrew, R' Itzke taught Talmud and grammar, and Mr Shuster taught nature studies.

We were enthralled - a school like "the others" had: recess, bells, a bit of recreation between the classes, holiday hikes, classroom dramatics.

We loved this school, but our parents were worried: how would their children fare, without knowledge of Polish? And so we were transferred to a Polish school. Here we learned new subjects: singing, art, gymnastics. Soon the Jewish students outdistanced the others; the result: seeds of envy and hatred.

The principal of the school, named Dolemba, was a good-natured but also a pleasure-hunting drunkard. The Jewish students didn't let this bad example deter them. They studied hard, so as to complete the courses and go on to higher education elsewhere. Their Jewish studies were provided by a noble person who taught us to love Hebrew - Benjamin Offseiewitz (Ovseyewitz). Those of us who managed to continue with our studies in the large cities always recalled him with love and affection. Other Korelitz teachers who held classes in their homes were Hershel Dobkes, Berl Feivel from Eishishok, Zelig der Schorser (who also did watch repairing) and Zvi Hirsh Chessler.

---

*[Pages XIX-XXI]*

*[Pages 100-101 - Yiddish]*
**Copied to Page 97**

# R' Zvi-Hershel Hacohen Boyarsky

## Zippora Katzenelson-Nachumov

Ignorance had no place in the *Old Shul*. There the folks studied Torah and Talmud day and night. Around it were the public institutions of the community: the Rabbi's home (the *Cold Shul*, so named because the temperature inside was always cooler than outside - summer <u>and</u> winter). Beyond was an even cooler spot - the cemetery, with its headstones sunken into the ground among the weeds - except the modest mausoleum of the deceased Rabbi, R' Yitzhok Yechiel, for whom Yitzhok Katzenelson was named. On the other end of the courtyard was the warmest spot in town - the *schvitzbod*, the Turkish bath, so-called.

Opposite the *Old Shul* and the cemetery was the Hassidic *shtibel* [a place for prayer and also a place for community gathering] of the Koidanover Rebbe. The First *Gabbai* of the *shtibel* was R' Zvi-Hershel Hacohen Boyarsky, a teacher by occupation and understandably a man of modest means. He was a jolly person, rotund and built close to the ground, and he sported a short black beard. He had unbounded faith and was ever in good spirits. His fine singing voice resounded through the alleys and lifted the hearts of his listeners. No *simcha* [joyful occasion] in the *shtibel* was worth the name without his presence, and his preparations to visit the Rebbe in his town was an event in Korelitz.

He was beloved for his gaiety by all his students. He was also a born teacher and knew how to handle the children; the pupils who lagged behind were taken into the smaller room for "private instruction" as in the main room the older pupils taught the younger ones. Yitzhok Katzenelson often spoke of the influence that these surroundings had upon him in his childhood days. This was the background of his future folk poem, "The Sun in Flames is Setting". He often returned to it in later years, visiting the Rabbi's house where his cradle was still standing. And on each occasion he would remark, sadly, that R' Zvi-Hershel was no longer among the living.

**Right to left:** Mordechai Trotzky, Kalman Morduchowitz, Israel Tzelkowitz, Moshe-Eliyahu Shuster, Nachum Krulevitzky

---

# KORELITZ: SAGES AND STUDENTS

*[Pages XXI-XXII]*
*[Pages 58-59 - Yiddish]*
**Copied to Page 49**

## The Poem of Korelitz's *Bet-Hamidrash*

### Yitzhak Katzenelson
**(unknown translator)**

There it stands, your *Bet-Hamidrash*! Deep in my heart
I feel a tug - you are known to me, yet unfamiliar...
This is the sacred spot where I used to romp abut,
Where portly young men used to chat, and the pious prayed.

This is the sacred site to which Jews once came
With aching hearts, and emerged requited;
This was the place where the speechless were heeded
And the weak refreshed with strength.

O Jewish Bet-Hamidrash, home for every Jew,

Recipient of supplication, repository of pain;
To you the Jew his joys recited,
Within your walls the exile lost its edge.

In summertime the birds chirped their song of praise,
Their melodies came through the open windows
Like birds on the wing and sunlight streaming in,
And in the winter nights we sought your warm comfort.

O Jewish *Bet-Hamidrash*, home of all homes!
O our only guardian - can anything replace you?
We the wanderers, you our guiding light.
The comforter who soothes our weary wandering.

Your door is ever open - whene'er I wish, I enter.
Your kindly *shamash* does not ask: Who and wherefrom are you?
If I wish, I pray; if not, silent I remain;
No other home so warms the heart.

Your Holy Ark is filled with Torah scroll,
Its curtain by pious brides embroidered;
A preacher's stand for quoting Scripture,
A lectern with two lions, carved into gentleness.

Your shelves are lined with ponderous volumes,
Ancient Talmud tomes and Rambam folios, books on end!
Over which pallid students pore and sway -
No! No house with such treasure troves is poor.

Your study lecterns, where wars are waged,
Was more worthy than most tranquil peace;
Your benches, for soul and body restful,
For slumber sweet and the best of dreams.

Lowly built, you rise above all others!
Unbeautiful, your beauty all exceeds!
Your loyal roof reflects the brightest sunshine,
The warmest ray through your windows stream.

**Published in "Hajnt", Warsaw, 1935, No. 265**

---

*[Pages XXIII-XXIV -English]* **Copied to page 50**
*[Pages 60-61 - Hebrew]*

# Once there was the Rabbi's House
## Yehoshua Ovseyewitz (Y. Ovsi)
*(See Photo page 50)*

Small and of meager means as it was, the town knew how to safeguard its way of life, its spiritual wholesomeness, its inner light and atmosphere, quietly spinning the continuous fabric of faith and tradition. It withstood adamantly the barbed shafts of assimilation, an island beset by an inimical environment.

The town's weapons in this relentless struggle were the institutions which it created and maintained: the houses of prayer, the schools and academies, the societies and organizations founded to support and supplement them: the Talmud Study group, the Visitation Society, Free Loan Aid, and others.

The Rabbi's house was one of these institutions, singular and outstanding, the center of kindliness and the core of understanding. Owned by the community, this house was the rabbi's residence during his tenure, which in many cases meant for life; (rabbis left at times to assume positions elsewhere; rarely was a rabbi dismissed). Within the walls of this house dwelled, in the course of many decades, Torah luminaries whose decision and impact was felt in the community's religious, social and cultural life. Theirs was the decisive voice in litigations between man and his neighbor, and their esteemed personality lent weight and credence to their judgment.

The Rabbi's House, in itself, lent a distinctive charm to the town, in comparison with the external aspect of Korelitz. The town's appearance was drab, at best. Its plainness was accentuated even more sharply by the beautiful expressions of nature all around it: hills, glades, meadows, and the bright blue skies above - all of which combined to show up the mossy houses and their crooked walls, their ragged roofs and smoke-stained windows, a blot on the creation of the Almighty.

Nor did the appearance of the town fare any better from its mundane life. The days were filled with the rasping sound of people engaged in earning a living, the harsh tumult of the masses, the peasants and the hangers on of the market place, uncouth, boorish and often closer in appearance to the animal world.

In this depressing atmosphere the Rabbi's House stood out in magic relief. It was located on the town's boundary line, on a tract of land adjoining the open fields. Its dignified exterior was matched by the serenity within its walls, by its cleanliness and soothing atmosphere. Here one could readily shed the barnacles of gray reality, straighten up, and face an uncontaminated world.

This was the Rabbi's House that I knew, the gathering place for the cleansing of the soul. Now it is gone, and the heart weeps over the destruction that overtook it, as it shared the fate of the town and its Jewish inhabitants.

*HADOAR*, **3** *Tevet* **5703, Vol.6. Poland Edition**
(*AB:* The Hebrew date translates to 11th December 1942)

---

*[Pages XXIV-XXV]*

# Men Of Stature And Scholarship

***Excerpts from the collection of stories about the Torah associations, written by the Hebrew writer and teacher Y. Ovsi (Yehoshua Ovseiewitz), a native of Korelitz***

The tradition of supporting Torah scholars is one of the most ingrained customs among Jews. It was not so long ago that many of the rabbis, in assuming a new post, would insist on the consent of the community leaders to support a certain number of Torah students. The communities gladly filled this condition.

In every *Bet-Midrash* where such an association held its sessions, there was always someone (usually the *shamash*) who arranged "meals-for-the-day" places for the out-of-town scholars. Every family in town regarded it as its sacred duty to provide meals daily for at least one scholar; the wealthier families invited two or three to partake of their meals.

Unlike the *yeshivot*, these associations were not supervised but were under the authority of the rabbi of the town. He and the other town scholars were aware of the capability, diligence and progress of each of the students.

In the small Jewish communities there were several pious women who provided food for every scholar for whom no other meal arrangements had been made. In Korelitz the woman was Dvorah Shimshelevitz [see elsewhere in this volume], affectionately known as Dvorah Pia Rashe's.

The following is a collection of brief sketches of some of Korelitz's Talmud Association members:

*[Pages XXVI-XXVIII – below –very abridged]*
*[Pages 64—89 in Hebrew – very detailed –* **see pages 53-86***]*

### Rabbi Zvi Menachem Zisling

Born in 1866. Father, Rabbi B.Z. Arye-Leib, was a writer for *Halevanon* ("The Lebanon", a Hebrew periodical). Settled in Eretz-Israel in 1914 and became instructor on Talmud in *Tachkemoni* High School in Tel Aviv. Longtime member of Tel-Aviv's Community Council and Municipal Council.

### Rabbi Meir Levin

Studied rabbinics and community administration under Rabbi Yechiel Yitzhok Davidson. Later was rabbi in Vilaika, near Wilna, and became active in political Zionism. Helped young rabbis in other communities to set up academies for Torah study.

### Dr. Yehuda Leib Davidson

Received fine Hebrew education, wrote poetry and prose. Went to Wilna and studied for matriculation certificate. Urged establishment of Academy for Jewish Studies in Russia. Wrote articles about farming and manufacturing among Russia's Jews. Received certificate in Warsaw (1882). Studied medicine in Warsaw University, received M.D. degree in 1890. Encouraged his relative Yitzhak Katzenelson to become a Hebrew poet, in Israel.

### Rabbi Michael Tannenbaum

Born in Motele, birthplace of Dr. Haim Weizmann (a relative). Married daughter of wealthy merchant; finding that the tumult of trade was interfering with his studying at home, he spent the weekdays in the Korelitz *Bet-Hamidrash*. His diligence with the Talmud was legendary. His wealthy father-in-law supported many of the students and provided for the widow of the rabbi of Korelitz. In 1887 was invited to serve as Rabbi of Lomze, and filled the post until his death in 1910.

### Rabbi Meir Hillel Zunser

A diligent Torah scholar, he studied Hebrew philology and other tongues, mathematics, social sciences and general history. Was ordained for the rabbinate but went into trade. Was accountant for large firms in Lodz and Warsaw, but maintained his scholar's schedule.

*[Pages XXVI-XXVII]*

# The Rabbis Of Korelitz

***(Material compiled by Moshe Cinowitz, Zvi Menachem Zisling, Noah Gottlieb and Batsheva Asherovitz)***

Much has been said in comment on the remarkable number of outstanding rabbis, scholars and Torah luminaries born in Korelitz or who had served its community over a score of decades. This volume would be incomplete without a record of their activities and contributions, and only lack of space prevents the publication of a fuller account of their lives and deeds.

### RABBI MOSHE *b'r* DOVID

Position as chief rabbinic authority in Korelitz was his first. Was appointed on recommendation of his father, head of the rabbinical court in Novohorodok. His Torah writings were published in Wilna in 1848. Was in his late twenties when he died.

### RABBI HAYYIM TUR

An outstanding scholar and commentator on difficult Talmud tractates (comments published in Wilna in 1873). Served in Korelitz from 1840 to 1856 and later became heard of the *Gmilut Hassadim* Congregration in Wilna until his death in 1874. In Wilna he helped many young men from Korelitz who came to the famous Lithuanian Torah center to pursue their studies.

### RABBI NAFTOLI HERTZ

Served in Korelitz from 1829-1835. First came there as an emissary of the Wolozhin (Volozyn) Yeshiva. Was instrumental in encouraging young men to intensify their studies under the *aegis* of the Yeshiva.

### RABBI YITZCHOK YECHIEL DAVIDSON

Among the most outstanding scholars, researchers and pietists of his generation, he added great luster to the name of Korelitz during his 17 years in the town (1857-1874). Fame as Talmud pedagogue drew many young men to Korelitz, among them Rabbi Yaacov Reiness, later a leading figure in religious Zionism. The Korelitzer landsmanschaft, organized in New York (April 4, 1904) as a congregation, with a Synagogue of its own, was named in his memory.

### RABBI ELIYOHU FEINSTEIN

The scion of an immensely learned family, he studied in Wolozhin and was the favorite of its leading spirits - Rabbi Naftali Zvi Yehuda Berlin and Rabbi Yossef Dov Soloveitchik. Became rabbi of Korelitz in 1874, succeeding his father-in-law, Rabbi

Yitzchok Yechiel. Served for five years before being called to larger communities in the region. Among his achievements in Korelitz: eased recruitment of Jews for the Russian army, arranged an orderly birth registry, established popular Torah classes to combat wave of "enlightenment", sent talented young men to *yeshivot*, and persuaded Baron Horatio Ginsburg to employ pious young men in his enterprises.

It is worth noting that his writings are referred to by his grandson, Rabbi Yossef Dov (*b'r* Moshe) Soloveitchik in his lectures at Yeshiva University.

### RABBI ELIYOHU BORUCH KAMAI

Encouraged community to build a hostel for poor travelers coming to Korelitz, and later persuaded it to build a medical clinic for the indigent in town. He reorganized the Talmud Torah in town and appointed a competent teaching staff. His fame drew offers from other communities, and he left Korelitz in 1887 for Wekeshne.

### RABBI MORDECHAI WEITZEL

Spirited away from a rival community (Bitten), he was in Korelitz from 1887 to 1891. Established *yeshiva* in the town. People flocked to ask his advice in such numbers that he had to plead, via announcements in the newspapers, to be allowed to fulfill his rabbinic duties. He was well-versed in medicine; he healed a Polish landowner and distributed his compensation among the poor.

### RABBI MEIR *b'r* YOSSEF FEIMER

Led frugal existence (of his salary of 18 rubles weekly, he gave 8 to augment salaries of town's judges). Was in Korelitz from 1893 to 1896 after serving in the large city of Slutzk. His son studied in Korelitz and later (1925) became rabbi of Bet-El Congregation in New York.

### RABBI AVROHOM YAACOV BRUCK

Born in Novohorodok, attended Mir Yeshiva, married daughter of Rabbi Mordechai Weitzel. Insisted on livelihood from manual labor (glazier). Expert in religious philosophy, an authority on Hebrew literature and an ardent Zionist (established Zionist branches in the region and attended Zionist conferences).

### RABBI AVROHOM YITZCHOK KOHEN

Came to Volozhin Yeshiva at 18, already famous for his scholarship. Called to Korelitz several years later. Issued call to communities in region to aid Korelitz when more than half the town was consumed by fire.

---

*[Page XXVIII]*

# Torah Scholars Born In Korelitz

### RABBI NISSAN BROIDAH

Was Rabbi of Shiniyawski, Krewei and Horodok; recommended for the last-named post by Rabbi Mordechai Weitzel. Was energetic public figure. Erected synagogue and community institutions in Horodok. Ardent Zionist and close worker with Rabbi Shmuel Mohilover. Elected delegate to the Third Zionist Congress in London. Joined Mizrachi when it was formed (1902) and called on religious Jewry and its rabbis to support the Zionist movement.

### RABBI YISROEL MICHAL YESHURUN

Appointed head of *yeshiva* attached to the Great Synagogue of Minsk, Described in "who's who" of Minsk's rabbis as "wise, of great intellect and a master of Torah...generous, industrious and inspiring." Edited works of Rabbi Duber Yoffe.

### RABBI URI DOVID *b'r* YOSSEF

His book *Aperion Dovid* (Wilna, 1872) gained him standing in the rabbinic world (Aperion was his family name). Inherited love for Torah study from long line of rabbis and judges. Carried on intensive correspondence with scholars, among them another native of Korelitz, Rabbi Yitzhok Yehoshua, a judge in Mir. Contributed to the Sir Moses Montefiore project in Jerusalem.

### RABBI ABRAZSHINSKY

Came to Korelitz from Mir. Known as a linguist and expert in literature. Was a successful merchant. Daughter Nechama married M. Gvirtzman, veteran of Hapoel Hamizrachi and former member of the Jerusalem Municipal Council.

### RABBI IDL ISAAC (ALTER) OSHEROWITZ

Left Korelitz at an early age to study in the yeshivot of Mir and Slabodka and was ordained for the rabbinate, but preferred to teach and accepted post of head of the "Ohel Yitzhok" Yeshiva in Kovno. Was drawn to Zionist movement and served as delegate to Mizrachi conferences in Lithuania. Sought to return to Korelitz but was prevented by the strained relations between Poland and Lithuania. Passed away at the age of 48.

### RABBI YOSSEF KORELITZER (SHIMSHELEVITZ)

Went to Eishishok at the age of 15 and became renowned Talmud authority Settled in Jerusalem and taught at one of its yeshivot. He was a favorite of Chief Rabbi Avrohom Yitzhok Hakohen Kuk.

[Pages XXIX – XXX]
[Pages 62-63 - Hebrew]
**As on page 52**

# The Korelitz Shochet
## (abridged English version)

## David Cohen - Kibbutz Alonim

*/ Reality and Legend/*

*\*In memory of the Korelitz community which was annihilated in the Holocaust years and its martyrs who were buried in a mass grave in the city of Novogrudek*

This happened two or three generations ago. Korelitz, pursuing its life at the slow pace of its Ruta River, the power source for the flour mills in the area, was already famous for the many sages and scholars in its midst. But the man whose fame spread with the advent of Zionism was R' Moshe Avrohom Volfin, the *shochet* of Korelitz, a pious man of learning whose soul yearned for Jerusalem and whose heart wept for it, in the midnight prayers which he offered for its redemption.

One wintery night the cold penetrated his lungs and laid him low with a high fever. The town physician, an expert on pneumonia, prescribed several drugs, plus goat's milk. Thus was a goat added to the *shochet's* household, a white goat which R' Moshe Avrohom prized greatly.

The news of the forthcoming First Zionist Congress reached Korelitz and at once R' Moshe Avrohom became an "active Zionist". During the days of the Congress he donned his Sabbath clothes and greeted his fellow Jews with *mazel tov*. As soon as the Congress proclaimed the establishment of the Palestine Bank *on the initiative of Dr Herzl\**, he began campaigning for the purchase of its stock. His main concern was to set an example for the others, but the shares cost money - a rare commodity with R' Moshe Avrohom.

The white goat! True R' Moshe Avrohom had grown attached to the animal but he would do it! He would sell the goat and buy a share, and let the people of Korelitz thus know how dearly he regarded the Zionist idea! He sold the goat, went to Novohorodok to acquire the share, and read what it said in Hebrew to the delighted congregants in the synagogue. They applauded heartily - and bought shares.

The story about the goat and the shares reached Vilna, and the Zionists there tendered lavish praise to Korelitz and its energetic and devoted Zionist. When the Second Zionist Congress came around and the shekel campaign was proclaimed, it was again R' Moshe Avrohom who spurred shekel sales in

Korelitz. When the authorities got word of it, they issued a warrant for R' Moshe Avrohom's arrest. As the constables came to get him, R' Moshe Avrohom stood up and pronounced the *Shehecheyonu* benediction, thanking the Almighty for having given him the privilege of being arrested for selling the Zionist shekel.

It is said that when Dr. Theodor Herzl was told about it, he said: "If I have such Zionist Jews as the shochet of Korelitz, it will be much easier to surmount all the difficulties that the Jewish nation will encounter on its way, to Zion and Jerusalem".

*\* added in from the Hebrew version*

---

*[Pages XXX-XXXI – English - slightly different and abridged]*
*[Pages 92-94- Yiddish]*
**See also page 88**

# The Story Of Korelitz's *Shochtim*

## Sarah Begin (Gal)

In R' Moshe Yitzhok Volfin the Jewish community of Korelitz had a real find: he was *shochet,* cantor and *mohel* all in one, and therefore saved the poor community a tidy sum. When R' Moshe Yizhok grew old and retired, he was followed by his son Chloineh. In time the community grew considerably; low economic state did not prevent the Jews of Korelitz from multiplying. In time, R' Chloineh ceded half his seniority to his son, R' Bertche, and the other half he gave as a dowry to his daughter Duske, later the wife of R' Kalman Begin, son of R' Yitzhok Dovid, the rabbinical judge of Kletzk.

R' Yitzhok Dovid gave his eight children a marvellous education: his daughter Freide Hinde was able to learn a *blatt Gemoreh*. R' Kalman engaged in *shechita*, and before his death he deeded his portion equally to his son Nachum-Eizik and, as dowry, to his daughter Sarah-Dvorah.

For a while R' Bertsche was the only *shochet* in Korelitz. Nachum-Eizik, having fallen victim to the wave of enlightenment and Zionist literature, had little desire to be a *shochet*. He wanted to leave the town and seek his future elsewhere, but he had little to say in the matter. He had to grow a beard and earlocks and to study *shechita*. Later, when he married his sister off to the son of R' Alter Morduchovitz, Rabbi of Baksht, he transferred to her his share and went to live in Minsk, where he went into business with his brother.

Toward the end of the First World War, a quarrel broke out in a town near Minsk, between the butchers and the *shochet*. The local rabbis decided that the official (Torah) verdict would have to be given by a *shochet* from another locality. Since R' Nachum-Eizik was no longer actively engaged in *shechita* he was invited to be the arbiter. On the morning after he had given the verdict, he was found on the ground, in his *tallit* and *tephilin*, stabbed to death. The news of the murder spread quickly throughout the region, but for certain reasons the whole matter was kept quiet. The roads were then clogged with soldiers, and it was impossible to bring the deceased to Korelitz for burial, and he was interred in the Minsk cemetery.

When R' Bertsche's eyes grew too weak for his calling he transferred his post to his son, R' Moshe Avrohom Volfin, the noted Zionist from Poltava. From that time until the destruction of the Korelitz community there were two *shochtim* in the town, the other being R' Avrohom Yitzhok, a neat, fine-looking man. The two were great friends, played chess together and gave Korelitz much of its good name. Since their sons were swept up in the Zionist movement and did not want to enter their fathers' field, the latter were the last of an illustrious Korelitz's dynasty of *shochtim*. Alter Morduchowitz was one of the very last *shochtim* prior to the annihilation of the Korelitz community by the Nazi murderers.

---

*[Pages XXXI-XXXIII - English]*
*[Pages 90-91- Yiddish]*
**Copied to Page 87**

# Dvorah And The Talmud Association

## Alter Gitlin

Dvorah, the provider for the *Kibbutz* (Talmud Association) in Korelitz, was well on in years, and so was her dwelling, a rambling structure so low that it seemed to be bowing before the Torah students that kept crossing its threshold. Inside, however, there was a sense of spaciousness. A long table, covered with a spotless white cloth, ran down the middle of the main room, and white benches paralleled it on either side. The room was bright even on bleak winter days, and the scholars (young men who were not invited by other households in town for meals) couldn't tell whether the light came from the pert white curtains at the small windows or from the fond look in Dvorah's eyes.

Dvorah had a system: each weekday morning she would make the rounds of the well-to-do and generous homes in the town and collect the funds which their owners had pledged. Then she would proceed to the market place, purchase the commodities she needed, and prepare a meal for the young men "worthy of Solomon's table". She knew who liked what, and delighted in preparing the special dishes. The scholars also knew what Dvorah liked - the lively sound of pilpulistic disputation, and they engaged in Talmudic debate as Dvorah kept refilling their plates. Then, as they recited the Grace After Meals, she received her reward: "May the Compassionate One bless the mistress of this house". Her eyes would fill with tears of gratitude for the privilege of serving Jewish scholars.

Dvorah also fried potato pancakes for all the Kibbutz scholars, poor and rich alike, and none dared not to partake of them, for to have done so was to run the risk of being charged with heresy. The scholars gathered at 1pm at Dvorah's home, crowding each other to get at the morsels. Dvorah apportioned the pancakes to each according to his scholarliness, and the largest portions went to those who spent longest hours on their studies. Amazingly, she knew exactly who was studying how hard, for, in the course of her rounds, she would go up to the women's gallery in the *Bet-HaMidrash* and look down on her charges, as they argued over a jot and fought over a tittle. If she spied a group sitting behind the stove and simply chatting, her face would darken and she would cry out: "Bums! Robbers! Why are you wasting your time? Back to your studies!" At the sound of her voice, all the young men in the place would rise to their feet and yell: "Long live Mama Dvorah", at which their benefactress, contrite because of the break in study that she had caused, would hastily withdraw.

Such was Dvorah's custom, for thirty years on end. When she died, the young men took apart the table and fashioned a coffin out of it. The entire town was at the funeral and three rabbis eulogized her. Many have since forgotten her - but not the young men whom she had fed so lovingly, and I, one of them, am paying her this tribute.

*"Hamizrachi"* 18 Shvat, 5681 (Third year, No. 4), 1921

---

# INSTITUTIONS AND ORGANIZATIONS

*[Pages XXXIII-XXXIV– English - abridged]*
*[Pages 167-168 Yiddish]*
**See also page 162**

## The Korelitz Bank And Free Loan Fund

### Fruma Gulkowich-Berger

Korelitz's Jews were never affluent, but they were known for their taking care on one another, sharing joy and sorrow alike and ever ready to lend a helping hand.

It was this sense of mutual responsibility which led to the founding of a people's bank and a free loan fund - two of the community's foremost institutions. The bank was established thanks to subsidies received from the *Yekope* Society of Wilna and its doors were open to everyone in need of financial assistance.

The manager and bookkeeper of the bank was Yitzhok-Meir Klatzkis, a former teacher and a devoted worker, and the Board of Directors consisted of three or four individuals (I recall the names of Gertz Namiat, the druggist; Getzl Relien, a merchant, and T. Klecicki, also a merchant). Borrowers had to have two guarantors and to pay interest. However, this arrangement was beyond the means of some of the people, and a Free Loan Fund was founded, operated mainly by the Artisans Guild, which made short-term, interest-free loans, mostly to artisans and the poorer members of the community. The Fund received gifts from America and from special events arranged in the town itself, among them theatre performances put on by the Drama Circle.

Among the Fund's administrators were Berl Bussel, Jacob Gershenovsky, Israel Rudi, Efroymsky and Berl Polizhesky, but others were co-opted to help in this important work. Many a Korelitzer had the bank and the Fund to thank for tiding him over some difficult situation.

---

*[Page XXXIV– English - abridged]*
*{Pages 168-172 – Yiddish]*
**See also page 163**

## The Drama Circle

Among the outstanding characteristics of Korelitz was its Jewish youth - talented, intelligent, resourceful. Youth groups flourished, particularly those engaged in the arts. Among these, the Drama Circle was the most distinguished, since professional theatre troupes rarely visited the town, the Circle was a major source of entertainment, and its income went to support worthy causes in the community.

Several of the Circle members possessed genuine dramatic talent: Bert Polizhesky, excellent in the role of the witch ("Koldunie"); Sheppe Klatchka, the stage director and outstanding actor who maintained a high group morale; Hayim Bussel, a teacher in the Jewish school still remembered for his role of Batyushka Prokop in "Hassia the Orphan"; Berl Obrinski, who turned in a passionate performance in "Yoshe Kalb"; the Gershenovsky brothers - Yankl, Moishe'le, Yashe and Ruchke, and the musicians Berl and David Lifshitz.

The women were no less talented: Rivka Yellin, the excellent comedienne; a bevy of beauties - Menuha Abramowich, Levitt, Chaya-Leike Shereshevsky; Menuha and Mania Kaganowich usually played the lead roles.

Several of the Circle members went abroad in quest of a better life, amongst them Chaike Dushkin and Ben-Zion Gulkowich.

The Circle put on a new performance for each holiday, and this was the social event of the season, not only in Korelitz but also in surrounding communities which the Circle visited.
The last play put on by the Circle was "God, Man and the Devil". The Devil - Hitler - put an end to the Circle, as he did to so many Korelitzes throughout Europe.

---

*[Pages XXXV- XXXVI – English - abridged]*
*[Pages 151-154 Yiddish]*
**See also page 148**

# Korelitz's Fire-Fighting Brigade

## Yaacov Abramowich

The Brigade was the pride of Korelitz - deservedly. Its structure, I recall, was highly formal; I also remember the names of the officers in my day:

**President**: the druggist Eliasberg
**Commander**: David Slutsky
**Deputy-Commander**: Savelie Klatzko
**Adjutant**: Mordechai Bezin
**Manager**: Gertz Namiat
**First Unit Commander**: Reuben Perevelutsky
**Second Unit Commander**: Israel Israelit
**Third Unit Commander**: Hayim Abramovich
**Water Director**: Boruch Zalkowich
**Orchestra Conductor**: Shimon Miller

I used to attend the band's rehearsals, but I wasn't accepted to the Brigade because I was too young. I also watched their drills - up the rope, high on the ladder, pumping the water. Later, as the years went by and I joined the Brigade, Commander David Slutzky appointed me House Commander, in charge of the firehouse and its contents. I had to see to it that the hoses didn't leak and the carriages were in good shape. I painted the wheels, greased the axles, saw that the barrels on the two-wheelers were always filled with water. If the job was beyond my capacity, I called in a professional. However, Commander Slutzky's first order was for me to go to the market place, buy material for my uniform and cap and take it to Shloimke Kabak the tailor. My joy was indescribable.

I spent more time in the firehouse than at home, under the tutelage of Noah Gershenovsky, who lived across the street and kept the keys to the place.

The drill schedule, on Sundays, was announced by Yasha Gershenovsky to all the members; later the job was taken over by his brother Yodke, David Lifshitz and Leibe Ozochovsky. The Brigade gathered in the firehouse yard, where Adjutant Bezin would already be waiting. The drill began with a parade, led by the band: Moishe Gershenovsky and Moishe Lifshitz -clarinet; Noah Gershenovsky - trombone; Yasha Gershenovsky and Berl Lifshitz - trumpet; David Lifshitz - tenor sax; Isaiah Gershenovsky, Markel Gershenovsky, Avreml Lipchon - drums; Azerovsky and Idl Savitzky - cymbals.

A few paces behind the orchestra marched the officers, the hook-and-ladder unit and the firefighters - brawny lads in copper helmets and uniforms, small axes thrust into the broad leather bands around their waists. Last came the water suppliers. The good people of Korelitz lined the streets and applauded mightily.

Back at the firehouse, the Brigade went into its drill, using all its equipment and apparatus. It then moved to the river for further manouevers.

The firehouse was maintained chiefly by the townspeople through a monthly tax. If a citizen showed signs of not wanting to pay (such as being in arrears), the Brigade would send a hose down his chimney and give him a choice: pay up or suffer the consequences of a flood. He would inevitably choose the obvious.

The firehouse also served as the town's theatre. Traveling troupes would pay for the use of the premises, which would be cleared of all the apparatus and have a stage set up. A local theatre group, directed first by Alter Boyarsky and later by Savelie Klatzko also gave performances in the firehouse, which benefited from the income. The cashier was the beloved Yudel Efroimsky, president of the Labor Association.

The firefighters also helped maintain law and order, particularly on market days, when the peasants, bolstered by liquor, would create disturbances and let their horses run wild. The Brigade was authorized to catch the horses and hose down their owners.

In time the Brigade received mechanized fire equipment from the authorities and was on call for fires in neighboring settlements as well.

---

*[Page XXXVII – English - abridged]*
*[Pages 156-158 Yiddish]*
**See also page 152**

# Korelitz's Sports Organizations

Korelitz had a Jewish soccer team, *Maccabi*, and the team had a field of sorts; it also practiced in the market place (Yeshayahu Bolotnitzky, who lived in the area, was custodian of the sports gear). The uniform consisted of khaki shorts and a white top embroidered with a blue *Magen David* and the words *Maccabi-Korelitz*. The team played in Novohorodek, Turetz and other teams in Korelitz itself, among them a Christian group headed by Tadek Yuzkewich, a son of the town's patron.

I recall a game with this team on a bright Sunday morning. One of our players was Mordechai Krulevitzky (now named Malkhieli), on a visit from Eretz-Israel. The game was tough and bitter. Our team emerged victorious, and the Yuzkewich group tried to make up for its defeat by attacking our players. Mordechai displayed the same prowess with his fists that he did with his feet.

I was instrumental in organizing a volleyball team. We (my brother Gabriel and Saul Zalmansky) fashioned a net, Berl Lubczansky forged two iron stakes, and we set out for the cattle market on Zafale Hill, cleaned the grounds a bit, put up the long stakes and stretched the net across the marked-out court. In time we became proficient and sent our team to neighboring communities. Once we came to Turetz on a Saturday and were nearly stoned...

The Polish high school in town also had a team of Christian students. We had a junior team of boys who also attended the same high school and often beat the "regulars". On several occasions, as visiting teams from other towns came to play, the Principal (Dolemba) would draw on our Jewish team (Gitl Kavalewich, Motke Polaszki and me) to reinforce the regular team.

Our women's team became so expert and popular that the wife of the Police Chief joined it. In fact, the good players were held in such esteem that when the town authorities were asked by the Germans to furnish them with the names of the Jewish players - the first to be deported - their names were not included in the list...

---

*[Pages XXXVIII-XL abridged]*
*[Pages 175-180 – Hebrew]*
**See also page 170**

# The Chalutz Youth In Korelitz
## Kalman Osherowich

(The History of the *Chalutz* and *Hashomer HaTza'ir*)

Korelitz is a genuine example of the pioneering Jewish youth in Europe which, about half a century ago, laid the groundwork for the Zionist program which found its expression in settlement and, later, in statehood.

When the First World War ended, Korelitz was mostly in ruins. The Jews slowly came back from their places of refuge - Grodno, Novohorodek - and began the painful work of reconstruction: first the synagogue and the school, later the houses and the shops. But no sooner was the beginning made than the town fell prey to the struggle between the Bolsheviks and the Poles. The latter finally gained control, and the community returned to a degree of normalcy.

Those were the days when Jewish communities in Eastern Europe were influenced by two major movements: the *Bund*, which sought economic and occupational equality for the Jewish proletariat, and the Zionist Movement. Korelitz tended towards the latter. Mordechai Krulevitzky was the 'live wire' Zionist. He organized the *Hechalutz HaTza'ir* (Young Pioneer), assisted by Hassia Oberzhansky; an older group, *Hechalutz*, was organized by Moshe-Eli Shuster, Nissan Zalmanowsky and Yossef Portnoy.

Zionist lecturers were brought in - Yosef Bankover and Byalopolsky - and a complete cultural program was instituted: Braina, the rabbi's daughter, taught Hebrew; Shuster taught geography; literary circles and a 'living newspaper' were established, the latter edited by Alter Rozovsky.

Zionist activity in Korelitz suffered a setback because of a rather curious happening: the *Hechalutz* central office, pleased with our work, assigned an immigration "certificate" to one of our members. Unfortunately the assignee was engaged in business and couldn't 'get away'. The disillusionment occasioned as a result caused many members to drop out, but the movement was too strong to die. Gradually we rebuilt it. We set about preparing ourselves for vocations: the boys were trained in carpentry and the girls in sewing. On winter nights we did charwomen's work in the school and set the money we earned aside for the Jewish National Fund and the worker's fund in Eretz-Israel. We took over the matzah baking for Passover and made money, for the same purpose.

In 1925-6 we received several certificates for *aliya*. The first to leave was Leima Polechuk (now in Ramat Hasharon), Yossef Portnoy (in Kfar Sava), Bracha Kaplan (in Kibbutz Hakovesh*), Gitl Lundin (Kibbutz Hakovesh*), Sheindl Perevolutzky (now Kuznitz, in Tel Aviv), Pessia Afroymsky (now Gurfinkel in Mishmar Hashelosha), Mordechai Krulevitzky (Malkhielei, in Hod Hasharon), Stoliar (returned to Europe and died in the Holocaust). All of these first joined Kibbutz Hakovesh* but later dispersed throughout the land. There was a great deal of excitement in the town.

The Movement suffered another reverse in 1927, when the economic situation in Eretz-Israel was so bad that two of our people came back to Korelitz. We, the veterans, were so put out that we padded the membership reports which we sent to the Central Office, paying membership dues out of our own pockets for the dropouts. The idea was Leah Kaplan's (now in Kibbutz Givat Haim); she just couldn't stand the disgrace...

At this point an energetic young man came to Korelitz - Hayim Bussel, a graduate of the *Hashomer HaTza'ir* - and proposed to set up a branch. The *Chalutz* members objected, but the new group flourished, attracting the youngsters and the adolescents. The groupings were given names of the Tribes of Israel; I found myself in charge of *Judah*. We maintained a full program of culture, sports and entertainment. On *Lag Ba'omer* we set up a camp in a nearby forest and tearfully sang *Hatikva*. By 1928 we were strong enough to hold a regional convention in Korelitz.

*Hashomer HaTza'ir* was not spared misfortune of its own. In 1929 the town was burned down, and the riots of 1929 brought the movement to an end.

But again history had its say. Jewish life in Poland grew more precarious. The young people strove to reach the Jewish homeland, and since certificates were not available they went there "illegally". Unfortunately, many remained behind and were annihilated, but those of Korelitz who found their way to their destination have added to the story of heroism known as the State of Israel.

* *Transcriber's note*: The correct name is "Kibbutz Ramat Hakovesh".

---

*[Page XL]*
*[Pages 187-188 –Hebrew]*
**See also page 182**

# BETAR

## Gutka Nachumovsky-Ganczewicz (Gantzevitz)

[This chapter is the same as the Hebrew on **Page 182**, with the addition of 2 different photos there - *AB*]

The *Betar* Club in Korelitz came into being as a result of the enthusiasm engendered by Zeev Jabotinsky's visit in Poland. Its founding was opposed by the already existing *Hashomer HaTza'ir* and *Hechalutz*, but with the help of veteran adult members of the Revisionist movement, the Club proceeded with its work. As the opposing groups increased their activities, the town was overcome by an avalanche of debates and disputations.

Eventually *Betar* members received their uniforms, and the first *Betar* commander of Korelitz made his *aliya*. Many others followed, for it was the *Betar*, in line with Jabotinsky's belief, which preached evacuation of Europe. Unfortunately, not enough heed was paid to the call, and Polish Jewry paid for it with its life.

*[Page XLI]*

**Directors of the Yiddish Library**; (sitting, left to right) Kalman Mordechowitz, Moishele Shuster, Rivka Shuster, Shimon Muller; (in front): Israel Tzelkowitz, Nissan Zalmanski.

**The Yiddish Drama Circle of Korelitz, 1925**

*[Page XLII]*

**Hechalutz HaTza'ir of Korelitz 5.VI.25 (13<sup>th</sup> *Sivan* 5685)**

From right to left: Yaacov Mazuretzky, Berl Gurevich, Fanya Lifshitz, Haya Leah Kaplan-Shereshevky, Hayim Bolotnitzky, Yosef Portnoy

**The *Judith* Club, 1928**

*[Page XLIII]*

The *Hechalutz* Club, 1929

**Pioneer Korelitz youth In training**: (from right) Hayim Bolotnitzky, Moishe Stoliar, Haya Leah Kaplan, Mordechai Krulevetzky (Malkieli), Fania Lifshitz, Hayim Kaplan, David Portnoy, Yitzhak Stoliar

# IMAGES AND PERSONALITIES

Note: All the following cameos are <u>abridged</u> English texts, and for more information, read the full versions originally written in Hebrew or Yiddish (Original pages 189-225; **in this book, pages 184-220**)

*[Page XLIV]*
*[Pages 189-190 –Yiddish]*
**See also page 184**
## Yitzhak Katzenelson In His Birthplace

**(From "Yitzhak Katzenelson: His Life and Works" by Zippora Katzenelson-Nachumov, Chapter 22, pp. 150 ff.)**

The visit of Yitzhak Katzenelson to his home town, following a tour of Jewish communities in Lithuania, had all the earmarks of a festival. He was given a public welcome at the railway station and taken to the home of his grandfather, Rabbi Yitzhak Yechiel, where his cradle was being kept as a memento of Korelitz's famous son.

He spent the few days of his visit with the young people, strolling with them along the road or across the fields, singing Hebrew and Yiddish songs, and talking about the Land of Israel. He urged his young compatriots to go there: "Dear Jewish sons and daughters, your place is in the Land of Israel. Go there and build a new life for yourselves."

---

*[Page XLIV - English - abridged]*
*[Page 192 –Yiddish]*
**See also page 187**
## Yaacov Binyamin Katzenelson

Born in Kapulie in 1859. Studied in Volozhin and Kovno. Author of *Olelot Efrayim* (1889), in which he described the vaunted *Maskilim* (enlightened) as rank opportunists. Under the pseudonym *Ben Yemini*, he wrote for the Hebrew encyclopedia, *Ha-Eshkol* (Warsaw), visiting Korelitz to see his wife, the daughter of Korelitz's rabbi, R. Yitzhak Yechiel Davidson. Their son Yitzhak was born in 1886.

In its eulogy, the newspaper *"Hajnt"* (November 28, 1931) said: "...He lived and breathed love for the Hebrew tongue and the Jewish people. His erudition in Judaica was immense, particularly in Jewish history... for many years he was engaged in pedagogy, and the generation of disciples whom he reared was always his pride and joy..."

---

*[Page XLV – English - abridged]*
*[Pages 194-196 –Yiddish]*
**See also page 190**

# My Father: Moshe Avrohom, son of R' Shoul Naftoli Osherowitz

### Kalman Osherowitz -- Raanana

One may say that my grandfather Shoul Naftoli was the victim of progress: the introduction of the railway into the area put his horse-and-wagon transport system out of business. He wanted his son to engage in a less exacting occupation, and had him learn the art of leatherworking for *tephillin* and Torah scrolls. My father also became active in the religious life of the community, as a clerk of the Rabbinical Court, *mesadder kedushin* (officiating at weddings), and advisor to young rabbis. He was also the *mohel* and advisor in special maternity cases. Much of his attention was given to the *Hevra Kaddisha* and the administration of the cemetery, and he still found time to conduct a class in *Mishnayot*.

As an ardent Zionist, it was always his dream to settle in Eretz-Israel. We helped him achieve it; we brought him to the Land of Israel, at the age of 78 and bought him a plot of land in Herzliya. He passed away at the age of 88.

---

*[Pages XLV-XLVI English – Abridged]*
*[Pages 196 – Hebrew, 197 – Yiddish]*
**See also pages 192, 193**

# Pesach Kaplan

### Hassia Turtel-Oberzhansky
### Y.H. Biletzky

A leading public figure in Korelitz, Pesach Kaplan was privileged to live in Eretz-Israel scores of years. His activities in Korelitz were legendary: he was concerned with communal welfare, education, intercession with the inimical Czarist authorities and, later, with the anti-Semitic Polish Republic. He spent a few years in the United States, and on his return became the English-language expert, writing letters for Korelitz residents to their relatives across the sea. He was very musical and served as cantor in the new synagogue. All of his children settled in Eretz-Israel, and toward the end of his days he lived with them in their kibbutzim and moshavim, where he was extremely popular.

He taught the new pioneers many things about their people and history. At the time of his death he was over 90.

---

*[Page XLVI - English – Abridged]*
*[Pages 198-199 – Yiddish]*
**See also page 194**

# Gershon Eliasberg

Born in Novohorodek in 1876, he chose his father's career - pharmacy, and after years of study and work in Russia returned to Korelitz. By that time he already had to his credit extensive experience in public affairs - youth leadership and professional branch organization. In Korelitz he devoted himself to the rehabilitation of the families which had undergone economic ruin, and formed ties of the *Yekope* aid association, later becoming a member of its board. He founded the People's Cooperative Bank in Korelitz, and was active in the Rebuilding Commission, Free Loan Society and various general welfare societies of the town, gaining the respect and gratitude of all its inhabitants.

---

*[Page XLVI - English -Abridged]*
*[Page 199 - Yiddish]*
**See also page 195**

# Shalom Cohen

Born into a rabbinic family (1880), he worked as a bookkeeper from the age of 18 to the outbreak of the World War. Deported from Korelitz by the Germans, he went to his father's family in Novohorodok, where he helped carry on the relief work among Jewish victims of the war in the area. After the war he continued with public affairs - Secretary to the first democratically elected Community Council in the town, a founder of the Folk School (he also taught there) and a member of the *Jakufa* (*Yekope*) Committee's Free Loan Society division.

---

*[Page XLVII – English – abridged]*
*[Page 200- Hebrew]*
**See also page 196**

# Rina Garabalsky

## Hassia Turtel-Obrezhansky

An avid student, she came to the United States in 1908, at the age of 17, to continue her studies and worked in the Jewish Division of the N.Y. Public

Library, continuing her studies in night school and later, when already married, at City College. Her ardent Zionism led her to Eretz-Israel in 1920, where she worked in the Mikveh-Israel Agricultural School and at Ein-Harod. She went back to the U.S. and in 1930 she came with her husband, the writer Moshe Stavy-Stavsky, to Korelitz, much to the excited delight of the Zionist youth in the town.

Thirty years later she was already high in the ranks of Israel's Working Mothers Association and the Soldiers' Welfare Committee, and was a member of President Shazar's Bible study circle.

---

*[Page XLVII – English – abridged]*
*[Pages 201-202 – Yiddish]*
**See also page 197**

# Alter Greenfeld

## Hassia Turtel Obrezhansky

A true cultural activist, his interests ranged from organizing a children's club and working with the Hehalutz Council to extensive travel all over the province to deliver lectures, editing bulletins and writing poems and essays. In Novohorodek he participated in the periodical *Navaredoker Leben*, signing his writings A. Gad. His volume of poetry, *Mir Iz Gut* (I have It Made) was published by the Korelitz Library in 1936,and his other manuscripts were awaiting publication, but when the Russian army entered Poland he went to Russia and was not heard from since.

---

*[Page XLVII English –abridged]*
*[Page 202 –Hebrew]*
**See also page 198**

# Yossel Zalamanker

## Leah Lubchansky-Kornfeld

He was childless, and all he had was his honesty and goodness of heart. Short of stature, blue-eyed, his face adorned with a gold-yellow beard, he would make his way quietly to the *Bet-Hamidrash*, looking about for someone to talk to on the way, except on Wednesday, when he sold eggs in the market place. Then he would come hurrying, his coat-tails flying, fearful lest he would be late for Mincha.

---

*[Page XLVIII – English - abridged]*
*[Page 203 –Yiddish]*
**See also page 199**

# Feivel Nisselevitz
## Yaacov Abramowich

He was the postman of the town, along with his being a coachman. Everyone who needed transportation to Novohorodok (21 kilometers) wanted to ride with Feivel. His tunes and anecdotes were much to the liking of his passengers, although he did ask them to walk up the steep inclines on the way to make it easier for the horses. The police at the Novohorodok checkpoint knew him well and waved him through without inspection.

His family was wiped out by the Nazis, except for one daughter, who left for Eretz-Israel before the war and settled in Tel Yosef.

---

*[Page XLVIII – English - abridged]*
*[Page 204 – Yiddish]*
**See also page 200**

# The Porush, Kalman Marashiner

## Yaacov Abramowich

He used to come to our school just before dismissal time, then take the boys with him to the *Bet-Hamidrash* and had them recite Psalms, in return for which he gave them gifts - a pencil, notebook and other small items of this kind.

He spent his entire day in the *Bet-Hamidrash*. Malkah, his wife, would bring his meals to him, and instead of sleeping he would lie on the wooden bench and take a brief nap, despite the sound of study around him.

In time he and his wife joined their children in Eretz-Israel.

---

# THE HOLOCAUST

*[Page XLIX– English - abridged]*
*[Pages 208-209 –Yiddish]*
**See also page 204**

## The Road Of Suffering

### Malka Pomerchik

The Russians entered Korelitz, at the outbreak of the German-Polish fighting, and began operating in Soviet style. First they "nationalized" the large buildings, then closed down the stores and set up one large shopping center. Immediately a shortage of commodities occurred, and long lines queued up for supplies. Everyone was put to work in cooperatives. I became a teacher in a Russian school, teaching German and working with the Fourth Grade. My prominent position in the town placed me in danger, and I left at the first opportunity for Russia, along with my husband, sister and brother-in-law, and one brother.

On the way, we became separated but managed to reunite and reach Tashkent, where we spent the war years. Returning to Korelitz we found there but a handful of Jews - too tired to move away. We went on to Austria, hoping to proceed to Eretz-Israel with *Aliya Bet*, but our child was too young. We had to wait until after the War of Liberation. Eventually we settled in Kfar Saba.

---

*[Pages XLIX–L - English - abridged]*
*[Page 212-225 –Yiddish]*
**See also page 209**

## On The Way To Destruction

### Ben Ir (A townsman)

The reputation of the Nazis preceded their arrival in Korelitz. It was reported that they were destroying bridges and mining the roads leading to Russia.

The Nazis entered Korelitz at the end of June 1941. At first the town was in chaos. From the surrounding areas, peasants came with sacks and empty wagons, and they left with pillaged Jewish goods.

The Germans set up headquarters in Yosef Bernstein's house and ordered the Jews to form a Council, which they forced Rabbi Viernik to organize. He formed it with Shimon Zelaviansky, Moshke Kivelevitch and Baruch Shimshelevitz. The first order issued to the Council by the Germans was to collect all Jewish valuables. Whenever they came to get the valuables, they subjected Rabbi Viernik to a beating.

The next step was the ghetto - Lifshitz's two-storey house; all the remaining Jews in Korelitz were herded into these quarters, under unspeakable conditions. The men were ordered to report to work; if any didn't show up, said the Nazis, the others would be shot. A list of all the able-bodied Jews was prepared for the Nazis by the Poles in Korelitz. These Jews - 105 in number - were taken to the synagogue before their departure for Novohorodek (where they were later killed). Those of their families who wanted to say goodbye to them were shot.

Transport by transport, the Jews were taken from the ghetto and shipped out to their death. By the end of 1942 Korelitz was *Judenrein* [free of Jews].

The indescribable barbarism and brutality of the Germans was matched by the vicious greed of the local populace. No sooner was a Jewish family taken away from its home by the Nazis - and already the non-Jews were there with their wagons, to take away whatever could be detached.

The few Jews from Korelitz who succeeded in escaping from the ghetto made their way to the Dworetz camp, near the forest. Here conditions were better: the Nazis needed lumber, and they made use of Jewish slave labor to get it.

Singly and in small groups, Jews from the area filtered into the forests to join the partisans. The struggle was conducted on two fronts: against the Germans and against the peasants who informed the Germans where the partisans had their camps. It was only when the partisans wiped out a family of informers that they were rid of this danger. But the war against the Nazis went on to the very end.

---

*[Page LI – English - abridged]*
*[Pages 256-261 –Yiddish]*
**See also pages 248-50**

# The Heroism Of The Korelitz Young Men

**Reuben Dushkin**, a meat dealer by occupation, was a quiet, honest, hard-working man with a large family. His eldest daughter, Sara, married Shlomo Navitsky, and the two men operated one meat market.

In 1941, as the Nazis drew near, the peasants and townspeople of Korelitz set about pillaging Jewish homes, going from one house to the next and dragging out furniture and other household goods.

A band of hooligans came to Reuben's home, sacks ready to be filled. But Reuben and his sons - Yankl, Motl and Hayyim - and son-in-law beat them back. The hooligans bided their time until the Germans came into Korelitz. But the Jews knew what was coming, and those who managed to flee and join the partisans gave a good account of themselves.

**Yaacov Slutsky** was a young farmer, but when he had to flee from Korelitz and joined the partisans he undertook an important task - to procure weapons. He went about the countryside, picking up discarded rifles and bits of metal, which he then fashioned into crude but serviceable firearms, mines and bombs, which he later used to blow up German communication lines.

**Hershl the Carpenter** (the best in Korelitz) was taken to the Novohorodek concentration camp in 1942 and put to work in his craft. But he also succeeded in fashioning an escape tunnel from the ghetto, and succeeded in getting to the partisan camps, where he fashioned stocks for rifles. After the war he made his way to Israel and joined his daughter Vitl in Jerusalem, where he continued with his craft.

---

*[Pages LII-LIV]*

# THE "BIELSHCHIKS"

## Hertzel Nohumovski

Tuvya Bielski          Asael Bielski          Zusia Bielski

All too often have we heard it said, or at least implied, that the Jews of Eastern Europe allowed themselves to be led like sheep to the Nazi slaughter-houses. This implication does a two-fold injustice to the memory of the martyrs: it glosses over their fate and - it is not true.

Understandably, these Jewish communities were in no position to match the armed strength of the Nazis or to check the vicious assaults of their "neighbors", the Poles, Ukranians and the other groups among whom Jews had been living, in some cases for hundreds of years. But there was resistance, and there were acts of heroism and self-sacrifice which matched the resistance of the Second Commonwealth to Roman rule 19 centuries ago.

The following account, by Herzl Nachumovsky, is but one of many such poignant and dramatic stories which are now part of Jewish history.

Like an underground fire, the word was passed from one ghetto to another: "The Bielsky brothers are organizing in the forest".

The forest - the only place which offered hiding from the Nazis - and which the Nazis, unable to bring in their armor, were reluctant to penetrate. Here the three Bielsky brothers - Tuvya, Zusya and Asael - organized the resistance movement, and inmates of the ghettos in the area filtered into the thick woods, some with old rifles which they had managed to get from the peasants, others empty-handed. All were welcome, and soon the "Bielschchiks" numbered 1,200 souls - men, women and children.

Arrivals were assigned to their group of townspeople, and each one was given a job to which he was best suited; the most coveted one, of course, was to bear arms against the enemy.

In time the groupings were broken up and reassembled into brigades, each with its commanding officer (among the officers: Hayim Abramowitz of Korelitz and Yisrael Yankelevitz, Yehuda Bielsky and Yudl Levin from Novohorodok). Tuvya Bielsky was the commander-in-chief and his brothers were his lieutenants - very much as in the case of Judah the Maccabee. Zusya turned raw youths into excellent scouts. (There was a fourth Bielsky - Archik, too young to assume command, but the most knowledgeable when it came to trailing and tracking). The rest of the General Staff consisted of Pessach Friedberg and Lazar Malbin.

It was the duty of the scouts to leave the forest on horseback, tour the farms and villages in the area for information, and lay the groundwork for action against the enemy. Two young men from Korelitz, Ben-Zion Gulkowich and Yaacov Abramowich, were among the best in the unit.

The sabotage unit was particularly active. Armed with home-made mines, they blew up bridges, railroad tracks, culverts and installations. The work was doubly dangerous because the crude mines also took their toll; this is how

Yaacov Slutsky of Korelitz, a quiet and truly noble youth, lost his life. Another active member of the unit was Shlomo Stoler, who later reached Israel and gave his life for the creation of the State.

Food was obviously a constant and pressing problem. The only way to get it was to go out at night to distant villages and ask the farmers; in most cases they met with refusal, and food had to be taken by force. Often several forays were made in a single night.

The arsenal of the Bielshchiks was woefully meager in the beginning, and there was only one way to get weapons: to ambush the enemy and take his arms and ammunition. Asael Bielsky was the leader of this unit, and he went out with his men in every instance. The usual procedure was to waylay convoys of Nazis or local police, at times after careful planning and at others on the basis of hasty information.

This activity went on for about a year. Then came an order from the central staff of the Soviet partisans to separate the fighters from the others, send the latter deeper into the forest, and be ready for further orders, in five days. The Jewish partisans became suspicious. Tuvya was particularly uneasy. He decided on the strategy of dividing the fighters into two groups: one remained with the non-fighters - the elderly, the women and the children - while the other, consisting of men selected by Tuvya, left under the cover of darkness, with their weapons.

Knowing that the forest would have to be their home for some time, the other Bielsky brothers and their followers set about converting the heart of the forest into a village. From the trees they felled they fashioned log cabins, accommodating about 800 souls. At the same time they built a bakery, a storehouse, a flour mill which they operated with three horses, a workshop for tailoring and shoe repair, even a smoked meats factory. Soon the new village (named "Jerusalem" by the surrounding groups) was the center of partisan life. Hershl Shkolnik of Korelitz managed the carpentry shop, which fashioned rifle stocks.

Most welcome of all, perhaps, was the Turkish bathhouse.

Came the spring of 1944. Life in the village was going on in orderly fashion. Then, on June 28, came the words that the Germans were in flight. Many were captured as they entered the forest but could not find their way out of it. The desire for vengeance was so great that many partisans abandoned the village in quest of the fleeing enemy - a move which almost ended in disaster, as a large group of fleeing Germans attacked the camp and almost overcame the few defenders.

On July 16 the surviving partisans took part in the mustering out in Novohorodok, and were praised by the Russian General Igorkov for the extraordinary courage and self-sacrifice of the "Bielshchiks" in the face of the Nazi foe.

---

*[Page LV-English-abridged]*
*[Pages 228-231 Yiddish]*
**See also page 223**

# What They Went Through
## (Excerpt from "Ghetto Recollections")

## Fruma Gulkowich-Berger

... My sisters had already found hiding in an attic. My sister-in-law Yehudit grabbed me by the arm and pulled me out of the barn, but I was as if turned to stone. Where could we find some hole to crawl into? We were as strangers to the earth; it would open and eject us. We went by a few dead bodies. I recognized one, a Korelitz girl, Merke Yellin; she had the courage to spit a German in his face.

We were now passing by the big outhouse in the center of the ghetto. Without hesitating we went in and lowered ourselves into the large cesspool, which was up to our chests. We found there two women, Esther Menaker and Masha Rabinowitz. We each took a corner; in case the breathing of one would be heard, the others might not be discovered...

The Germans came with their dogs. Our hiding place was discovered. The Germans shot into the cesspool. A bullet hit Esther Menaker; she went under without a sound. Another bullet went through my dress and slightly grazed my arm. The Germans withdrew, saying to each other that anyone still in the cesspool would die anyway.

We were there six days, without food. Every time someone came in, our hearts almost stopped beating...

By this time, most of the Jews in the Ghetto had either been killed or deported. The ghetto was made smaller, leaving the outhouse outside the walls. We were "saved"...

---

[Pages LV – LVI -abridged]
[Pages 250-254  - Hebrew]
**See also page 241**

# IDEL KAGAN

The stories of the Holocaust, of what the Germans and their allies did to the Jewish communities of Eastern Europe, are of one pattern and the same content - only the details vie with each other in revealing the utter bestiality of the criminals. If there are variations, they are to be found in the personal experiences of the survivors.

One of these is Idel Kagan. Born in Novohorodek, but bound to Korelitz by the marriage of his father and uncle to the Gurevitz sisters of that town, his last visit there was when the German occupation was already in force; he was sent there with several others to report on the situation. It was already hopeless. He was only 12 at the time.

Survival was now a matter of miracles. Once he faced a firing squad which was called off at the last minute because the Germans though that death by bullets was too simple. On another occasion, as the Germans lined up Jewish children to be shot, he managed to put on his father's coat and was passed over.

By a daring move Idel managed to escape and get to the forests, to join the partisans. But he had to be careful; the Polish partisans were all too happy to inform on the Jews. In the course of his wanderings Idel had to cross an icy river. His feet became frozen, and he barely managed to make it back to the ghetto, where he was no longer registered, and was there "operated" with a kitchen knife. A few days later the Germans made another round of their selections. Idel's mother and sister were murdered. Idel himself, lying on a bed of wooden boards under a pile of rags and pillows, was not discovered. At night he crawled out of the emptied ghetto. How he managed to stay alive he does not know to this day.

Idel was 15 when the war ended. A series of surgeries improved the condition of his feet. He managed to reach England and join a distant member of the family. A new world opened before him - security, peace of mind - with all the horrible memories - opportunity. He began as a wage earner, and in the course of the years grew to be a captain of industry. The Kagan family was resurrected; he married Barbara Steinfeld, and their three children are named for his father, mother and uncle. The eternity of the Jewish people shall not be denied.

---

# AFTERMATH

*[Pages LVII-LVIII]*
*[Pages 270-272 – Yiddish]*
**See also page 260**

## A Visit To Korelitz After The War

### BEN IR (a Townsman)

*Note : In the (orginal) Yiddish text, Yaacov Abramowich is the author.*
*This English version is very similar but in the Yiddish text there is more information*
*and more names of people are given.*
*However the English version below also gives some information which does NOT*
*appear in the Yiddish text.*

Ben-Zion Gulkowich and I left Novohorodek in a cart and headed for Korelitz, 21 kilometers away. As we neared the town, our hearts began to beat faster and our faces changed color. We looked at each other wordlessly, knowing well what our thoughts were at that moment.

As we neared the power mill which once belonged to Reuben Bezin and his partners Yitzhok Stoler and Hayyim Mishkin, we found many farmers with their grain-laden wagons, awaiting their turn to mill the grain. We vainly looked for a Jewish face - perhaps Bezin's ever-smiling countenance - but he was gone, and everyone elso was gone.

With aching hearts we drove on. We passed the Zalmanke well, where we used to get fresh water. Not a soul around.

And now we were where the smithies once stood, near Zapale hill. Once the place resounded with hammers pounding the anvils: Yudke the blacksmith, Yaacov Slutsky, Abraham Lipchin and his sons, Alter Abrahamovitch. Everything was silent, in ruins.

Feige-Zirl's hotel - empty, abandoned.

And here was Yankel Zalemanski's house. Yankel with his red beard was a shrewd egg-dealer. As the farmers from Zapelie, Liesok and Kalzenoi came by on their way to town to sell their produce, Yankel and his children would halt them and lead them into their yard, where they bought up all the eggs. The yard was like a marketplace. Now - silent as a grave.

We drew near to our home. Again the heart started pounding and tears came running down. Inside we found a family of peasants. I told them that I was the former owner of the house, born there, lived there for many years, until the Germans came and drove us out.

The peasants invited us to sit down and have something to eat. They were from Russia, they said, and had been given the house; they were not to blame for the disaster which had befallen us. They gave us some bread, butter and a few eggs, and we left. I said farewell to my home, to the memories - all gone!

We drove by Shloimke Oberzhanski's tavern, the town "club", where we used to drink beer, smoke, chat. Deserted.

Good God! There wasn't a single Jew left in Korelitz.

Here was our school and its large yard, where children's voices resounded in song and play.

And here were the two synagogues...Rabbi Vernik's house, where words of Torah never ceased. People used to come to the Rabbi to seek answers to their problems, to voice complaints. Now it was so silent that it was hard to believe people once lived there.

Even the cemetery. Here it was always quiet, but now all the tombstones had been smashed beyond recognition of any names.

We came to the large house of my Uncle Ezra Pomerchik, where I had spent my childhood years. I recalled those wonderful Saturday nights, where my Aunt Libbe used to make supper for the whole gang, at times hearty barley soup and *latkes*, or bean soup and herring and potatoes. My Uncle and Aunt took part in the chatting, just like the young folks.

Here we found a peasant. He had another house in town, but this one was larger and better built - and it cost him nothing. I asked him: "Where are the owners?" He turned away.

On Mill Street we met a Christian woman, Todoretzka. She recognized us. "You're still alive?" she wondered.
"We're looking for Jews" I replied.
"Well, Zelda Moshka the carpenter's daughter is still here... Sadye the leather worker Michael Kagan, Motl the leather worker and his son Leibe."

Together we went to look for them and we all wept.

We returned to Novohorodek, our hearts broken. It was a sad farewell to our beloved little town. We shall probably never see it again.

[Pages LIX-LXI]
[Pages 292-295 Yiddish]
See also page 285

# The Korelitzer Society Of America, Inc.

## Morris Kessler
## Guttel Simon

*Coordinator's Note: This text has been **copied** to **page 285**, and **in addition**, the **Constitution Committee names and roles and Constitution of the Society** appear there (Pages **287-289**). In addition, there are different **photographs** from those in the English Section.*

In New York there is an organization which bears the name "Korelitzer Society". The organization was formed on April 4, 1904, by a group of individuals born in Korelitz, at the home of Benjamin and Golda (Rochel Zlatess) Horwitz.

Early in the twentieth century, the decrees, oppression and pogroms perpetuated against the Jews by Czarist Russia set into motion a large-scale immigration to America. The situation of Russia's Jews was very bad. Many Jews were being persecuted because of political activity - particularly the young people who belonged to revolutionary organizations. Jews living within the Pale of Settlement were impoverished, and the vision of "Golden America" attracted masses of them to the New World. But when they did arrive in America, they found themselves in difficult circumstances. The native tongue was foreign to them; the customs were alien, and work in the sweatshops was hard. The entire country was then in the process of development, but jobs did not come so readily, and the pay was poor.

Depressed and confused in the tumult of New York, they clung to each other and to their friends. Most of the immigrants were men who had left their families behind in the Old World and were expected to send them sustenance, until they were able to bring them to America, and a few of them were single. Those who had relatives in America moved in with them, sleeping wherever there was room - on the floor, on a cot, and living as cheaply as possible, since every American dollar meant two rubles.

The difficult circumstances and the loneliness of the newly-arrived immigrants were bound to bring about organization into *landsmannschaften*, such as the *Korelitzer landsmannschaft* in New York. The organization was named *Chevra B'nai Yitzhak-Yechiel Anshel Korelitz*: a place was rented in which the *Chevra* established its own Synagogue. It was named for Rabbi Yitzhak-Yehiel, for many years the illustrious rabbi of Korelitz (and grandfather of the martyred Hebrew poet Yitzhak Katzenelson).

The following attended the founding meeting of the Society:
Nissan Rabinowich o.b.m. (the first President); Isaac David Itzkowitz; Joseph Chessler; Gedalyahu Becker; Abraham-Samuel Shimenowitz; Yaacov-Joseph Pomerantz; Alter Shimenowitz; Leibe-Itche Kaplan; Yitzhak-Yona Itzkowitz; Tevel Hurewitz; Feivel Polusky, and Harry Barrish.

The first aim of the Korelitzer Society was mutual aid and a sick fund. Each member paid membership dues. The income was used for various purposes - the acquisition of a cemetery plot for any Korelitzer who passed away, the rental of a hall for the semi-monthly meetings, and similar purposes.

The carpenters among the Korelitzer donated an Ark, bought a Scroll of the Torah for the Korelitzer synagogue; on Sabbaths, holidays, and even weekdays the synagogue was packed with worshippers. The synagogue was the only place where the Korelitzer met regularly. As was the custom among the Jews in Korelitz itself, Torah honors (*aliyot*) were apportioned. The custom was in effect for many years.

In the Second World War the situation changed completely. Many people came up from the South to New York, adding to the congestion. Living quarters became scarce. Until then the Korelitzer lived in the poorer sections of New York, and the newcomers kept penetrating more and more deeply into the Jewish sections. The large influx of the population forced a move to the surrounding towns.

The financial situation of the new immigrants began to improve, and many among the Korelitzer began moving out of New York. The meetings were not well attended.

The organization was then re-chartered under the laws of the State of New York and renamed "The Korelitzer Society". The religious coloration of the society also underwent change. The meeting date was shifted from Saturday night to Sunday afternoon and the meetings were held once monthly. Since 1970 it has been meeting four times a year.

The Korelitzer Society presently numbers 150 members, of which 40 are widows.

The following are the Presidents who served the society since its formation:

Nissan Rabinowitz, Tevel Hurewitz, Gedalya Becker, Mendel Tobias, Note Levine, Feivel Poluzky, Jacob Pomerantz, Gutel Shimenowitz (Simon). Louis Simenowitz, Joseph Chessler, Harry Barrish, Meyer Itzkowitz, Joseph

Mendelson, Sender Mendelson, Max Zussman, Meyer Rotkoff, Hayyim Abramowitz, Hyman Itzkowitz, the current president Morris Kessler, Moshe-Kopel Abramowitz, Louis Cohen, Isaac Geshvisky. Some also served as Vice-Presidents, and Moshe-Kopel Abramowitz also served as Protocol Secretary.

*[Page LXI]*

**A meeting of the Board of the Korelitzer Society, U.S.A.**

# INDEX

*Note: This index refers to the material before page 400 and does not include the material in the appendices that follow.*

## L

Yudelvitch, 12

# Z

Zaks, 91, 357
Zalamanker, 198, 304, 386
Zalamansky, 110
Zalemanski, 260, 395
Zaleviansky, 20
Zalivansky, 233
Zalkowich, 374
Zalman, 12, 57, 58, 68, 76, 89, 164, 166, 187, 214, 215, 218, 294, 295, 296
Zalmanovsky, 171

Zalmanowsky, 377
Zalmanski, 380
Zalmansky, 111, 139, 153, 293, 376
Zamushchick, 293
Zamushchik, 293
Ze'ev, 37, 78, 301
Zelaviansky, 210, 388
Zelivansky, 293
Zisling, 83, 365, 366
Zochovitzky,, 101
Zolmbe, 160
Zunser, 85, 86, 365
Zussman, 271, 285, 286, 287, 293, 398

# Appendices to the Korelitz Yizkor Book

1. Early Emigration from Korelitz
   A. The **Polusky-Turetzky** families (including connections with **Nash, Goodman and Tobias** families) in South Africa and the USA *(Merle Horwitz, Marion Polusky-Nakash, Bernard Paul, Bradley Nash, Mark Tobias)*
   B. The **Sapolsky and Kolczycki** families in the USA *(David Abelson)*
   C. The **Kartorzynski** family *(Ken Domeshek)*
   D. The **Faivelovitz** family in New Zealand *(Solly Faine, Ann Belinsky)*
   E. The **Fajwelewicz** family in France *(Paulette Lubelski)*
   F. The **Fivelevitz** family in the USA *(Targum, Duchan, Pagano and Musikar families)*

2. Korelitz Between the Wars
   G. Leah **Lubchansky** *(Rosemarie Koren, Nurit Buchweitz)*
   H. Berl **Domesek** *(Ken Domeshek)*
   I. The **Nisselevitz** family *(Hana Golan)*
   J. The **Fivelovich** family in Korelitz in WWII *(Hillel Orgad)*

3. World War II – the Partisans
   K. Fruma **Gulkowich** *(Ralph and Albert Berger)*
   L. Yaacov **Abramowich** *(Zahava Elbaz and Dina Abramoviz Karmy)*
   M. Gutke **Gantzevitz** (Tova **Nohomovski**) *(Chana Messer)*

4. World War II and After – Escaping to Life in Russia and then in the DP Camps
   N. Malka and Yaacov **Poluzhsky** *(Gershon Poleg, Avigail Poleg-Dvir, Yogev Bargad)*

5. Korelitz today
   O. **A visit to Korelitz** in 2010  *(Merle Horwitz)*

# Appendix A

# The Polusky-Turetzky Family

## (including connections with
# Nash, Goodman and Tobias families)

### Collated by Ann Belinsky

Meyer Polusky (Poluzhsky) was born in Karelitz in the Minsk province, to Feivel and Faie. He had 3 siblings, Maishe, Berl and Chaim.

Meyer married **Nechama Turetsky** (Zuretsky) and they immigrated with their family to Wellington, South Africa, just before the outbreak of the First World War. Two granddaughters **Merle Horwitz** (nee Adler), the first co-ordinator of the translation of the Korelitz Yizkor Book; and **Marion Nakash-Polusky**; and a grandson **Bernard Paul**, have provided much of the material below. From correspondence with **Bradley Nash** and **Mary Goodman** in the USA, a tentative family tree for the Polusky family was prepared, connecting the South African family with relatives in the USA.

Similarly, from correspondence Merle had with **Karin McQuillan**, and recent correspondence with **Mark Tobias**, a tentative family tree for the Turetsky family was prepared, connecting the South African family with Tobias relatives in the USA.

In both instances, we discovered that the USA relatives were very active in the Korelitzer Society of America.

## The Polusky (Poluzhsky) Family

Meyer and Nechama had 7 children: Annie, Sarah, Tilly, Abie (all born in Korelitz), Barney (Marion Polusky's father), Fanny (Bernard Paul's mother) and Rebecca –Becky (Merle Horwitz's mother), and many other grandchildren.

**Fig. 1**
Meyer and Nechama Polusky in Paarl (South Africa)

**Fig. 2**
Nechama holding the baby Barney, and Barney as an adult
---------

Merle Horwitz (nee Adler) grew up in the house of her grandparents, Nechama and Meyer Polusky. She inherited the candlesticks and wine cup, which were both probably brought from Korelitz.

**Fig. 3**
Candlesticks and wine cup (becher)

**Fig. 4**
**Wedding of Fanny POLUSKY to Mendel PAUL in the early 1940's.**

**Left to right** - Tilly Polusky, Becky Polusky, Ali Paul, Fanny Polusky, Mendel Paul, unknown, Hannah (Nechama) & Meyer Polusky. Bridesmaid Vilma (daughter of Tilly)
Not at wedding - Barney Polusky, Sarah Polusky, Annie Polusky and deceased Abie Polusky

# Bradley Nash, Mary Goodman, and the Polusky Connection

In 2004, Bradley Nash contacted Merle, seeking information about the Polusky family. He wrote that his great-grandfather Isaac Neshvisky -anglicized to NASH - had twin cousins Feivel (Phillip) and Shlemeh (Sam) Poluszky, involved the construction business in the USA. He had been in contact with a Mary Goodman, who confirmed in a letter in 2004 that her grandfather Feivel (Phillip) and his twin brother were also in the construction business. Thus their genealogical connection seems verified. The not-yet-corroborated part is whether the father of the twins - Dov Baer (Berl) Polusky is indeed the same brother of Meyer Polusky, grandfather of Marion and Merle (and of course other family members). We have not been able to make contact with Mary Goodman for more information. However in 2004 she did send the photo below to Bernard Paul:

**Fig. 5**
**40<sup>th</sup> Anniversary of the Korelitzer Society Inc. 1902-1942**
Feivel Phillip Polusky is standing in the top row 2nd from the right.

Feivel Polusky was a Founder and served as one of the Presidents of the Korelitzer Society in New York. His name appears on pages 285-87 and 398-399 of book. He was also a Trustee of the Benevolent Society (Page 287) and the Cemetery (*Gader*) Committee (below).

# BRADLEY NASH

Bradley writes: "My great-grandfather, **Isaac Neshwisky** (later changed to Nash; he also used the first names Ike, Irwin, Irving and Isadore at various points), was born in Korelitz *ca* 1886 and immigrated to New York in 1913. I have a copy of the ship manifest, showing his arrival in NY, on February 13, 1913, apparently under the name "Aisik Iswiski". The manifest lists "Karelz, Russia" as his last permanent residence. On the second page, Feivel Polusky (residing at 280 Madison Street on the Lower East Side of Manhattan) is listed as the relative he was "going to join". I believe Feivel was a first cousin of Isaac. Feivel and Isaac were both carpenters and were partners in a construction business for many years.

Isaac was a member and at times an officer, of the Korelitzer Society. The Yizkor Book mentions him in a few places in English and Yiddish – but with one exception incorrectly gives the last name as "Geshvisky". The two Geshvisky references (in Yiddish on page 286 and its English transliteration on page 399) indicate that he was a past president. The name does appear correctly as "Neshvisky" in Yiddish in the list of members of the Society's Constitution Committee (page 287). Feivel Polusky appears on the same list as an "Old Age Trustee" and *Gemilas Chesed* Trustee.

My grandfather, **Hyman (Chaim) Nash**, was also a member of the Korelitzer Society, and in its later years an officer. He appears in a picture of a board meeting in the English section of this book (page 399) standing in the back row on the right end, with a hat). My grandfather never set foot in Korelitz himself. He was born in a nearby shtetl, Horodishche, in 1908. When Isaac left in 1913 to get himself established in America, my grandfather remained in Horodishche with his mother (Rochel/Rose) and his two siblings (a brother Anshul (Arthur) and Musha (Mae)) in his grandfather's house. They were displaced during World War I, and lost contact with Isaac, who was already in America, for an extended period, but they eventually joined him in New York in 1923. I learned a great deal about Horodishche from my grandfather, but he didn't know much about Korelitz. He did tell a story about his grandfather, Moshe Aaron Neshwisky, who walked from Korelitz to Horodishche to visit the family. It was summertime, and they were sleeping outside. My grandfather recalls being awakened by an old man in a long black kapote, who said, *Ikh bin dayn zeyde fun Korelitz.* (I'm your grandpa from Korelitz). He visited with them briefly, and then went home."

**Fig. 6**
Rochel and Isaac Neshwisky-Nash, in the Bronx, 1950's

Bradley has sent photographs of the tombstones of Feivel and Sam Polusky, buried in the Mount Judah Cemetery in Ridgewood Queens where the Korelitzer Society had its original cemetery. He also has sent photos of the elaborate gate for the *Chevra B'nai Yitzkhok Yechiel Anshei Korelitz* (The original name of the Korelitzer Society in America). Isaac Neshwisky is listed on one side as a Trustee; Feivel Polusky is listed on the other side, as a member of the Fence Committee.

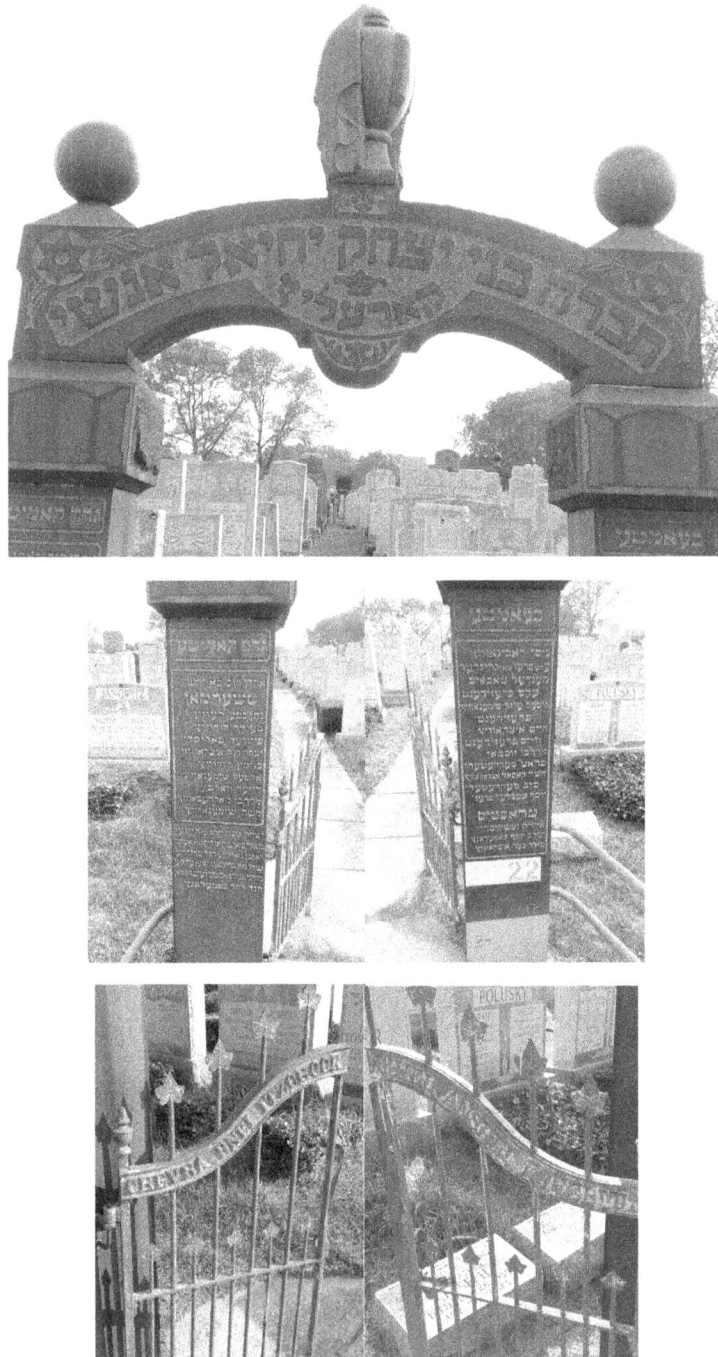

**Fig. 7**
**The entrance portal to the Korelitzer Section of the Mount Judah Cemetery in Ridgewood**
**Queens where the Korelitzer Society had its original cemetery.**
At the top and on the gates - written in Hebrew and English - *Chevra B'nai Yitzkhok Yechiel*
*Anshei Korelitz*. Translation: The B'nai Yitzkhok Yechiel Society of Korelitzers.
The right hand pillar lists names of the Committee members and the left hand pillar lists the
Fence Committee members (the names are listed below, opposite Figs 8 and 9).

**Fig. 8**
**Pillar of the Committee (unknown date) of the Korelitzer Society**
**(Mount Judah cemetery in Ridgewood)**
Translation opposite.

## Translation of the Committee Pillar:

# COMMITTEE

Nissan Rabinowich
First President and Founder

Mendel Tobias
Ex-President

Guttel Ozer Shimonovitz
PRESIDENT

Haim Itzkowitz
Vice President

Mordechai Zussman
Protocol Secretary

Moshe-Kopel Abramovitz
Financial Secretary

Yosef Chessler
Treasurer
~~~~~~~~~~~~~~~~~
Trustees:

Isaac Neshwisky

Yaacov Yosef Pomerantz

Meir Ber Itzkowitz

**Fig. 9**
**Pillar of the Fence Committee (unknown date) of the Korelitzer Society**
**(Mount Judah cemetery in Ridgewood)**
Translation opposite.

**Translation of the Fence Committee Pillar:**

# FENCE COMMITTEE

Aharon Dov Barish – **CHAIRMAN**

Nathan Netta Levine

Tevel Horwitz

Feivel Polusky

Yitzhak David Itzikovitz

Meyer Wolfin

Mordechai Mordechovitz

Moshe Shimonovitz

``````````````````

Yitzhak Ginzburg with his wife Raizel

Morris Itzikowitz with his wife Esther

Reuven Galvin with his wife Rachel Frieda

Shlomo Grimowitz with his wife Elka

Mordechai Avraham son of Dusha Yaacov Zussman

Chana Rachel Pomerantz
``````````````````

# The Turetzky Family
## With connections to the Tobias and McQuillan families

**Figs. 10 and 11**
**Photos of relatives of Nechama Turetsky**
Possibly brothers or brothers-in-law.

Nechama (Hannah) was the youngest daughter of Leah and Meyer Turetzky, who was the unofficial mayor of Mir. She had 2 or 3 brothers and at least one sister who emigrated either to or via Cardiff (Wales UK) to the United States. Nechama married Meyer Polusky.

Merle Horwitz knew her grandmother Nechama had a married sister with the surname Tobias in the United States, but had never managed to find any relatives.

Merle received information from **Karin McQuillan** in 2010: her grandmother was Rose Therese, born 1894, daughter of Anna Tobias (nee Turetsky), whose father was the unofficial mayor of Mir. Anna, who immigrated to the USA, had 2 sisters - one of whom married a Rabbi and went to Palestine, and one of whom married a shoe manufacturer and went to South Africa. This seems to fit in with the information that Merle had, that Nechama's sister's married name was Tobias. Later, a family tree with the names Menachem Mendel and Anna Turetsky was found on the internet, with descendants including Karen McQuillan.

# Mark Tobias and the Turetsky Connection

Then I (Ann Belinsky) received correspondence from **Mark Tobias**, also searching for family records, who sent me photos of the gravestones of Anna and Menachem Mendel (Max) Tobias from the Korelitzer Section in the Mt Zion Cemetery in Flushing Meadows, New York, and so closed off the circle.

**Fig. 12**
**In the Korelitzer Section of Mt Zion Cemetery, Flushing Meadows**

LHS: *In Hebrew - CHANA MALKA, daughter of MEYER TOYBAS* (the surname is <u>probably</u> a mistake as Toybas (Tobias) is her married name). Beloved mother **ANNA TOBIAS**. Died April 22, 1958 aged 88 years.

RHS: *In Hebrew - YISRAEL MENACHEM MENDEL, son of DOV BAER TOYBAS.* Beloved husband and father **MAX TOBIAS**. Died February 17 1941 aged 72 years.

According to the above dates, Max and Anna would have been born around 1870, which is logical. We still have to corroborate that Anna is indeed related to the above Turetsky family (as daughter of Meir and Leah and sister of Nechama), since her father's surname is apparently not indicated correctly.

It is not yet clear if Mark himself is related, if at all, to Anna and Max, and there are indeed several graves of Korelitzers with Tobias surnames buried in the same section, including Mark's grandparents **Rachel and Morris Tobias**, and another couple, Rachel and Max Tobias.

Mark Tobias's great-grandparents, Morris (born 1873) and Rachel (born 1876, nee Levine) Tobias, were born in Korelitz. They came to the USA in 1899, and lived in New York until 1915-16, when they moved to Bridgeport, Connecticut. Morris was a member of the Korelitzer Society. Their 5 children were Joseph-Abraham, Irving, Edward, Victoria Jean, Rose and Sam (Mark's grandfather). The Korelitzer Society lists in the David Abelson Appendix B include the names Moses and Issar Tobias, 409 Hawley Avenue, Bridgeport Connecticut. This has been verified as Mark's great-grandfather, Morris (Moses) (died 1937) and Morris's brother Irving (Issar) lived at one stage in Hawley Avenue, Bridgeport!

This genealogical investigation is not complete. However it has been an interesting exercise to try and put all the names together, and I hope that the families involved will maybe carry on from here to further corroborate the relationships.

**Fig. 13**
**The Mt Zion Cemetery (Flushing): Korelitzer Section.**
**Cemetery Committee Officers (unknown date)**
Max Tobias – Ex. President; David Horowitz – President; Morris Tobias – Vice-President; Julius Turetzky – Secretary; Abraham Davidson – Treasurer; Meyer Itzkowitz – 1st Trustee; Jacob Pomerantz – 2nd Trustee; Morris Zarinsky 3rd Trustee

# Appendix B
# The Sapolsky and Kolczycki Families
## and their Descendants

## By David M. Abelson

My maternal grandmother, Mae Sapolsky, was born in Korelitz in September 1903. Mae and her parents, Joseph and Alice (maiden name Kolczycki), immigrated to the United States. Joseph arrived at Ellis Island in March 1903 on the SS Patricia, leaving behind a pregnant wife. Mae and her mother arrived at Ellis Island in July 1906 aboard the RMS Carmania.

Joseph's brother, Kopel, entered the United States at Ellis Island in 1904. There is no record to suggest that Joseph and Kopel's parents, Jacob and Minnie Riva (maiden name Slutzky), emigrated from Korelitz, but both Joseph and Kopel stated in their immigration papers that they would be staying with their brother, Abraham, in New York City on the lower eastside. We know of no other mention of Abraham. The name Sapolsky was later changed to Spaulder.

Alice's twin sister, Ida, and their parents, Moshe and Gita Kolczycki (maiden name Goldberg), also immigrated. We do not know when, and the only record we have of Moshe and Gita being in the United States is a photograph from approximately 1910. Kolczycki was shortened to Koltz. *(Also transliterated as Koltsitsky - AB)*

These families settled in and around New York City.

In 1928, Mae Sapolsky married Jacob Goldberg. Jacob, known as Jack, was born in 1898 in New York City. His parents emigrated from Russia, but when and from where is unclear. Mae and Jack have two children, Joan and Elaine (my mother). They both live in New York City. While Joseph, Alice and Ida were fixtures during Joan and Elaine's younger years, Mae did not speak of her family in Poland other than to say she had cousins, and certainly did not speak of the atrocities they faced during WWII. Following the war with the rise of McCarthyism, Mae, like other Jews of her generation, was deceptive about when and where she was born as she was fearful that she would be deported even though she became a United States citizen in 1931.

In addition to Alice and Ida, Moshe and Gita Kolczycki had two older boys, Marcus and Tuvia. Tuvia stayed in Korelitz, where he married Chasia and had three daughters. He was murdered in Korelitz in 1942. (More information about his family can be found on Page 327) Marcus moved to Lodz, Poland where he married Chana Kaja, and raised a family. Marcus, Chana, son

Natan and his wife Miriam, and other family members were first sent to the Lodz ghetto. In August 1944, they were sent to Auschwitz, where they were murdered. Natan and Miriam's daughter, Zofia, survived the camps. Zofia's story and that of her husband, Jurek Flajszman, is recounted in the book, "Polish Witness to the Shoah". Natan's brother, Tadeusz, also survived the war. Like Zofia, Tadeusz returned to Lodz, where he lived until he died in 1962. Zofia (known as Zosia) and Jurek had a daughter, Katja.

Mae and Jack were in contact with Tadeusz during the 1950s. For reasons that are unknown to us, just as Mae and Jack did not talk about family in Poland, Tadeusz did not tell Zosia that she had family in the United States. Until winter 2015, my family's connection to Korelitz was unclear, but through the power of the internet and the help of Teresa Pollin of the United States Holocaust Memorial Museum, we now know our family history—and now the two sides of the family are in touch.

Zosia, Jurek and Katja moved to Upsalla, Sweden in 1969 after the *de facto* expulsion of Jews from Poland by the communist government. Jurek died in August 2017. Katja Flajszman and I, two of Moshe and Gita Kolczycki's great-great grandchildren, live in Boulder, Colorado.

## The Korelitzer Society Name and Address List

Mae died in 1994. Among her possessions was a list of people (first names, surnames and addresses) who probably belonged to the Korelitzer Society in the New York City area. The list, likely from the 1930s, was written on the back of a printed form (Figure 1) inviting members to a Special General meeting. The form is in English and Yiddish. The list was likely made/held by Mae's parents, perhaps as a way of keeping in touch with other ex-Korelitzers, or perhaps they had a role in the Society and had made the list for mailing/financial purposes connected to the Society. The Korelitzer Society disbanded in 1980.

Chevra Bnai Yizchok Yechiel Anshei Korelitz

Dear Brother:

You are requested to attend a SPECIAL GENERAL MEETING on SATURDAY,...................................193..., 8 P. M., at our Local

Subject: **First Payment** **Second Payment**

We hope that you will not fail to attend this meeting.

By order of the President,

......................................... Fin. Sec'y.

| YOU OWE: | Dol. | Cents | זי שולדען אן: |
|---|---|---|---|
| Arrears | | | ריקשטענדע |
| Quarterly Dues | 2 | 75 | קווארטאל בײַטרענע |
| Cemetery Tax | | | סעמעטערי |
| Loan Fund | | 10 | גמילת חסד |
| Old Age Fund | | 5 | אלד אײדזש פאנד |
| Registered Letters | | | רעדזשיסטרירטע לעטערס |
| Fine | | | שטראפען |
| Total | | | טאטאל |
| Received | | | בעצאהלט |
| Balance | | | באלאנס |

In case of moving, notify Secretary at once.
ווען א ברודער מופט, לאזט גלײך וויסען דעם סעקרעטער,

Please present this bill at the meeting

חברה בני יצחק יחיאל
אנשי קארעליץ

ווערטהער ברודער:—

איהר זײַט העפליכסט אײַנגעלאדען צו אין דושענעראל (ספּעשעל) פערזאמלונג וועלכע וועט שטאטפינדען אם שבת, דעם......מען ה. מ. אום 8 אוהר אבענדס, אין אונזער לאקאל,.................

צוועק: ערשטע אײַנצאהלונג. צווייטע אײַנצאהלונג.

יעדער מעמבער מוז אפמענדען די מיטינגען. פאר ניט אפמענדען קען ער באשטראפט ווערען מים 50 סענטס.

אים אויפפראגע דעם פרעזידענט,

......................................... סעקרעטאר

LAST PAYMENT .......................................... לעצטע אײַנצאהלונג:

ווען א ברודער באצאהלט ניט זײַן שולדען בײַלעצטע אײַנצאהלונג, איז ער צו קיינע בענעפיטס ניט בערעכטיגם.

If a Brother is in arrears after Last Payment, he is not entitled to benefit

Suspension night .......................................... שטרײַך אווענד איז

ווען א ברודער אטענדעט ניט א פונעראל, דארף ער באצאהלען א דאלאר אדער מעהר. ווען א ברודער פעהלט צו קומען צו א סיק קאמיטע, אדער שבעה קאמיטע מוז ער באצאהלען 50 סענטס שטראף פאר ניט קומען און 50 סענטס שטראף פאר ניט בעריכטען.

For non-attendance at funeral a Brother will have to pay one dollar or more.
If a Brother fails to attend a Sick or Shive Committee he will have to pay 50c fine for non-attendance and 50c fine for not reporting.

אלעם צו מעלדען צום רעקארדינג סעקרעטער

**Fig. 1** **Original form (in English and Yiddish) for inviting members of the Korelitzer Society to Special General Meetings**

## *Additional Notes by Ann Belinsky:*

The original list (Figs 2a and b) is in phonetic Yiddish/Hebrew letters. It seems that the list had been copied into the Hebrew script from an English source, as the names go according to the English alphabetical order and not according to the Yiddish (Hebrew) alphabet. These lists are written/transliterated using a Yiddish pronunciation.

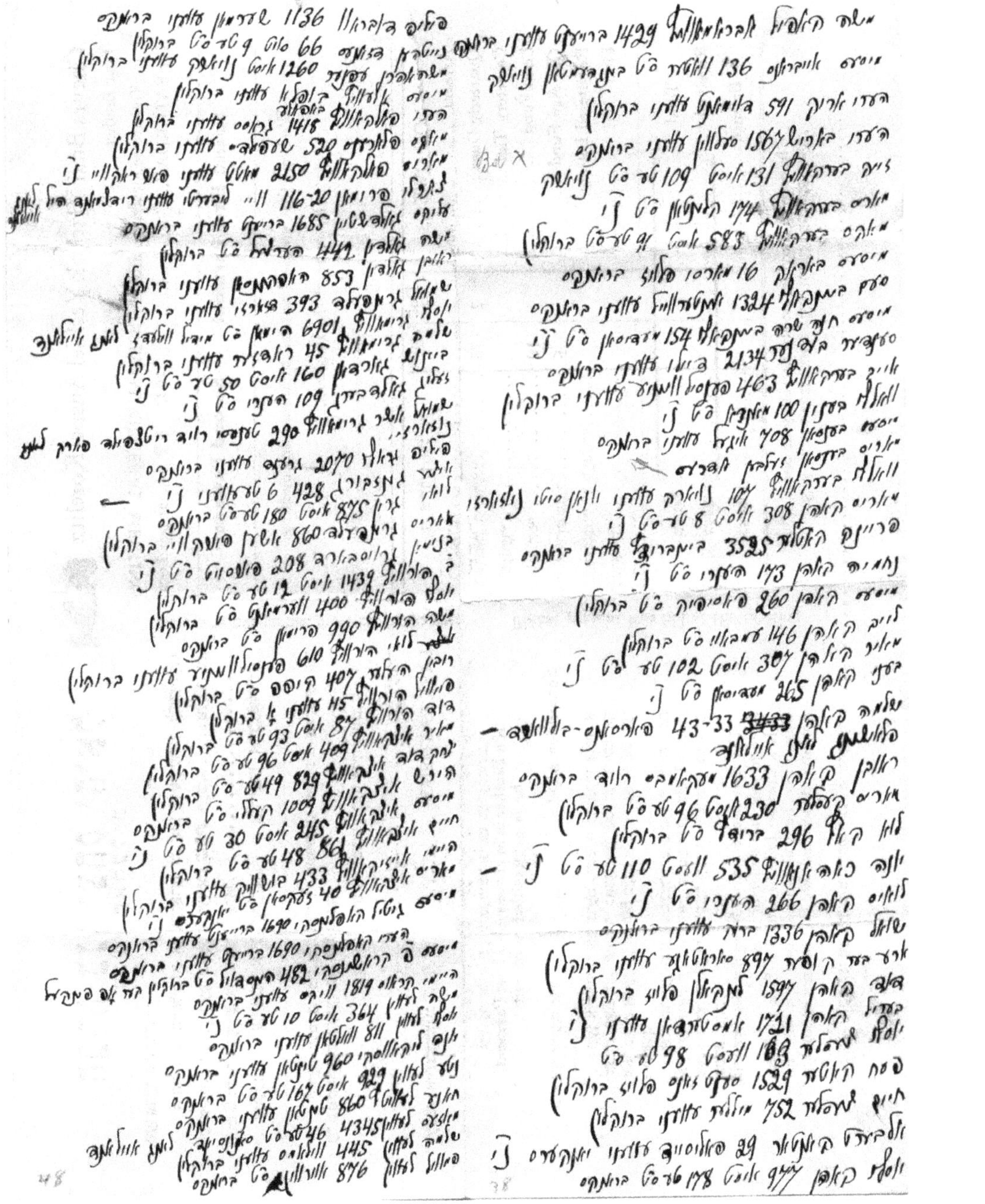

Fig. 2a: The first page of the list of Korelitzer Society members, 1930's

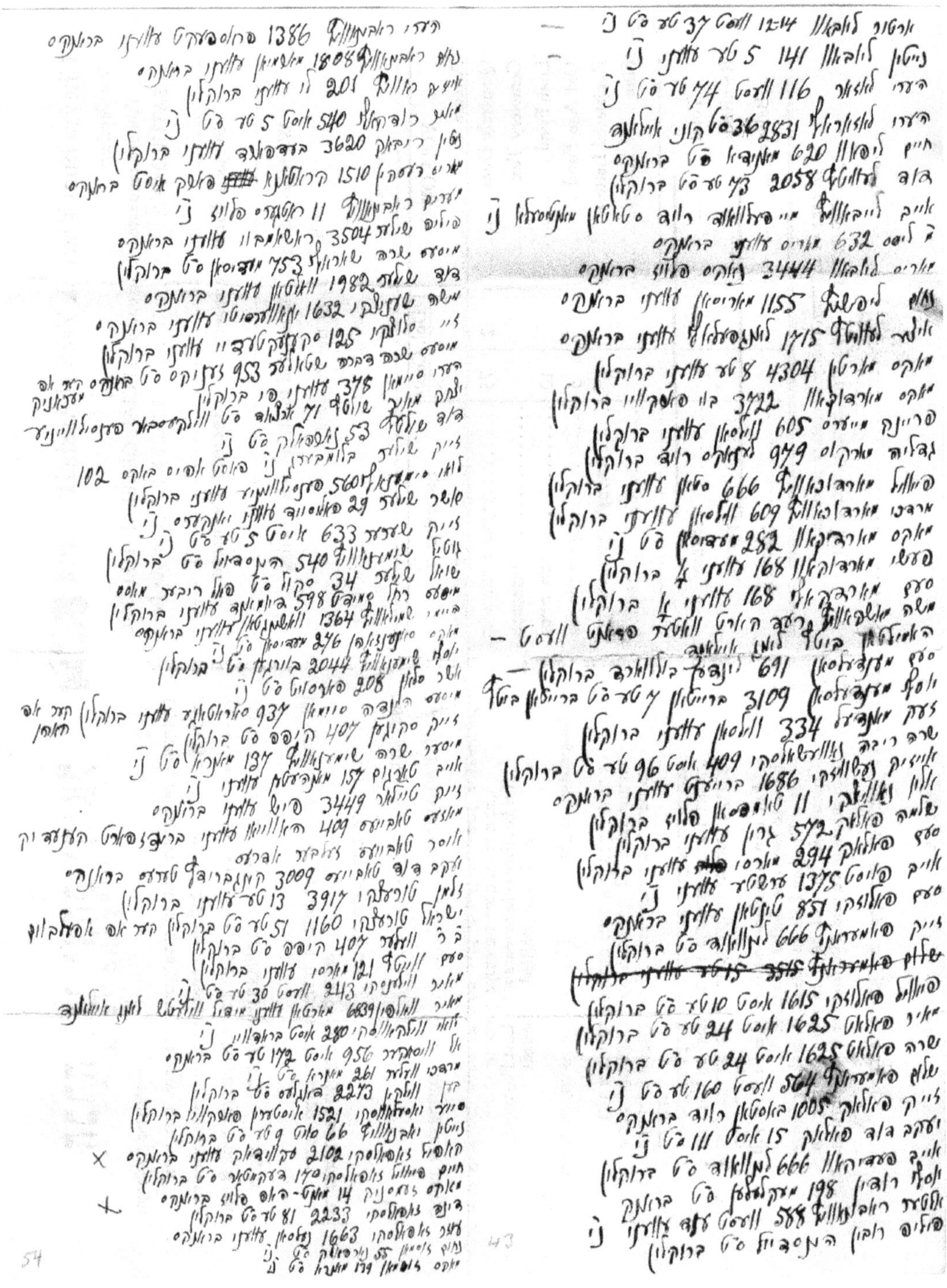

Fig. 2h: The second page of the list of Korelitzer Society members, 1930's

I transliterated these lists back into the English alphabet (Table 1). I understand Hebrew but not always the Yiddish pronunciation, so that the meaning of the original street name was not always clear. Luckily there are lists of Brooklyn and Bronx Streets available online so I could compare the names and correct spelling in English and be sure that I had transliterated back to English correctly!

I also used the Korelitzer Society list available on the JewishGen website (contributed by Jerry Seligson) and where the same name appeared in both lists, used the Seligson spelling to make it easier for the reader to compare. I also googled locations other than Brooklyn and Bronx, to try and find the correct names and spelling. There are still some names which have eluded me, which appear in *italics*. Thanks also to Harvey Spitzer for help with some names.

However, since the original list in English has probably been lost, these lists are a valuable historical and genealogical tool.

Below is the transliterated list of all the above names in Figs. 2a and 2b:

### Table 1: Abelson  List of Korelitzer Society members in the 1930's - names and addresses

| Surname | First name | Address | Region |
|---|---|---|---|

**PAGE 1**
**RIGHT HAND SIDE**

**A**

| Surname | First name | Address | Region |
|---|---|---|---|
| Abramovitz | Moshe Kopel | 1429 Bryant Avenue | Bronx |
| Abrams | Moses | 136 Water Street, Binghamton | New York |
| Arick | Harry | *591  ?Doymont Avenue ?Diamond Street* | Brooklyn |

**B**

| Surname | First name | Address | Region |
|---|---|---|---|
| Bareish | Harry | 1567 Selwyn Avenue | Bronx |
| Berkowitz | Jake | 131 East 109th Street | New York |
| Berkowitz | Morris | 174 Clinton Street | New York |
| Berkowitz | Max | 583 East 91st Street | Brooklyn |
| Berek | Moses | 16 Marcy Place | Bronx |
| Bankof (Bainkof) | Sam Moses Hannah | 1324 Intervale Avenue | Bronx |
| Bankof (Bainkof) | Sarah | 154 Madison Street | New York |
| Budner | Sander | 2134 Daly Avenue | Bronx |
| Berkowitz | Abe | 463 Pennsylvania Avenue | Brooklyn |
| Bennin | Wolf | 100 Monroe Street | New York |
| Benson | Moses | 708 Eagle Avenue | Bronx |
| Benson | Morris | Same address as Moses Benson | Bronx |
| Berkowitz | Wolf | 107 New York Avenue, Union City | New Jersey |

## C

| Cohen | Morris | 308 East 8th Street | New York |
|---|---|---|---|
| Cutler (Kutler) | Frank | 3525 Bainbridge Avenue | Bronx |
| Cohen | Nechemia | 173 Henry Street | New York |
| Cohen | Moses | 260 Pacific Street | Brooklyn |
| Cohen | Leib | 146 Amboy Street | Brooklyn |
| Cohen | Meir | 307 East 102 Street | New York |
| Cohen | Benny | 265 Madison Street | New York |
| Cohen | Shlomo | 43-33 Parsons Boulevard, Flushing | Long Island |
| Cohen | Reuven | 1633 Macombs Road | Bronx |
| Kessler (Chessler) | Morris | 230 East 96th Street | Brooklyn |
| Katz | Lou | 296 Bridge Street | Brooklyn |
| Kahanovitz (Kakanowitz) | Yona (J) | 535 West 110th Street | New York |
| Cohen | Louis | 266 Henry Street | New York |
| Cohen | Shaul | 1336 Brook Avenue | Bronx |
| Cooper | *?Ira Baer* | 897 Saratoga Avenue | Brooklyn |
| Cohen | David | 1597 Lincoln Place | Brooklyn |
| Cohen | Berel | 1721 Amsterdam Avenue | New York |
| Chessler | (I)Yosef | 163 West 98th Street | not given |
| Carter | Pesach (Phillip) | 1529 Saint (St.) John's Place | Brookyn |
| Chessler | Haim | 752 Miller Avenue | Brooklyn |
| Cantor (?Kantor) | Albert | 29 Palisade Avenue, Yonkers | New York |
| Cohen | Yosef | 977 East 178th Street | Bronx |

## PAGE 1
## LEFT HAND SIDE

## D

| Dubrow | Phillip | 1136 Sherman Avenue | Bronx |
|---|---|---|---|
| *Desolnas?Julnes* | Nathan | 66 South 9th Street | Brooklyn |

## E

| Epner | Moshe Aharon | 1260 East New York Avenue | Brooklyn |
|---|---|---|---|
| *?Elovitz* | Moses | Buffalo Avenue | Brooklyn |

## F

| Falkowitz | Harry | 1418  ?Grass Grace Avenue* | Brooklyn |
|---|---|---|---|
| | | *No Grace Avenue in Brooklyn. There is a Grace Avenue in Bronx* | |
| Florentz | Max | 520 Sheffield Avenue | Brooklyn |
| Falkowitz | Morris | 2150 Mott Avenue, Far Rockaway | Queens |
| | | 116-20 (?Wye) Liberty Avenue | |
| Freeman | Charlie | Richmond Hill | Long Island |

## G

| Goldstein | Alex | 1685 Bryant Avenue | Bronx |
|---|---|---|---|
| Goldin | Moshe | 442 Herzl Street | Brooklyn |
| Goldin | Reuven | 853 Hopkinson Avenue | Brooklyn |
| Greenfield | Shmuel | 393  Jersey Avenue | Brooklyn |
| Grumowitz | Yosef | 6901 Hyman Street=Ave?, Model Village | Long Island |
| Grumowitz | Shlomo | 45 Rogers Avenue | Brooklyn |

| Gordin | Beynish (?) | 160 East 50th Street | New York |
|---|---|---|---|
| Goldberg | Zelig | 109 Henry Street | New York |
| Grumowitz | Shmuel Asher | 290 *Tennessee?*\* Road, Ridgefield Park<br>\* No Tennessee Road in Ridgefield Park | New Jersey |
| Graller or Grallo | Phillip | 2070 Grand Avenue | Bronx |
| Ginzburg | ? | 428 6th Avenue | New York |
| Green | Louis | 875 East 180th Street | Bronx |
| Greenfield | Morris | 860 Ocean Parkway | Brooklyn |
| Grossbard | Benjamin | 208 Forsyth Street, Manhattan | New York |

**H**

| Horowitz | B. | 1439 East 12th Street | Brooklyn |
|---|---|---|---|
| Horowitz | Yosef | 400 Vermont Street | Brooklyn |
| Horowitz | Moshe | 990 Freeman Street | Bronx |
| Horowitz | Louis | 610 Pennsylvania Avenue | Brooklyn |
| Heller | Rubin | 407 Cooper Street | Brooklyn |
| Horowitz | Faivel | 115 Avenue A | Brooklyn |
| Horowitz | David | 87 East 93rd Street | Brooklyn |

**I**

| Itskowitz | Meyer | 409 East 96th Street | Brooklyn |
|---|---|---|---|
| Itskowitz | Yitzhak David | 829 49th Street | Brooklyn |
| Itskowitz | Hirsch | 1009 Kelly Street | Bronx |
| Itskowitz | Moses | 245 East 30th Street | New York |
| Itskowitz | Haim | 861 48th Street | Brooklyn |
| Izikovitch (Aiscowich) | Haim | 433 Bushwick Avenue | Brooklyn |
| Itskowitz | Morris | 40 Jackson Street, Yonkers | New York |

**K**

| Kaplinsky | Moses Gittel | 1690 Bryant Avenue | Bronx |
|---|---|---|---|
| Kaplinsky | Harry | 1690 Bryant Avenue (same) | Bronx |
| Krashtinsky | Moses P. | 482 Hinsdale Street | Brooklyn |
| Kraus | Hymie | 1819 Weeks Avenue | Bronx |

**L**

| Levine | Moshe | 364 East 10th Street | New York |
|---|---|---|---|
| Levine | Yosef | 811 Walton Avenue | Bronx |
| Likofsky | Yona | 960 Tinton Avenue | Bronx |
| Levine | Netta | 929 East 167th Street | Bronx |
| Levich | Chana | 860 Tinton Avenue | Bronx |
| Levine | Moses | 4345 46th Street, Sunnyside | Long Island |
| Levine | Shlomo | 445 Williams Avenue | Brooklyn |
| Levine | Samuel | 876 Overing Street | Bronx |

**Page 2**
**RIGHT HAND SIDE**
**L**

| Lubow | Arthur | 12-14 West 37th Street | New York |
|---|---|---|---|
| Lubow | Nathan | 141 5th Avenue | New York |
| Lazar | Harry | 116 West 74th Street | New York |

| | | | |
|---|---|---|---|
| Lazaroff | Harry | 2831 36th Street | Coney Island |
| Lipaw | Chaim | 620 Manida Street | Bronx |
| Lovitz | David | 2058 73rd Street | Brooklyn |
| Leibovitz | Abe | Maplewood Road Staten *M...* | New York |
| Liss | M. | Morris Avenue | Bronx |
| Lovell | Morris | 3444 Knox Place | Bronx |
| Lipshitz | Nachum | 1155 Morrison Avenue | Bronx |
| Lovitz | Itche | 1715 Longfellow Avenue | Bronx |

**M**

| | | | |
|---|---|---|---|
| Martin | Max | 4304 8th Avenue | Brooklyn |
| Mardikon | Max | 3722 Bay Parkway | Brooklyn |
| Myers | Frank | 605 Wilson Avenue | Brooklyn |
| Marcus | Gedalia | 979 Lenox Road | Brooklyn |
| Mordochowitz | Faivel | 666 Stone Avenue | Brooklyn |
| Mordochowitz | Mordechai | 609 Wilson Avenue | Brooklyn |
| Mardikon | Max | 282 Madison Street | New York |
| Mordokoff | Pashy | 168 Avenue A | Brooklyn |
| Mardkoff | Sam | 168 Avenue A | Brooklyn |
| Moskowitz | Moshe | Hart Road Waterfront West, Hamilton Beach | Long Island |
| Mendelson | Sam | 691 Linden Boulevard | Brooklyn |
| Mendelson | Yosef | 3109 Brighton 7th Street | Brighton Beach |
| Mandel | Jack | 334 Wilson Avenue | Brooklyn |

**N**

| | | | |
|---|---|---|---|
| Navashalsky | Sarah Reeva | 409 East 96th Street | Brooklyn |
| Nashomsky | Isaac | 1686 Bryant Avenue | Bronx |
| Navalky? Novitzky? | Alon?Alan | 11 Thompson Place (Present name: McKeever Pl.) | Brooklyn |

**P**

| | | | |
|---|---|---|---|
| Pollack | Shlomo | 572 Greene Avenue | Brooklyn |
| Pollack | Sam | 294 Marcy Avenue | Brooklyn |
| Poyst (or Foyst) | Abe | 1375 First Avenue , Manhattan | New York |
| Polusky/Palusky | Sam | 851 Tinton Avenue | Bronx |
| Pomerantz | Jake, Zach | 666 Linwood Street | Brooklyn |
| Pomerantz | Shalom | 3515 15th Avenue **(LINE DELETED)** | Brooklyn |
| Polusky/Palusky | Faivel | 1615 East 10th Street | Brooklyn |
| Pallet/Pollet | Meir | 1625 East 24th Street | Brooklyn |
| Pallet/Pollet | Sarah | 1625 East 24th Street | Brooklyn |
| Pomerantz | Shalom | 564 West 160th Street | New York |
| Pollack | Jake, Zach | 1005 Boston Road | Bronx |
| Pollack | Yaacov David | 15 East 111th Street | New York |
| Paticoff | Abe | 666 Linwood Street | Brooklyn |

**R**

| | | | |
|---|---|---|---|
| Rudin | Yosef | 198 Mcclellan Street | Bronx |
| Rabinowitz | Alter | 588 West End Avenue | New York |
| Rubin | Phillip | Hinsdale Street | Brooklyn |

**Page 2**
**LEFT HAND SIDE**
**R ctd.**

| | | | |
|---|---|---|---|
| Rabinowitz | Harry | 1386 Prospect Avenue | Bronx |
| Rabinowitz | Nachum | 1808 Marmion Avenue | Bronx |
| Ravitz | Isaac | 201 Lee Avenue | Brooklyn |
| Rutkoff | Meyer | 540 East 5th Street | New York |
| Ribuck | Nathan | 3620 Bedford Avenue | Brooklyn |
| Raskin | Morris | 1510 Crotona Park East | Bronx |
| Rabinowitz | Miriam, Meyeram | 11 Rutgers Place | New York |

**S**

| | | | |
|---|---|---|---|
| Schiller | Phillip | 3504 Rochambeau Avenue | Bronx |
| Sharaf | Moses Sarah | 753 Madison Street | New York |
| Schiller | David | 1982 Walton Avenue | Bronx |
| Sonitzky | Moshe | 1632 University Avenue | Bronx |
| Slutzky | Jay | 125 Schenectady Avenue | Brooklyn |
| | Moses Sarah | | |
| Shtollar | Deborah | 953  Street | Bronx |
| Simon | Harry | 378 Avenue P | Brooklyn |
| Schultz | Yitzchak Meir | 71 Orchard Street Wilkinsburg | Pennsylvania |
| Schultz | David | 53 Norfolk Street | New York |
| Schiller | Jake | Bloomberry, New York. PO Box 102 | New York |
| Simanoff | Leo, Louis | 5601 Pennsylvania Avenue | Brooklyn |
| Schiller | Asher | 29 Palmswood Avenue, Yonkers | New York |
| Sherer, Shirer? | Jake | 633 East 5th Street | New York |
| Simonowitz | Guttel | 540 Hinsdale Street | Brooklyn |
| Schiller | Shaul | 34 School Street, Fall River | Mass. |
| Schmidt | Moses Rachel | 598 --- Avenue | Brooklyn |
| Shmullowitz | Hymie | 1364 Washington Avenue | Bronx |
| Sonenson | Max | 276 Madison Street | New York |
| Simonowitz | Yosef | 2044 Bergen Street | Brooklyn |
| Sloane | Asher | 208 Forsyth Street, Manhattan | New York |
| Simon | Moses Hinda | 937 Saratoga Avenue | Brooklyn |
| Skigan | Jake | 407 Keap Street | Brooklyn |
| Shimonovitz | Musar, Sarah | 137 Monroe Street | New York |

**T**

| | | | |
|---|---|---|---|
| Targum (Taryum) | Abe | 157 Manhattan Avenue | New York |
| Taylor | Jake | 3449 Fish Avenue | Bronx |
| Tobias | Moses | 409 Hawley Avenue Bridgeport | Connecticut |
| Tobias | Ossar/Issar? | same address (409 Hawley, Bridgeport) | Connecticut |
| Tobias | Jacob David | 3009 Kingsbridge Terrace | Brooklyn |
| Turetsky | Zalman | 3917 13th Avenue | Brooklyn |
| Turetsky | Yisrael | 1160 51st Street | Brooklyn |

**W**

| | | | |
|---|---|---|---|
| Weller | B.R. | 407 Keap Street | Brooklyn |
| Weitz | Sam | 121 Marcy Avenue | Brooklyn |
| Willensky | Meyer | 243 West 30th Street | New York |
| Wolfin | Meyer | 6839 Marten Avenue, Model Village | Long Island |

| | | | |
|---|---|---|---|
| Willkovsky | Louis | 280 East Broadway | New York |
| Wysoker | Al | 956 East 172nd Street | Bronx |
| Weller | Mordechai | 261 Monroe Street | New York |
| Wilkin | Ben | 2273 Douglass Street | Brooklyn |

**Y**

| | | | |
|---|---|---|---|
| Yoselovsky | *Sva?* | 1521 Eastern Parkview | Brooklyn |
| Yavnovitz (Janowitz?) | Nathan | 66 South 9th Street | Brooklyn |

**Z**

| | | | |
|---|---|---|---|
| Zapolsky (Sapolsky) | Kopel | 2102 Aqueduct Avenue | Bronx |
| Zapolsky (Sapolsky) | Chaim Faivel | 170 Decatur Street | Bronx |
| Zamshnick | Max | 14 Mount Hope Place | Bronx |
| Zapolsky (Sapolsky) | Dina | 2233 81st Street | Brooklyn |
| Zapolsky (Sapolsky) | Ozer | 1663 Nelson Avenue | Bronx |
| Zussman (?Sussman) | Nachum | 55 Norfolk Street | New York |
| Zussman (?Sussman) | Max | 139 Monroe Street | New York |

Another valuable piece of information sent by David Abelson is a photo of Korelitz taken before 1906. (Fig 3). The sentences on the back of the photo read:

*Korelitz Guberny Minsk Street Zalemanky*

*i.e.* The town of Korelitz in the Minsk Province, Zalemanky Street.

This fits into the hand-drawn street map of Korelitz (page 4) where in the lower left we see Zalemanky Street, which continues as Church Lane, where the Korelichi Church of Saints Peter and Paul is located (on the left-hand side).

**Fig. 3**
**Zalemanky Street in the town of Korelitz in the Minsk Province (before 1906)**

Note: This photo is similar to that which appears on page 8 in this book, but is taken at a different time of the year - the trees above have no leaves, as compared to those in full foliage on Page 8. *(AB)*

# Appendix C
# The Kartorzynski's
## The Story of a U.S. Korelitzer Society Family

## By Kenneth A. Domeshek*

The Kartorzynski family name appears in Korelitz, Nowogrudek and Negnewicze, three nearby towns in present day Belarus. Descendants do not know how long this family was in that area, but there are records in the 1800's to early 1900's. One reference from 1880 identifies Movsha Yankel Kartorzynski from Negnewicze as evading the draft. Enta Kartorzynski, a grocer, appears in a business directory for Korelitz in 1911. Avram Dovid Kartorzynski and Girsh Yankel Kartorzynski were voters in Nowogrudek in 1906. This same Avram was probably the father/husband of the people in this story.

Avram had a very large family. He fathered seven children with his first wife, Nettie (maiden name unknown). After Nettie passed away, Avram married Chaja (Ida) Schiller, and together added five more children to the family. There were three additional children who died, born to either Nettie or Chaja. The names of these three deceased children may now be lost to history.

The family rented a house on a dairy farm owned by a doctor. The farm had milk cows and made cheese. The house was at the front of the property and a cook lived in the back. We believe the farm was near Negnewicze, which was a small shtetl ten miles east of Nowogrudek and five miles southeast of Korelitz.

Imagine this quiet farming existence being transformed into a war zone in 1919 and 1920. During these years, the army of the Second Polish Republic attempted to secure an eastern boundary for the country by battling the Soviet Ukraine army through this part of Belarus and into present day Ukraine. Then the Soviet Russian army counter-attacked westward, forcing the Poles all the way to the Polish capital city of Warsaw, where a ceasefire was declared. The Kartorzynski ancestral area became a battlefield…twice.

These events helped accelerate the mass emigration of Jews from this specific area. Jews were already leaving Europe. This had been happening for decades. However, as written in the introduction to Shalom Cholawski's book, *The Jews of Bielorussia During World War II**, the exodus of Jews from the Nowogrudek district during this tumultuous time was extremely high. The Jewish population in this district declined by 60 percent from census years 1897 to 1921.

Suffice it to say, life was hard for poor Jews renting their home on a farm, with their communities scarred by war, and with an annexation boundary about to divide this region into different countries. Like many other Jews, the Kartorzynski family decided to leave. The first group to come to New York City was six of the seven older children (Sam, Max, Charles, Louis, Mary and Rose).

These children were from Nettie. We do not know when they arrived, but they were already established in New York when the second group came in 1921.

The second group hid money, buried in a field at their farm, until enough was saved to pay for passage to New York. Shraga Feivel (Phil) was the leader of this group of seven. Based on ages, it appears he was one of Nettie's sons. He stayed behind in the old country with his step-mother and younger siblings, after the brothers and sisters of his age left for the U.S. In addition to Feivel at 30 years old, the second group was comprised of the second wife Chaja (Ida, 48 years), and her children Estera (Ester, 15), Anna (14), Musia (May, 13), Sonia (Sadie or Susie, 11) and Ilcka (Irving, 9). They came to Ellis Island in September of 1921.

When Sonia arrived at Ellis Island, she was coughing. The authorities guarded against diseases like tuberculosis and diphtheria, and young Sonia was denied entry. A sick 11 year old girl who spoke no English was not about to travel alone. So Feivel took Sonia back to Hamburg, Germany on the same passenger ship, the SS Mount Clay. A couple months later, Sonia's cough had cleared, and she and Feivel were back in New York via the SS Stockholm out of Sweden. This time, they were admitted and all thirteen family members were finally reunited.

However, Avram Kartorzynski did not make the trip. He was aging and crippled with arthritis. He sent his family off for a better life, knowing he was unable to join them. Avram Kartorzynski died in the old country at about 80 years old. We have no further knowledge of him.

**Fig. 1**
**Polish passport photos of Shraga Feivel Kartorzynski from 1921, known as Phil Carter in the U.S., and his wife Shirley, date unknown.**

Some time after everyone arrived in New York, they changed their last name to Carter (although one brother had to be different and picked Karter). They also anglicized their first names. Thus, Feivel became Phil. He became a U.S. citizen, married Shirley Edelstein, and opened a hardware and home furnishings store on the ground floor of a building in Brooklyn. His family lived in an apartment on the third floor, and Phil worked very long hours, six and a half days every week. Phil was also the glue that kept all his brothers and sisters together as a family. He acted as the patriarch of the second group of arrivals, and assumed responsibilities that might normally have been reserved for the now absent father, Avram.

## The Korelitzer Society

At some point after arriving in New York City, Phil Carter joined the Korelitzer Society. There are membership records for 1938, 1942 and 1963, and he is listed in all of them. His life-long participation is evidence that Phil was committed to this society. But he also believed in the role behind the formation of the society, which was to help Korelitz Jews in the U.S. and in the old country. Like many Korelitzer members, this is because Phil did more than just pay dues. Warren Carter (Phil's U.S. born son) remembers going with his parents to special fund raising events for the *Lantzman* (landsmen or countrymen) that were still "on the other side" (in the old country). Tickets for these fund raisers were probably available through the many benefit organizations in New York, including the Korelitzer Society, as Jews from all over New York City attended. Warren remembers these events were often plays, where the actors spoke Yiddish.

It may have been that Phil Carter wasn't the first family member to join the Korelitzer Society. That might have been the matriarch, Ida. Unfortunately, membership records have not been found that go back to when Ida was alive.

Frances, the U.S born daughter of May (Musia) Horowitz nee Carter, remembers that her mother had a Korelitzer Society serving tray during the 1930's and 1940's. This tray was hammered aluminum, with upturned edges, and engraved with the Korelitzer Society name. This tray did not go with May's family when they moved to California in 1944 and has since been lost.

To the best of our knowledge, May was not a member of the Korelitzer Society. We believe the tray came to May from her mother Ida, when Ida passed away in 1932. That points to Ida being a member of the society and it fits with other observations. When daughter Frances interviewed May about the family history from the old country, there was a notation that someone was "born in Karenitz". This was most likely a misspelling or misunderstanding of Korelitz, and we surmise the person born there was either May, her mother Ida, or her father Avram. (Based on the citation for Enta Kartorzynski, the grocer, we know the family name was definitely in Korelitz during the right time-frame.)

There is also the fact that Ida is among the early burials in the Korelitzer Society section of Mount Judah Cemetery in New York. She rests in plot 16. The family descendants can only guess why Ida wanted to be affiliated with Korelitz for the rest of eternity. Could it be that Korelitz was Ida's hometown?

Or might this have been her way of connecting with Avram, the husband she had to leave behind in the old country?

## KORELITZER SOCIETY, Inc.

קארעליצער סאסייעטי, אינק.

Meets Every 2nd and 4th Saturday Evening
at ACADEMY HALL, 853 Broadway, New York

October 27th, 1955

KORELITZER SOCIETY, INC. hereby ACKNOWLEDGES

the receipt of One Hundred Fifty and 00/100 ($150.00) Dollars from

Mr. Philip Carter, residing at 1529 St. Johns Place, Brooklyn 13,

New York, and the Korelitzer Society, Inc. promises to reserve

Grave No. 100 next to Grave No. 101 of your deceased wife, Shirley

Carter, in Mt. Judea Cemetery, in Cypress Hills, Brooklyn, New

York, as your personal property, provided however that you, Mr.

Philip Carter, are a member in good standing with the Korelitzer

Society, Inc. at that time.

_S. Mendelson_ President

### Fig. 2
Official correspondence in 1955 between the Korelitzer Society and Phil Carter. This reserved the Korelitzer burial plot in Mount Judah for Phil, adjacent to the plot for his wife who had just passed away. The seal on the lower left is difficult to read. It says the society organized in 1904 and incorporated in New York in 1934.

KORELITZER   SOCIETY   INC.

HERMAN ITZKOWITZ PRES.
P.O.BOX 472
FAR ROCKAWAY N.Y. 11690
FA-7-1460

MORRIS KESLER VICE-PRES.
9407 KINGS HIGHWAY
BROOKLYN N.Y.
DI-5-3867

ALBERT O. PATICOFF  FIN. SEC'Y
1859  53rd Street
BROOKLYN N.Y.
CL-9-3608

IRVING FLORENTZ SEC'Y.
2365 EAST 13th Street
Brooklyn N.Y. 11229
743-6128

DEAR FRIEND AND FELLOW MEMBER:

S. Mendelson
117 West 13th Street
New York, N.Y.

Mr. Philip Carter

1529 St. Johns Place

Brooklyn 13, N.Y.

**Fig. 3**

**The burial plot correspondence from the Korelitzer Society was mailed to Phil Carter in this envelope.**
**In the same papers, an early list of Korelitzer Society officers was found - the top portion of a letter, date and content unknown, addressed to Korelitzer Society friends and fellow members.**

We also presume that Korelitz had special meaning to Phil.  After all, he was a long-time member of the Korelitzer Society and also chose to be buried in the Korelitzer section of Mount Judah Cemetery.  In fact, he took care of all the final arrangements for step mother Ida, himself, and his wife Shirley.  When Shirley passed in 1955, she was buried in plot 101.  Phil lived another 20 years, but had already reserved Korelitzer plot 100.  That is where he rests today, next to Shirley.

*The author is the grandson of Sonia Kartorzynska (became Sadie/Susie Domeshek nee Carter), the little girl who was sent back because of a cough. His father Allen Domeshek and Carter cousins Warren and Frances were tremendously helpful in putting this story together. Warren found the old passports, photos, and Korelitzer Society correspondence.*

**Bibliography:
Cholawski, S. The Jews of Bielorussia During World War II. Harwood Academic Publishers, Amsterdam, 1998. 333 pages

# Appendix D
# The Faivelovitz (Faine), Gershovitz and Mendelovitz Families

## Solly Faine (Melbourne, Australia)
## and Ann Belinsky (Israel)**

## The origins of the Faine-Faivelovitz family

Our maternal grandfather was Jacob David (Yankel Dovid) Faivelovitz. He was born in approximately 1870 in Korelitz to his parents Yochanan and Batya Henia Faivelovitz.

Fig. 1            Fig. 2            Fig. 3

Figs 1 and 2: Jacob David Faine about 1927 (left) and in 1932 (center).

The photograph on the right, Fig. 3, taken in Minsk, probably in the late 1800s, is of unknown ancestors. Jacob David Faine had it framed and hung in his house in Stratford. His family never knew who they were – probably his parents.

Jacob David had a sister called Rivkah, who married Yosef Lewin, originally Chernovsky) as well as 2 other sisters, Gittel and Feigeh (Pia) We cannot trace any other Faivelovitz's who are directly related to our family, although we have had contact with several other Faivelovitz's whose family came from Korelitz (see separate Appendices).

Jacob David's first wife was Chaya* Sorka Gershovitz. They married in 1892 and had three children: Yochanan (John-Joe), Rachel (Ray) and Rivka (Becky). About 1900, he went to work in South Africa in a boot factory in Capetown.

He seems to have remained in South Africa until he returned to Korelitz, probably 1901, after Vita Sorka died. We have no pictures of her, nor have the descendants of her family in the USA. In fact they thought she had emigrated. Apparently she fell off a "stove", the large tiled all-purpose heating cooking and sleeping equipment that dominated the living space in their homes. Not only was it warm in winter but the elderly and frail slept on it for warmth.

Chaya Vitka Sorka was the eldest of 10 siblings, children of Chaim Moshe (Morris) Gershowitz and his wife Feige (Florance), from Korelitz. Eight children went to USA. One child, Noah, was refused admission to USA because of trachoma, an eye infection, so he went back and then to Palestine. His son Ezra was in Italy with the Jewish Brigade during World War 2. In Israel, the family name is Gershoni. Ezra Gershoni died in 1952. He had 2 children, Avi and Moshe. The rest of the Gershovitz family in USA are known as Hershovitz, Gershovitz and Harris. The family is centered in Albany and in Chicago.

**Fig. 4**

**L-R: Feige and Morris (Moshe Chaim) Gershovitz about 1897. Their eldest daughter Vita Sorka may have looked similar to one of her sisters Mira Liebe (left) or Dora (right). There are no pictures of her**.

Jacob David remarried quite quickly, to Esther Mendelovitz. They had a child - Yaisef Maishe - Joseph Maurice (born 1906).

After that, he left again and went to New Zealand, We don't know why he didn't go back to South Africa, or to Australia. Jacob David arrived in Wellington, New Zealand in August 1908, on the ship *Wimmera*. After 3 or 4 years in New Zealand he must have made enough money to send for his wife and children. Esther and the four young children arrived by ship from probably Gdynia (Gdansk) or Hamburg to London. They stayed at the Jewish Shelter in Leman Street for several weeks waiting in London for a passage to New Zealand, and then traveled several weeks on the ship *Mamari* to Wellington, New Zealand arriving at the end of 1912.

*Chaya's name was anglicised to Vita and to the diminutive derivative Vitka.

**Fig. 5**
**Approx. 1905: John-Joe (standing). Esther Faivelovitz (nee Mendelovitz)**
**Lower L-R: (children) Rachel, Joseph, Rivka**

They settled in a small town called Stratford. There was one other Jewish family in the town (perhaps 1000 people then). Jacob David travelled around the countryside with a horse and wagon, repairing shoes and boots, selling clothing and household goods to farmers. He had got a *shechita* qualification for poultry killing before he went to New Zealand, so they could eat chicken, otherwise a parcel of meat from the kosher butcher in the capital city of Wellington was occasionally sent. Jacob David anglicized the family surname to Faine at least as early as 1913. He was naturalized in July 1920.

His sisters apparently remained in Russia (Later Poland and now Belarus). His sister Rivka lived in the nearby town of Lubtch (Lyubcha). Rivka was widowed and impoverished after WW1. Her sons left for the USA and South Africa. Rivka's sad but illuminating letters in Yiddish sent to her brother in New Zealand were the key to discovering the South African family in 2003. Rivka died about the same time as Jacob David, in 1934. Her youngest daughter Pasha Malka went to South Africa shortly after. Another daughter, Mina Reizel, her husband Reuven Movshowitz and 3 young children were murdered by the Nazis in 1942. Three other daughters of Minna Reizel managed to come to Palestine in 1932. These were Chemda Gittel, (m. Yosef Simchoni); Elka (m. Chaim Jankelowitz) and Batya (m.Yaacov Chechik).

## The Mendelovitz family:

Esther was the youngest of 5 children born in 1883 to Moshe and Sheyna Mendelovitz in Korelitz. The other children were: Reuben, Hanna Minna, Benjamin and Velvul.

Esther married Jacob David and left Korelitz in 1912. In New Zealand, Esther and Jacob had 4 children: Jean (Shayna), Bessie, Alick and Harry.

**Fig. 6**
**Esther Mendelovitz-Faivelovitz, 1932**

The family has 2 letters written in Yiddish by her brother Benjamin in 1913 from New York, where he writes that: *"our brother Reuben Mendelovitz. ... is with me 5 months, he was with his son Fylka for half a year... To Fylka is born a daughter –Mazeltov to us!*

He mentions Reuben's daughter Pasha Leah and son-in-law: *I can write about Reuben's son-in-law.... He - Pasha Leah's husband - came to America –to me..."*

**Fig. 7**
**Reuven Mendelovitz, Esther's brother**

In 2004, after publishing this letter in the Belarus SIG Forum on the JewishGen website, we received a letter from Pasha-Leah's daughter, Natalie Kaplan (nee Engel) living in New York, and discovered a whole new branch of the Mendelovitz family in the USA.

One interesting part of this story is that we discovered that Sarah (Sorka) Kushilevitz, the daughter of Feigeh Pia (Jacob-David's sister), married Fylka Mendelovitz, son of Reuben (Esther's brother), *i.e.* Sorka and Fylka were both cousins to Jacob-David and Esther's children! They came to live in Houston in 1911, where they were known as Sarah and Leon Mendelovitz. Their descendants live in Houston, and other cities in the USA.

Thus the Faivelovitz family tree as we know it, has increased, from about 30 in New Zealand, to at least 300, dispersed in New Zealand, Australia, South Africa, the USA and Israel.

*\*\* Solly Faine is the son of Yochanan (John-Joe) and Luba Faine.*
*Ann Belinsky is the daughter of Bessie (Faine) and Morry Goldstein.*
*Solly and Ann have a common grandfather (Jacob David Faine) but different grandmothers – Chaya-Vitka and Esther, respectively.*

# Appendix E

# Paulette Lubelski (Fajwelewicz)

## Collated by Ann Belinsky

In the JewishGen BELARUS Digest for Wednesday, October 31, 2007, the following title appeared:

*Search for FAJWELEWICZ family*

Paulette Lubelski wrote as follows:

*...I'm looking for details about the place where my father was born and about his family. My father's name was SZIMON FAJWELEWICZ and he was born in 1905 in KARELIECZ which is a small town near NOVOGRODEK... His father's name was Alter and he was a baker, his mother's name was Hana Jenta.*

*My father left KARELIECZ at the late twenties for Paris, France where I was born. I made "Aliya" and came to Israel in 1970. As far as I know my father had brothers and sisters that I believe were all murdered during the Holocaust... I do wish, though, that there are relatives that have survived this horrible period. I would very much like to get to know them and/or their descendants, and to be in touch with them. ...I will be grateful to all those who will contact me.*

Following up on this letter, I met with Paulette and can summarize as follows: Alter and Hana Jenta FAJWELEWICZ (Faivelovitz) lived in Korelitz and had 7 children, three of whom died in the Holocaust. Those who survived, or emigrated before WWII were:

- Moshe (Moshkeh) – was married with children. His wife and children died in the Holocaust but he survived and came to Paris after the war, married again but had no children and died in 1960.

- Mandel - came to Paris some time between 1925-28. Mandel had 2 children: Maurice (surname changed to Failevic) (who lives in France) and Huguette, who went to the States.

- Szimon (b. about 1905) - was a communist in Korelitz, and as such, was put into prison there. His brother Mandel sent money to bail him out, and then he came to Paris, in 1929 or 1930. He married Huma Wajnwurcel (born in Deblin – near Warsaw) and they had 2 daughters, Claire (b.1933) and Paulette (b. 1936). During WWII the children lived in a village 200 km from Paris with an adopted family and were brought up Catholic. Paulette's father stayed in Paris and was active in the French Resistance. Her mother went to Lacreuse, where she worked on a farm. She would send money to the adoptive family, and send eggs and chickens to her husband so that he could sell them on the Black Market. When the war was over, their mother came to collect them. They stayed with their mother for a year in the village, and in 1946 went back to Paris.

- Ida (Itka) -came to Paris in 1933. Ida's married name was Shenkman, and she had two boys -Albert and Charles. All live in Paris.

Paulette's father and mother only received French citizenship about 1960. Up till then, they were *apatride* -without citizenship.

At present we have no direct evidence or documentation of a connection to the New Zealand Faivelovitz family.

# Appendix F

# Descendants of Maier and Sarah Fivelevitch

## Collated by Ann Belinsky*

According to the family tree, Maier Fivelevitch married Sarah (maiden name unknown) about 1875 and their son Samuel (Shimon), was born in 1877 in Korelitz. They had two other children – Bessie and Esther Rose. Samuel married Masha Abramowitz in Korelitz and they had one or two sons and two daughters: Sarah (Saura), born 25 Dec 1892 in Korelitz, Russia and died in the USA on 17 Jan 1974; and Molly (Malka), born 1900 in Korelitz, Russia, married Abraham Pulver and died in the USA in 1988.

Masha Abramowitz's parents were Zalman and Shaina, also from Korelitz. They had 3 daughters - Masha, Sara-Feigel and another daughter of unknown name who married (unknown) Berman. The latter 2 emigrated to the USA. The Bermans lived in Chicago.

Jason Pagano (Sarah's great-grandson) - relates that he heard from his great-aunt Charlotte Duchan (the daughter of Sarah Fivelevitch/Fine) that her father Sam left for America around 1900-1903 and sent money back. Soon, he paid for the family to come, but, heartbroken at the thought of leaving her parents, Sarah's mother (Masha) died in Korelitz before their trip. Sarah, her younger sister Molly (Malka) and one or two brothers set off on the 400+ mile journey from Korelitz to Gdansk in Poland. Her brother(s) did not survive the trip, dying of diphtheria, so 13 year-old Sarah and her 9 year-old sister continued to America alone, where they reunited with their father, Samuel who had changed his surname to **FINE** and remarried.

Sarah would go on to marry Abraham Targum, a fellow Korelitzer, on June 10, 1910 in Orange County, New York. Sarah and Abraham Targum were members of the New York Korelitzer Society. They ran a candy/stationery/newspaper store in New York City and had three children: (Emanuel (deceased) George (deceased) and Charlotte (now in her upper 90s); besides nine grandchildren, there are now 15 great-grandchildren and three great-great grandchildren. The family lives mostly in the Northeastern United States (Boston to Washington, DC), mostly clustered around New York City. Members of the family are buried with other landsmen from the same *shtetl* of Korelitz in the Beth Moses Cemetery in Farmingdale, NY.

*Information from Charlotte and Brian Duchan, Barbara Musikar, Jason Pagano and Shari Targum.

**Fig. 1**
**Sarah (Fivelevitch) Targum in the 1960's**

**Fig. 2**
**Avraham Targum and his daughter Charlotte**

**Fig. 3**
**L-R: Emanuel and George Targum**

Abraham Targum had a sister, Rebecca. Their parents were Shlomo Targum and Yetta Horowitz. Rebecca married Harry Levine and had three children: Charles, Joseph and Frances.

Samuel Fine remarried to Tillie (Dina/Rivi) Slonimsky from Slonim on 12th May 1906 in Manhattan, New York. Their children were Max, Natie, Rose and Alexander (Sender). Tillie had a daughter Fannie from an earlier marriage.

Molly Fivelevitch married Abraham Pulver, who was from Rumania. Abe was born in 1889 to Reuben Pulver and Hanna (nee) Brownstein, naturalized in 1913, and died in 1981. Abe had two brothers: Jack and Max.

Molly and Abe had two children: Mildred and Norman (Nathan). Mildred married Jerry Hockheiser and had two children, a boy, Zef, and a girl, Beth. Norman married Arlene Schall, daughter of Jack Schall and Ruth. They had no children.

**Fig. 4**

**Molly (Fivelevitch) Pulver and her niece Charlotte (Targum) Duchan**

At present we have no direct evidence or documentation of a connection to the New Zealand Faivelovitz family.

# Appendix G

# Leah Lubchansky-Kornfeld (1913-2015)

### With thanks to Rosemarie Koren and Nurit Buchweitz

Leah Lubchansky arrived in *Eretz Israel* in 1932 as described below.
After the Holocaust she was very active in the Korelitz organization and on the Committee of the Korelitzer Society (pages **271, 348**). Photos of her martyred family appear on page **325** in this book.

### An interview at her home 16 Yigal Alon Street, Herzlia on 22.09.2007
### Recorded by Zvi Miller in Hebrew - Translation by Ann Belinsky

I was born in 1913 in Poland, in the town of Korelitz, near Novogrudek, in the district of Vilnius. When I was about three and a half we became refugees for four years. I remember these years as very bad. My parents, grandparents and the children wandered from place to place.

The family was in the grain trade and we had a large barn in the yard, divided up for the different types of grain so that they wouldn't get mixed together. One day German-speaking people arrived and settled in our house, they had guns and bombs, and in the morning I saw that they were taking bags and filling them with grains of all the different types. I was happy because I thought they were buying it, but they took the bags and also filled all sorts of other containers that they found and the rest they began to throw around the building. I complained to my mother that she was letting them throw the grains around, but she would never let me play with the grains. But my mother did not answer, she only packed the contents of the house in boxes and sheets and threw them outside and said to my father Haim to put them in the wagon. We lived at the end of town so we always had a horse and wagon. Once all was packed, my mother called us and said "come children, we're going to visit grandfather". Grandfather lived in the town and I was pleased. After a while I smelt fire and told mother. She replied that our house is burning and we shouldn't look back to see our house on fire. We arrived at grandfather's house at night and in the morning the siren sounded and everyone went into the cellars and basements were full of people and it was crowded and smelly. I started crying and the people yelled at me that if I cry they will hear and kill everyone. My aunt took me and we went outside. A Cossack on a horse, with a long spear, passed by. When he saw us he turned around and looked at us but then he gave the horse a blow with his whip and rode off. We went back to the basement and since then I do not cry.

We wandered and wandered until we reached a town where there were Russians with prisoners. They needed someone to translate for them, so they would call my father. We stayed there for probably four years. It was in the Belobez Forest, (*AB - Puszcza Bialowieska?*) one of the biggest forests in Europe, there were animals and mosquitoes and we became ill with malaria. The villagers did not like Jews, there was only one Jewish family and of course my friends were all gentiles. There was one girl I loved, but her father did not allow her to play with me, she would look out the window at us playing, but she wasn't allowed to go outside. Once her father called me and I was so happy. When I went in she was lying in bed and her father told me to play with her. She had a high fever and she did not even look at me. He gave me her handkerchief to wipe my face as if I had dirt on it. Another Russian entered the room and asked her father what this Jewish child is doing here? After all, you never have let your daughter play with her. So her father then answered that his daughter has smallpox and he wants me to get infected by the disease. The Russian told him to throw me out, because the Jews were not infected with smallpox, since they have a vaccine.

From this period, what I remember most is that there was a teacher in the village, because I really wanted to learn and get knowledge. Mother would tell us what she knew from the Bible about the book of Genesis and more. One day a man came into the town and agreed to teach children in three villages, each week a different village in return for lodgings and food. On Saturdays he would stay with us. The first week I didn't learn because I was sick, but when they reached the third week, one of the families changed their mind and said they didn't have anything to feed him, even potatoes were scarce and there was hunger, so the arrangement was cancelled. Afterwards my aunt took my brother to her house in the village to learn and I stayed in the town without any schooling. Then a gentile man came and said he teaches children and that I could come and study. I was so happy because I wanted so much to know and learn. With all the joy and excitement, I could not fall asleep, but suddenly I overheard a conversation between my parents - "What if he tells her to cross herself?" I thought to myself, what does it mean to cross myself? I had crossed myself together with all the gentile girls, and it was not a big thing, but then I realized it was something bad to cross oneself and I really could not sleep. I decided I would only pretend to cross myself, but because he wanted to force me to cross myself, I stopped studying with him and regretted it very much.

My father's name was Haim and my mother's name was Ita. I had four brothers Shaul, Simcha, Berl and Yisrael and a sister Rachel. Simcha was killed as a soldier in the Polish army. My father, mother, sister Rachel, brother Yisrael and Simcha's family perished in the Holocaust.

I was in the *HaShomer HaTsa'ir* Youth Group. I did not attribute any significance to the fact that I was in *HaShomer HaTsa'ir* but I wanted to be independent. My older brother Shaul was already in South Africa and I wanted to go to *Eretz Israel*. I approached my mother and told her I wanted to go to

*Eretz Israel.* She replied that if I wanted to go there, "we will allow you, but you should know that there will never be quiet", and I remember that to this day. There were no *certificates*\* but a trip was being organized to Israel and I signed up. My grandfather was also a Zionist and had a son there and he wanted to go too and also put his name down, but in the end he didn't go.

On the 11th of August 1932, we started the trip and travelled for eighteen days. We went to Warsaw and were in Romania and Turkey and Beirut in Lebanon, where we had a very difficult week. From Beirut we went by taxi to Rosh Hanikra and from there we were taken to Haifa. We were very happy but were told to disperse quickly because the English will realize that we are not just happy tourists. I went with two girls from our town to their relatives in Haifa and the next day I arrived in Ra'anana. On the same ship called *Dacha* (which was later sold for transporting animals), were one hundred and eighty "travelers" from Poland. It was after the *Maccabiah* (Jewish sports event held in *Eretz Israel*), when some of the visitors had managed to remain in the country, and we thought that we would also be absorbed. Later it turned out that it was a single attempt to make *aliyah* in this way, there was controversy on the subject, *aliyah* officials who succeeded with the *Maccabiah* feared that the English would be angry that they had been deceived and tourism officials feared that the English would prevent tourism and thus this method was suspended. In Ra'anana I stayed with my uncle Bezalel (Kalman) Osherovich. He warned me that an Arab who understood Yiddish was "mending shoes", however he was not exactly a cobbler but British police informer who reported illegal new immigrants to them.

When visiting Herzliya I met my husband Kalman Kornfeld (from Vertogen in Bessarabia) and we were married a few months later. My husband also didn't have Palestinian citizenship yet and when he requested it so that he could bring his mother, he was refused because of me. My husband finally got citizenship and I remained as an illegal immigrant until the State was established. It was suggested that I go to Beirut for two days and when I come back I would get a certificate, but I refused, because a whole family could come on that certificate. When my husband got his citizenship, my name was listed on the folder in brackets and the children were listed with a father but without a mother.

In November 1932, I came to Herzliya and worked picking oranges. I kept on with that even after the birth of my children. We built a hut on Rav Kook Street and my husband bought a plot together with his friend. The friend built a hut and lived in it with his wife and child, afterwards he moved to Kfar Haim and took the hut with him. We built a new hut with one room and a small kitchenette and lived there for a short time - two years. We bought a bigger plot in Ahad Ha'am Street which was then called Manski Road and built a larger hut with two rooms, a kitchen and toilets. The house on Yigal Alon Street (formerly known as Shachar) was not easy to build, it was after the war and there were no building materials and I think we built it over more than two years. In this house on Yigal Alon Street we have lived since 1952.

We had two children, a daughter and son - Tsafrira and Abraham. Our daughter died in a car accident. I have three grandchildren and five great-grandchildren, may they be healthy.

My brother Berl was in the Russian army and went to fight in Finland for Russia. He told us that some were given Finnish uniforms and some were given Russian uniforms and told to do an exercise to see if they know how to shoot and they shot at each other. His fingers were injured and a hospital nurse amputated them. He remained an invalid and after the war he came to Israel as an illegal immigrant. He could not find work because of his disability and the family sent him to Johannesburg, South Africa. There he established and managed a successful business and was very happy there. He visited Israel several times and the last time he visited, he had a heart attack and was buried in Herzliya.

I volunteered for the *Hagana* and then as medical volunteer in *Magen David Adom* (Red Star of David) and during the War of Independence we were on shifts on Saturdays and organized blood donor drives. We had a list of seventy blood donors, the "jabbers" were Aaron Taichner and Dr. Weinschnak. Today I take care of the flowers of my yard and water the trees if necessary.

Our house was used as a family gathering place for the whole family, the Passover *Seder* was always with me but now the grandchildren alternate in holding it.

------------------------------------------------------------------------------------

*certificate - the British government restricted immigration during the mandate period and fixed a quota for immigration certificates.

**Fig. 1**
**Esther Leah, the grandmother of Leah Lubchansky's mother**

Fig. 2
Seated: Leah Lubchansky's parents, Ita and Haim
Standing between them (light colored dress): Leah Lubchansky
Others not identified

**Fig. 3**

המצבה מעל קבר האחים בליטובקה ( ליד נובוגרודק)

של 5500 הקדושים ז"ל מקהילות נובוגרודק , לובטש , קרליץ
סליב והסביבה, שנרצחו ע"י הנאצים ועוזריהם
בשחיטה השניה הגדולה ב– כד אב תש"ב ( 42 . 8 . 7 )
ובשחיטה השלישית הגדולה ב– כט' שבט תש"ג (43 . 2 . 4 )
המצבה הוקמה בקיץ 1993 בפעלו ובמימונו של
יקירנו , בן – עירנו מר קגן ג'ק מלונדון

## The Memorial on the mass grave in Litovka (by Novogrudek)

To the 5500 martyrs from the communities of Novogrudek, Lubtch, Karelitz, Selyub and the environs, who were murdered by the Nazis and their helpers in the Second Big Slaughter on 7th August, 1942 and in the Third Big Slaughter on 4th February, 1943.
The Memorial was erected in the summer of 1993 with the aid and financing of our dear friend, born in Novogrudek, Mr Jack Kagan from London.

# Appendix H
# An Unexpected Link to Korelitz

## Kenneth A. Domeshek *

Both of my paternal grandparents came from the same part of present day Belarus. They arrived separately in New York in 1922 and started new lives. Neither of them spoke much about their memories from the old country. After the letters from Belarus suddenly stopped, never to resume, a conversation about memories became even more difficult.

Today, U.S. descendants are piecing together the missing family history. Kartorzynski is the maiden name of my grandmother. This name appears in Korelitz, Nowogrudek and Negnewicze, which are Jewish towns clustered within a dozen miles of each other. Damesek is the name of my grandfather's family. For generations, this name appears in the town of Nesvizh, which is about 30 miles away.

Fig. 1 The family of Rabbi Shmuel and Ida Damesek, Nesvizh, circa 1912.

Standing, L-R: Berl (aged 12), Leibel, Israel, Chana, Joseph. Sitting, L-R: Ida (nee Schiller), Lazar (Eliezer), Shmuel (Samuel), Leymeh (standing next to Shmuel).

During this ongoing research, it was a welcome surprise to find a Damesek in Korelitz. It was even more surprising to discover that this Damesek was my grandfather's brother, Berl, of whom we had lost track. The last knowledge we had of Berl was when he was 12 years old, living with his family (standing far left, above) in Nesvizh.

We have since learned that Berl became a teacher, like his father. Berl married Buzeh (nee Kahonovitz) and they lived in Korelitz. Their children were Shaul (Sulia) and Yehudit. Berl and his family were murdered in 1942. Berl was 42, Buzeh 40, Shaul 13, and Yehudit 8. They were commemorated in Pages of Testimony at Yad Vashem in Jerusalem by Yaacov Abramowich, Mania Ritz and Leah (Lubchansky) Kornfeld.

The U.S. Damesek descendants were excited when Ann Belinsky, who is the translation coordinator of this book, located Dina Abramoviz in Israel, the daughter of Yaacov. Dina had a school photo taken in Korelitz in 1926. Berl, then 26 years old, is the teacher sitting in the middle row, far right.

**Fig. 2**
**Korelicze school photograph from 1926, courtesy of Hana Golan.**

(This same photo is owned by both Hana Golan and Dina Abramoviz. The copy owned by Dina has been covered with handwritten names by her father Yaacov Abramowich, and we preferred to bring the clearer copy, owned by Hana Golan, here.)

Shortly thereafter, the U.S. descendants were given one more piece of good news. Ann Belinsky noticed that a picture of Berl was already published in the original version of Sefer Korelitz. The Damesek descendants had no record of Berl after he was 12 years old, and all of a sudden, here was a photo of Berl (at about 40 years) and his family. That photo is below. The descendants can confirm with certainty that this is our Berl. He looks remarkably like the only two family members to leave Nesvizh and come to America before the Holocaust, his brothers Joseph and Lazar.

**Fig. 3**
**This is a Kahonovitz family photograph from Korelitz, originally published with all the names on page 341.** The middle row contains the Kahonovitz parents and three married daughters, including Mania Ritz (middle row, far left, and together with her husband Eliezer, standing behind her, are the only survivors in this photo), who submitted Pages of Testimony for the Dameseks. In the back row, the husbands are standing behind their respective wives. Berl Damesek is back row, far right. His wife Buzeh is middle row, far right. Their children are sitting in the front row, with Shaul on the right and Yehudit in the middle.

* The author is the grandson of Lazar (Eliezer) Damesek of Nesvizh, who came to New York in 1921 after living for one year in Montreal, Canada. After arriving in New York, Lazar married Sonia Kartorzynska, who coincidentally lived very near Korelitz as a child. They became naturalized U.S. citizens and changed their names to Louis and Sadie (Susie) Domeshek. The author's family is grateful to and wishes to thank Dina Abramoviz and Ann Belinsky for their help in bringing a memory of Berl Damesek and his family in Korelitz.

# Appendix I

# The Nissilevitz family
## As related by Hana Golan (Hanik Nisselevitz/Nitzani)

### Collated by Ann Belinsky

David and Sara Nisselevitz of Korelitz had four children: Abba, Luba, Feivel, and Feigel.

Feivel Nissilevitz was born in Korelitz in 1913. Because he was a gifted student, he was sent to study at a high school in Vilnius. There he met his future wife Fruma Klotz and they married in Vilnius in 1932.
They then came to Eretz Israel, where he changed his name to Shraga Nitzani. They lived with the Gordonia group at Givat Hakibutzim for one year and he worked in the building industry. After one year the Gordonia group went to Kibbutz Degania Bet, but Shraga and Fruma left them and went to live in Rehovot.
All the rest of the family remained in Korelitz and died in the Holocaust after being sent to the Novogrudek Ghetto in 1941. However, in 1939, David Nisselevitz was arrested and tortured by the Russians and may have died then (see Page 19).

Hana (Chanik) Golan is the daughter of Feivel/Shraga Nisselevitz and granddaughter of David Nisselevitz.
Feivel/Shraga had three other children: Yekhezkel Nitzani, Sara Braudo-Nitzani, and Davidit Mintzer-Nitzani, plus a total of eleven grandchildren.

Photos from the family album appear below.

בתיה קלאץ - ווילנא -1912
נפטרה רחובות – 1987

כ"ץ נסילביץ פייביל קורעליץ - 1913
שכא ניצן נפטרה-1980

**Fig. 1**

| Fruma Klotz – born 1912 Vilna | Feivel Nissilevitz – born 1913 Korelitz |
|---|---|
| married Shraga Nitzani | (name changed to Shraga Nitzani) |
| died in Rehovot (Israel) 1987 | died in Rehovot (Israel) 1980 |

**Fig. 2**
**Class V 1926**
**Feivel Nissilevitz - top row, 3<sup>rd</sup> from left**
**The teacher Berl Domesek -middle row, 1<sup>st</sup> right**

Fig. 3 Family photos. Legend on opposite page.

## Figure 3 legend:

**Top left (L-R)**: Sara, Luba and David Nissilevitz
On the back of this photo is a **dedication**:
"A keepsake (memory)
For my dear ones - my children Feivel, Fruma, Hana'leh
Korelitz 9/VIII." (probably 1938)

**Top right (L-R):** Luba Nissilevitz and unknown
**Center (L-R):** left - Abba's wife; lower left - Luba Nissilevitz; right - a cousin?
**Bottom Left**: Abba Nissilevitz
**Bottom Right**: Upper left - Luba Nissilevitz; lower left: unknown; upper right –
Malka Becker; lower right – Miriam Shkolnik –Lev

**Fig. 4 - 1934.**
**Standing: L-R: ---, ---, Menucha Abramowich, Abba Nissilevitz, ---, ---**
**Sitting, L-R: Koneh Meyerovich, Rachel Bussel, ---, ---, ---**

Dedication on the back of the photo (in Polish): For Mnusia herself
Korelicze, July 7, 1934

Fig. 5
Standing: 2nd from left: Menucha Abramowich
Sitting: 2nd from left: Abba Nissilevitz

Fig. 6 1936.
Bottom, L-R: Koneh Meyerovich, Rachel Bussel, ---, Abba Nissilevitz, ---, Luba Nissilevitz
Middle; L-R: ----
Top, L-R: ----
Dedication on the back of the photo: Korelicze, May 1936. Before departure for Palestine.
Sabyna Szachter[owna]

Hana Golan (born in Israel) has written 3 poems about Korelitz.

**1.** She had a cousin in Korelitz, also called Hana Nissilevitz, the daughter of Abba Nissilevitz, and also probably born in the same year, 1937. They were the same age, but had never met. Hana died in the Holocaust and Hana Golan writes about their parallel lives:

## THE OTHER HANA'LEH

Born in Korelitz in White Russia
Like her Sabra cousin
At the beginning of World War Two

At the age of three or four
She was marched to the forest
Or to the pits
Her last birthday was celebrated
With gas
Or with an axe

And her cousin -
They continued to celebrate with flowers and cake
And presented her with
A war every decade
The loss of dear ones
And continuous anxiety

p.38 *In*: Hanik Golan-Nitzani, 2011. *Halon Ha'hasheka Hakhula* (in Hebrew) (=Blue Darkness) Iton Books 2011, 66pp.

**2.** Hana Golan prepares herself for a "Roots" visit to Korelitz

# LAMENTATION FOR KORELITZ
(before the journey to Korelitz)


When I will come to the earth
Soaked with blood
Of my father's family.

The fir trees by the river
Observed the convoy
Lashed with whips
From their treetops

How long
Were the quiet waters
Colored red?

My father knew nothing,
Only believed
That when they were annihilated
They remembered
That Fyvka,
Their young son
Was alive
And forgave him.


June 2009


p.30 *In*: Hanik Golan-Nitzani, 2011. *Halon Ha'hasheka Hakhula* (in Hebrew) (=Blue Darkness) Iton Books , 66pp.

**3.** After visiting the town of Korelitz

# CRYSTALS OF *KADDISH**

On the lawns of the Korelitz Museum
Arose within me "*Yitkadal v'yitkadesh*"
The words flew around with
The crystals of flowers
Of the birch trees
To the silent heavens
As at that time.

With trembling fingers
I held the photos
Of the Nissilevitz family
Sixty seven years
One spring
Spring
Silent were the words
Of the *Kaddish*
For my father's
Family

June 2009

p.31 *In*: Hanik Golan-Nitzani, 2011. *Halon Ha'hasheka Hakhula* (in Hebrew) (=Blue Darkness) Iton Books, 66pp.

*A prayer recited in the daily synagogue services and by mourners after the death of a close relative.

David Nisselevitz (Hana's grandfather) also had a brother named Feivel, who was the postman/coachman in Korelitz (see page 199). Feivel was married to Masha and their daughter Feigeh (Tzipporah) obtained a Palestine Immigration Certificate and made *aliyah* to Eretz Yisrael in 1933 to Kibbutz Tel Yosef.

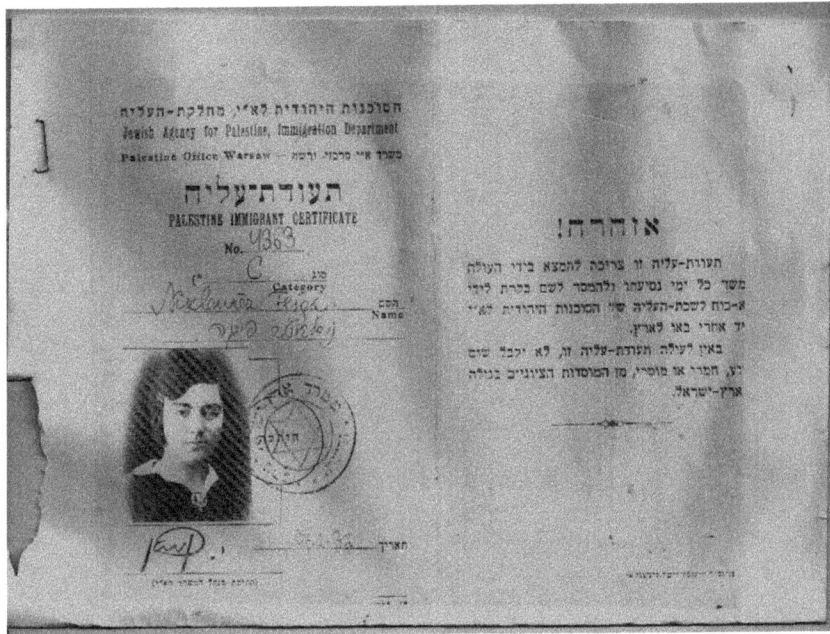

**Fig. 7**
**Official Palestine Immigration Certificate**
**Issued to Feigeh Nissilevitz 28.2.1933.**

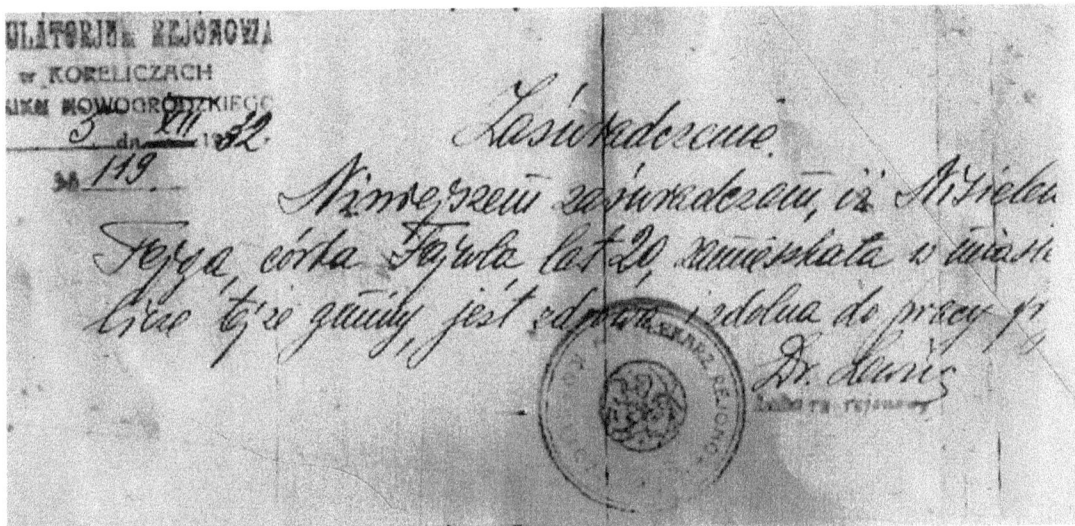

**Fig. 8**
**Confirmation (in Polish) in 1932 that Feigeh Nissilevitz has permission to leave Korelitz and emigrate to Palestine**

From the family album

**Fig. 9**
*HaShomer Hatzair* Youth group

**Fig. 10**
Unknown (also *Hashomer Hatzair*?). Standing - Chaim Bussel?

# Appendix J
# Benyamin (Yomen) Fivelovich

## collated by Ann Belinsky

Benyamin (Yomen) Fivelovich (Fajwelowicz) was born in Korelitz in 1925.

We know that his father was a trader in wood. His parents' names were Hillel and Chana. Not much more is known about his past as he did not speak about it to his family in Israel.

He had 3 siblings: Itka, Avraham and Haya Rachel, all of whom died in the Holocaust, along with his parents.

Benjamin was in the ghetto in Korelitz or Novogrudek, and his friends encouraged him to run away to the forests. There he met up with the partisans and stayed with them, going out at night to look for food. At one stage he was attacked by a dog which bit his leg very deeply -there was a prominent scar.

He had a cousin, Masha, who hid in the cesspool when the Germans came and was saved. (This is Masha Rabinovitch whose story was written by Fruma Gulkowich on page 225). She came to Haifa after the war and has a son.

In Israel, Benyamin was a fireman. He did attend the Novogrudek meetings in Israel until he passed away on 6th April 1996. He is buried in Jerusalem.

Benyamin's son and daughter are named Hillel and Chana respectively, after their grandparents. There is another daughter, Shifra Haya Fivelovich. Hillel, who lives in Petach Tikva, has changed his surname to Orgad. Chana (married surname – Tamam) lives in Jerusalem.

**Fig. 1 Benyamin Fivelovich**

At present we have no direct evidence or documentation of a connection to the New Zealand Faivelovitz family.

In the Yad Vashem Database there are 2 Pages of Testimony written by Benjamin Fivelovich for his family who died in the Holocaust
(the names are recorded according to the Polish script - Fajwelowicz):

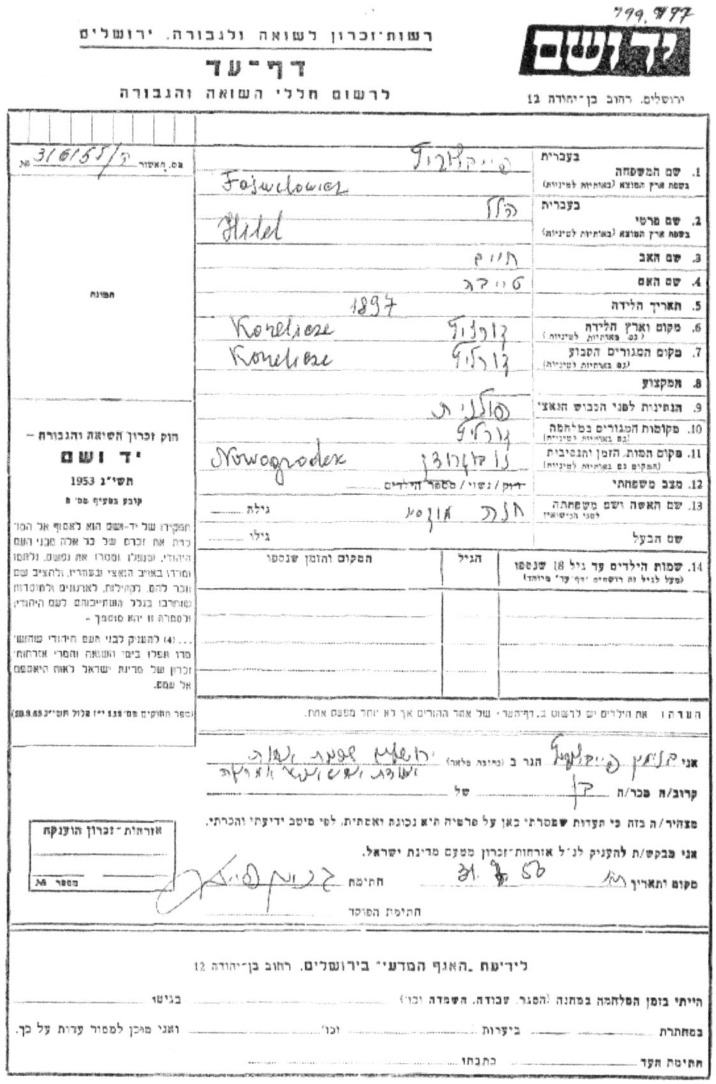
799,977

רשות־זכרון לשואה ולגבורה. ירושלים

דף־עד

לרשום חללי השואה והגבורה

יד ושם

ירושלים. רחוב בן־יהודה 12

1. שם המשפחה — Fajwelowicz
2. שם פרטי — Hillel
3. שם האב
4. שם האם
5. תאריך הלידה — 1897
6. מקום וארץ הלידה — Korelicze
7. מקום המגורים הקבוע — Korelicze
8. המקצוע
9. הנתינות לפני הכיבוש הנאצי
10. מקומות המגורים במלחמה
11. מקום המות, הזמן והנסיבות — Nowogrodek
12. מצב משפחתי
13. שם האשה ושם משפחתה
14. שמות הילדים עד גיל 18 שנספו

31. 7. 56

**Fig 2. Yad Vashem Testimony for Hillel Fajwelowicz**

Surname: **Fajwelowicz** Given Name: **Hillel**; Born: 1897
**Father's name**: Haim: **Mother's name**: Taibeh
Birthplace and Permanent Address: **Korelitz**; Nationality before the Nazi Conquest: **Polish**
Address During the War: **Korelitz** Region: Novogrudek
Wife's name and maiden name: **Chana Moksai**
Signed by **Benjamin Fajwelowicz (son). 31.7.56**

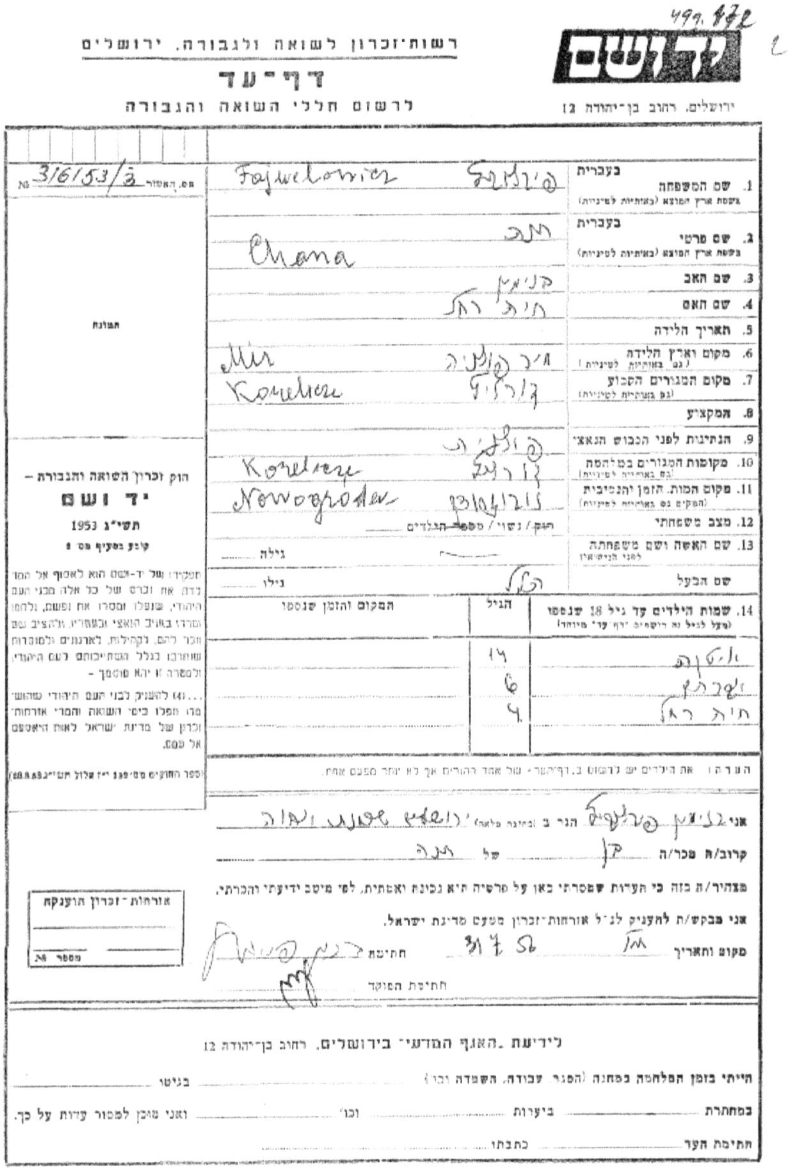

רשות־זכרון לשואה ולגבורה. ירושלים

**יד - ושם**

לרשום חללי השואה והגבורה

ירושלים. רחוב בן-יהודה 12

| | | |
|---|---|---|
| No. 3/6/53/3 | Fajwelowicz | בעברית 1. שם המשפחה |
| | | בעברית 2. שם פרטי |
| | Chana | |
| | | 3. שם האב |
| | | 4. שם האם |
| | | 5. תאריך הלידה |
| | Mir | 6. מקום וארץ הלידה |
| | Korelitz | 7. מקום המגורים הקבוע |
| | | 8. המקצוע |
| | | 9. הנתינות לפני הכבוש הנאצי |
| | Korelitz | 10. מקומות הסגורים במלחמה |
| | Nowogroder | 11. מקום המות. הזמן והנסיבות |
| | | 12. מצב משפחתי |
| | | 13. שם האשה ושם משפחתה |
| | | שם הבעל |

14. שמות הילדים עד גיל 18 שנספו

| הגיל | המקום והזמן שנספו |
|---|---|
| 14 | |
| 6 | |
| 4 | |

אני... קרוב/ה מכר/ה... של...

מקום ותאריך... 31.7.56

Fig. 3. Yad Vashem Testimony for Chana Fajwelowicz

Surname: **Fajwelowicz** Given Name: **Chana**;      Born: -
Father's name: **Benjamin**;    Mother's name: **Haya Rachel**
Birthplace: **Mir** Permanent Address: **Korelitz**; Nationality before the Nazi Conquest: **Polish**
Address During the War: **Korelitz** Region: **Novogrudek**
Husband's name: **Hillel**
Children who died in the Holocaust and their age:  **Itka 14; Avraham 6; Haya Rachel 4**
Signed by:  **Benjamin Fajwelowicz (son). 31.7.56**

# Appendix K

# Fruma Gulkowich Berger

## Collated by Ann Belinsky

Fruma Gulkowich was born in Lublin in 1918 and grew up in Korelitz, together with 3 sisters and one brother, Ben-Zion.

She was active in the Zionist Youth Movements and hoped to go to Palestine or to South Africa but war broke out and she remained with the family in Korelitz. Her mother was beaten and died in the ghetto there, and her father and 3 sisters were killed during the big massacre on August 7th 1942. After hiding in a cesspool for a week together with her sister-in-law Yehudis (Judy), they were pulled out by her brother Ben-Zion, and after several weeks all three left the ghetto and joined the Bielski Partisan Brigade, headed by Tuvia Bielski. Fruma was the first of the girls to get a rifle, stand guard and participate in various activities. There she met her future husband, Murray Berger, from the town of Vyselub (Wseilub, Selub) close to Korelitz. Ben-Zion excelled as a scout. They remained in the forest for 2 years until the Russians forced the Germans to retreat. Murray and his brother Ellie, Ben-Zion, Judy and Fruma returned to Novogrudek and stayed there till the end of 1944. They hoped to travel to Palestine illegally and were sent to a DP camp (*Kibbutz Tulda*) in Romania, then to Italy (*Kibbutz Anzio*). They searched for relatives overseas and Murray's brother Harry in the U.S. sent them an affidavit which permitted them to immigrate to the States. There they started their lives anew and raised their two children, Ralph and Albert. Fruma died in 1995 and Murray in 1999.

Fruma and Murray's story is told in the book *With Courage Shall We Fight: The Memoirs and Poetry of Holocaust Resistance Fighters Frances "Fruma" Gulkowich Berger and Murray "Motke" Berger, edited by Ralph S. Berger and Albert S. Berger 2010. ComteQ Publishing, New Jersey.*

Fruma found solace in writing poetry in Yiddish relating to her experiences during the Holocaust. Many of these poems appear in this Yizkor book. In addition, Fruma wrote several of the chapters in this book, as did her brother Ben-Zion.

Below we publish several photos from the book "With Courage Shall We Fight" with acknowledgment to Ralph and Albert Berger who gave us permission to use these photos and to also use the translations of Fruma's poems from that book.

Photos of Fruma's sisters, Feigele, Grunia and daughter Mirele, and Brina, who were all murdered in the Holocaust, can be seen on page 319.

**Fig. 1**
**Korelitz, 1938**
Fruma with aunt Rivka Ullman and cousin Ephraim Gulkowich
(Ephraim died May, 1944 in the Tchkalovske Brigade
- see also the poem "The Partisan Ephraim", Page 256)

**Fig. 2**
**Ben-Zion Gulkowich, 1930's**

Fig. 3
Murray Berger (first on right) with cousins, Wseilub, 1939-40

Fig. 4
Sora Rivka, Murray Berger's mother, before the war

**Fig. 5**
**Members of the *Kibbutz Anzio*, Italy, 1946-47**

Front, left to right: Yaacov Abramowitz, Chaim Leibowitz, Ben-Zion Gulkowich
2$^{nd}$ row: ---, Murray Berger, ---, Yocheved Abramowitz, Fruma Gulkowich, ----
3$^{rd}$ Row:  Lazar Malbin is between unknown lady 1$^{st}$ left and Murray Berger

**Fig. 6**
**Former Bielski Partisans, Rome 1946-47**

Standing, L-R: Chaim Leibowitz, ---, Sonia Oshman, ---. Murray Berger, ---, Elliot Berger
Seated, L-R: Fruma Gulkowich Berger, Aaron Oshman, holding his and Sonia's son, Matthew,
Lazar Malbin, Mr. _____ Benson, holding his daughter, Yolanda.

Fig. 7
Wedding Photo of Fruma and Murray, Rome 1947

Fig. 8
Ben-Zion and Judy Gulkow (Gulkowich) with son Albert, Rome, 1946

# Appendix L
# Yaacov and Yocheved Abramowich
## (Abramowicz, Abramowitz)

## Compiled by Ann Belinsky

Yaacov (Jakob, Yankel) Abramowich was born in 1913 in Korelitz, to Eliezer (Lazer) and Dushka - Dina (nee Pomerchik). He had two siblings, Menucha and Gabriel. Eliezer and Dushka had a shop which sold cloth. Yaacov studied at the Tarbut School in Novogrudek. His sister Menucha went to Israel in 1936 to Kfar Maas. Yaacov's brother and parents died in the Holocaust.

Yaacov helped establish the *HaShomer HaTza'ir* youth movement in Korelitz, and later moved over to the *HeChalutz* youth movement. He was also very active in fundraising for the *Keren Kayemet LeYisrael*.

When the Germans occupied the area in 1941, he escaped to the Naliboki forest, and joined Tuvia Bielski's partisan Kalinin battalion, where he participated in many daring military operations. He was commander of the horsemen, a saboteur and also served as bodyguard to Asael Bielski, the deputy commander of the battalion. After leaving the Soviet Union, he was active in the *PaKhaKh* (*Pachach*) (Partisans, Soldiers and Pioneers) movement in Italy and Germany in the Displaced Persons camps, to help the Jews there. He also organized groups of Jews for the "illegal immigration" to pre-1948 Palestine. Yaacov died on 12th October, 2009.

Yocheved Abramowich nee Slutzky was born in April 1919 in the town of Nowogrodek. She was one of five children born to her parents Golda and David Slutzky. Theirs was a warm and hospitable family, also noted for giving to the needy. With the outbreak of the Second World War they were forced to leave their home and move to the ghetto. Yocheved and her brother Yehudah escaped to the nearby forest and joined the partisan group of Tuvia Bielski and his brothers. There she met Yaacov. After the war they lived in Anzio, Italy for three years, where they married and their first daughter Zehava was born. They then fulfilled their dream to immigrate to Israel in 1947, where they built their house in Petah Tikva, where their daughter Dina was born. Yocheved died on *Tu B'Av* 1994.

Below are photos and documents from their legacy. Many thanks to their daughters Zehava Elbaz and Dina Abramoviz Karmy, who made the material available.

# Before the Holocaust

**Fig. 1**
**15 June 1936**

**Fig. 2**
**31 March 1934**

In both photos: L-R: Menucha, Dushka, Yaacov, Below: Gabriel Abramowich

**Fig. 3**
**16th May, 1923**
**Left:** Yanes     **Right:** Mishke Abramowitz.
(Uncles of Yaacov. Maybe moved to Argentina)

**Fig. 4**
**Ice Skating in Korelitz**

**Fig. 5**

**Inscription: For Yankel-Yankel**
**A memory, from my heart.  Feigel Zilberman**

**Fig. 6**
**Menucha Abramowich - Yaacov's sister**, who came to Eretz Israel in 1936
Inscription: From Yashke Abramowicz
to Reeva Katzman (from Mogilev)10. I .41

**Fig. 7**                                    **Fig. 8**
Left: **Yocheved (Slutzki**) and her first husband (--- Moltchatchky) 1930
Right:  Yehuda Slutzki, Yocheved, ---Moltchatchky

## PARTISANS DURING THE WAR

**Fig. 9: Newspaper Photo with 2 partisans**
**Left: Yaacov Abramowich     Right: Yudel Levin**

Yudel and Yaacov returned to Novogrudek in 1944, when the Germans were still in the city. They met a German living in Yudel's house and asked him to photograph them, Yudel later obtained the photo as a newspaper cutting, in the town of Fuehrenwald (Fernwald) in Germany.

This same photo was enlarged and appeared on the wall of the Museum of Kibbutz Lochamey Haghettaot.

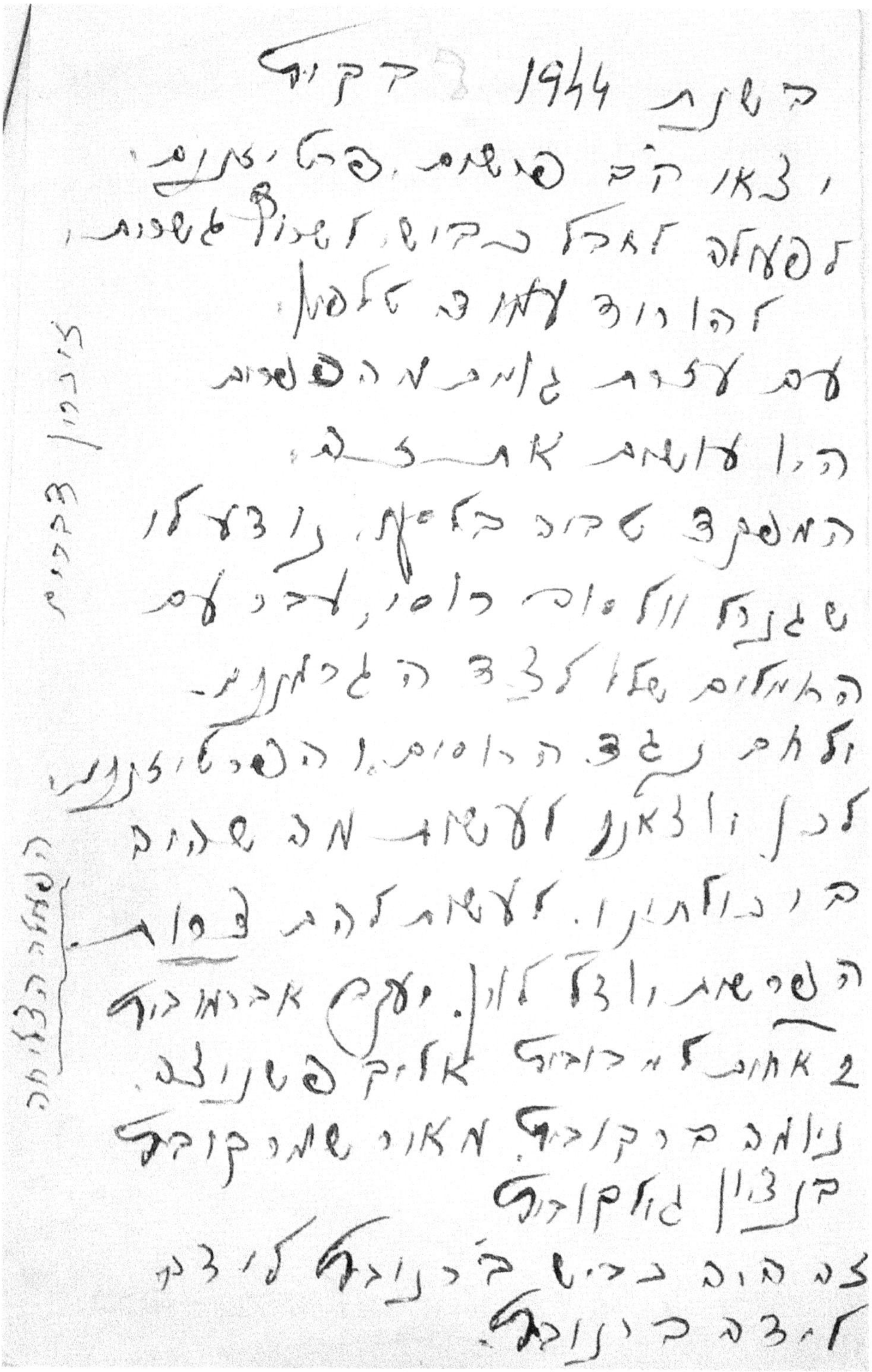

Fig. 10
Recollection of a Successful Operation (Translation on page 7), handwritten by Yaacov

Translation of Fig. 10:

## **Recollection of a Successful Operation (Page 6)**

In the summer of 1944, 12* partisan horsemen left for an operation to sabotage roads, to burn bridges, to fell telegraph poles. With the help of Gentiles from the villages they did this.

Commander Tuvia Bielski heard that the (Russian) General Vlasov had crossed over to the German side, with many of his soldiers, and fought against the Russians and the partisans. Thus we went out to do what we could, to cause them troubles. The horsemen were Yudel Levin, Yaacov Abramowich, 2 brothers Leibovitch, Alick Pashintza, Nyoma Berkovitch, Meir Shmerkovitz, BenZion Gulkowich.
This happened on the Baranovitz-Lida Road, by Baranovitz.

(*on the side*: Recollection.       The Operation was Successful)

*The original Hebrew number is 102 but this is obviously a mistake. 12 is the number mentioned in his memoir on Page 216 in this book.

**Fig. 11**
L-R: Shmuel Zalman Leibowich, Yaacov Abramowich, BenZion Gulkowich

**Fig. 12**
**Holding the photo of their Commander: Asael Bielski**
Sitting L-R: Zalman Leibowich, BenZion Gulkowich
Standing L-R: Yaacov Abramowich, Leibel Abramowitz, Michael - ---, Yoel Meyerovich

## IN POST WAR EUROPE

**Fig. 13**
**A group of women from the Bielski Camp, holding the photo of**
**Asael Bielski**
Sitting left: Yocheved Slutzki (Abramowich)
Kibbutz Aqua Santa, Italy

**Fig. 14**
Left: Yaacov and Yocheved Abramowich
Right: Avraham and Haya Maggid
Italy 1945, on their joint wedding day.
They received clothes and suits only on the day of the wedding.

**Fig. 15**
Standing: - Unknown
Sitting, L-R: Yaacov and Yocheved Abramowich, Avraham and Haya Maggid

**Fig. 16**
**In Landsberg, Germany on *Shlichut*.**
L-R: ---, Shmuel Oppenheim, Yashkeh Mazavietski, ---, Yaacov Abramowich, Yudel Levine,
David Palotnik, Pinchus Boldo, Reuven Oppenheim

**Fig. 17**
**Partisans in Germany, 1945.**
L-R David Palotnik, Yaacov Abramowich, Yudel Levine, Pinchus Boldo, Yitzhak Berkovich

**Fig. 18**
**1945, Partisans and family in Fernwald Germany**
**Standing. L-R:** Yashkeh Mazavietski, ---, David Palotnik, ---, ---, ---, Yehoshua Oppenheim, Shmuel Oppenheim, Pinchuk Boldo, Ita Dzienciolski, Rochel Boldo.
**Middle, L-R:** ---, ---, ---, Luba Boldo, Yaacov Abramowich, Raya Boldo
**Front, L-R:** Shlomo Dzienciolski, ---, Haya Gershoni (nee Boldo), holding her child Assaela Bielski, ---, ---

**Fig. 19**
**In the forest, 1945**
L-R: Luba Boldo, Pinchus (Pinik) Boldo, Raya Boldo, baby - Assaela Bielski, Haya Gershoni (mother of Assaela), Yaacov Abramowich, Ita Dzienciolski, Rachel Boldo

## Relationships of those in the photos:

Ita Dzienciolski was mother of Rachel and Haya.

Rachel married Hanan Boldo and was mother of Yosef, Pinchus and Luba.

Raya --- married Yosef Boldo.

Haya Dzienciolski and Asael Bielski's daughter is Assaela. Haya later married Asher Gershoni.

Luba Boldo married Ephraim Sinder

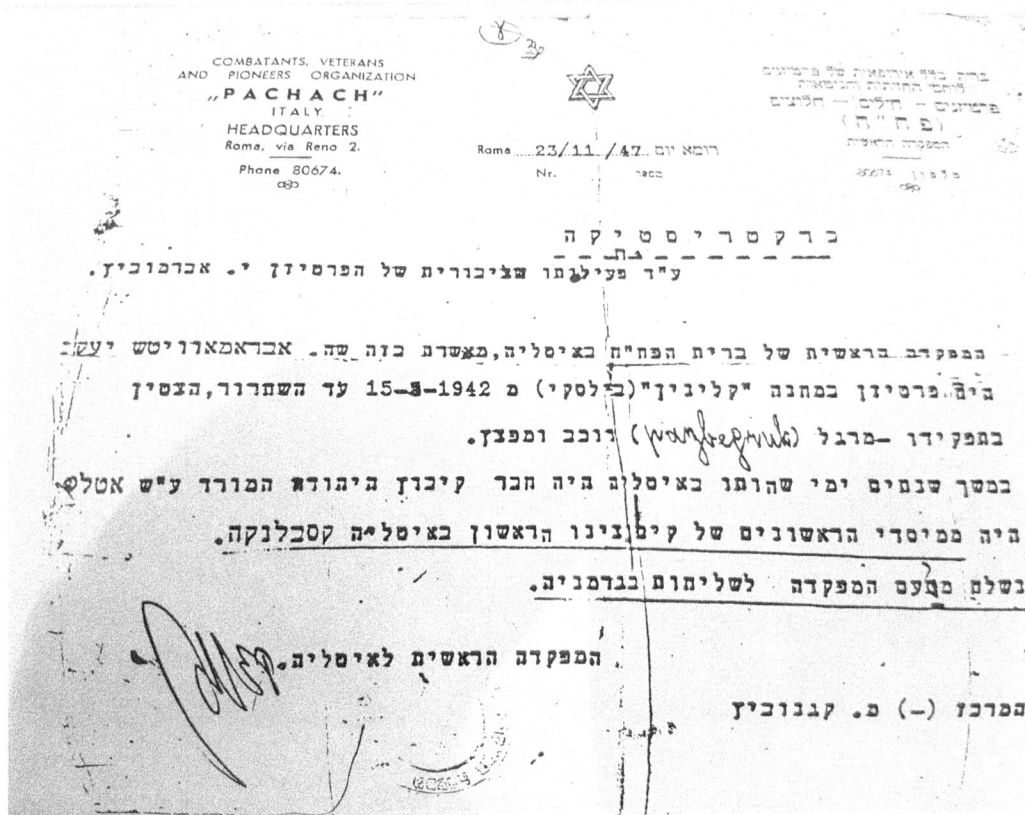

**Fig. 20**

COMBATANTS, VETERANS
AND PIONEERS ORGANIZATIONS
**"PACHACH'**
ITALY
HEADQUARTERS
Rome, via Reno 2
Phone 80674

Rome 23/11/47

## "Characteristica" - Personal Reference

Concerning the public activities of the partisan **Y. Abramowitz**

In the main headquarters of the "Pachach" organization in Italy, we confirm that Abramowitz Yaacov was a partisan in the "Kalinin" (Bielski) camp from 15.3.1942 until the liberation, and excelled in his role as Spy, Horseman and Saboteur.
During the two years in Italy he was a member of the *Yehudi Hamored* Atlas Kibbutz.
He was one of the first founders of our first *kibbutz* in Italy - Casablanca.
He was sent by the Headquarters on *Shlichut* (a mission) to Germany.

The Chief Italian Headquarters (signature)

The Center (-) M. Kaganovich

**Fig. 21**
**On *Shlichut* in Munich.**
**A group of partisans sent to bring Jews to Eretz Israel, 1946**
L-R:  ---, Yashkeh Mazavietski, ---,---,---,---,---, David Palotnik, ---, ---. ---, Yaacov Abramowich

**Fig. 22**
**Partisans at a conference in Munich, Germany**
L-R: Yashkeh Mazavietski, Yaacov Abramowich, --------, David Palotnik,

**Fig. 23**
**In Italy**
**Standing: ---** (David Slutsky. Yeshaya Resnick ---Unknown order)
**Sitting L-R**: Haim Abramowitz, Yashke Mazavietski, David Palotnik, Lazar Malbin
**Front: L-R**: Friedman, Leybush, Yaacov Abramowich

**Fig. 24**
**Partisans on *Shlichut***
Front: Yashkeh Mazavietski, Yaacov Abramowich, David Palotnik

**Fig. 25**
**Munich, Germany**
**L-R:** Eynha, Yashkeh Mazavietski, Yaacov Abramowich,
On *Shlichut*, at a partisan conference

**Fig. 26**
**1946**
**On *Shlichut* to Germany, with the *Pakhakh* Organization,**
**sent to bring Jews to Eretz Israel.**
**L-R:** David Palotnik, Hibutchnik, Yaacov Abramowich, Yeshahayu Bruk, ---,
Yashkeh Mazavietski

**Fig. 27**
**In Italy**
**L-R:** Yoel Meyerovitch, Murray Berger, Fruma Gulkowich Berger, Yosef Shkolnik, Yaacov
Abramowich, Ben-Zion Gulkow (Gulkowich)

**Fig. 28**
**In the kitchen in *Kibbutz Anzio*, Italy**
Yochevcd Abramowich in a black dress, front right

*Abramowich was a founder of Kibbutz Aqua Santa, which was later renamed Anzio Nettuna*

**Fig. 29**
**Italy**
**L-R**: Yaacov and Yocheved Abramowich, Yoel Meyerovich

**Fig. 30**
**In Milano**
**L-R:** Friedman, Yaacov Abramowich, Yashke Mazavietski, David Palotnik

**IN ISRAEL**

**Fig. 31**
**Moshe Rabinowitz, Yocheved and Yaacov Abramovich**
Moshe, who had made Aliyah at age 14, came to meet survivors of his family in Israel
Yocheved Slutzky was Moshe's cousin. Yocheved's mother Golda, was sister to Moshe's
mother, Nechama.

**Meetings of ex-partisans in Israel. Those who survived became "family".**

**Fig. 32 - March 23 1965 (in Belgium)**
**Standing, L-R**: Haya Gerstzovsky, Reika (Raya) Boldo, Haya Gershoni, Malka-a lady host in
Belgium , Yaacov Abramowich , Batya –a daughter of Bella Rabinovitz, Arkeh Gertzovsky,
Yocheved Abramowich, Lilka Kravitz.
**Sitting, L-R**: Haim Kravitz, Bella Rabinovitz

## The Partisans always had Reunions in a Forest, in Israel

**Fig. 33**
**L-R:** Yaacov Abramowich, ---, Hertzel Nohomovski, ---

**Fig. 34**
**Left:** Yaacov Abramowich
**Right:** Lazer Malbin

**Fig. 35**
**L-R:** Tuvia Bielski, Yaacov Abramowich, ---. ---, ---

**Fig. 36**
**Sitting, R-L:** Tova Nohomovski, ---, Haya Gershoni, Rest unknown
**Standing, R-L:** ---, ---, ---, Sonia Peck, Yocheved Abramowich and behind her, Yaacov Abramowich,
**Standing 2nd left:** Raya Kaplinski. Rest unknown

# TUVIA BIELSKI (1906-1987)

**Fig. 37**
**Tuvia Bielski in his youth**
(Photo from the internet)

Tuvia Bielski, together with his brothers Zus, Asael and Aron and friends who had escaped from the local villages and ghettos, set up a partisan camp in the Naliboki Forest to save Jews fleeing from the extermination squads. His camp was extraordinary in that it did not take in only those who would fight as partisans, but also families, the old and the young, and in this way saved 1200 people by the end of the war. The story is told on page 390 in this book.

Their story was also made into a film "Defiance" (2008), directed by Edward Zwick and set during the occupation of Belarus by Nazi Germany. The screenplay by Clayton Frohman and Zwick was based on Nechama Tec's book "Defiance: The Bielski Partisans", University Press, Oxford, 1993.

The letter below was written in 1953, confirming Yaacov Abramowich's role as a partisan in Tuvia's camp.

4

בלסקי טוביה
מפקד לשעבר על מחנה "
הגר ברמח גן ביאליק 13.

א י ש ו ר

הנני מאשר בזה שמר אברמוביץ יעקב היה פרטיזן
במחנה שלי על שם קלינין בשנת 1942 עד השחרור 1944
זמן ממושך בתפקיד מפקד הפרשים ואחרי כן עבר לפי
בקשתו לקבוצת חבלנים.

הנ"ל נפצע מספר פעמים בשעת מלוי תפקידים שונים
בחזה בסביבות יערות נליבוקי, רוסיה הלבנה ע"י נהר
ברזינה, בשנת 1943, פעם שניה נפצע הנ"ל בצלעות
בצד השמאלי, כפעולת הפצצת כביש ע"י כפר בלצ'יץ
בסביבות נבדרוק, ע"י חיילי " וולסוב" בשנת 044 1944.

טיפול רפואי נתן לו ע"י רופא איסלר שהיה בזמנו
רופא המחנה. הפרטיזן אברמוסיץ .יעקב היה חייל מסור
ונאמן, ביצע פעולות מסוכנות ביותר שנמסרו לו עקב
תפקידו לביצוע ע"י המפקדה.

מילא את פעולותיו באהבה ולא נרתע לסכן את נפשו
שבשעת הצורך.

מפקד מחנה הפרטיזנים
ע"ש קלינין

טוביה בלסקי

.53

תאריך: 12.7.53

**Fig. 38**
**Letter from Tuvia Bielski, 1953, confirming that Yaacov Abramowich was a partisan in the Kalinin Brigade of the Bielski Unit**
Translation opposite

**Translation of the letter from Tuvia Bielski on page 23**

Bielski Tuvia
Past Commander of the Camp
Living in Ramat Gan, Bialik 13

Confirmation

I hereby confirm that Mr Abramowitz Yaacov was a partisan in [my] Kalinin camp in 1942 until the liberation in 1944. For a long time he was Commander of the Horsemen and afterwards, according to his request, he transferred to the Saboteur Group.

The above was wounded a number of times in his chest while fulfilling his role in the area of the Naliboki Forest, White Russia, by the Breznia River, in 1943. The second time he was wounded in his left side ribs, in an operation bombing the road by the village of Belchitz in the area of Novogrudek, by "Vlasov" soldiers in 1944.

He was given medical treatment by Doctor Islad who at that time was doctor of the Camp. The partisan Abramowitz Yaacov was a devoted and trustworthy soldier, who carried out extremely dangerous operations with relevance to his role, which were issued to him by the headquarters.

He carried out his actions with love and did not recoil from endangering his soul when necessary.

Commander of the Kalinin Partisan Camp
(signature)
Tuvia Bielski

12th July 1953.

Later Tuvia went to live in New York with his wife Lilka. The partisans kept in touch with him and celebrated his 80th birthday there. After his death he was buried in Jerusalem with full state honors.

**Fig. 39 Partisans at Tuvia's 80th birthday celebration in New York
(Identifications thanks to Ralph Berger and Bella Rubin (Taibe Seltzer's daughter)**

1. Lola Seltzer
2. Sonia Oshman
3. Yaacov Abramowich
4. Ann Monka
5. Irving Stoll (Ann's brother)
6. Sonia Bielski
7. Leah Johnson
8. Leah Friedberg
9. Pesach Friedberg
10. Zus Bielski
11. Rae Kushner
12. Taibe (Toby) Seltzer (Tuvia's sister).
13. Rae Kushner's sister
14. Aaron Oshman
15. Tuvia Bielski
16. Lilka Bielski
17. Judy Gulkow
18. Frances (Fruma) Gulkowich Berger
19. Murray Berger
20. Yocheved Abramowich
21. Fannie Brodsky
22. Irving Resnick
23. Irving's wife

# Appendix M
# Gutke Gantzevitz
## (later known in Israel as **Tova Nohomovski**)

### Collated by Ann Belinsky and Chana Messer

**Gutke Gantzevitz** was born 1st August 1920 and raised in **Korelitz.** Her parents were **Devoshke and Zelig**. They owned a small grocery shop.
She had one sister named **Luba** and three brothers - **Moshe-David, Yudel** and **Itzhak- Berl**.
Gutke was the only one of the family to survive the Holocaust. She joined the Bielski brigade in the Naliboki forest - there she met her future husband, **Hertzel Nohomovski** (from Novogrudek). Hertzel went to a Hebrew high school in Vilna and spoke fluent Hebrew, while Gutke was a dental technician before the war.

Gutke and Hertzel illegally immigrated to Israel in 1946 on the ship Enzo Sireni and were kept in the Atlit Detention camp until Hertzel's family from Gedera obtained *certificatim* (permits) for them and they moved to Gedera.

Hertzel worked in the orange groves, as a builder, and volunteered for the *Etzel* group fighting against the British. In 1947 he joined the army and fought for Israel during the War of Independence. He then joined the police and was an officer in the police force until he retired. Hertzel committed his life to his family and to commemorating the history of the family that he lost during the Holocaust. He educated children, gave lectures in schools, and wrote articles and memoirs.

Their children are Chana Messer (now in USA) and Azriel Nevo (Israel).

Tova (Gutke) worked in different jobs, especially with children. She lived to be a great-grandmother. She dedicated her life to her family and never stopped talking and telling stories about her family that she lost during the Holocaust. Tova was an extraordinary woman. She was admired by her family and everyone that met her. She was a true inspiration of courage and survival.

Hertzel passed away in February 1995 and Tova (Gutke) died 2nd October 2013.

Below are family photos.

Fig. 1 (L-R) Dvoshke (nee Slutzky) and Zelig Gantzevitz

Fig. 2.    L-R:  Itzhak, Yudel and Luba Gantzevitz

Fig. 3
Cousin Basha Rabinovitz

Fig. 4
Tamara (nee Lubetsky) Gantzevitz
(Zelig's mother)

**Fig. 5 A group of Korelitz youth, 1936**

**Fig. 6 Betar Youth Group, Novogrudek, 3rd May, 1934**

**Fig. 7. Hertzel Nohomovski with his father Kusha**

**Fig. 8. Tova (Gutke) Nohomovski, 1948, Gedera, Israel**

Fig. 9  Hertzel and Tova (Gutke) Nohomovski (Gantzevitz) on their arrival in Israel, 1946

# Appendix N

## Malka Poluzhsky (nee Pomerchik)
### (8th February 1912 - 16th April 2006)

**Translated from her life story\* by Ann Belinsky**

Malka was born to her parents Ezra and Ahuva Leiba Pomerchik in the town of Turetz. She grew up in the town of Yeremich, on the banks of the Neyman River, 13 km east of Korelitz, and went to school there until the age of 14. She then continued in the Gymnasia (high school) in the city of Novogrudek.

In 1929 her parents decided to leave Yeremich, and move to Korelitz. For Malka it was difficult to not to return to Yeremich, with her memories of a happy and free childhood. However eventually she found that Korelitz also had its own beauty and she was very impressed with the wonderful idealistically motivated Jewish youth. The Pilsodsky government was socialist and tolerant towards the Jews, the high schools filled with Jewish youth and a Jewish *Tarbut* school was opened. Many went to Eretz Israel and their enthusiastic letters, especially from *HaShomer HaTsa'ir* graduates inspired her even more. She spent more and more time in that youth movement, which was to pave her future.

\*Malka Poluzhsky – *The Song of My Life - Shirat Chayai (in Hebrew and Yiddish)*, 2010. Ed. Sara Poleg. Achital Publishing, Hod Hasharon, Israel. 151 pp.

In 1934 Pilsodsky died and with his death came dramatic changes towards the Jews. The universities and high schools restricted the number of Jewish students. So she returned to Korelitz and devoted all her time to making *aliyah*. Together with a small group of youth, she re-organized *Hashomer HaTsa'ir* and managed attract most of the young people, and influence their parents.

**Fig. 1**
**Community Elders in Korelitz before WWII, together with the Rabbi**

Malka went to *hachshara* in Grodno to learn how to live life on a kibbutz in Israel. It was very difficult. Full of romantic enthusiasm, she found tired youth, who had been living there in terrible conditions for 4 years, with no hope of receiving certificates to enter Eretz Israel. Some of the women managed to make fictional marriages to men from Eretz Israel and evade the British to get there.

In 1939 the Germans invaded Poland. The Molotov-Ribbentrop agreement divided Poland into two, Western Poland to Germany and Eastern Poland to Soviet Russia. There was chaos as the Polish government officials fled. The Soviets entered on 17th September 1939 and took over the government. They released all the political prisoners, destroyed the palace and nationalized Jewish houses above a certain size. Malka had learnt Russian at school and her knowledge drew attention of the authorities, who raised her in rank until she became a delegate to the local council. Then the government passed from the local population to people from Moscow and a new order started. Small businesses disappeared, shops attached to houses became rooms for the increasing population. The authorities tried their utmost to influence the youth to study Russian and to become members of the communist party. Malka decided she must go to Eretz Israel and join her sister who was there already. In 1941, when the pact was cancelled by Hitler, the Russian officials left and the Jews remained helpless. Not all realized the impending danger, but Malka knew that as a prominent personality in the town, she must leave. Encouraged by her understanding mother, she tried to convince others to leave but only succeeded in influencing her brother Feivel Pomerchik, her sister Hadassah (Hodeh) and her husband Shaul Zalamansky and of course Malka's beloved husband Yaacov Poluzhsky.

Malka's older brother Berl-Dov decided to remain with his parents. Within 2 weeks of the German invasion, he and 150 others would be murdered. And those remaining would also suffer a similar fate after much suffering.

After farewelling her grandmother Michal in Turetz, they set out, moving in the direction of Minsk, in the hope of catching a train. They met up with a truckload of people from the area, who agreed only to take Malka to Minsk as her feet had swollen so much. They planned to meet up in Minsk and continue their journey. However Minsk was destroyed and burnt city. The truck ran out of gas and Malka decided to continue without her family via the villages. The roads were being bombed and even as they arrived at the village of Trashkova, where they had planned to rest, bombers flew over and they heard that German paratroopers had landed in the village. Thus they were forced to leave in panic. They were advised by the Christian people amongst them to destroy all documents indicating their Jewishness. Malka destroyed all Soviet documents but kept her identity card.

The people she had walked with were Russian citizens and the minute they reached Russian soil they left her and joined the Soviet army. Malka's feet were very swollen and she continued walking barefoot, apathetic to the bombing, until she reached the town of Brezino. There she met many refugees including from Korelitz among them Golodiatz, a refugee from Vilna who lodged with her aunt Dushka, Reuven Kalmanovitz (son of Shmuel Hirshel) and Aharon Perevolotsky, brother of her best girlfriend. She continued with Golodiatz into Russia, hoping to find a train.

*Continuing in her own words, from the book:*

"Almost all the stations were destroyed and the carriages lying on their sides. German bombers caused destruction almost without opposition. The refugees ran around like poisoned mice, crying, looking for each other and still dreaming of a train. After 12 days of wandering, full of suffering, despair and disappointment, we arrived at the city of Smolensk, a beautiful historical city on the banks of the Dniepa that stood almost complete, despite the bombing.

We succeeded in getting on a train, distancing ourselves from the battlefields. However some time later, the train was bombed, and destroyed, there were many killed and much weeping. Again we started walking to get away from the danger.

Only then did I start to feel despair and think that it had not been worthwhile, I was alone and far from my loved ones, in a strange country, stuck in a cruel war with an unbeatable enemy. I was sure that my dear husband Yaacov, my brother Feivel, Hadassah and Shaul had been killed and I would never see them again. At the end of my strength and in complete apathy we arrived at the *kolkhoz* (a Russian collective farm) in the Tambov district and rested there. I started to ask the other refugees if by chance they had seen my family, and surprise – within all the chaos in this huge foreign country, I strangely managed to find them all.

According to the information I had received, I left the *kolkhoz* and went into the city of Tambov. They too, had passed many dangers and arrived at Tambov where the men had been drafted into the army. I found the school where they had lived, but unfortunately they were not there. They had been sent several days previously to a large army camp in the forest area, 13 km from Tambov. Without thinking twice I began to walk in that direction, until I found myself in front of a sentry at the "Reddy" Camp. I begged him to let me in, he understood me and let me into the camp. I will never forget the warm attitude of the Russian soldiers. Each helped and brought me to places where I could possibly find them. I went from headquarter to headquarter, looked at lists, spoke to officers, who they themselves had lost relatives. Towards evening I succeeded with my stubbornness to find them.

Our happiness knew no boundaries, despite our miserable situation. From them I learned where my younger sister Hadassah, was staying in Tambov. I found her in despair and desolation. When I suddenly appeared, I brought her happiness and regards from all her loved ones in the camp. I was the first woman who had dared to go into the guarded army camp. After me, other women started to visit their relatives and bring food and clothes in those cold and rainy autumn days. Being together, Hadassah and I decided to return to my *kolkhoz*, work there till the end of the war and wait for the men's return. We got in a bus, and waited for the driver, who did not hurry to leave. It started raining, which covered the truck and us with sticky mud. Three days the rain continued and we couldn't move. On the fourth day it started to clear. We were about to leave and suddenly our men appeared! They had been released from the army as they were former Polish citizens. According to the agreement with Wanda Wasilewska, a separate Polish division of the Soviet Red Army would be formed. We got off the truck and decided to go south, to a warmer climate, in view of the approaching winter. Almost all the Polish refugees decided to leave Siberia with its cold and snow. We got on a freight train and started our journey. This time the trip was more pleasant. We were together again, caring for one another as in the past. For many days the train pulled the open carriages, full of people seeking refuge. The destination was Tashkent.

We arrived at night time. Loud knocks and a deep bass voice told us that our trip was over, now we must leave the carriages and travel to the *kolkhozy* which had emptied of men and needed manpower. We were happy, we did not fear work and hoped that thus we would go through the war together and still return to our home town and reunite with the rest of our families. We arrived at the Kalinin *Kolkhoz*, the reception was friendly, but poverty and scarcity were everywhere. We started to work, though others immediately went to look for easier jobs. We worked in various jobs in the fields, in buildings, in drainage. We had a good name everywhere, but for all the thousands of hours worked, we saw no money. We did not suffer more than the *kolkhoz* inhabitants, who lived in poverty since all the agricultural produce had been nationalized for the war needs. In addition, the management board stole and wasted all the rest. The Uzbeks were embittered. Even previously they hated the Soviets, who had forced them into the *kolkhoz*. Every time there was an announcement that at the front the Russians had lost and the Germans were advancing, they were happy. We got on with them but were fearful of what would happen. At the same time there were reports from Molotov on the destruction of whole Jewish communities in the area conquered by the Germans. We read of the horrors and torture of prisoners of wars, on cruel executions of thousands of people and then we understood that our dear parents and brother were no longer alive. Understanding of the situation penetrated our consciousness, but the heart could not come to grips with it.

In Uzbekistan we endured many incidents. First, my brother Feivel sickened with typhus and we had to hospitalize him in a hospital where many people died daily from this disease. There was a serious earthquake where our hut almost collapsed on us. Feivel was still in the hospital when my husband Yaacov, sister Hadassah and Shaul her husband traveled far from the *kolkhoz* to work on building the North Tashkent canal, and I remained alone to look after my sick brother. I visited him daily in the city, 5 km away from our *kolkhoz*. We thought he would return home after several days as his condition was improving. Already on the first evening the complete stock of firewood which my friends had prepared for heating and cooking was stolen. Feivel was not released and I was forced to wait a whole week in the miserable hut. To this day, I don't know where I got the strength. Finally he was released, well but very weak. I fed him and got him back on his legs. We heard nothing from the others and they didn't know about us. Yaacov couldn't bear it and left the camp without permission, got on a train without a ticket and returned to the *kolkhoz* after 500 kilometers as a stowaway. It was very dangerous. After he saw us, he prepared wood and returned to work on the canal. Thanks to their hard work at the canal we saved some oil and flour, the basic necessity, and could exist in the *kolkhoz* for some time. The war continued and became worse and worse. Bread and other foods were rationed. We decided to leave and seek work in the city of Namangan (Uzbekistan). First was Shaul, my brother-in-law, who found work there, while we remained and worked in the cotton. Suddenly Yaacov received a draft notice to do forced labor in distant Siberia. We were in shock. We had thought that here in the hinterland, we would succeed in "passing the deluge". Luckily Yaacov suddenly got typhus, and with a fever he was sent to the hospital. Next day it turned out that also Hadassah was feverish and signs of typhus covered her body. We brought her to the hospital. For three critical weeks the two fought for their lives against the terrible disease, which cut down hundreds and thousands of refugees. Finally they overcame it, recuperated and returned home. We then left the *kolkhoz* and went to Namangan.

A new chapter started. There was no work and it was difficult to find an apartment. We found one in Talman Street, a deserted ruin. But we had an address, and already Yaacov and Feivel received work at the army factory. Yaacov was still weak and walked with a stick, but there was no choice, we had to work. Aharon Perevolotsky came to live with us. He was already in Namangan and worked in the sanitation department. The men worked, and Hadassah and I began to sell things in the market, because the men's salaries were not enough.

Hadassah had always been a good saleswoman, fast and aggressive, and I helped her. There were difficulties and sometimes troubles: the police demanded bribes, more than once our wares were confiscated or we were taken to the police station. But Hadassah aggressively stood opposite them with confidence and determination until they gave in. She fought for our existence like a lion. Feivel and Yaacov would come over to the market in their breaks to help us, but more than once caused new trouble. The inspectors pounced on Yaacov, he was called to the police department and sat several days in arrest. Despite all, somehow, we managed.

**Fig. 2**
**Uzbekistan, Namangan, September 1941**
**Standing L-R: Aharon Prevolutsky, from Korelitz; Feivel Pomerchik**
**Sitting, L-R: Shaul (Shayal) Zalamansky, Hadassah's first husband; Hadassah (Hoda)**
**Perlman, Malka Poluzhsky; Yaacov Poluzhsky**
**(Feivel, Malka and Hadassah were siblings)**

The biggest misfortune was the day that Yaacov and Feivel received draft notices. After the Soviets had warded off the Germans from Stalingrad, more and more people were being swallowed by the front. There was no longer any obligation towards Polish citizens. Even people above 60 were being drafted and sent to the front. They went and we didn't hear anything from them. And when there was a letter finally, it was very grievous. Feivel was badly wounded and Shaul had fallen in battle. This was a terrible blow, but we had to continue. Feivel needed us more than ever, we didn't imagine how close to death he was in the army hospital in distant Novosibirsk. We worked harder to save money and send him things. We didn't know that the parcels never arrived to him at all. He fought a long time against the injury and finally overcame it. We received his first letter with tears of joy and began to hope that maybe we could return home and by some miracle our dear ones would still be alive.

In the town center, the radio boomed out daily of new victories over the Germans, their victims and prisoners of war. The Soviet army advanced rapidly towards Poland and towards Berlin. We waited breathlessly for peace and the final defeat of the German army. Many days passed, with many victims on both sides. Many Soviet soldiers died before they reached Berlin. And then the second front opened and the British and American troops joined and together finally overpowered the Germans and gave the final crushing blow to the Nazi monster.

Berlin fell and was burnt down, Hitler committed suicide together with his mistress Eva Braun. European countries together with Russia and the Americans celebrated on the ruins of the capital of Germany, Berlin, which had been destined in Hitler's plans to be "Capital of the World".

We began plans to return home. This too, was not easy. Yaacov was bound to his important work and his superiors did not agree to let him go. We had to show them an official document from our workplace before the war. We lacked money and clothing. Also. I was pregnant and we were scared in my situation to make a long and arduous journey. But nothing stands in front of desire, we received a letter from Feivel that he was returning to Korelitz and hoped to meet us there. We finally received all the required documents and an authorization from Yaacov's boss and we parted from the place where we had passed most of the war years. The trains were full of returning soldiers and refugees returning to their homes in the towns and villages in every corner of liberated Russia and Poland. Exhausted soldiers, full of yearning for their dear ones, for whom they had shed much blood, pushed their way forcefully into the carriages. It was difficult for people like us, with no elbows, to make our way through and to get on to a train.

Again we were lucky. Fate pushed us into the right place and towards merciful and good people. We travelled in terrible crowded conditions for many kilometers, we passed by destroyed cities, abandoned villages, silent towns, until we reached Minsk. Here we felt very close to our destination, only 100 kilometers separated us from Korelitz. But unexpectedly in Minsk a terrible surprise waited for us. When we got on the Minsk-Baronovitch train, a fight began between the soldiers on the train and those trying to get on it. Guns were pulled and they began to shoot at us. It was then I saw how my Yaacov was so devoted to me and willing to give up his life for me. He stood opposite the shooter with us behind him, ready for any result. Luckily the train started moving and distanced us from what could have been a tragedy.

We arrived at Korelitz in the early evening. Thin autumn snow covered the roads and we almost didn't recognize the town, despite that most of the houses were standing in their place. Greyness, sadness and depression filled the air, a strange silence. No one came out to meet us, no one was waiting for us, the Gentiles who had located themselves in the Jewish houses were scared to come out for fear of revenge. A few Jews who had survived with the help of the partisans had settled in a half-destroyed house. These were couples that after the loss of their partners, children and families, had bonded their fates with each other without any formal ceremony and begun to rebuild a new home. These were people who were beyond despair, people who wanted to live the moment, even these such miserable lives. In the background of the mass grave where all their loved ones were buried, they lived and worried about their livelihood.

We also crowded into their house in a dark and modest corner and did not dare to ask questions. In the meanwhile Feivel returned and together we began to think of future plans. One thing was clear – Our way is to Eretz Israel, of which we had dreamed, to which we had yearned all the years of wandering. We found two uncles alive, Malchiel and Eliezer, who had been partisans and returned to Turetz, their birthplace and the burial place of their families. We took them in with us and slightly encouraged, prepared to travel. A serious problem arose financially. We needed a minimal amount of money in order to leave with such a number of people. We began to influence the remnants of the two towns Korelitz and Turetz, to join us and leave the land soaked with the blood of their dear ones. This task was very difficult, they had lost all hope, were attached to the mass grave outside the town and did not want to leave. From the pain and despair, the yearnings and loneliness, they had become addicted to alcohol wherein they found forgetfulness. We did not give up, we started trying to get back our property which had been nationalized during the war and then given to the Soviets. The local government tried to influence us to stay and help restore what had been destroyed. We didn't want to do this, nor give up on our property. We turned to the court and they delayed us endlessly in order to wear us out. The governor threatened us, the person in charge of the house expelled us from his office and there seemed to be no chance of winning in court. All of a sudden an idea came to me to write to Moscow about the big injustice that the local clerks were doing to us, in addition to all the troubles that we had gone through and the sacrifices we had made for the Soviet homeland. The letter was very moving, well formulated and based on rightful requests, and also written by a woman who before the war had been a dedicated Soviet delegate. The answer came quickly. Within a week the trial took place and the government returned us our house.

The money problem had been solved, we sold the house and moved to Turetz, to convince our uncles to agree to join us. Several months of my pregnancy passed and it was now necessary to wait until the birth. We stayed in my uncle's house, where also another Gentile family lived. According to a court order they could not be removed. The house was old and musty, dirty and full of lice, and made us very depressed. We remembered it as it had been - full of life and happiness, made clean and neat by my aunt Mussia. In this house I gave birth to my beloved daughter who according to the family tree was the fifth and the last to be attached to this house. To bring up a baby in these conditions, in a house so miserable and sad, was almost impossible. It was hard to get milk, and hygienic conditions were nonexistent. Life in the town was just beginning again, institutions had been hastily set up without skills or knowledge of management and the lack of basic necessities all encouraged us to decide to leave as soon as possible while we still could.

At the end of the war, a law had been passed about exchanging Polish citizens. Those who had lived in Russia during the war could return to Poland and the Russians who lived in Poland could return to Russia if they wished. This law was especially passed for those people living on the Polish-Russian border, who at the end of World War I had received these areas, worked them, married and raised families there. The main point was that they had "preserved" the Polish borders. At the end of WWII they expressed their desire to return to Poland, their homeland, leaving all their property to the Soviets. This loophole was exploited by the Jewish survivors, who returned together with them to Poland, with the aim to emigrate to Eretz Israel or to America. We also registered and waited for the day to leave for Eretz Israel. We had two good reasons to postpone the journey to a later date: First, Ahuva'leh, our daughter, was still too small to endure the travel, and secondly, no less important, Yaacov's brother. Mordechai, was about to be released from the Soviet army and join us. However none of these reasons helped because the last date for the end of the project was approaching and could close all future possibilities of emigration. We packed our meagre baggage and the two week old baby and started on our journey. The uncles continued to refuse and nothing helped. With no choice, we left without them. It is strange that if fate wants to point us in a different direction, something always happens which will help it. When we arrived at the train station in Gorodia, it turned out that the train would only be leaving in the early morning. Yaacov, with much initiative, did not waste time, rented a truck, returned to Turetz and put the facts in front of the uncles and others. It worked wonderfully, within several hours everyone packed their belongings and returned in the truck to us in the station. In the morning the train set out into the territory of Poland.

1946. At the end of the war there was chaos and lack of civilian security, as happens after every war. In the forests and along the ways there are violent types of people wandering around, who looted and murdered. We travelled in closed carriages and were scared to open them even for inspection. We passed the Soviet border quietly and entered the area of Poland. A terrible surprise awaited us there, the Kielce Pogrom.

We arrived at Kielce on exactly the day of the pogrom. The rabble, incited by anti-Semitic elements, fell upon group of Jews who had managed to survive the Holocaust, and slaughtered them like sheep. For a long time we could not get over the shock and insult of their actions. We left that damned town with hate and continued to Wroclaw (pronounced *Vrotslav*). A city of tall, cracked skeletons, a ghost town with bitter memories, a revengeful town. The sight of a city with long streams of German refugees, struggling on their feet with little pushcarts of their belongings, reminded us of ourselves five years previously, filled our souls with satisfaction and a righteous sense of justice. We saw with our own eyes, the humiliation and punishment of a whole people who thought they could dominate the world, that they were a superior race.

We started to get organized in our new place. We found a large house, many floors, with lots of rooms, but open and completely destroyed. With no choice we settled down in several of the better rooms as good Polish citizens. After the victory, Silesia was annexed to Poland. We lacked everything –there was no milk for the babies, no hygiene and no food. The Germans destroyed everything before they left. We managed somehow but our thoughts were our way to Eretz Israel. In the city of Wroclaw, the *Bricha* [the underground organized effort that helped Jewish Holocaust survivors escape post–World War II Europe to the British Mandate for Palestine] was working at full steam, friends from Eretz Israel and also energetic Zionistic youth from the survivors organized *kibbutzim* [groups], concentrated the survivors and sent them to Eretz Israel, by illegal means, naturally. *Kibbutzim* sprang up from all streams of Judaism and all had the same long-awaited goal, to make *aliyah* to Eretz Israel.

Naturally I turned to the *Hashomer HaTsa'ir* kibbutz. In light of my many activities in the past we were all accepted. All the partisan family including with the tiny baby, and we were even promised first place on the list for *aliya*, when it would come.

We moved to the *kibbutz*. It consisted of people younger than us, who knew and valued our willingness to help them with all our strength and experience. The conditions were very difficult, especially to manage with the needs of my baby, who was the only one in the whole *kibbutz*. Despite the considerate attitude, we could not give little Ahuva'leh the milk she needed and she reacted with loud vocal concerts in the middle of the night, something that disturbed the sleep of the members who had to leave every day to work. Also here in Wroclaw, we didn't have complete quiet. More than once there were attacks on the *kibbutz*, but the members were already daring and skilled and knew how to defend and ward off the Polish hooligans. There were hidden arms and the young ones received training in self-defense from people from the Eretz Israeli *Haganah*. At the first opportunity as we had been promised, our group started out.

We arrived in a truck to the border and then several of the *Bricha* activists appeared and transferred us to Czech territory. We passed a very superficial check. Czechoslovakia was then the only country in Europe that opened its borders to the wave of refugees on their way to Eretz Israel. Before we got on the train, we were asked to destroy all our Jewish documents, and be in the disguise as Greek refugees returning to their homeland. We continued our way to the border of Austria, which was used as a transfer station. We got to Vienna, from there we were transferred in groups to the refugee camps spread out all over Austria. We were brought to the Ebensee Camp. We saw long huts, dark and depressing, and nearby, the crematoria that had not yet been destroyed. We wanted to run away but the people of the *Bricha* convinced us to stay in the meanwhile, until we could be moved to a better camp. It was already winter, a freezing cold pierced to our bones, we lived in large unheated rooms, bed to bed and in darkness. Army blankets from the Joint were distributed. The experienced partisan men improvised a heater, they brought logs from the nearby forest and the place became friendlier. We were given food from the shared kitchen, standard meals three times a day. It was hard for me with Ahuva'leh who couldn't eat the long noodles or beans in the soup. The Joint took care of everything for us, but for some reason forgot about the babies. I don't know what the situation was in other camps that winter. For us in Ebensee it was terrible.

**Fig. 3**
**In the DP camp. Survivors of the Pomerchik Family**
1. Yaacov Poluzhsky 2. Malka (Pomerchik) Poluzhsky 3. Malchiel Pomerchik
4. Velvul Perlman 5. Hadassah (Pomerchik – Zalamansky) Perlman
6. Alta Rachel Pomerchik (married to Feivel) 7. Feivel Pomerchik
8. Leyzer Pomerchik 9. (baby) Ahuva Poluzhsky (now married to Itzik Postan)

At the beginning of spring we moved to the Hallein camp near Salzberg. This also had been a concentration camp previously and the barracks had been used by the SS with their dogs and other accessories that had been utilized to destroy the unfortunate inhabitants. These were long huts with many rooms and an endless corridor. The rooms were empty with no furniture, but instead, they were full of fleas. We did a thorough disinfection and made the rooms livable. Our situation improved. There was a room for each family, at the end of the corridor was a place for washing clothes with many useable taps which gave unlimited water. The kitchen was shared, but there was more food rich in vitamins, both for the adults and for the children. The camp was close to the city of Hallein, which we visited quite often for shopping or culture. We began to enter order into our social life, a camp committee was chosen according to the list of political parties, and political and social arguments began. *Shlichim* (emissaries) came from Eretz Israel, organized the youth to into defense units, secreted in several guns for training so that they could prepare for the struggle that was going on in Israel, so that they could join the *Haganah* the minute that the homeland would call them to the flag. Of course all this was done in complete secrecy.

To all appearances, regular life continued. The barracks of *HaShomer HaTsa'ir* was number 6 and was the most active, ebullient and especially reputable. Almost all the members of *HaShomer HaTza'ir* came from the movement from before the war, enthusiastic people with an ideological attitude. Barracks 6 attracted attention for its complete cleanliness. We argued with people who wanted to emigrate to America or another country. Our people did not have dealings with the Austrians, did not knock on their doors, as others did. The camp itself received slowly a look of a small Jewish town. A general shop opened, a butcher shop provided enough kosher meat. Social and cultural life were organized. A small theatre was built where classical plays were performed. We tried, as much as was possible, to give content to our lives, until we could go to Eretz Israel. In Hallein I gave birth to my son Gershon. Looking after him was already much easier than to Ahuva'leh. Despite the easier life, we waited impatiently for the chance to emigrate. There also those who had got tired of waiting, and tried their luck in illegal ways to get there. Several succeeded, but most remained in Italy or were returned to the camp. We, the partisan family, remained still in one place for various reasons. Yaacov was a member of the committee, very active, and I was very busy with two young children. News that I received from those who had left to try illegal ways was not good. The English had increased their siege on the coasts and refugees who had come by sea were caught and sent to Cyprus. With no choice we sat and waited for the big and wonderful moment of the announcement of the State. We were privileged to hear on the radio the festive voice of David Ben Gurion informing the people of Israel and all the Jews in the Diaspora of the establishment of the State of Israel. I was not especially surprised. In my heart I was so convinced that it would happen, that it had to happen. We deserved it, we had paid enough with our blood. It only remained for us to pack our suitcases and start on our journey. But again we were delayed because Yaacov had to take care of others, especially the youngsters who were already drafted into the underground to the Israel Defense Forces.

All the years of our wanderings we tried, the family of partisans, to be together, to support each other, to strengthen each other's spirits in times of stress and breaking. When we began *aliyah*, the package broke up, and each found a solution to his problems according to his wishes and opinions.

In 25th May 1949 we boarded the ship *Galila* which brought us to the coast of Haifa on the 29th May 1949. We had finally reached our destination, we came to Israel to live and be built there. On the soil of the young homeland the second part of my life began."

# Yaacov Poluzhsky

Yaacov Poluzhsky was born in Korelitz on Purim, 1913 and died 3rd November 1983. His mother Esther and brother Moshe were murdered in the Holocaust - see page **343** (his father Gershon died earlier). He survived by leaving with Malka and part of her family in 1941 when war broke out. Yaacov and Malka Pomerchik were married on the day that the German invasion began - 22nd June 1941. Yaacov's brother Mordechai also survived, after fighting with the Soviet army and living through the siege of Leningrad. He returned to Korelitz after the war and lived in Novogrudek until he could make *aliyah* to Israel in 1960 with his family.

**Fig. 4**
**Yaacov and Malka Poluzhsky**

In the DP camp after WWII, Yaacov was active in helping with immigration to Palestine/Eretz Israel, and also worked for the Jewish National Fund.

**Fig. 5**
**A reference letter from the "Central Aliyah Office in Austria" No. 220 15.5.1949:**
"We confirm that Mr Poluzhsky Yaacov from the Hallein Camp near Salzberg
was an active, loyal Zionist and was of great help in our work.
Stamp: The Palestine Immigration Office"

Yaacov was in touch with ex-partisans from the Korelitz area, who were also active in organization of immigration before the establishment of the State of Israel.

**Fig. 6**
**Yaacov Poluzhsky (right) with 3 ex-partisans at a DP camp**

Malka and Yaacov were both very active in the Remembrance Committees of Korelitz. Malka was on the Sefer Korelitz Publication Committee and Yaacov on the Committee of Korelitz Survivors in Israel (see pages **347-348**). Malka made several contributions to the Sefer Yizkor –see pages **177, 179, 204**. She also wrote poems in Yiddish and one of them appears on Page **106**.

**Fig. 7**
**Meeting of the Sefer Korelitz Publication Committee with President Ephraim Katzir, 1973**

L-R: Malka Poluzhsky, Michael Beigin, President Ephraim Katzir, Yaacov Abramowich, Hassia Turtel Oberzhansky (possibly), --------

Many thanks to Gershon Poleg, Avigail Poleg-Dvir and Yogev Bargad, for supplying the Book of Memorial to Malka (*Shirat Chayai*), photos and other information.

# Appendix O

# A visit to Korelitz in 2010

**Merle Horwitz** visited Korelitz in 2010. She found no signs of the town of Korelitz as it was between the wars. There is not even a plaque in commemoration of the town's Jewish population.

**Fig. 1**

**Merle Horwitz at the entrance to the town of Korelichi (established 1395)**

**Fig. 2**
**The area where the Jewish cemetery was located.**
Now there is not even one tombstone to be seen.

**Fig. 3**
**The field where the Jews were taken before being expelled from Korelitz**

Fig. 4
The area where the synagogues once stood

Fig. 5
Apartments where once a synagogue stood

**Fig. 6**
**Plaque outside the Korelitz Museum**
Translation: Ministry of Culture of the Republic of Belarus.
Karelichi Regional Local Historical Museum

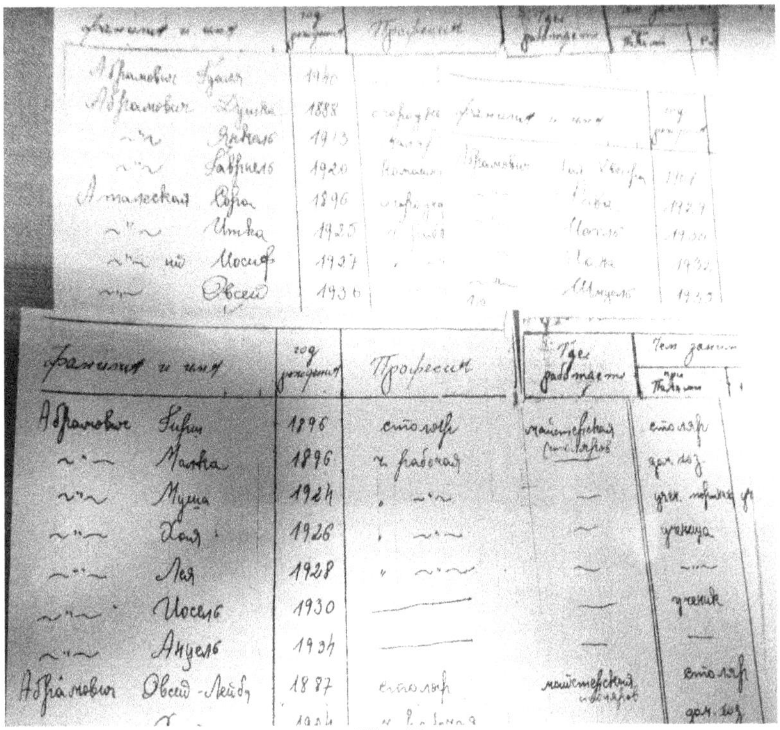

**Fig. 7**
**Korelitz Museum**
<u>**List of Names, Birthdates and occupations of people in Korelitz**</u>

<u>**Column headings, left to right:**</u> Name and surname, birth year, profession, work place, occupation. The last 3 columns are partly covered on the top list. If the list was from ghetto - everyone had to work or have a profession, so as not to be sent to death.

**Upper list LHS**: Abramovich Gdalia, 1940
Abramovich Dushka, 1888, *ogorodnik* – vegetable gardener
" Yankel, 1913, painter
" Gavriel, 1920, ?
Amalesky Sora 1896 - gardener, Itka 1925, Joseph1927 and Ovsej 1936

**Upper list RHS:** Abramovich Chaya-Dveira, 1907
" Riva, 1929
" Yossel, 1930
" Chana, 1932
" Shmuel, 1935

**Lower list:** Abramovich Girsch, 1896, Carpenter workshop - carpenter
" Malka, 1896, worker - housewife
" Musha, 1924, seamstress's apprentice
" Chaya, 1926, pupil (female)
" Leah, 1928,---
" Yossel, 1930,  pupil (male)-
" Yankel, 1934 ---
Abramovich Ovsej-Leibe, 1887, carpenter